MY LIFE OF MUSIC

MY LIFE OF MUSIC

by

HENRY J. WOOD

With an Introduction by
SIR HUGH ALLEN

LONDON
VICTOR GOLLANCZ LTD

First published October 1938
Second impression (first cheap edition) 1946
Third impression May 1948
Fourth impression September 1949

DEDICATED TO THOSE

who feel about music as I have always felt that it is a benediction put within the reach of human nature. Commercialism should never touch its heart (tho' sometimes it must affect its exterior presentment). But if we care intensely enough about that part—the inner indestructible part—a concession here or there with the changing years should not, and need not, obscure the chief point —that its care is a sacred thing. To those who think this way this book is dedicated.

HENRY J. WOOD

London

October 1938

★

PRINTED IN GREAT BRITAIN BY PURNELL AND SONS, LTD. (T.U.)
PAULTON (SOMERSET) AND LONDON

INTRODUCTION

SIR HENRY WOOD holds a unique position in our musical world. His name is a household word. His influence on our music as a conductor has made itself felt for fully fifty years in a remarkable way and with beneficent results.

He has indeed good reason to be proud of all he has done, and we to be grateful for it.

How comes it that he has made for himself such a position in this country as a conductor? He started life with the serious handicap of being a real Britisher born and bred. He had remarkable gifts. He learned all his music in this country and has exercised his profession unremittingly in England for England. No one has had greater influence on the music of his time and generation, nor given himself so unsparingly to its service.

More than most he has come into close touch with our music-making in every part of the kingdom and has always stimulated it. He has never visited any music society or organization that was not the better for the contact.

Sir Henry learned his job by actual experience and never took anything at second hand. He has some practical solution for every problem that presents itself. The effect of this is that everybody trusts him, for they know that he will always "deliver the goods."

When he calls a rehearsal for ten o'clock you may set your watch by the first beat he makes at it. If a composer is promised that his work shall be rehearsed at 11.10 he will hear it rehearsed at that time.

This reliability, this immense range of experience—of musical sympathy, this power of administration—these unique gifts of musicianship and of leadership are factors in the hold he possesses on the goodwill and imagination of us all.

As an almost exact contemporary I well remember standing, at the age of thirteen, beside a newly built organ in the Fisheries Exhibition while a black-haired little fellow (whose name was Henry Wood) gave a recital. I was filled with an emotion

5

which at the time I took to be envy, but which I now realize was suppressed admiration.

So to speak I took off my hat to that boy. And today all these years afterwards, I raise my hat again to Henry Wood in the spirit of gratitude and of affection.

September, 1938. H. P. A.

FOREWORD

I HAD DETERMINED never to write Memoirs—a suggestion put to me many times by publishers and friends of Music—because, full as my *Life of Music* has been, I felt it would prove dull reading to those who look for anecdote and travel in an autobiography. Of anecdotes I have a full store, but as these are so often unkind I decided that most of them would have to be omitted; while travel has been denied me since, from 1895, the Promenade Concerts, Symphony and Sunday Concerts at Queen's Hall have held me prisoner in England.

But my friends have at last prevailed upon me to write this book, as they say I am the only one left to give the true history of these now famous concerts—and in it I endeavour to do so. In it too, I take the opportunity of thanking my public for its kindness and faithful—I may say loving—support all these years. It is to them, and to the unfailing loyalty of my Orchestral Musicians, that England can boast a stronghold of Music which cannot be emulated by any other country. When I looked round Queen's Hall these August and September nights gratitude overwhelms me as I note the numbers of young men and women standing and listening in rapt attention to the Great Masters whom my years of Music in and for England have taught them to love and revere.

To Sir Hugh Allen I offer my thanks for so kindly writing the Preface to this book, and to my Publisher I owe gratitude for his foresight in issuing it at a price within the means of the Vast General Public of Music Lovers. I also thank the Editors of *The Times*, the *Daily Telegraph*, the *Yorkshire Post*, and the *Oxford Bulletin* for their kind permission to quote from articles originally printed in their publications.

London, W.1.   H. J. W.
    September, 1938.

CONTENTS

I

EARLY DAYS

A TERRIBLE SCREAM—that of my darling mother—is my first recollection. A broken nose the first souvenir of my inborn love for music. . . .

I was born in London on the 3rd of March, 1869, at 318, Oxford Street.[1] Of this period I have no recollection save that of my mother's scream when I must have been nearly three. An old Italian used to play his hurdy-gurdy outside our house. I was strapped in my little tub chair and placed on a table near the window where I could watch the antics of the man and his funny little monkey. One day, they tell me, I was so excited that, before our little nursemaid could reach me I had fallen off the table on to my nose. The result was a fracture which, though carefully set, gave me a crooked nose for the rest of my life. My souvenir.

My mother, though not in the room, heard the thud and knew instinctively what had happened. Her scream I can hear to this day. My first recollection.

Soon after this my parents moved to Pond Street, Hampstead, as my father had taken a shop in Oxford Street where no living accommodation was included. He travelled to and from business each day by bus.

In his way he was a unique personality. By trade an optician—as were his father and brother and several members of his family including Thomas Armstrong Bros. of Deansgate, Manchester, by nature he was a lover of books, painting and, above all, music. He should really have been a professional tenor singer because he had such a beautiful voice.

While at boarding-school in Finchley he devoted every spare moment to constructing model stationary engines. He was in partnership with his second brother when he married my mother, but this partnership was dissolved as his brother did not consider him in a position to marry.

For six months my father wandered about London in search of a job. As he met with no success my mother persuaded him to open a shop as an optician and model engineer with the little money she had saved and his own very small capital. She often told me how anxious she was until the first customer arrived on

[1] Old numbering.

the day the shop was opened. The first article sold was neither a pair of spectacles nor yet a barometer, but a small vertical steam engine and boiler priced at three guineas. From that day my father slowly but surely prospered; but I am certain he would never have begun anything of the kind had it not been for the guidance and dominating influence of my mother who was a splendid business woman.

Eventually my father's business became known throughout Great Britain, for every schoolboy knew H. J. Wood's model engine shop in Oxford Street. I often wonder how many old Etonians and Harrovians who patronized him still retain examples of his work.

As time went on he made magnificent scale models of famous railway locomotives at his little factory in Battersea. Indian Army officers and wealthy Americans ordered his creations. Entranced, I would watch Pike (his best workman) filing a square lump of brass, four by two inches, with the truth and flatness of a modern planing machine.

Pike was wonderfully skilled. In the course of thirty or forty years he and his assistant, under the guidance of my father, turned out some beautiful locomotives selling at anything from £45 to £300. Cornish, the other assistant, devoted himself to the model horizontal stationary engines. It has always been a regret to me that I did not keep one of these fine examples of model engineering.

Another outlet for my father's undoubted genius was the carrying-out of scientific experiments for Oxford and Cambridge University Professors. I clearly recollect the excitement caused during the testing of a new type of copper tubular boiler when —with the pressure-gauge registering nearly 600 lb. to the square inch—a nut holding one of the stays stripped its thread and shot through a panel of a door at the back of the premises.

While we were living in Hampstead my mother spent much of her time taking me out in my pram each day on the Heath. It was here, during my babyhood, that she would take me on her knee and give me my first lessons in music as well as the alphabet. Although so early in life, I can still remember those lessons. She would take my tiny hands and place them palms upwards; then, with the forefinger of my right hand she would help me to touch the outstretched fingers of my left, counting 'one, two, three, four, five. . . .'

" These, darling," she said, "are the five musical lines—the lovely musical notes E.G.B.D.F." I would look into her eyes while she repeated: "E for *every*; G for *good*; B for *Briton*; D for *deals*; F for *fairly*. *Every good Briton deals fairly*."

Each afternoon these delightful lessons proceed until, as a result of her patient teaching, I could point to the finger representing any one of these notes. Later came the second stage when she would make me slide my right index finger between those of my left hand, explaining that the gaps were the spaces of the stave, each a musical note and spelling the word F.A.C.E.

As the learning of my notes remains a mind picture, so the learning of my alphabet remains a tangible one, for I still possess my old rag book with its quaint pictures of nursery rhymes in alphabetical order, which my mother also explained to me. It interests me, even now, to realize that in these baby days I displayed my love of art—later to take shape in such earnest, for on the blank space at the back of the pictures I painted a 'puff-puff' and an omnibus in violent, intense colours: blackest of black, darkest of blue, deepest of crimson. As a small child, a paint-box was always my greatest treasure.

From my earliest years I remember my mother's beautiful soprano (the real Welsh) voice, and her singing to me old songs of Wales in her native tongue which she spoke so prettily and never seemed to forget in spite of having lived so many years in London. Often she read to me her own favourite hymns and sang me to sleep with a Welsh air—*All thro' the Night* or *The Ash Grove* or the *March of the Men of Harlech*. Now, as I look back and reflect, I know that of these tunes I preferred the last because of its rhythmic energy.

I did not attend school until I was nearly nine, but my mother gave me lessons regularly between my games every morning and afternoon, and I spent much of my time each day strumming triads to myself on an excellent Broadwood cottage piano. Often my mother helped me in this, but I did not have what I could call a real piano lesson until I was much older. Every evening, on his return from business, my father practised his 'cello for an hour or more, and I still carry the memory of his beautiful tone in my mind. I now know that his technique was not great, though his intonation was exceptionally good.

II

AN OLD-WORLD COTTAGE HOME

WE DID NOT remain in Hampstead very long as my father found the daily journeys took up too much of his time. He wanted every spare moment for his beloved 'cello and singing. We therefore returned to Oxford Street—to a new shop (then numbered 185) a few doors east of Buzzard's. We rented the whole building comprising the shop and a three-storied house above. At the back, beyond a paved yard, was an old cottage with a red-tiled roof. In this we lived. I was given the run of the front premises, first as a playground and later as a studio where eventually I was to teach, paint, and study music.

This cottage-in-the-garden was an old-world affair—the real original type of Oxford Street home a hundred and fifty years ago—a most charming and comfortable house. Incidentally, it was on the long front gardens that the shops were eventually built.

Some time before my father took them over, the premises had belonged to a well-known tobacconist. At the back of the cottage was a large room lighted by a skylight and fitted up as a workshop. I remember this room well. It must have been unique for it was paved with large stone slabs, except in the centre where there was a wide circle of tiny kidney cobbles, worn and bright, which in times past a pony travelled round and round attached to the mill-shaft in its daily task of grinding tobacco for snuff.

Our return to Oxford Street made my mother anxious lest I should miss the air of the Heath. She therefore kept me out in my pram in Hyde Park or Kensington Gardens to give me as much fresh air as possible. Later on I bought a small yacht to sail on the Round Pond. This seemed to please my mother as much as myself. We were very happy together and our long walks taught me to know my London fairly well.

On our way home from the Park one day my mother suddenly remembered she wanted to buy a comb. We came out at Marble Arch and walked a short distance down Edgware Road to a hairdresser's. Seeing a comb she fancied in the window, my mother went in to ask the price of it.

"How much is the comb on the shelf in the window?" she asked.

From the back of the shop a curious voice said: "How much is the comb on the shelf in the window, *damn your eyes!*"

The assistant named the price.

"Let me see it, please!"

Again the voice: "Let me see it, please, *damn your eyes!*"

I could see my mother was becoming rather agitated.

"I must apologize for my new parrot repeating your words, Madam," said the assistant, "but the sailor who brought him to me taught him to swear and I can't break him of it."

"What a curious bird!" said my mother.

"What a curious bird, *damn your eyes!*" said the parrot.

Another story of these early days exemplifies a trait in my character which developed as time went on and created in me almost a one-line thought until my object was achieved. Whenever my mother took me out I would always try to steer her to a certain cookshop in Market Street, now a side window in Waring's. I would then glue my nose to the window, looking intently at the floor of the shop. Attempts on the part of my parent to discover what I was trying to see were met with an embarrassed silence until one day, after prolonged questioning, I confessed my secret.

"I want to see the black dogs," I said.

"What black dogs?"

"The black dogs Uncle Thomas says they always keep under the counter."

"What for?"

"He says they never wash the plates in cookshops. They just hold them under the counter and the black dogs lick them clean."

One of my father's favourite pastimes was visiting London pawnbrokers' shops where he picked up really good violins for a mere song. He was friendly with (and had lessons from) an Italian named Pernorma, and it was during these lessons that I learned a good deal about stringed instruments, for they discussed them at great length—the violin and the 'cello especially. Pernorma played on one of my father's 'cellos whenever he came to the house, and my interest became so intense that I worried until he gave me a violin. On this I spent much time scraping out tunes in between my piano-strumming efforts. Harmony, however, soon took complete possession of the musical part of me, and I abandoned the violin until I had turned fourteen.

It is over sixty years since I lived in that old-world cottage home, but I can still remember every nook and cranny in it.

III

THE ORGAN IN ST. SEPULCHRE'S

My father was a regular church-goer, rarely if ever missing a service at St. Sepulchre's, Holborn Viaduct, where (from the time his voice broke) he was principal tenor for some years. Frequently on a Sunday afternoon he would go to St. Paul's Cathedral where his friend Sir John Stainer was organist. Sometimes he went to sing at the special Sunday evening choir service either in St. Paul's or the Abbey. At other times he visited the Temple Church where the organist, Dr. E. J. Hopkins, was also a great friend. My father greatly admired Hopkins's improvisations.

As soon as I could toddle my parents would take me to the Sunday morning service at St. Sepulchre's. From later experience and a good memory I now know that I was thus given an early opportunity of regularly hearing one of the best mixed choirs in London rendering some of the finest English cathedral music. The soprano leader there was Margaret Hoare who later became a well-known concert and oratorio singer. I remember my mother was quite jealous because my father always walked home with Margaret, while she herself had to walk behind with me—and Margaret was a very pretty woman!

Amongst my cherished recollections of St. Sepulchre's is the splendid organ, then in the west gallery. The choir sat on either side of it. How excited Mother and I were when Father sang a tenor solo in the anthem! I can still hear his beautiful voice and finished rendering of *If with all your hearts*, the choir following with *Cast thy burden*. My father was also a lifelong member of the Sacred Harmonic Society whose concerts were given in Exeter Hall, Strand. Sims Reeves often sang there, and my father came to know him intimately. Upon his renderings he modelled his own.

I can distinctly recall many discussions between my father and his friends, for I nearly always managed to be present at these. I remember, for instance, his opinion of John Hullah as a conductor not being particularly high, for he often related how in the *finale* of Schumann's piano concerto (at the syncopated subject) Hullah completely lost his head and went round in circles. Hullah, on the other hand, admired my father's exceedingly vigorous and even tenor voice, and on several occasions tried to persuade him to take up singing professionally. Sir Michael Costa also expressed admiration for his voice and style; he, too, advised him to give up business and become professional. All to no purpose; music remained a loved hobby.

Santley's first appearance in London was in the *Creation* at Exeter Hall soon after he had returned from his studies in Italy. My father used to relate how Santley broke down in the duet *Graceful Consort* owing to nerves; but the audience, loving his glorious voice and style, burst into kindly applause and bade him go on. He did—from one triumph to another. I know my father thought Santley a very great singer with magnificent technique. His declamatory and rhythmic style won universal admiration, but, in my father's opinion, Santley's *Elijah* did not equal that of William Ludwig, whose conception was so noble. (Then, later, came dear Ffrangçon-Davies who seemed to live the Prophet over again.)

All this, of course, was just my father's amateur opinion, but the day came when I was able to form my own. Still, it was a very good training for me to hear these discussions. Young as I was, I learned to listen to singers with insight and appreciation, and I now realize that my father's association with St. Sepulchre's, and the opportunities of hearing that fine organist George Cooper, bred in me the love I retain to this day for the organ, for organists, and for organ music.

Mrs. Cooper took a great fancy to me. In 1876, when I was only seven, she would send for me on a Sunday morning as soon as I had arrived with my parents, and allow me to sit with her in the organ-loft. She always played the first part of the morning service for her husband, who himself played for an early service at the Bluecoat School, after which he had to go on to St. Paul's Cathedral for the 10.30 service, only getting back to St. Sepulchre's in time to play the concluding hymn and the outgoing voluntary. No man I ever heard played Handel's choruses with the same dignity and breadth as George Cooper.

A little later the Coopers would take me home with them to Sunday dinner. We travelled in a four-wheeler hired for the whole day. These treats were a delight to me, even though I knew my parents missed me at their own meal. Hearing either of the Coopers play on the magnificent Renatus Harris organ in St. Sepulchre's, with its wonderful diapasons and ten stops on the pedals, filled me with wonder and admiration; but I was overjoyed when, at the age of ten, I was told I might practise on the organ so long as Mr. Cooper was not giving lessons.

I remember standing under the dome in St. Paul's Cathedral with my father at the funeral service for George Cooper in October, 1876, when my father introduced me to dear old Sir John Goss, telling me afterwards that I had shaken hands with one of the most distinguished musicians of the day, and one who was a pupil of Thomas Attwood who in his turn was a pupil of Mozart.

My father used to take me for those practices at St. Sepulchre's on the top of a 'knife-board' omnibus (generally a green *Bayswater*, but sometimes a yellow *Paddington*) from Tottenham Court Road to Newgate Street. It was not, however, until I was twelve that I was allowed to go alone. Never shall I forget the comic little person who used to blow for my practices. On Sundays three men blew, but I had to make do with one and play quietly. I asked the blower his name.

"Ain't got no nyme, sir," he said. "But they calls me *Ky-legs*. If you awsks for *Ky-legs*, you'll get *me* all right!"

A good name, for he was so knock-kneed that his legs formed a perfect capital K. He was a good-natured little Cockney, but I fear I often played a little joke on him by pulling out the heavy reeds at the end of a Bach fugue. He would come rushing round with only his trousers on, dripping with perspiration.

"Three men's job this mornin', sir! Werf more'n a bob a hour!" I usually gave him a tip of sixpence and he would depart to the *Saracen's Head*, donning his coat as he went, and would return refreshed and amiable as ever.

My uncle—William Thomas Wood, a watch and clock maker—would often come in from his shop at 18, Barbican, to hear me practise. He was a real 'City Father' and worshipped everything connected with London—myself included. Indeed, one of his boasts was that he had eaten more City dinners than any other City churchwarden. He was a good fellow and I loved him. He was friendly with the vicar and churchwarden of St. Mary Aldermanbury where the organist had refused to play a Wednesday evening service without increase in salary. My uncle proposed me as deputy. Naturally, at ten years of age, I was overjoyed at the prospect of playing for an evening service and of gaining experience on a new organ.

On the Saturday preceding my first service at St. Mary's my uncle took me to try the instrument. He was a nervous, fidgety man, and the sight of me balancing my small body on about two inches of seat (so that my feet could touch the pedals) was almost too much for him, for even in this attitude I could only touch certain pedals by balancing from one leg to the other. My pedalling, I fear, was restricted to the dominant and tonic cadence at the end of a hymn.

Such was my first professional engagement. No payment—except from my uncle who slipped half-a-crown into my hand at the end of the service. This I saved to purchase more organ music.

Organ music! How the mention of it conjures up in my mind the memory of the days when I used to buy candles so that I could study music in my bedroom late at night! Perhaps this was the only thing I did of which my parents disapproved; but I came near to undermining my health over it. A slight facial paralysis set in which our family doctor, a man named Bannister, immediately assigned to overwork. Consequently I was forbidden to do anything for at least three months. The right side of my mouth and right eye were affected, the mouth being drawn up and the eye almost closed; but rest put me right again. I remember the pain caused through an attempt to effect a cure by means of a beastly little electrical appliance. It did no good. However, I turned farmer for six weeks at Crickheath Hall, near Oswestry, where I stayed with relatives of my mother named Lewis, and rapidly recovered. For all that, the inequality of the right and left side of my face is still apparent. While here, I was able to indulge in my love of art and made many sketches.

My mother conceived the notion of selling some of these through art dealers. Arming herself with two or three canvases at a time, she hawked them round to every artist's colourman and picture framemaker within a three or four-mile radius of Oxford Street. This took many months to accomplish. Doubtless her winsome smile and sweet speech were mainly responsible for the dealers putting my sketches in their windows. It afforded me great amusement, when out walking with her, to see these exhibits of which she kept a very precise list with the title of each picture and the date when left. After two or three years, polite notes would reach us from the various dealers asking her kindly to call for Master Wood's sketches, as they were unable to house them any longer. I need hardly say that not a single sketch sold by this means, and a bonfire should have ended this waste of paint and canvas. However, I used the canvases again and again.

The mention of Dr. Bannister reminds me of the amusement caused by a story my mother used to tell of my being persuaded, after repeated invitations, to go to tea with him and his wife.

On arrival the first thing I said was: "I can only stop twenty minutes. I am very busy." Mrs. Bannister told my mother that all through tea I did nothing but fidget to get back to work.

Needless to say, I was *not* invited again.

IV

I HAVE MY OWN ROOM

In 1878 two important things happened; I was sent to school and was given my own room in the main house overlooking Oxford Street while my parents continued to occupy our cottage in the garden. The school was in Argyle Street, run by a Mr. and Mrs. Vie. There I remained until I was fifteen. I learned very little, for I was not a brilliant scholar in the general sense of the term; but I carried off every prize for painting, drawing, and music.

I had one really musical friend at school—a dear fellow named Augustus Toop. He had the palest face I ever saw, but he possessed a beautiful treble voice and, at eleven, joined Steadman's School for Choristers. He sang most artistically. When his voice broke he went on to Trinity College and afterwards became organist of St. Peter's, Vere Street—Dr. Roberts's church. Curiously enough, we never made music together nor even discussed it; he looked upon me as a student of painting; I regarded him one of music.

From the age of nine my parents made me feel I could stand on my own feet and follow my own devices with their implicit trust—a trust I can in all truth say I never betrayed. Now that I am a man of years I derive much happiness from the sweet memory I have carried throughout my life of my beloved father and mother, realizing that to them I owe what success I have achieved. I am quite sure my soundness of ear is due to my father's persistent training. When I was still a young child no meal ever passed without a tap on a tumbler, cup, table—*anything*—with—"What note's that, Joe?"

Lord! How I hated that name! Many a time I would not answer, pretending not to hear until he said "*Henry, dear!*" Then only would I answer. If ever he himself felt in doubt he verified my answer at the piano. I thus gained the sense of absolute pitch which I have never lost except for a period of about three years after the high Philharmonic pitch was lowered to French diapason normal (A.435.5) in 1895 with the opening of the Promenade concerts. Then, temporarily, my ear certainly did go astray, but I gradually became accustomed to the change.

We had pianos in the dining-room, the drawing-room, and in my bedroom as far back as I can remember. Now that I had been given my own quarters in the main building, the fine large drawing-room (with the folding doors removed) was fitted up for me as a music-room and contained my own Broadwood grand as well as an Alexander harmonium. This I bought at Metzler's. I had the run of Metzler's as my father's friend Munro Coward—an uncle of Noel Coward, by the way—was very kind to me. He must have been of immense value to them by reason of his amazing skill on these instruments. He could make them sound really grand. A three-guinea harmonium in his hands sounded like an instrument worth a hundred pounds. People used to come into Metzler's and he would demonstrate on perhaps quite a cheap instrument. It would be bought and delivered. A day or two after the purchaser would come back and ask whether the same instrument had been sent up. Mr. Coward would assure them it was so and suggest he came to their house. He did, and played so wonderfully that there was no doubt; but the instrument never sounded the same as when he played it. I used to be greatly entertained with these stories, I remember.

This incident reminds me of Noel Coward himself. His output for his years is prodigious, his extraordinary stage technique having been acquired by sheer experience. He was, so to speak, born and bred on the stage, and is, in addition, very musical. To think that so young a man should have conceived that wonderful *Cavalcade* and play after play is amazing! In addition he is a gifted musician with a flair for writing tuneful melodies and is withal a fascinating actor in his own particular genre. I much appreciate the fact that he engages a suitable orchestra for his productions—would that every producer would do the same!

Between my parents' bedroom and mine I fitted up a speaking-tube with mouthpieces and whistles. I bought the necessary lead piping, etc., at Matthew's, the ironmongers in Oxford Street (now in Charing Cross Road), and fitted up the tube myself, much to the admiration of my parents. One of my delights was to blow the whistle before they went to sleep and get my father to sing to me. As a rule my favourite aria *The enemy said* (*Israel in Egypt*) came through the tube, after which my mother's voice: "Henry, dear, it is past eleven. You must go to sleep or you will be fit for nothing in the morning." They little knew on how many nights I removed the whistle from my end of the tube and replaced it with a tightly-fitting cork so that they could not hear my little Bord pianette. I think in this perhaps I *did* betray the trust they placed in me, but when they knew they were not angry and only understood the more how deeply rooted music was in me.

On the second floor was my combined laboratory and play-room in which I could indulge my numerous scientific and mechanical hobbies. The ceiling was low, and I shall never forget my mother coming in one day and looking aghast at the black blobs on it after I had been indulging in a little football practice.

All round this room, on wooden trestles, I fixed up a double railway line of 3½-inch gauge. It owned a station which I named *Richmond Junction*, and there were points for switching from one line to another, a train composed of a locomotive and tender—this was made by my father—a first-class carriage, and a guard's van. Nothing gave my pals or myself greater pleasure than getting up steam with a little spirit-lamp placed underneath the engine boiler, and running the train round the room. Once, I remember, through travelling too fast on the sharper curves of the *Inner Circle*, the train came off the lines and the four bogey wheels were put out of truth. This meant a visit to my father's workshop. While the damage was being repaired I had to fall back on a horizontal engine which I had set up on a large board with a vertical tubular boiler; but although it drove shafting and working models it was never as much fun as the *Richmond Express*.

The back room on the same floor was given up to livestock. Here I kept a collection of white mice. For these I made a large tread-wheel, but it proved too heavy for the twenty-four little feet of six mice to turn; I was therefore compelled to construct a smaller model.

Silkworms also found a place in my menagerie. I reared them for several years but could never quite accept the fact that my mother was unable to make use of the little silken skeins with which I presented her from time to time. I kept a rabbit for a short time but, for once, my mother insisted rather than requested and I had to give him to the baker's boy. Another thing I loved was the quick result obtained from growing mustard-and-cress on a piece of damp blanket on my windowsill.

My interest in model engines gradually flagged. I then turned to electricity and, with my father's help, constructed a large electrical machine. My joy was great when I was able to charge up a big Leyden jar from which I could produce a fat, crackling spark. When my school friends came to see my 'Lab' I fear I let the spark loose amongst the uninitiated.

By far the most important of my electrical appliances were my Bunsen batteries. I began with four but eventually possessed twelve, the height of my ambition being to have electric light in the sconces of my pianette in the room below. Great was my parents' excitement when at last I was successful in fitting up two tiny electric lamps, one in each sconce. As a whole the experiment was a success, but I had reckoned without the cost of the batteries which seemed to have a perfect mania for 'holing'. I had better confess I often went to bed having forgotten to take the zinc plates out of the solution. Some years later I sent the whole of my electrical apparatus to Stevens's auction rooms where it sold for the noble sum of one pound—with which, of course, I purchased still more music.

Reflecting on this exciting laboratory-cum-menagerie I now realize why my dear mother, on entering it, always put her little handkerchief to her nose until she had become accustomed to the 'atmosphere'; for twelve Bunsen batteries, six white mice, a couple of guinea pigs, a canary, and some linnets—well, I leave it to you, as George Robey used to say in his famous song!

The large room behind my bedroom on the second floor I arranged as a studio because it had the advantage of a splendid light. Here I dabbled in painting and drawing. I was immensely proud of the two easels which were always set up; moreover, my father very generously had the large casement removed and two plate glass panes inserted to gain all the light available. On the long side of the room I put up shelves for books and scientific literature, of which collection I was very proud. I was never a great novel-reader and have always bought books rather than borrowed them—chiefly because I have a habit of underlining passages that particularly arrest my attention and to which I may wish to refer at some future time.

During this period my Monday evenings were devoted to chamber-music performed in my music-room, a fine large room which ran over the shop and store-room. We had come to know two excellent amateur violinists, Peter Jerome and William Gunthorpe. The latter's daughter, some years later, became one of the only two pupils to whom I ever taught piano-playing; the other was that brilliant entertainer Margaret Cooper. She also studied singing with me. Splendidly equipped, both as pianist and vocalist, and possessed of considerable charm of manner; she achieved great success in her own particular line—indeed, this kind of entertainment seemed to die with her.

These chamber-music Mondays were a regular institution until I was seventeen. I played the piano part in trios by Haydn, Mozart, Beethoven, and (later) by Brahms and César Franck. If Jerome could not come to take the violin part, Gunthorpe did—and *vice versa*; so that, with my father playing the 'cello, we were always sure of a complete trio. In the early days of these meetings we never ventured on anything beyond Haydn; sometimes, I fear, we went so far as to descend to Gurlitt. By way of a change Jerome might play a Handel sonata with me, and I distinctly remember my first acquaintance with Beethoven's *Horn Sonata* in which my father played the horn part on his 'cello. Another of his favourites was a Mendelssohn sonata; but it was a great day when I essayed for the first time Bach's duet in D minor for two violins with Jerome. I remember I took the second part and played abominably.

From this time onwards I resumed my interest in the violin and progressed well, but I was anxious to play in the quartets of Haydn, Mozart, Beethoven, Schubert, Schumann, and Brahms, for which reason I took up the viola.

Those were grand evenings, but I will not answer for the standard of the performances. Still, they undoubtedly laid the foundation of a knowledge of chamber-music for me. We generally began at eight and rarely finished before midnight—sometimes later. The result was that my breakfast was brought up to my room by my ever-watchful mother on Tuesday mornings. Then my father began to send me to the Saturday and Monday 'Pops' at St. James's Hall which stood on the site of the present Piccadilly Hotel. The wonderful Joachim Quartet was then at the zenith of its fame, but there were many celebrated singers, Santley amongst them. He seemed always to be singing *Let the dreadful engines* (Purcell); if not that, it was *Ich grolle nicht* of Schumann, both of which recall memories of marvellous tone and rhythm.

At the 'Pops' I first met Mary Wakefield, a contralto singer who appeared there once only. Many years later I was again to meet her as President of the Westmorland Competitive Festival at Kendal. It was entirely due to her initiative that the competitive festival movement was set on foot. I shall speak of her later, but it is worth recording here that what she did proved of inestimable value in breeding a desire to cultivate music, for the competitive spirit has always been strong in British people. All to the good, so long as the prizewinners do not fancy themselves as soloists and try to turn professional. Because a prizewinner may be considered the best baritone of his local centre he is not necessarily good enough to swell the ranks of professional singers and players.

I think it must have been in 1881 that my father left St. Sepulchre's choir. Sunday mornings now being free, I devoted mine to painting. My cousin Edgar Thomas Wood, well known as a water-colour artist, frequently came in and we worked together. I still have one of these first efforts, a picture called *Apples*.

An architect friend of my father's, a Mr. Nesfield, took the greatest interest in my painting and wrote on the back of this sketch: 'Dear Henry Wood, if you ever want to sell this little picture, I will give you £10 for it.

ERNEST NESFIELD.'

I made this little sketch in my Oxford Street studio while another friend of my parents—Sir Philip York of Erddigg Hall, Wrexham—painted the same subject in water colours. (I used oils.) For a year or two we sketched together, particularly in Richmond Park on Saturday mornings. These sketches are still in my possession.

I had taken to painting still life a good deal and became attracted to a certain kind of background for fruit pictures. This was made by covering a new canvas with flake white and raw umber. After adding a slightly darker tone in one corner— usually the top left hand—I took my longest palette knife and wiped down the canvas from top to bottom, leaving sufficient paint to show the texture. I am sure that many of the backgrounds in Fantin-Latour's flower pictures were painted in this way. Years later I adopted the same method for some miserably wretched portraits I tried to paint of friends. Although I painted a good deal from the nude at various art schools, I never succeeded in doing a good head.

While I was at St. John's Wood Art School distinguished artists visited the students there once a month. One day Whistler came in, almost unnoticed. He stood looking at a canvas on which a young girl student was working.

"Don't you think you have a little too much green in the shadow of that elbow?" he asked.

"Oh, I don't think so," replied the girl. "I always *paint* what I *see*."

Whistler moved off.

"H'm!" he grunted—"and you'll get the shock of your life when you *see* what you *paint*."

V

THE FISHERIES EXHIBITION OF 1883

MY FATHER NEVER missed a chance of taking me to anything of importance in London—comedy, farce, drama, Shakespeare, concerts, or opera. We saw and heard everything. Always in the pit or gallery. How I revelled in the season of Italian opera at Covent Garden! Or the wonderment of attending five performances at the Lyceum of Verdi's *Othello* (just produced) under the direction of the great Italian conductor Faccio, with Tamagno in the title-rôle and a complete cast, orchestra, and chorus from Milan!

Naturally we went to the Fisheries Exhibition in June of 1883. During one of these visits I went up to the organ which stood at the end of one of the long galleries. It was a fine example of Lewis's work; not large—merely two manuals and thirty-five stops—but its diapasons were the finest I had heard, apart from those by Harris at St. Sepulchre's. I had heard so many organs that I had learned to make comparisons. It may appear far-fetched that I should speak so definitely of my organ knowledge at so early an age, but I had never let an opportunity go by of learning all I could from an organist. If his explanation was beyond my comprehension I just plagued him for a more simple one. So that diapason-tone was something I really understood.

While we were looking at this organ a strange little man with jet-black hair, small head, flat nose and protruding jaw came up to us and asked whether my father would care to try the instrument. My father said: "No! I don't play the organ, but my son would like to try it." After a little persuasion I sat down and played the E minor prelude and fugue of Bach from memory. A small crowd collected and I rambled on for half an hour or so.

Our new acquaintance was Hermann Smith, an acoustician whose friendship I was to enjoy for nearly thirty years. He asked my father to let me give two or three organ recitals a week during the run of the Exhibition. You can imagine how keen I was to do this. I gave recitals each week until the Exhibition closed. Here is my first programme:

1. Great Dagon (*Samson*)   Handel
2. Minuet and Trio (from a symphony)   Haydn
3. Gavotte   Rameau

4. Air "The Lullaby" (*The Pirates*)   Storace
5. Marcia Religioso (*arr*. Spark)   Gluck
6. Trio, Andante and Rondo   Haydn
7. Minuet (*Samson*)   Handel
8. Pastoral Prelude (*arr*. Whittingham)   Gordigiani
9. March (*Judas Maccabaeus*)   Handel
10. Movement from a Piano Sonata   Beethoven
11. Wedding March (*arr*. Westbrook)   Mendelssohn

Two years later I gave another series of recitals on Wedlake's organ at the Inventions Exhibition. This was a twofold delight because in the intervals between my recitals I could go off and look at the scientific inventions and collections of instruments in the top gallery of the Albert Hall nearby. I remember I heard some appalling recitals given by a man named Tamplin who played nothing but the veriest tosh. I gave a third series of recitals at the Folkestone Art Treasures Exhibition in July, 1886.

About this time there were Sunday evening recitals at St. Sepulchre's given for a short period by a flashy player named James Loring. He was succeeded by Dr. Edwin M. Lott, my acquaintance with whom led to my becoming his assistant. As he was away a good deal I frequently played for what were almost cathedral services. My father, with his usual forethought, placed me under Lott for organ, piano, and harmony.

Lott dressed like the Abbé Liszt. He was of striking appearance—over six feet in height and very broad, a native of Jersey. He wrote pieces for the piano—somewhat in the style of Thalberg—which he published with Ashdown and Parry. I believe he was their reader.

I shall never forget my first organ lesson with him. I was to play Bach's F major *Toccata*. We discussed its registration, and I began. Lott said he would listen in the nave. I played and waited for his criticism. As he did not come I tackled the *Passacaglia*. Still no Lott. I then went down the church and found he had apparently gone. At the vestry door I inquired of the little gold-braided beadle if he had seen Dr. Lott. He imitated the action of drinking and jerked his thumb towards the *Viaduct Tavern*. I went back to the organ and, in a few minutes, Lott stood beside me.

"Bravo, my boy!" he said. "Splendid! Excuse my rushing off, but I have another appointment; but come and practise whenever you like. I shall see you at home on Tuesday for your piano and harmony." (The fee my father paid for this so-called lesson was one guinea.)

My lessons at Lott's home in Notting Hill consisted of piano-playing at half-past eight in the morning until nine, followed by harmony till half-past nine. (Fee: £1 5s.)

These lessons were even more farcical than those on the organ. The piano part of the business began with ten minutes of scales and exercises (edited and fingered by Edwin M. Lott; published by Ashdown and Parry); a piece by Hummel or Moscheles; another piece—one of his own creations in the shape of a *valse de concert* or a *tarantella* (published by Ashdown and Parry).

Lott dragged out the piano lesson until the hour was nearly up. Then I was hurried down into the dining-room where he looked through my harmony exercises. At 9.30 sharp I was pushed through the front door, sometimes without a harmony lesson at all. Useless to tell him I had done more than he asked for, or that there was some composition for him to examine. It was always: "Yes, yes! All right, my boy! They'll keep till next week." And the book from which I learned my harmony? *The Elements of Harmony*, by Edwin M. Lott (published by Ashdown and Parry).

I was determined, however, to keep my teacher at my side during those organ lessons *somehow*. At the second of them he disappeared down the church "to hear the effect". I gave him two minutes. Then I followed him to the *Viaduct Tavern* which stood on the corner of Newgate Street. The doors of the saloon bar were held open by a couple of straps. I peered through the gap. There was Edwin M. Lott with a churchwarden and a well-known parishioner.

"*Dr. Lott! Your organ pupil wants you!*" This in as penetrating a voice as I could muster. He turned round sharply, upsetting his whisky.

"Coming, my boy! Coming!"

Nothing more was said, but it cured him. He never left me again during the three months I remained his pupil. That summer he left me in charge of the services for six weeks. This brought me an organ pupil—a nephew of the Rev. James Jackson, for many years vicar of St. Sepulchre's. The vicar, incidentally, gave me a splendid testimonial as an organist and choir trainer. I still have it in my possession.

VI

I GO TO THE ROYAL ACADEMY

After my brief period of farcical tuition under Dr. Lott my father placed me in the care of Ebenezer Prout and his son Louis. I know that I owe to these two great teachers my knowledge of harmony, counterpoint, fugue, form, and instrumentation. Until I actually went to the Academy I devoted two hours every Tuesday and Friday to my lessons with them at their home in Dalston.

Louis Prout took me through the *Macfarren Day Theory* and also through *Tristan and Isolde* for harmonic analysis; but it was old Ebenezer who really played the chief part in my musical development because he persuaded my father to send me to the R.A.M. so that I could study all subjects under one roof and benefit from rubbing shoulders with other students. So I left the little school in Argyle Street and, at the age of nearly sixteen, became a whole-time student of music.

My Professors were Walter Macfarren (piano), Charles Steggall (organ), Prout (composition), Garcia (singing). I loved my two years there, during which period many of my compositions were tried out. Two of these were performed at the R.A.M. Public Concerts at St. James's Hall on July 9, 1890, both being songs sung by Ben Grove. They were *The sea hath its pearls* and *When on my couch I am lying*. All rules were broken by the audience who enthusiastically called for me.

When I became accompanist to the operatic class I formed a lasting friendship with Gustav Garcia who directed it. I also accompanied for singing lessons given by Manuel Garcia, W. H. Cummings, Fiori, Edwin Holland, Duvivier, Randegger, Arthur Thompson and Fred Walker. It was a great chance for me because I learned the traditional renderings of classical arias as taught by these great teachers. Young as I was, I realized that such experience would fit me for the future I had planned, for love of the human voice had taken hold of me just as the organ had done in my earlier days. Determined to be a teacher of singing, I took lessons from every professor available and heard every vocalist of the day.

Accompanying for Manuel Garcia's pupils was a privilege and an artistic experience of the greatest value—both in what to do and what not to do—but although I consider he was the finest teacher of his day, I must say he was at times quite violent with his pupils. It was nothing for him to fling a book at an unsuspecting head during a lesson. It never seemed to occur to him that the poor soul was in no fit state to learn anything further—at least, during that lesson.

Occasionally I came in for it also. A mezzo-soprano was singing *I will sing of Thy great mercy* (*St. Paul*) which she rather dragged. So did I.

"You're dragging!" stormed Garcia.

The next second he cannoned me on to the floor, taking the keys from under my fingers. The singer went on, and any on-looker might have thought it part of the game, so naturally was it done. David Hughes, a Welsh baritone, also suffered from Garcia's book-throwing, but he had been trained as a boxer and always managed to dodge.

Garcia was a real character. One day he showed me an advertisement in a daily paper.

"Look at this, Henry!" he shouted. . . . "Voice production! What's *voice production? We* teach *singing* here!"

I also remember a Welsh miner who came to the R.A.M. to study singing. He had a fine though somewhat throaty baritone voice and was nothing of a musician. However, Garcia did wonders with his voice in six months, mainly by giving him vocal exercises and training his ear to be alert to his own tone —certainly not by talking about voice production. Indeed, after four years' study this man won several prizes.

It so happened that the students knew that Randegger some-times offered engagements to baritones, especially if he were producing Saint-Saëns's *Heaven's declare*, in which there is a baritone quartet, or perhaps for the double quartet in *Elijah*. This was an attraction, and it was the thing to get into Randeg-ger's class. I thoroughly enjoyed myself the morning the Welsh baritone approached Garcia and broke the news that *he* wanted to join Randegger's class.

"Please, sir," he said in a voice that was hardly *robusto*, "I'm sorry, but I want to leave your class at the end of the term and go to Randegger."

I held my breath. I watched those fierce Spanish eyes flash fire, and prepared for the storm I knew must break. Garcia stared at the man for a moment. Then, in a voice of thunder:

"*Could you sing a note when you came to me?*"

"N-no, sir!" (This very tremulously.)

"*Had you any vocal technique?*"

"Er . . . n-no, sir!"

"Had you any repertoire ?"

"N-no, s-sir!" (Hardly audible.)

"Then GET OUT OF MY ROOM, and never let me see your face again. Out you go or I'll *kick* you out—even though I *am* very nearly a hundred!"

The Welshman fled. Garcia followed him to the door.

"I'm a teacher of singing," he roared, "*not* a concert agent!"

That taught *me* a lesson, too. I always told my pupils I could not undertake to find them engagements, and took care to inquire whether they were coming for real singing lessons or merely to try to make use of my influence.

Soon after I went to the R.A.M. the Principal (Sir G. A. Macfarren) died, and Joseph Barnby took over the choir and orchestra. I admired him intensely. No matter whether it was his own choir at St. Anne's, Soho, or the Royal Choral Society, he possessed in far greater degree than any other conductor I have ever met the ability to obtain phrasing, expression, diction and tone-colour from his choirs. He even made Macfarren's dull and laboured oratorio *St. John the Baptist* a thing of beauty. I remember so well his handling of *Hear my Prayer* with the R.A.M. students: he made me realize how much he could make out of what is really an ordinary anthem. With his oratorio singers he was amazing; he could give them a lesson in diction and phrasing without letting them know he was doing so—not always easy in front of a choir.

At a later concert under Barnby I played with the orchestra the organ concerto in E minor by Prout on that terrible box of whistles at St. James's Hall—a performance that brought me much praise both from Barnby and Prout himself.

There was at the R.A.M. an exceedingly gifted organist and violinist named H. C. Tonking, a raw Cornishman who had been under Prosper Sainton for violin and Steggall for organ. My father thought so much of him that I became his private pupil for both instruments. He was then a sub-professor.

Tonking was a curious fellow and a tremendous worker. He taught me to play Bach's organ preludes and fugues. His phrasing and registration of the 'Great G Minor' and the Toccata and Fugue in D minor were masterly; and here I may add (in regard to the latter) 'Klenovsky' learned a great deal.

Tonking's brother frequently stayed with us at Oxford Street. He was a medical student at Bart's, and from him I derived an interest in physiology and anatomy—and, incidentally, my

[1] See page 333.

bad habit of underlining passages in books. His father was the proprietor of a chemist's shop in Camborne. One summer I spent a holiday there. Rather a busman's holiday, I fear, for Tonking and I gave recitals in places such as Plymouth and Penzance, he playing the violin and I the organ or piano.

I was greatly entertained with the chemist's shop. One day, I remember, a burly tin-miner came in and asked in a beery voice for a pick-me-up. He then proceeded to collapse on to a chair. The assistant (who must surely have been new to the job) produced a powder, but instead of stirring it in water until it effervesced, he tipped the powder into the man's mouth and told him to drink the water. He frothed and foamed so much that we all thought he was going to die; but he recovered in a few minutes and, jumping up, exclaimed: "My God! That was some pick-me-up! How much?"

My friendship with Tonking ended in a disagreeable manner. One Sunday morning he called for me and we drove to Westminster Chapel, Buckingham Gate, where for some years he had been organist: but I knew nothing of the fact that he had been dismissed the previous Sunday. We went into the upper gallery from which we watched the new organist about to begin a quiet voluntary. He drew the correct stops, but instead of quiet diapason tone the heaviest reeds (both eight and sixteen ft.) blared out, complete with the three- and five-rank mixtures.

Tonking was convulsed with merriment. "I changed the loud and soft draw-knobs last night," he told me in evident delight.

"What a filthy trick!" I said in disgust, and left him there and then.

I never saw him again, but the unhappy memory of his beastly prank came to me years later when, in that same chapel, I held my first chorus rehearsal (with two thousand five hundred voices) for the Handel Festival of 1926—conducting, I remember, from the pulpit.

VII

I MEET EDWARD GERMAN

EDWARD GERMAN WAS a fellow-student of mine at the R.A.M. We were both in Ebenezer Prout's composition class. German nicknamed me 'Wood in C' because I wrote a symphony—a long one, too—modelled on Schubert's in the same key which I had heard old August Manns produce at the

Crystal Palace. During the same term I also wrote a Romance in C for violin and orchestra, so that the nickname was perhaps well deserved.

German was a delightful, unassuming man whose talents were displayed even in his earliest compositions. How proud we all were when he brought his first symphony to Prout's class for analysis! Randegger took the greatest interest in German's career, and when Richard Mansfield (the great American actor) came over here to produce *Richard III* Randegger arranged for German to write the overture, entr'actes, and incidental music. The overture was afterwards produced at the Norwich and Leeds festivals, and his E minor symphony was performed by Manns at the Crystal Palace in 1890. German's fame, however, at this period rested chiefly on his *Henry VIII Dances* written for Irving's production of this play at the Lyceum. At various times I have produced all German's orchestral works at Queen's Hall; in 1898 I performed his symphonic poem *Hamlet* and worked very hard to obtain a sudden *subito piano* for the whole orchestra as directed in his score—one not easy to bring off neatly. German came in to the final rehearsal. We made that *subito piano* with extraordinary unanimity. I was delighted—that is, until I heard German calling out to me:

"Dear Henry!" he said in his delightful way, "cut out that *subito piano*, will you? I don't like it."

Much shuffling of feet—the orchestral musicians' way of showing displeasure or disappointment—followed. I confess I was a bit disappointed myself, but the incident goes to prove that even experienced composers cannot always be sure of their effects until they actually hear them. Some maintain they derive more pleasure from reading a score in an armchair than by actually hearing the work performed. Vaughan Williams once told me he thought that was 'swank'. I think I am inclined to agree with him.

German presented me with the full score of his *Norwich Symphony in F* which he published at his own expense some little time before he died. I revived it after publication and, incidentally, played the slow movement at the R.A.M. students' concert at Queen's Hall on December 4, 1936, in his memory after his death.

His *Henry VIII Dances,* the *Welsh Rhapsody,* and the *Theme and Six Diversions* will always live. His *Valse Gracieuse* is, in my opinion, one of the most charming and melodious five-minute pieces I know, and I am certain that if Novello circulated it amongst American and Continental conductors it would often

find a place in their programmes. Lionel Tertis loves this little work as much as I do.

Julia Neilson was a student at the R.A.M. in my time. I chiefly remember her for her almost angelic beauty. Never have I seen a young girl so graceful and with such charm of manner. As a matter of fact, hers was the one head I tried many times to paint (unbeknown to her, for she never sat for me) but my efforts proved that I should never become a portrait painter; for when I saw her the next time I almost burned with shame that my hands should so belie my vision.

In her student days she had ideas of going into grand opera; but all her professors told her no male singer would ever be found to match her in stature, although I may observe at this point that Jean de Reszke had not then appeared. What a figure of a man—and what a singer!

Julia Neilson's was indeed a sweet voice. I remember her singing *O for the wings of a dove* with a tenderness that touched me deeply. Since then she and her dear husband Fred Terry have given me many evenings of delight with their historical plays and delightful comedies. (Was she ever more charming than as *Sweet Nell ?*)

Two other students of singing in the Academy at this time were Hannah Jones, a Welsh contralto, and Ben Grove, an American bass. They sang several of my songs which were given an enthusiastic reception both by my friends and the Press. Subsequently I published these (among other songs) but some years later bought back the plates from the publishers in order to destroy these fruits of early exuberance.

Thinking of Edward German's nickname for me (Wood in C) reminds me that I wrote a Mass in C which I dedicated to Cardinal Vaughan. I gratefully remember he was pleased to accept a copy which I had specially bound in Cardinal colours. At one time I directed services at St. Joseph's Retreat in Highgate, where the organ and choir, as usual, were accommodated in the gallery. Above this gallery was a spiral staircase leading to a room in the tower used as a library. My librarian was a man named Edmund Grist whose system of cataloguing was remarkable. He had been employed at the British Museum from the age of twelve onward, which probably accounted for his skill. His librarianship at St. Joseph's, however, was not a paid job and, as he was free after four in the afternoons, he was anxious to obtain library-work in the evenings. I arranged for him to come to me, and invaluable I found him. His skill in binding band parts was amazing; moreover, I never knew

what it was to have to think about my scores and parts. He never failed me.

Grist was a colourless kind of man who rarely if ever smiled and certainly had no sense of humour. One day a telegram arrived, addressed to me at Queen's Hall. It was from Tosta de Benici, the well-known Swedish pianist, who was to appear at a Promenade concert. It read: TELL CHRIST TO PUT OUT THE BAND PARTS OF THE GRIEG CONCERTO. I handed it to Grist—who read it, and turned to me without trace of a smile: "She's spelt my name wrongly—it's not Christ —it's Grist."

I was fortunate in securing the services of Mr. W. H. Tabb when Grist retired. My Librarian's task is no easy business, and when one remembers that at least five hundred works with the thousands of band parts are handled during a Promenade concert season, one realizes the monumental task and responsibility of such a position—and Mr. Tabb has never failed me. When the changes came in 1927, I was glad the B.B.C. took him over, so that I felt quite safe, as my Library is still used during the Promenade season—only novelties being supplied from the B.B.C. library.

VIII

MY FLIGHT FROM THE ACADEMY

My exit from the Academy was somewhat dramatic. *I ran away.*

During the Handel Festival at the Crystal Palace I heard my ideal of a great organist—W. T. Best—play a newly-edited concerto in B flat with an elaborate and complicated cadenza upon which I myself had been working for some weeks with the idea of playing it at one of the R.A.M. concerts. It was put down for a Friday rehearsal. After the first few bars Mackenzie, who had now succeeded Macfarren as Principal of the Academy, turned to an organ student and said: "You can conduct this. You are an organist and should know Handel's concertos."

It so happened that the student had never conducted before. Consequently the orchestra broke down several times in the first movement—much to my disgust, for I had expected Mackenzie would himself conduct, and that the merits or otherwise of my playing would be judged by my performance under his direction. With rapidly rising ire I went through the first and second movements, and began the third. When we came to the *finale*, although Mackenzie was doing his best in dumb-show to keep conductor and orchestra together, I completely lost my temper, jumped off the seat, and fled from the hall. It was not until I had gone some distance that I realized I had left my hat and coat behind. For all I know, they are there now. Perhaps they kept them as a memento of my bad temper?

I received two bronze and two silver medals during my two years at the R.A.M. but did not resume my studies after this incident. However, I had undoubtedly completed the musical education that was to equip me for my future career. Although I left in a rage, Mackenzie and I remained friends throughout his life; and when the Great War broke out he invited me to take over Dr. Lierhammer's Vocal class at the Academy.

While I am about it, I had better make a clean breast of it and confess I ran away from Walter Macfarren's class as well. That was over Paderewski, who had been giving recitals. He had just appeared as a pianist and had created a sensation in London. All the students were raving about him, myself not least. At the end of a lesson I enthusiastically asked Macfarren whether he had heard Paderewski.

"No," he said indifferently. "I'm not particularly interested."

"Not *interested*, sir?"

"No. I have heard the man can't play his scales."

"But his technique, sir—the greatest since Rubinstein."

"Probably. I am not interested in him."

I was so furious that I never had another lesson with Macfarren.

After my Academy days I plunged whole-heartedly into my chosen profession as a teacher of singing and an orchestral and choral conductor. I soon found I had more singing pupils than I could comfortably deal with. Strangely enough, they were of all nationalities; and before I was nineteen I was earning a considerable income. I charged half a guinea for an hour's lesson which I gave in my music-room at 185, Oxford Street. For all that, my good parents still financed me to a great extent because my ideas were a trifle ambitious, one of them being to form a complete music library of my own.

Every Saturday morning I visited Augener's (then in Foubert's Place, Regent Street) in order to search for new organ music and to purchase full scores. Even though I was undoubtedly destined for a musical career, I realize now that I might never have achieved such success as has been mine but for the loving enthusiasm and generosity—sometimes, perhaps, too lavish—of my parents. I learned later that my father spent every penny he possessed on my artistic education. Not every aspirant to an artistic career is in the enviable position that I was of having parents who were able to advise the step-by-step advance. No hurry; no urge to begin to earn; only a careful, never-ceasing vigil and counsel that guided me until I was able to take my future in my own hands. My father was responsible for my becoming conductor of many societies in and round London; for he always insisted that if I wished to become a conductor worthy the name I must conduct an orchestra or choir (or both) every night of my life. I often think that if many young students had parents who made the tremendous sacrifices mine did they might stand a real chance of achieving success.

From my thirteenth year I had acted as accompanist at innumerable concerts. Although I had now set my mind on learning all I could of the art of conducting by practical experience I never lost touch with my piano. *A teacher of singing is seriously handicapped unless he is a good accompanist.*

One of these societies was that of All Saints', Clapton East, with which I gave the first concert for which I received payment on January 1, 1888. Thus January 1, 1938, marks my fifty years of professional conducting. The first part, I remember, consisted of Macfarren's cantata *May Day*. He had died on October 31, 1887, and we gave it in his memory as vice-president of the society. The artists taking part were all fellow-students of mine: Benoni Brewer, A. E. Spittle, Allen Gill (who later became so well known as Conductor of The Alexandra Palace Choral Society), Kate Norman, Padarn Lewis, Hannah Jones, and Ben Grove who, many years later, was to look after my father.

There was also the Bayswater Orchestral Society. A happy and keen little body it was, whose weekly rehearsals were held in the crypt of a large chapel in Lancaster Gate. It was run by two brothers named Palmer. One was a very bad double-bass player, and the other quite a good viola player, and, incidentally, an excellent secretary to the society.

I well remember their timpanist coming up to me—very irate—after my third rehearsal. "Young man," he said sternly, "you didn't give me every cue to come in; nor did you give me a look the beat *before* I came in. That's why I *didn't* come in!" I have kept an eye on timpanists ever since.

In addition to the foregoing I started the Hackney Orchestral Society. Thus at least three nights out of every week were devoted to obtaining the practical experience my father was so anxious for me to have. I very much wanted to conduct opera, largely because I saw clearly enough that, unless I had strong church influence, I might have to wait almost indefinitely before obtaining a cathedral appointment. Organ-recital engagements were few and far between and ill-paid at that; consequently I gradually gave up the instrument at which I had worked so hard and which I loved so well.

The only organ appointment I ever held with a choirmastership combined was at St. John's, Fulham. I was paid £60 a year, but only remained there twelve months. During that time, however, I improved the singing of the choir enormously; I know they told me I worked them nearly to death. At all events, my success must have amounted to something because I was always losing my solo boy. Other churches offered more than St. John's which could only afford to pay £3 per annum.

I suppose every organist makes a howler at some time in his career. I made mine there. I played a funeral march, but changed my mind about it when I chanced to notice not a coffin, but a charming bride waiting for me to play a wedding march in her honour.

As I have said before, my father saw to it that I heard everything in music worth hearing. He did not restrict me to London or even England, but sent me to Germany, Bavaria, France, Belgium, and America. My European travels were made comparatively simple for me because he always sent me off equipped with return tickets and Cook's coupons for the hotels. America did not offer the latter facility when I was dispatched to Boston to hear the famous symphony orchestra under George Henschel, and I must confess to feeling very young and inexperienced when I had to pay my hotel bill for the first time.

This long journey had been undertaken because my father had heard that the Boston Symphony Orchestra was the finest in the world. I have never forgotten my extraordinary exhilaration and wonderment when I heard them play the *Eroica* with woodwind and brass such as I had never dreamed of, while the warmth and glow of the string quality was simply entrancing. What a debt of gratitude musicians owe to the man who financed this marvellous orchestra—Colonel Higginson!

On one of my journeys to Germany I did too much sightseeing and allowed my pocket-money to dwindle to 1 mark 25 pfennigs —and this on the morning of my departure from the *Hotel Disch*, one of the smartest in Cologne. It was the custom there, on the departure of a guest, to ring a bell—the signal for the mobilization of every member of the staff who could possibly claim a tip. I ran the gauntlet, bag in hand, staring with as convincing an expression of absentmindedness as I was capable of producing. I managed fairly well until the hall porter loomed up before me. On him I bestowed my last mark.

On reaching London I took a cab home—for which, I need hardly add, my father paid.

IX

I WORK WITH SULLIVAN—AND OTHERS

In 1888 I was accompanist for François Cellier's rehearsals at the Savoy Theatre for the *Yeomen of the Guard*—Sullivan's own favourite opera. He told me he thought it his best. I remember how worried he was over *I have a Song to Sing-o*. I played several versions of it, none of which satisfied Gilbert, rhythmically, from the point of view of his lyric.

Sullivan had been sitting up night after night scoring the whole work and came into rehearsal one morning looking very tired. He put before me the latest version of the number. When I played it Gilbert was delighted with the melody over the drone bass. "The very thing!" he told Sullivan. George Grossmith fell in love with it, too, and we all predicted it would be the most successful number in the opera.

I remember how disappointed and hurt Sullivan was when he found the audience talked all through his overture. "I shall never take the trouble to write another," he told me. "Next time I shall get you or Ernest Ford to score a medley of the tunes."

I felt sorry for him. One of the worst habits of the British public is this tendency to talk through overtures and entr'actes. This was most evident at the production of Debussy's *Pelléas and Mélisande* where some of the loveliest music is played between the acts with the curtain down. For this reason that beautiful work will never be popular over here because English audiences will not accept a stage production if they are to keep silence between the acts. It is the same with our orchestras who compare badly with those on the Continent. Abroad, when a section of an orchestra has nothing to do for a few bars, the members listen to what the others are doing *and listen with interest and respect*. In England they talk if they get a chance. I have often been sorely tried at rehearsals and have had many times to be severe. Still, I will give our orchestras their due: when it comes to the final rehearsal and performance they are unequalled anywhere in the world.

Committees, in whose hand the appointment of conductors often lies, seem to me to aid and abet this lack of seriousness. The conductor who aims at popularity by *hilarity* often secures an appointment. The late Sir Frederick Bridge was an example. I remember his appointment as conductor of the Royal Choral Society which, under Barnby, was second to none. Bridge himself described to me his interview with the committee before his appointment.

"I fired off a joke as soon as I entered the room," he said. "I kept 'em in roars of laughter all through the interview . . . and that, my boy, was how I got the job."

Nothing as to his ability as a choral conductor. At least, not then. That came some years later. Bridge came to me in difficulties after he had been asked to conduct Wagner.

"I'm down to conduct a selection from *Parsifal*," he announced. "Never conducted a bar of Wagner in my life, my boy! Do I beat eight or four in a bar in the Grail Scene?"

I attended that performance. On every downbeat his heavy baton tapped a metal upright in his music stand, reverberating through the hall with dreadful insistence.

This lack of reverence for the great masters extends to private concerts. I remember Lady Cory's delightful musical At Homes. I suppose they are about the last of such *salons*, but she took care to engage artists like Kreisler, Casals, and Paderewski; yet many a time I have seen Kreisler fail to obtain silence even after his accompanist (Charlton Keith) had played a few preliminary bars. Not until Kreisler had played for several seconds would the silence due to such an artist and such music prevail.

The whole attitude is so *unworthy*. I have many times noticed that professors and guests who come into rehearsals will talk and hold conversation. I have taken to stopping when this occurs, for I do think that a conductor's attention need not be distracted; and at least it can be said that it is an evil that is being handed on to the young student. *We are bad listeners in England!*

The lay public is not only to blame. Professional musicians, who ought to know better, are just as bad. I have often noticed at rehearsals that singers not actually engaged for the moment will sit in the body of the hall and talk. Dear Clara Butt once offended me greatly in this respect. She came into Queen's Hall during a rehearsal of Beethoven's ninth symphony laughing and chatting as though she were in a restaurant. I fear I turned on her.

"Madame Butt! We are rehearsing Beethoven."

"I beg your pardon."

All the same, she annoyed me again—this time when we were making records of the *Dream of Gerontius* at the Columbia studios. She came in with her entire family and some of her friends. Arthur Brookes, the recording manager, came forward and told her that nothing could be done unless he could have complete silence; she forthwith packed her relatives and friends off home. She was always inclined to be a law unto herself but she was the idol of the concert public. I doubt whether any artist did half as much as she during the War; the public responded magnificently to her calls upon them—I believe she raised something like £100,000—and she sang songs to the wounded and won their deepest gratitude. After her marriage to Kennerley Rumford her singing and vocal style steadily advanced. He is a typical English gentleman whose birthright shone through every bar he sang.

To return to Sullivan. I often saw him at Mrs. Ronalds's Sunday afternoon musical At Homes where I shared duties of accompanist with Wilhelm Ganz and Henry Bird. At her house in Cadogan Square every artist of the day was to be seen; indeed, it was a *rendezvous* for musicians of every nationality.

In May, 1890, Sullivan asked me to act as *répétiteur* for his production of *Ivanhoe* at D'Oyly Carte's new opera-house in Cambridge Circus. This meant working under François Cellier and Ernest Ford, and being entrusted with the training of Lucille Hill, François Noyes and others for their parts, Sullivan personally paying my fees.

A few weeks before the production I was at a rehearsal playing the piano on the prompter's bridge over the orchestra. In the Robin Hood scene there is a recitative accompanied by a tremolo. I hung on to this in the 'till ready' style, and waited for Locksley to begin *What folly have we here?* Nothing happened.

Then some of the chorus pushed forward a big burly fellow.

"Go on! It's your part!"

He found the middle of the stage and began—a third too high. But he stuck to it, pointing to the castle though keeping his eyes fixed on Sullivan who was in front. After a few bars Sullivan rapped on the stage with his stick.

"Who is this man?" he said to Carte.

Carte shook his head. "I don't know."

"Do you know him?" This to Cellier.

"Never seen him before."

Sullivan grunted.

"Do you know him, Mr. Wood?"

"No, sir!"

"I suppose Mrs. Carte must have engaged him," mused Sullivan. "Will somebody have the goodness to find her?"

Mrs. Carte came on stage and there was a whispered conference, the unknown singer watching the proceedings with interest.

"Strike this scene!" commanded Sullivan. "We'll get on with the next act." He then turned to me.

"Take this fellow home with you this evening," he said. "Give him all the time you can, and for goodness' sake loosen his throaty production. Make him put some inflection into his recitatives—*and teach him his part*. He doesn't know it."

The singer proved to be a man named William Stevens, a young Cornish tenor. His self-esteem received a rude shock, for he was easily the most conceited individual I ever met in the profession. Even so, Sullivan paid for him to continue his lessons with me. *But we never found out who gave him the engagement.*

This meeting with Stevens, however, had a wonderful sequel for me. He brought to my studio the Princess Olga Ouroussoff who wished to take singing lessons. Her coming indeed marked a milestone in my life for, later, she was to become my wife.

It may be remembered that Ffrangçon-Davies began his career in the Church but later became one of England's really great singers. He provided an amusing incident during the run of *Ivanhoe* in which he took the part of Cedric the Saxon. After the opera had been running a few weeks and he had become well installed in his part, he danced on in the tournament scene one night in a strangely frisky manner, making comic asides to the evident amusement of the chorus ladies whom he insisted on chucking under the chin. He had obviously dined well rather than wisely; but, as there was no understudy in the theatre he had to go through with it, despite the titterings of the audience.

The next morning he was summoned before the management. I shall never forget the superb aplomb with which he walked on to the stage to face Sullivan, Carte, Cellier and myself.

"Good morning, gentlemen!" he said breezily. "This is an unexpected pleasure."

Carte nudged Sullivan and Sullivan nudged Cellier and Cellier nudged me. Carte then opened fire.

"Er . . . we had to send for you this morning, Mr. Ffrangçon-

Davies, because of the somewhat extraordinary performance you gave last night. Perhaps you can explain matters?"

Ffrangçon beamed.

"Quite easily," he said, "quite easily. You see, gentlemen, my *wife* was sitting in the stalls. I was so nervous that I had to take a restorative."

Carte had nothing to say. Nor had anyone else. At last: "Er . . . thank you, Mr. Davies. Good morning!"

Thus ended the interview with the still breezy Ffrangçon.

My association with Sullivan was very happy, and the production of *Ivanhoe* sealed a long friendship. Probably the public had never seen grand opera so superbly mounted or so splendidly stage-managed—the credit for which goes to Hugh Moss. Undoubtedly the principals and chorus were the finest obtainable.

Ivanhoe contains great moments, even if there are too many scenes. If D'Oyly Carte had had a repertory of six operas instead of only one, I believe he would have established English opera in London for all time. Towards the end of the run of *Ivanhoe* I was already preparing the *Flying Dutchman* with Eugène Oudin in the name part. He would have been superb. However, plans were altered and the Dutchman was shelved.

Among many letters Sullivan wrote me, the following illustrates the charming simplicity of the man—although I was so much his junior, he could seek my advice—"I am again conducting the *B Minor Mass*. You know your Bach well. Tell me! How is it that half-way through this superb work I feel everybody becomes bored and sick of it?"

"In my opinion," I replied, "it is because twelve double-basses are sawing away for two and a half hours without cessation. I suggest you look through the bass part. Wherever possible—in the arias and duets especially—rest the basses and let the 'cellos become the eight-feet bass. I have learned this from the great organists who never pedal continuously throughout a service. I suffer as much as you do from too much sixteen-feet bass (and the first violins) in choral performances of Bach and Handel."

This letter to Sullivan foreshadowed my ceaseless endeavour to balance tone between chorus and orchestra; hence my re-scoring of Handel in the *Messiah, Solomon*, and *Samson*, and of Bach in the *Mass*, the *Matthew Passion*, and over sixty of the cantatas. The 'let-us-have-it-as-written' doctrine (as preached by a certain set) is, in my view, wrong. We can never afford to do without the interpretative artist. In the first days of the pianola and the Welté-Mignon piano-player it was an education to hear, for instance, a Chopin *ballade* played by Carreño, D'Albert, Busoni, Pugno, or Bauer, and to *compare* them. All *great*—but how different in interpretation!

It is the same with painting. A great painter transfers a landscape or a head through his interpretative vision, giving us fresh beauties invisible to our eyes in the original. A conductor may appear tomorrow who will give us the Beethoven symphonies in an entirely new light. If so, I shall never complain, for the last thing I want is a *standardized* method of interpretation. I want *individual* interpretations. I have not yet forgotten the last words that most inspired of all conductors, Arthur Nikisch, ever spoke to me—when we parted on the quay at Ostend in 1921!

"Make all your performances a grand improvisation!"

To my mind this modifies the doctrine which preaches the gospel of a standard reading of the classics. Busoni varied Nikisch's dictum. He once said to me: *"everything* we do is a transcription."[1]

On the other hand, Toscanini once said that every note should be as the composer set it down. With all due respect to Toscanini's greatness as a conductor, I think that cannot be taken as a maxim. Beethoven, who was stone deaf for so many years, might have altered much of what he wrote if only he could have *heard* it. I remember my surprise when Stanford, commenting on his performance of Bach, said: "That's just as the old man would have liked it." *How could Stanford have known that?*

Art is ever in a state of flux. Of that I am convinced. If we are to have only the composer's notes we must have only his instruments and his conditions. I once had an oboe made of boxwood—a replica of those used in Handel's day, with the same broad reed. The result was appalling—so raucous and strong, so entirely different from the beautiful-toned woodwind of today. Historical performances of classical masterpieces are all very well but they should be heard in a very small hall under conditions which reigned when they were written. If we are only to have the great masters in the original I have committed a few sins. All the same, I am in good company. Liszt

[1] My impressions have been gathered from a host of conductors whom I watched at work in my early days. They include Theodore Thomas, Seidl, Mahler, Safonoff, Frank and Walter Damrosch, Bodanzky, Mengelberg, Gerecke, Manns, Fielded, Rabaud, Lamoureux, Colonne, Chevillard, Wolff, Monteaux, Stock, Ysaÿe, Rothwell, Verbrugghen, Hertz, Lohse, Faccio, Mancinelli, Steinbach, Mottl, Schalk, Vogt, Dvorak, Kees, Sarafin, Neruda, Hallé, Levi, Nikisch, Richter, and others.

successfully disarranged Schubert, and even Brahms was not altogether guiltless!

My final association with St. Sepulchre's brought me into contact with a retired solicitor named J. Mason Allen, a friend of Peter Jerome. On Sunday nights my father and I would walk with him to his rooms in Gray's Inn where he had one of the finest Steinway Grands I ever touched. He bought it at Steinway's factory in New York. In those days there was a vast difference between German and American Steinways. Allen had met Wagner in London in 1877 and had discussed many of his operas with him. I already knew Wagner's early operas, but through Allen I made the acquaintance of the *Ring, Tristan,* and *Parsifal.*

These Sunday evening sessions made my mother anxious about my health, for we usually reached home well after midnight. My fault, largely; my father always silently signified that he felt we should be going, but I could never drag myself away from Wagner and that Steinway. When we got home we always found my mother sitting up waiting for us. She never complained, but I often think her silence was really a tender reproach.

Allen was a remarkable sightreader. He could sing both alto and bass. He entertained me by turning on an excellent *falsetto* for Isolda which he alternated with a bass for King Mark. He was a staunch believer in my musical work, and for years afterwards I used to see him standing in the Promenade at Queen's Hall.

Then there were the holidays, the thought of which takes me back to early days again. I can see my mother now, getting me ready to go away—with her unfailing care over buttons and laces. As a youngster I wore the kilt for best, and for every day my suits—made by my mother—were of velvet in blue or black, sometimes a dark shade of mauve. I remember her cutting them out from a pattern, and the fuss there was over the diamond-shaped silvered buttons with their raised centres. Everything had to be exact.

While my mother concentrated on overhauling my wardrobe my father made arrangements for the journey to Crickheath Hall, Oswestry, where I had stayed after my facial paralysis in my early days. Sometimes I went to Llansantffraid (Montgomery) where I played for the Sunday services on a funny little one-manual organ by Bishop. The regular organist was Mrs. Ward of Blodwell Hall.

On one of these visits I remember her distress because there was a dumb note in the organ. (The tuner only came once a year.) During my first voluntary I noticed that the right lip of one of the front-row painted pipes was flattened in over the cutter. During the sermon I straightened it with my jack-knife and made it speak—much to Mrs. Ward's delight.

It was on one of these holidays that I first met the great Henry Leslie, founder of that unique body known as Henry Leslie's Select Choir. He was a native of Llansantffraid but had retired.

Hermann Smith, with whom I became acquainted at the Fisheries Exhibition, was a keen acoustician and whetted my appetite for further knowledge of pitch pipes and harmonium reeds. Every time we met we went into his theories regarding the air column in organ pipes. I think he must have known Helmholtz's *Sensations of Tone* by heart, and was a great friend of A. J. Ellis, the translator from the German of this monumental work. Ellis actually quotes Smith in the appendix of the work on free reeds, and it was through Smith's introduction to Ellis that I became interested in phonetics and his system of glossic spelling. I was so interested that I actually went to Daniel Jones (Professor of Phonetics at University College) and studied the subject. I have found the knowledge thus gained very helpful in teaching and training choirs because it made me alert to vowel analysis and the action of consonants.

Smith had gone into the subject thoroughly. He showed me varied qualities of tone obtained from resonance-caverns of differing shapes and materials. For these experiments he had four octaves of harmonium reeds blown by two feeders working below a windchest, the pressure of which was kept uniform by three spiral springs. One of his fads was buying every size of wooden box he could—usually from Oriental shops in London. He then cut away one side and bored a vent-hole in varying positions. He next placed the boxes above his row of reeds and showed me the effect of the resonance-caverns on the tone-quality issuing from the free reed. After James Baillie Hamilton exhibited his free-reed organ called the *Vocalion* he consulted Smith in all matters concerning its improvement.

Smith was very keen on what he called 'the tone of the air'. He fashioned a set of sticks about four feet long. These were of all shapes—round, oval, square, triangular, flat; some had blunt and some had sharp edges. These he used to swish through the air.

"*It is the shape of the vacuum produced at the back of the stick,* and the air rushing into this vacuum, that makes the difference in sound between the various sticks," he told me. "I can show you the same thing with the cutter of an organ pipe. The cutter, of course, acts as the air reed."

I still have a small collection of organ pipes ranging from six to eighteen inches in length. Also a vast number of tuning forks including a box of twelve given to me by Smith. Ellis had left them to him. The forks were originally made for the great German acoustician Professor Koenig. I have as well a small harmonium specially tuned to unequal temperament which serves to remind me of what the tuning of keyed instruments was before Bach brought out his well tempered clavier and wrote his forty-eight Preludes and Fugues to show that the twelve major and minor keys were now usable.

Hermann Smith often related to me his experiences when he accompanied the great Emerson on a lecture tour. He described Emerson's habit of carrying slips of paper about with him. These were about the size of an ordinary luggage label and on them he jotted down notes of things he saw or heard. When he arrived home he distributed these slips in an enormous nest of pigeon holes which hung on the wall over his desk. Later, when he settled down to serious writing he culled subjects and ideas from these notes. Smith said he was sure they were an inspiration for some of his greatest works.

As I say, Smith interested me vastly. He was an amazing man, intimate with Tennyson and Charles Dickens—indeed, with most of the literary men of the day. I soon shared his enthusiasm for Emerson and shortly afterwards acquired his complete works. My real literary hero, however, was Ruskin whom I was privileged to meet a year or two before his death in 1900.

X

I MEET RUSKIN

My MEETING WITH Ruskin in his home in Brantwood came about during my stay with Mary Wakefield and her brother at Grange-over-Sands. I remember how intense was my excitement in anticipation of meeting this great man of letters. When we arrived, however, he could not be found; but, guided by Mr. and Miss Severn with whom he lived, or who lived with him—I never actually discovered which—we eventually came across him in a reverie, leaning against a wall in the garden and looking out over his beloved Coniston Water.

At this time Ruskin was an old man, given to long silences and melancholy. We approached him in some trepidation; but Mary Wakefield, in her charming buoyant manner, easily broke the silence and presented me.

"This is young Henry Wood of Queen's Hall, London. He is going to direct my festival[1] next month. He is going to become a great choral conductor because he understands the voice and the art of singing better than anyone I know. He also paints."

During this somewhat lengthy introduction Ruskin's eyes had gradually grown less dreamy. He now looked at me with an air of interest. After a moment I plucked up enough courage to address him.

"Sir, I have read everything you have written about painting and drawing, and have spent days in the National Gallery studying Turner as a result." I added that I was familiar with many of Turner's four thousand water-colour sketches in the National Gallery.

"Do you know his *Swans*?" asked Ruskin.

"No, sir, but I shall make it my business to *get* to know it."

Actually it took me over two years to discover this white-and-sepia chalk drawing on brown paper. That was because, in those days, only three hundred and fifty of the drawings could be exhibited in the show cases at one time, the curator changing them about every three months. I actually made a copy of *Swans* which I still possess.

"Do you teach music?" was Ruskin's next question.

"Only singing."

"Well, I don't know much about singing, but if you teach your pupils to make a clear-voiced little instrument of *themselves* on which they can always depend, it is all you need try to achieve."

Conversation again turned to painting. Constable was a favourite of mine, and I ventured to mention him as a fine landscape artist.

Ruskin grunted.

"H'm . . . yes . . ." he admitted grudgingly, "but when I look at a picture of his I always want to put up an umbrella!"

[1] The Westmorland Musical Festival.

During my stay in Westmorland, Mary Wakefield introduced me to William Collingwood (Ruskin's secretary); the Croppers of Ellergreen; the Willinks of Whitefoot in whose delightful home I have since spent so many happy hours; Fred Yeats the painter, his wife and daughter. Of Miss Yeats's beautiful models of dancing figures and sheep and lambs I still have many replicas. I have also a little oil landscape which I painted in Ruskin's garden at Coniston Water. This I showed at the St. John's Wood Art School where it was admired by Sigismund Goetze whose great picture *He was despised* toured England and met with much appreciation.

Mr. Cropper was a fine-looking man and very keen on making a success of the biennial Westmorland Music Festival. The Willinks were equally enthusiastic. They helped to organize an art exhibition in Kendal with a view to augmenting generous gifts—made by themselves and many other music lovers in the Lake District—in aid of a laudable scheme to transfer the Festival from a very uncomfortable drill hall—where the platform was constructed of planks supported on barrels—to St. George's Hall.

I lent twenty of my own oil pictures for this show and Yeats worked like a Trojan hanging and cataloguing the exhibits. Although most of these were for sale, I did not wish to part with mine. However, at the close of the show, Mr. Cropper begged me to sell him one for £10. As the sale was in aid of the fund I could hardly refuse. I must say that, after my very early sketches, I have never wished to part with any of my canvases, but I still have the pleasure of seeing this, my *Sunlit Cornfield*, whenever I go to his house at Ellergreen where it is delightfully hung.

At this exhibition I first came across the water-colour sketches of Dr. Herbert Thompson, the well-known art and music critic of the *Yorkshire Post* whom I met in person in the early days of Sir Augustus Harris's Italian opera season at Covent Garden. I have met him since at most of my Philharmonic concerts in Hull when we always stay at the Royal Station Hotel and enjoy chats about art during breakfast the next morning. He is the only musical critic of my acquaintance who is also a practical painter. I have always enjoyed his musical commentaries because they are free from bias and cant.

One report of a concert of mine at Hull did, however, puzzle me. It concerned Elgar's *Enigma Variations*. The variation known as *Nimrod* was described as 'a fitting memorial in its elegant note'. The next time I met Thompson I asked him what he meant.

"An illustration of the evils of telegraphing notices," he replied. "What I said was *elegiac* note."

Dr. Thompson gave a fine series of lectures on art at the Leeds University some years ago; I still possess a copy of his chronological chart of British painters.

Returning to Westmorland festivals, I call to mind what an excellent chorus master George Rathbone was, a fact evident by his popularity in the villages whence the contingents came. Moreover, he was an extraordinarily good pianist which helped in no small measure during his preliminary rehearsals. Later on, my friend Arthur Willink took over the direction and training of the chorus with splendid results.

These festivals often furnished us with odd and amusing situations, two or three of which I recall happening this year. The Princess Christian was to give the prizes resulting from nineteen village competitions. She was accompanied by the Countess Bective, and I shall never forget how diligently Mary Wakefield worked during the whole morning to train the prize-winners to curtsy and walk backwards before Her Royal Highness, and how we rocked with merriment watching her train two policemen in the latter movement.

The policemen were to bring the Princess into the hall, this being the only sign of officialdom we could muster. The local officer, in accordance with Mary Wakefield's request to 'send two of your best men', sent one fine-looking constable about six-foot-four and the other somewhere about five feet. It was too ridiculous to watch these men walk up the centre gangway preceding the Princess; and I personally was hard put to keep a straight face when the Countess, following up, tipped me a broad wink while I directed (with as much dignity as I could command) the National Anthem.

Then followed the prize-giving during which one small girl clutched the Princess's knee to steady herself during her curtsy, while a couple of large boys would persist (in spite of many dumb signs to them) in walking backwards towards the edge of the platform, facing the Princess whose horror was audibly expressed when she saw that they must step off into space and probably land on top of Mrs. Rosa Newmarch who was sitting in the stalls just below. However, Providence (or something akin) prevented the catastrophe with the first boy's consciousness intervening just as his heel was going over the edge.

At this same Kendal festival we had forgathered at our hotel, and had been discussing the unfortunate habit of foreign publishers in getting their translations made at home. Mrs.

Newmarch declared she remembered in her youth the translation of a famous ballad called *The Wolf* which a great artist had sung at one of the 'Pop' concerts. The English words, she declared, ran something like this:

> When the Wolf, with glitt'ring shout
> Crieth ' t-whit, to-whoo! *Get out!* '
> Out he came with fierce persistence;
> Maidens shrieked—but no assistance.

Later in the afternoon, Ernest Newman produced a newly-published album of German classics, and pointed to a gem of translation in a line which ran: *O, Maiden, take the bloody rose!*

We were convulsed with laughter and heard in our imaginations a musical curate or a very prim and youthful soprano declaiming this text from the platform. Before the day was out we had formed a secret circle on mediæval lines—a sort of Rosicrucian sect. We each received a card of membership with roses painted on them in red toothpaste by Ernest Newman, and we also invented the *Sign of the Bloody Rose* which I was to make with my baton before starting the evening concert. Naturally, the audience (with the exception of Mary Wakefield) had no idea what this cabalistic sign really meant. They probably regarded it as one of my 'little affectations' as a conductor. The *Bloody Rose Society* continued to exist for some time. These were jolly days indeed—and, of course, we were all very young.

XI

I GO ON TOUR

The Arthur Rousbey Grand English Opera Company. Experienced conductor required. Tour commencing August 1. This week: West London Theatre, Edgware rd. Write Manager.

WHETHER IT WAS in the *Stage* or the *Era* that I read this advertisement I have completely forgotten. It was in one or the other. Perhaps the word *grand* caught my fancy. I cannot say; but I remember showing it to my mother who wisely suggested that we attended one of the company's performances. On reference to a daily paper we found they were giving *Faust* that night, and decided to go.

Despite the extravagance, my mother took a stage box. The orchestra was deplorable, the most important instruments being absent; but the conductor attempted to fill in the gaps with his left hand on an upright piano which was not even in tune.

The chorus, however, was excellent. Marguerite, poor dear, had a very pronounced cast in one eye, but her voice was solid and strong. Faust was a barrel of a man who sang throatily. The bass was the best, the baritone (Valentine) being taken by Rousbey himself. A pompous little fellow with an extremely penetrating voice, he barked and notched every phrase and sang all slurred phrases with marked aspirates. (Qui-hi-het home I-hi-hi leave behind.)

I thought of old Garcia. Had this man been in his class he would have had a book at his head. He wore the heaviest make-up I have ever seen on the stage. His eyelashes looked like the railings in Hyde Park, and he persisted in singing into his hand, holding the locket which was about the size of a plate. My mother was disgusted.

"My dear Henry, you can't possibly conduct a crowd like this," she said to me after the first act.

"But, Mother, think of the experience of controlling and training such a crowd!"

At all events, I answered the advertisement. The result was an interview with Rousbey, a smartly-dressed little man with a deep voice and manner intended, I imagine, to convey the idea that he was a dramatic baritone. In this overpowering presence I felt exceedingly conscious of my youthful appearance, for although I had carefully cultivated a fluffy bit of wool round my chin in the hope it might add to my years in appearance, I felt he was looking through the wool and through me as well. Fortunately he did not ask me my age. I handed him my splendid testimonial from Gustav Garcia.

"This is—ah—a very fine testimonial, Mr. Wood," he said impressively. "May I inquire what experience you have had? Of course you know our splendid repertoire," he continued without giving me a chance to say anything. "We have done *Maritana*, *Bohemian Girl*, *Martha*, *Figaro*, *Carmen*, and *Il Trovatore*. Next season I shall do *Don Giovanni* and a new opera, by a young Leeds composer, called *Belfigore*."

"I know all except *Belfigore*," I said.

"What operas have you conducted in public?"

"*Mignon* at the Royalty; *The Mock Doctor* at the Crystal Palace; *Pepita* (Lecocq), as well as my own *Returning the Compliment*, *A Hundred Years Ago*, *Daisy*, *Zuleika*, and *Nacoochee*."

"That seems all right. What salary for the first year?"

I went into a cold perspiration. I had to choose then and there between my pupils and this chance of conducting opera. Fearing I might ask too much—not having the slightest idea what salary I should receive in this class of company—I stammered something about two guineas a week. Rousbey turned to his manager.

"Make out a contract for three years. Two guineas a week for the first year; four for the second; eight for the third."

He turned to me and held out his hand.

"Good morning, Mr. Wood!"

The next moment I was out in the street. This hustled contract taught me a valuable lesson—one which all young students might well remember. When fees are being discussed with hard-headed business men, on no account should a direct answer be given right away. Every one is entitled to ask for an hour to consider a business proposition during which time a student may be able to consult a parent or a teacher.

My return home with this contract in my pocket surprised my parents. They were amazed, but the 'Henry-can-do-no-wrong' theory was still their law and, as usual, they backed me up in my new scheme.

I had to explain to my pupils that I should be away, but I said nothing as to the period it was likely to be. I was giving up a lucrative teaching connection—but experience came first.

A week or so before we opened I attended piano rehearsals at Mortimer Hall (Mortimer Street) where, to my surprise, I found Henry Hayes who had been a student in Holland's class at the Academy. He was taking small baritone parts. I had actually seen him and told him what I was about to do, but he had mentioned nothing about joining the cast himself.

The full company assembled at Charing Cross station, and I found myself with a chorus of forty, a travelling orchestra of six, ten principals, a wardrobe master and mistress, an advance booking agent, and a stage manager—all bound for Ramsgate. Of Rousbey himself I had seen nothing since the original interview. He was much too grand to attend piano rehearsals, and Hayes was his understudy.

I was now too grown-up to be seen off by my parents, but my mother went on by an earlier train to be sure her dear boy had comfortable lodgings. She had a bad time of it. There was a heavy storm raging, and she went from apartment to apartment without success. Not surprising—at Ramsgate on August 1st. However, half an hour before our train arrived, she found lodgings some distance from the theatre. She met me at the station and waited while I deposited my nice new trunk in the cloakroom. The other trunk travelled with the theatrical baggage. It was a huge affair, packed with scores, band parts, tuning forks, and many books. Everybody seemed to object to this trunk owing to its weight, and I took a youthful delight in watching the surprise of the porters when they tackled it.

The rooms were not lovely, but they were clean. The rent—this my mother broke gently to me—was two guineas a week. I was aghast.

"But I only *earn* that a week," I protested. As usual, I was told not to worry; my father would see me through. My mother then returned to town after giving me a tremendous tea. She seemed gratified at the idea of starting me off with a good meal.

The first days were spent in rehearsing. The orchestra—as usual—was hopeless. I fear I became sarcastic and upset things a little by asking the violins whether they were sure they were playing on the right string. The woodwind played so out of tune that I begged them not to *transpose*—a remark that did not go down very well.

The climax, however, came on the opening night. The stage band for the march in *Faust* was a local affair. The rehearsal was fixed for six o'clock. The local band turned up, but most of them appeared to be a little 'Saturday-afternoonish', the bass drummer especially. This band sometimes played on the pier and consisted of two cornets, two saxhorns, and a base drum. Not having to appear until the third act, these gentlemen retired for further refreshment. And a fine sight they made at their entry, the drummer wearing his cap at a rakish angle! He played his part abominably, landing after the beat rather than on it, with special effects on each bar-*line*. I fixed him with a glare that ought to have sobered him for all time, left the chorus and orchestra to take care of themselves, and dug out the second and fourth beats, leaning half over the prompt box. The chorus loved it, of course; especially when he lurched off-stage to the accompaniment of derisive cheers from a packed house.

After living by myself for a fortnight, I joined Hayes—at his suggestion. It was a good idea because he could attend to the catering. We were giving eight shows a week, and rehearsals were from ten till five—so that I had little time to spare for such mundane things as food.

The venture worked admirably and Hayes was a delightful companion. One day I asked him how Rousbey came to engage him merely to play small parts and to understudy. I was touched by his reply.

"I heard you were to conduct," he said simply. He then told me that his mother had advanced £100, returnable as salary at 25s. a week, as there was no actual vacancy. All this to be with me!

One Sunday morning we were preparing to leave a northern town, and I glanced down our bill for the week. One item arrested my attention: *use of cruet 4s. 6d.* We were used to *use of cruet 2s. 6d.*, but this seemed excessive. However, the landlady refused to give way when I questioned it. I paid up—*and took the cruet*, despite the protests of the landlady and her daughter who followed us to the station. I had a grand reception from the company when I arrived on the platform with the cruet dangling from my little finger. I explained that I had bought it for 4s. 6d.—a better one could be bought nowadays from Woolworths for sixpence—but as the train moved off I gave it back to the weeping girl. This brought a roar of cheering from the rest of the company who were watching from the carriage windows.

We opened in a small Lancashire town with *Don Giovanni*, during a rehearsal for which I noticed an altercation going on between Rouseby and the local stage carpenter. Rousbey was evidently thinking of the Commandatore's requirements in the last act.

"I must have a horse."

"Ain't got no 'orse!"

Rousbey paced up and down. The carpenter thought hard.

"Ah've got it, sir!"

"Well?"

"Christmas panto at Middlesboro' oop younder 'ave got cow what I can paint white and cut down into a 'orse. Send t'van this afternoon, get cow, and I can see 'bout it."

During Tuesday's band rehearsal the cow arrived. A crowd of children watched it being pushed in through the scene-shifters' slot at the back of the stage. It was an unlovely animal —merely a silhouette cut out of one-inch board. They brought it in and fixed it to the floor whereupon the carpenter sawed its tummy off, trimmed its horns, and lopped its tufty tail. He then outlined what he considered were the proper contours of a horse and painted it a greyish white.

The next morning Rousbey inspected it. Gilbert King swore he could not sit on that knife-edge for half an hour and sing the Commandatore's part with any sense of dignity.

More thought by the carpenter. More pacing by Rousbey. At last: "Eh, lad, Ah've got it! I'll lend thee t'bike saddle." That night King mounted his gee-gee with the aid of a short pair of steps. His right leg was cocked over the animal's back with the toe of his boot in a stirrup; his left foot rested on a false step at the back. He was a heavy man and his deep breathing efforts made the horse wobble so much that more screws and struts were necessary to steady it. I had my work cut out to keep the orchestra from laughing, and had already told Rousbey that the audience would not take the last act seriously. The gallery comments subsequently proved my contention.

"Taak it 'ome! Thaat were't no 'orse! Thaat's a bloody cow!"

The difficulties did not end there. Rousbey told me the Middlesbrough people protested that he had returned them a horse whereas they had lent him a cow. They wanted their cow back.

There was much amusement the night we did *Faust*. When we came to where Marguerite and Faust were singing the duet a cat shot across the stage pursued by a small terrier dog. The unfortunate artists craned their necks to discover why the audience was laughing.

After a month of this sort of thing I tackled Rousbey and told him I could not possibly go on at the salary.

"I gave you what you asked," he reminded me.

"I know, but you were too quick for me."

He was very charming and offered a new contract for £6 for the first season, and £10 and £12 respectively for the other two; but I had already overworked and arrived home at the end of the first season a bundle of nerves. I had to break the contract and some rather difficult letters had to be written; but it came all right in the end because Rousbey himself had ideas of being a conductor. As I had given him tuition, and as he had conducted an act as many as three times in a week, he was now able and willing to take on the direction himself.

XII

MORE GRAND OPERA

After a short rest I resumed my teaching and went into partnership with Gustav Garcia in his operatic school in Berners Street. I also attended evening art classes at Heatherly's school in Newman Street. I always visualize dear old Heatherly in his velvet coat, coming round about every three weeks to examine my work. I then studied under the great Legros and, later, under Brown and Tonks at the Slade School of Art. Two years afterwards I went to the St. John's Wood Art School and studied under Ward to whom I was greatly attached. Later still I was under Walenn who, by the way, was a member of the well-known musical family.

I directed a few concerts at St. James's Hall during this period. At one of them (run by Daniel Mayer) Mark Hambourg played three concertos. Hambourg was then fifteen. His wonderful technique created a deep impression, and he was considered to be another Rubinstein. Incidentally, he resembled him in appearance. Busoni told me a few years later that he thought he possessed the greatest talent in the piano world at that time.

My next engagement was to conduct Marie Roze's farewell operatic tour with the Carl Rosa Company. She was the idol of the British public—equal in popularity with Patti and Melba —and the memories of this tour are amongst the sweetest of my life of music.

Unlike Rousbey, Marie Roze was *not* too grand to attend my piano rehearsals. Ganz, I remember, presented me to her as 'the young conductor of whom Mrs. Carl Rosa thinks so much'. She herself introduced me to almost everyone she knew. No small favour, for through her I met Irving, Ellen Terry, Bancroft, Hare, the Kendals, Forbes-Robertson, Mary Anderson, etcetera.

Our company included fine singers: Lily Moody, Durward Lely, Wilfred Howard and Lily Hunt; and we travelled with a splendid orchestra of ten. As we only visited the larger cities, I found the local orchestras better than those I met in the days of Rousbey's company. However, one unfortunate incident I vividly recall.

A few hours before the opening of *Carmen* our flautist fell ill. We hurriedly engaged a local man who was recommended by the manager of the theatre. There was no chance for rehearsal which naturally made me very anxious, but I was assured that he was a splendid flautist and would require no rehearsing.

He failed to take his first entrance and again the second. The orchestra, knowing the work so well, filled in his parts—a violin here, a viola there—while I practically conducted him alone throughout the first act. I was blazing and, at the last bar—seeing he was the first to make for the exit—rushed round, caught, and confronted him with: '*You impostor !* I thought you could play the flute!''

"So did I, and it's a bit of a sook for both of us," he yelled at me—and fled. We finished without a flute, the part being filled in by our leader.

We had a delightful manager named Pitt whom we called 'Blinkin' Pitt' because he continually blinked. He later became manager of the Lyric Theatre in Shaftesbury Avenue. (He was no relation of Percy Pitt.)

As for Marie Roze, her triumph was phenomenal. Police had to be called out to deal with the crowds which welcomed her at the railway stations when she arrived; still greater throngs gathered before her hotel, often refusing to go away until she had appeared on the balcony and had sung them a song. They took the horses from the shafts of her carriage outside the theatre, the stage door of which was unapproachable for an hour after the performance.

One night, after a perfectly terrific stage-door demonstration, the crowds practically lifted Marie into her carriage. As soon as we were inside she made me pull down the blinds and, in order to get away at all, I waved my hand from underneath the blind and had it shaken and kissed by the excited crowd who, doubtless, thought it was hers.

I had many happy hours with this radiant personality. She told me tales of her student days in Paris and of her meetings with Massé, Berlioz, Gounod, Bizet, Godard, and Massenet whose *Manon* she adored. She was herself ideal in the name part. She told me how she attended the wounded during the siege of Paris in 1870, and how she received—every day during the siege—a tiny loaf of white bread tied up with blue ribbon. She never discovered who sent it.

This tour lasted three months. I then resumed teaching and my work with Garcia. My next operatic venture was with Leslie Crotty and Georgina Burns, probably the most popular baritone and soprano Carl Rosa ever had. They had retired from the company and were very well off, having drawn large salaries for a number of years. They now ran a company of their own with myself as conductor. This was the best-paid operatic engagement I ever held. Crotty's voice was brilliant—not unlike Santley's, but he was not such a good actor.

Tom Robertson, a distant relative of Crotty, had prepared an English version of *La Cenerentola* (Rossini) to arrange which Crotty paid me a lump sum, asking me to touch up the score in places. This I did, and inserted extra choruses from Rossini's other operas. It was a great success in the musical and dramatic sense but, despite Georgina Burns' admirable singing and the comedy of Alice Bath and Charlie Morand, the opera failed to draw a public. Crotty must have lost heavily.

He was angry at this lack of support, especially as he knew that if he had produced *Faust* or *The Bohemian Girl* he would have seen a return; but he did not wish to encroach upon the repertory of the Carl Rosa. His company he paid liberally and every member of it loved and respected him.

Three months later I received a letter from Lago, the impresario of the Imperial Opera Company of St. Petersburg. Lago was in London engaging a company for a twelve weeks' season of Italian opera at the Olympic Theatre, off the Strand. His letter enclosed one from Gustav Garcia. In it he said he required a young English conductor to be second in command to Arditi. Garcia had recommended me. Lago wanted to open with *Eugène Onegin* (Tchaikovsky) and to produce both *Lohengrin* and *Oberon* in Italian. Tchaikovsky was almost unknown in London at that time, and this was my introduction to his works. I wired an acceptance provided Crotty would release me.

The company was in Edinburgh where I arrived late on a Sunday afternoon. I found the score of *Onegin* awaiting me. I wanted to go through it but there was no piano in my hotel. I took a cab and called upon several members of the company to see whether there was a piano in their lodgings. It must have been seven o'clock before I found one in rooms shared by Kate Hemming and another singer. Kate Hemming read the contralto part of the Nurse and her friend that of Tatiana. After twenty minutes or so there was a knock, and a very dour-looking Scots landlady stood outside.

"It's the Sabbath," she informed me. "Ye must no' sing but sacred music."

We mollified her and resumed. In another ten minutes she was there again.

"The gentleman in the rooms above has been doon," she said. "He says ye must no' sing but sacred music."

"We are," I said. "It's called *The Meeting of the Holy Apostles* by a new Russian composer." However, it was no good. She returned for the third time and told Miss Hemming that if she *must* sing she could find other lodgings. I returned to my hotel and read the score until the early hours of the morning.

I was now more keen than ever to conduct for Lago. I had an interview with Crotty the next day. He was sympathetic and agreed to release me so long as I provided *and coached* another conductor, came down each Sunday evening to rehearse the orchestra the following morning, and conducted the opening in each new town every Monday night. He offered a generous fee and I thought there would be no difficulty in getting a conductor. I telegraphed to friends at the R.A.M. and advertised in *The Times* and *Telegraph*. Knowing Allen Gill's ambition was to conduct, I invited him; but he would not give up his organist post—"in case," he said, "the tour does not last."

Every two or three days I invited a prospective conductor to my hotel, expenses paid. The day was spent in going through the score; at night I sat by him in the orchestra. One night he would direct a first act; the next a second, and so on. During the interval I would go to Crotty's dressing-room for an opinion.

"My dear man, he is no good. He has no control over the orchestra and never gives the singers their cues. He follows the voice so badly, too. Might be all right in Wagner; no good for Rossini."

This went on for five weeks. I was in despair. At last a young German, whose name I forget now, proved to be my liberator.

Lago had a rival in Sir Augustus Harris who was plainly jealous of him. The previous autumn (1891) Lago had produced *Cavalleria Rusticana* for the first time in England at the newly-built Shaftesbury Theatre. Vignas sang Turiddu and created a *furore*. Harris, however, refused to lease either Covent Garden or Drury Lane to Lago, who was forced to take the New Olympic —a perfect barn of a place. Indeed, this season was known as 'the battle of the operas' owing to Harris's attitude towards Lago. Although Lago had Albani at the Olympic, Harris opposed him at Covent Garden. As a result neither succeeded.

My leader was J. T. Carrodus whom Robert Newman engaged to lead for me at the Promenade concerts at Queen's Hall in 1895. Unfortunately, however, he died shortly before they were opened. I met other musicians who were eventually to be associated with the Promenades, amongst whom were Adolph Borsdorf (horn), Lalande (oboe), Wotton and James (bassoon), and Solomon, whose trumpet-playing I still enjoy at my students' concerts at the R.A.M. where he has been professor for many years.

The production of *Eugène Onegin* established me as a conductor.

I shared the conductorship with old Signor Arditi (who died in 1903 at Hove, aged eighty-one). His knowledge of English was very limited and the orchestra derived great pleasure from wilfully misunderstanding him. Almost every day at band rehearsal he would tap and stop, look towards a particular section of the orchestra and cry in a piping *falsetto* : "Play nice, play nice!" By the third week of the season the band began to get fed up with this continual 'play nice!' and one morning Arditi turned to the double-basses, among whom was Hider [1] whose voice and size matched his instrument. Unable to control himself any longer when admonished to 'play nice', Hider replied in a stentorian bass voice: "I AM playing nice!" That cured Arditi of his 'play nice'.

However, he still continued to tap every first beat of the bar on the top of a Bechstein conductor's piano whenever the music was at all complicated. I remember that so well because, years afterwards, I bought that actual instrument from Elliott's of Watford.

During this season I first met Granville Bantock, a man of expansive mind whose *Omar Khayyàm* I admire so intensely. His outlook is big and noble in every way; many a man has been helped by this generous-minded musician.

Bantock's early work was definitely Wagnerian. Many of his later orchestral compositions contain very fine, original ideas and I regret that they are not more often performed. *The Pierrot of the Minute*, a comedy overture, is admittedly difficult and requires careful rehearsal, but had it been written by Debussy or Ravel there would have been no question about it: it would have been played the world over. His *Sappho Songs* are most beautifully written with wonderful insight for the voice. The same may be said of his Chinese songs, the words of which are superb translations from ancient Chinese poets.

Lady Bantock, who is a clever linguist, has made many translations for her husband's choral works and songs. She is evidently very understanding in regard to his expansiveness, for the following occurred without a word of remonstrance on her part. One day I was lunching with them at their home near Birmingham in company with Tovey and Anderton (who was known to us all as 'the Colonel' and who was Bantock's lifelong

[1] Known in the string world as the maker of a popular resin.

friend) when Lady Bantock suddenly exclaimed: "Good gracious! Here's a farmer's cart coming up the drive! What ever can be in it?"

Before the cart was near enough for us to see what it contained, we saw a second and a third pass the window loaded with full sacks.

"Where did these come from?" asked Lady Bantock. "Someone must have sent them to the wrong house."

"Well, no!" said Granville. "I had a little time to wait in Birmingham the other day and saw an auction sale of bulbs and things. I had heard you say you wanted a few, so I went in and bid. A 'lot' that seemed very cheap was knocked down to me. I suppose that is it."

Dear Granville! I am proud to say our early friendship has not diminished with the years.

My first—and last—taste of grand opera-conducting came to an unfortunate ending. After *Onegin* had run for some weeks Lago disappeared, leaving us all high and dry. I then rejoined Garcia's opera school and directed *Martha* (Flotow), *Semiramide* (Rossini) and *The Barber of Seville*. I remember Marie Garcia, a gifted singer and actress, and also Smallwood Metcalfe, a pupil of mine who became well known as a teacher of singing in Eastbourne and afterwards chorus master of the Queen's Hall Choral Society. He, by the way, was nephew to William Smallwood whose famous *Piano Tutor* must have earned for him a small fortune. I often met Smallwood Metcalfe at Kendal.

The next rung on the ladder was an engagement as conductor of Marie Roze's farewell concert tour under the direction of N. Vert. The tour extended from December, 1893 to March, 1894, during which time we visited forty-two towns.

We rehearsed in a fine room in Archibald Ramsden's piano galleries in Bond Street. An astute business man, Ramsden, and a typical rough Yorkshireman. He was a good judge of pictures and always managed to sell at a profit those he purchased. He took up an agency for the Schiedmayer pianos which were made in Stuttgart. At this time the most acceptable English piano was probably the Broadwood, but Ramsden popularized the Schiedmayer and sold hundreds of them.

He came in one morning to a rehearsal of *Cavalleria*.

"Henry Wood accompanies on the piano like a full orchestra," he told Vert, "but he'll never keep it up like that for a three months' tour."

"Don't you worry," I said without turning round. "I shall keep it up all right." Which I can honestly say I did. At all events, Ramsden was so delighted with me that he made me a member of his *U.B. Quiet Club*, so called from his habit of saying "You be quiet! I'll tell you all about it."

The 'club' met in a small room above his piano galleries. Any afternoon I could meet such men as Richter, Edward Lloyd, Andrew Black, A. J. Ellis, Vert, Arbos, Barrett of the *Morning Post*, Kalisch, etcetera. There would always be a couple of bottles of whisky and half a dozen 'Pollies' to cheer those who cared for it.

My association with Marie Roze was again a happy one. She regarded us all as her big family and, as usual, went triumphantly from one town to another. She sang a concert version of Santuzza's part in *Cavalleria* in the first half, the second being miscellaneous. One item was always a piano solo by her son Raymond, who was a dear boy but who never studied or worked. His professor (Arthur de Greef) would often write to his mother from Brussels saying he did not know what to do with young Raymond, for the boy spent all his time taking young ladies out to lunch, with the result that his memory was of the very worst and his piano solos were becoming shorter and shorter.

I was the only one who knew this, and told his mother so. She would then sometimes sit behind a screen, listen, and severely admonish him for his evident want of study. Later on he began to fancy himself as a composer, but on looking through his songs (which his mother sometimes showed me) I could detect no talent for composition. His writing for orchestra was hopeless, for it was evident from his score that he did not know the correct compass of the instrument for which he wrote, at this early stage.

Yet, through his mother's friendship with Irving and Tree, some years later, he became musical director to their London theatres and wrote incidental music for their stage productions. In 1913 he brought out his opera *Joan of Arc* at Covent Garden. I was naturally interested in his career and dropped in to several of his performances, but invariably came away with the impression of having spent half an hour with the well-known composers! Arthur de Greef, by the way, cannot be held responsible; he only taught Raymond the piano at Brussels.

At the end of the tour Marie Roze gave up her home in Regent's Park and went to teach in Paris. I never went there myself without visiting her and she always came to my concerts. I remember she told me the night I conducted Lamoureux's orchestra that her musical friends thought me un-English in appearance.

"They expected a bald-headed, big-toothed man—not a fluffy-headed bearded youngster," she told me.

Marie Roze was one of the world's beauties—the equal, probably, of Lily Langtry. She was a great actress but not a great singer.

While I think of it, I ought to say here that I owe a debt of gratitude both to Bernard Shaw and Robert Hichens who greatly encouraged me by their thoughtful criticisms in the *World* and *Saturday Review* at this time.

I often met George Bernard Shaw in those days at Mrs. Pattison's house in Brompton Square. "I like Marie's performances," he said, "but I keep my eyes open and my ears shut." This was a reference to her habit of singing out of tune, but undoubtedly she always charmed (and disarmed) her critics. Incidentally, I could name more than one lady who sings regularly out of tune, but I never see the fact commented on by our present-day music critics. They must be tone deaf. I have heard Saint-Saëns, Debussy, Ysaÿe, Strauss, and Elgar all attempt to sing when illustrating something. Some sang in the queerest voices—*but always dead in tune*. It is all a question of ear-training. My voice is the world's worst but I never sing out of tune. Even Bernard Shaw would agree, though I doubt whether his remark about open eyes and closed ears would apply in my case!

One last memory of Marie Roze. I was to conduct Gounod's *Redemption* at the Winter Gardens, Blackpool, then under Holland's management. It was Christmas-time and a thick fog caused us to arrive six hours late. Marie was in a fever about the fog and swore she would not be able to sing her part; but I had coached her and knew that she was musically certain of it.

We assembled at two o'clock for rehearsal. The orchestra was mainly composed of the Hallé players. I remember dear old Speilman led the violas and Carl Fuchs the 'cellos. The four trumpets for *Unfold, ye Portals!* were in two of the boxes. After an hour's rehearsal Holland, who had been pacing the stalls gangway, pulled my coat tails.

"Ah saay, Mr. Wood! The four troompets up in boxes ain't plaayed a nawte yet!"

"All right, Mr. Holland! They don't come in until *Unfold, ye Portals!*"

Half an hour later:

"Ah saay, Mr. Wood! Ah'm not paayin' them troompets to sit oop there and look pretty!"

"All right, Mr. Holland! *Unfold, ye Portals!*"

At last came the cue. The trumpeters nearly blew their heads off. . . .

"Eh, ba Goom! That were champion! *Let 'em do it again!* "

I now prevailed upon my father to give up business and become my secretary. One of my clearest memories of these days is returning from the last Marie Roze concert at Dublin on March 3, 1894—my twenty-fifth birthday—and going to a new home at No. 1, Langham Place (on the corner of Mortimer Street and Upper Regent Street) where I installed my dear mother with an efficient staff so that she could indulge her flair for entertaining.

And there . . . just a few doors away . . . was a *new* building. It's name was . . . QUEEN'S HALL.

Little did I realize the significance of its nearness!

XIII

I MEET FELIX MOTTL

I FIRST VISITED BAYREUTH for the festival the year Liszt died (1886) since when I have made it the scene of many pilgrimages. The London agent for these festivals was Schultz-Curtius who became my constant companion during these visits, introducing me to the great German artists and conductors. In 1903 Schultz-Curtius started his wonderful series of orchestral concerts at Queen's Hall, bringing over great Wagnerian conductors such as Levi, Mottl, Weingartner, Seidl, Siegfried Wagner, and many famous artists including Ternina, Vogl, van Rooy, Schumann-Heink and others. He appointed me musical adviser for his London concerts as he himself was not a musician. My work was to arrange the lay-out of his programmes, as well as to correct, section, letter, and—most important of all —to add the finishes to the concert excerpts from Wagner's operas, these having been given me by Levi and Mottl. I have used these endings all my life, and it greatly amuses me when the Press criticize them as 'Wood tampering with Wagner'.

One of the conductors I met at Bayreuth was Mottl. Conversation was something of an effort as neither of us was fluent in the other's language. Mottl liked me, and he took great interest in my conducting of Wagner and demonstrated his own interpretations at the piano, explaining many traditional points.

These have been invaluable to me, not alone when conducting concert excerpts, but when teaching Wagnerian roles.

My full scores of the *Ring* contain many of his remarks; most valuable of all are his orchestral finishes for concert use in his own handwriting. I am proud to possess them.

This experience was of the greatest importance inasmuch as it laid the foundations of my eventual success as a conductor of Wagner. This was of inestimable value to me because—apart from a superb performance at Frankfort of the *Meistersinger* overture and the Prelude and *Liebestod* from *Tristan* under the great Hans von Bülow—I had only heard Wagner done indifferently by Manns at the Crystal Palace.

It is true that I had attended Richter's concerts at St. James's Hall as a very young man, but I failed to appreciate his great qualities. I fear his performances left me cold and unmoved. Yet, strangely enough, when I heard him in Vienna, Berlin, Munich, and Bayreuth he thrilled me with his masterly grip.

I have a suspicion that many foreign conductors in those days entertained the mistaken notion that we in England did not understand music. Handel told Gluck as much one day when they met in Piccadilly; Carl Muck once expressed the same sentiment to me when I ventured to criticize a performance of the *Dutchman* under his direction at Covent Garden. All I actually said was: "What a bad performance! Full of mistakes both in the orchestra and on the stage."

Muck laughed sneeringly.

"Anything is good enough for England," he said. "Nobody understands."

I was furious.

"Dr. Muck," I said, "I paid 25*s.* for my stall tonight, and I *do* understand."

The scene of this little 'breeze' was the German Club and in the presence of several members of the London Wagner Society, including the genial Armbruster. Perhaps it would be fair to say that, many years after this, I heard the Boston Symphony Orchestra under Carl Muck when he gave some very inspired and perfect performances.

Perhaps Richter held this same view about English people not understanding music? And yet I recall a certain Monday evening at St. James's Hall when he gave a most inspired performance of the *Prelude* and *Liebestod* (*Tristan*) in the presence of Cosima Wagner who was sitting in the front row of stalls surrounded by all the German musical crowd of London.

During this period I was again teaching and found I had gained something of a reputation in America. This I owed to pupils like Alice Esty, Harriet Foster and Herbert Witherspoon, who themselves had succeeded in the States. Gustav Garcia kept me busy directing grand opera for him at the end of term and training pupils to act. Fortunately, I had kept plans of stage scenes of twenty-five operas. These I now found useful in marking vocal scores with stage positions and directions.

Garcia's dramatic class was run by Edgar B. Skeet. Sometimes we found ourselves short of a pupil for a part and had to step in ourselves. My great effort, which caused much amusement, was when I appeared at Kilburn Town Hall as a French waiter.

Even with these extra activities I continued to accept engagements as piano accompanist and found the Duchess of Wellington a good friend to me. She gave a special At Home in the wonderful picture gallery of Apsley House to introduce me to her influential friends. Four of my best pupils sang at this At Home; as a result of their performances my reputation as a teacher of singing was enhanced. I found myself teaching many days from nine till seven; but the long hours brought their reward, for I was carving out a career and making money.

Among my pupils was a certain Mrs. F. J. Harris whose husband produced plays in partnership with William Greet. Although busy teaching, I accepted his invitation to conduct *The Lady Slavey* written by George (later Sir George) Dance. It was produced at the Avenue Theatre, now the Playhouse. The principal part was taken by May Yohe, the most extraordinary prima donna I ever met.

XIV

THE INAUGURATION OF THE PROMENADE CONCERTS

In CHAPTER XII I described my home-coming on my twenty-fifth birthday from the Marie Roze tour, and my moving to Langham Place. Queen's Hall had been open for a few months only—to be exact, since the previous December when Robert Newman gave a concert with the Queen's Hall Choir which he had formed from the old Middlesex Choral Union. Cowen conducted this concert and I was engaged as organist and accompanist, this being my first association with Newman.

As a matter of fact, a message from him was waiting for me on my arrival from the tour. I remember every word of our conversation the morning he took me into the hall to see the arena cleared of all seats. Newman had a brisk, business-like manner and never wasted words. We stood looking down into the arena with its brownish carpet that blended with the dull-fawnish colour of the walls. Queen's Hall has been blue-green since then, and now it has been redecorated and given a splendid ventilation plant; but I can still see it as it was then.

"What do you think of the idea of having Promenade concerts here?" asked Newman suddenly.

"Well, with your knowledge of concerts, and given the right orchestra and artists, it should be a grand success."

"Right! Come over to Pagani's and have lunch. We can talk about it there."

I was greatly impressed with Newman over that lunch. I had never met a manager who knew anything about music. Newman did. He possessed both business acumen and artistic ideals. *He wanted the public to come to love great music.*

"I am going to run nightly concerts and train the public by easy stages," he said. "Popular at first, gradually raising the standard until I have *created* a public for classical and modern music. I shall have to get the *hall* known first; but I shall let it for City dinners and dances whether it actually pays me or not. Nobody seems to know this part of Regent Street at all, but once the hall is known, I shall run Promenade concerts with a permanent orchestra and conductor."

Newman will bear a little personal description. He was always brisk and busy but the moment he discussed music his blue eyes—they were *very* blue—lighted up as with fire, and the soft inner kindness of the man showed him to be a deep lover of music. He must have misled many by his abrupt manner, but once he spoke of art all that disappeared. He had had plenty of experience in running Promenade concerts at His Majesty's, so that he knew what he was about.

I did not meet him again until he called on me in February, 1895. With hardly a word of greeting he tackled the question of what was obviously uppermost in his mind.

"I have decided to run those Promenade concerts I told you about last year. I want you to be the conductor of a permanent Queen's Hall Orchestra. We'll run a ten weeks' season."

I can still feel the thrill of that moment. An orchestra . . . in Queen's Hall . . . *My* orchestra. . . .

"But you have never seen me conduct."

"Oh, yes I have! As often as I could—wherever you were. Given the right orchestra, you will become a *great* conductor. Anyhow, I mean to run you and *make* you. The public will support us. The time is ripe for an English conductor . . . and now . . . can you put up a little capital—say two or three thousand pounds?"

"I'm afraid not. I haven't such a sum to risk, and don't know anyone who has."

"Never mind! I'll see what can be done, *for I mean to run those concerts !*"

I left him with his words ringing in my ears and walked on air from the hall to my home. A man with a real vision; a man determined to carry out his ideals. What a chance for me!

It was at this time that I also came into contact with the lawyer Rubinstein. He was no relation to the pianist, but acted for the owners of the Queen's Hall. I subsequently attended many of his delightful musical At Homes and the family friendship continues to the present day through his clever lawyer son, my dear friend Stanley Rubinstein.

I gave a lesson later in the day to W. A. Peterkin, a Scot with a fine bass voice. Very often a friend of his came in during the lesson and sat quietly at the far end of my large music-room. He always listened intently. During a short rest in the lesson I told Peterkin about Robert Newman and said I only wished I could find the money.

Came a voice from the other end of the room: "Please tell me more about this project, Mr. Wood."

I was then formally introduced to Dr. George Cathcart, the ear and throat specialist, who (it transpired) had sent Peterkin to me for lessons. I told Dr. Cathcart exactly what Newman had said.

"I want you to introduce me to Newman," he said. "I might put up the money if he will do two things: one is to establish the *low pitch* and the other to engage you as his only conductor."

The first of these conditions was interesting in itself. Dr. Cathcart, as a throat specialist, understood the human voice and the harm the English high pitch was doing to singers. The low pitch was in vogue on the Continent; every great master had written in it. With the high pitch it was very nearly impossible to sing opera or oratorio. English singers, even then, were putting up a good fight for the low pitch, but it was by no means established. Sims Reeves refused to sing in a Handel Festival unless the low pitch were used, but organs and wind instruments were built to high pitch—for which Sir Michael Costa was to blame.

The Doctor's second condition, which had rather puzzled me, was the outcome, I learned later, of a discussion at the German Club. Carl Armbruster and others were discussing Wagner, the opinion being that English conductors did not understand him. Dr. Cathcart flatly contradicted this assertion.

"I know *one* Englishman who can conduct Wagner."

He was greeted with jeers.

"An *Englishman* conduct Wagner? Rubbish!" ·

This had rankled in the Doctor's mind—hence the condition. He guessed that my flair for Wagner would assure his works finding a big place in my programmes. At all events, I introduced him to Newman who agreed to the second condition without hesitation, but was reluctant about the first. He *liked* the high pitch. However, he succumbed to Dr. Cathcart's better judgment. Of what the financial arrangements were, I knew practically nothing—I know very little even now; but I *do* know that Dr. Cathcart was directly responsible for the inception of the Promenade concerts in August, 1895.

His condition about the pitch must have cost him a good deal, for it meant new wind instruments. The players refused to buy them, for they (like Newman) had no faith in the establishment of the low pitch. I went to Victor Mahillon's place in Wardour Street to buy these instruments which were lent to the players for the season. Most of them, however, bought them from Dr. Cathcart at the end of the first season—an acknowledgment that he had won his battle for the low pitch in England. The organ was lowered to A.439 at 59 dcg. F., to be in tune with A.435.5 in a heated hall.

I now entered into a contract with Newman as Musical Director of the Promenade concerts at a better figure than my two-guinea affair with Rousbey! I then set about engaging my orchestra, selecting it from among the young players in the London orchestras. Carrodus, you will remember, was engaged as leader but died a few weeks before the opening date. Fry Parker took his place for one season and was followed by Arthur Payne who led for so many years. The accompanist for the first season was H. Lane Wilson, the gifted song-writer.

As for Dr. Cathcart, the friendship which originated in so unconventional a manner in my studio forty-three years ago still remains unbroken. Barely a week passes without our meeting. If you were to ask him why he risked all that money he would tell you he was young at the time and had no idea what the entire cost of financing the concerts would prove to be. He has helped many people since, but still declares that I am his only real success. Of this I am convinced: had Dr. Cathcart not come forward with the capital, Newman would have found a way to further his scheme—*but the high pitch would have ruled* because, as I have said before, he did not share the Doctor's view on this point.

That my good friend would lose money on this first season was a foregone conclusion. However, he has never regretted it. He still comes to the Promenades. Sometimes he sits in the audience, but more often just behind those little curtains that have ushered in so many unknown composers and performers to success and prosperity.

XV

THE FIRST PROMENADE CONCERT

August the tenth, 1895, *at eight o'clock in the evening*.
I can see that packed house now and hear the welcome I received. Many such welcomes have been mine since then; but the first will always remain green in my memory—not only because it so encouraged me at the time, or even because it *was* the first, but because I doubt whether more than twenty people in that crowded audience had ever seen me raise a baton.

The prices were within the reach of everyone. The promenade was a shilling, the balcony two shillings, and the grand circle (numbered and reserved) three and five shillings. The programmes, I remember, were printed in single-sheet form. They cost the large sum of twopence but they contained excellent analytical notes by Edgar Jacques who continued to write them for some years.

Newman displayed great foresight. He issued a transferable season ticket for the promenade at one guinea for the whole season, for the balcony at two guineas and the grand circle at three and five guineas. The permanent orchestra numbered eighty players.

I here reproduce the entire programme of the first Promenade concert as a matter of interest. How many of my young Promenaders could stand and listen to it if I repeated it nowadays I leave to their judgment. I doubt whether I could tolerate it myself, but both they and I must remember the conditions ruling then. This was a new venture, and as such *it had to be popular.* A programme with five singers and three solo instrumentalists, and only the lightest of orchestral items. Here is the complete programme:

Overture	Rienzi	Wagner
Song	Prologue (*I Pagliacci*)	Leoncavallo
	Mr. Ffrangçon-Davies	
(a)	Havanera	Chabrier
(b)	Polonaise in A	Chopin
	(orchestrated by Glazounov)	
Song	Swiss Song	Eckert
	Madame Marie Duma	
Flute Solos	(a) Idylle	Benjamin Godard
	(b) Valse from Suite	
	Mr. A. Fransella	
Song	Thou hast come	Kennington
	Mr. Ivor McKay	

Chromatic Concert Valses from Opera
  Eulenspiegel
                  (First performance in England) Cyrill Kistler

Song	My Heart, thy sweet Voice	Saint-Saëns
	Mrs. Van der Vere Green	
Gavotte from	*Mignon*	Ambroise Thomas
Song	Vulcan's Songs (*Philemon and Baucis*)	Gounod
	Mr. W. A. Peterkin	

Hungarian Rhapsody in D minor and G major
  (No. 2)   Liszt

INTERVAL OF FIFTEEN MINUTES

Grand Selection	*Carmen*	Bizet
	(arranged by Cellier)	
Song	Largo al Factotum	Rossini
	Mr. Ffrangçon-Davies	
Overture	*Mignon*	Ambroise Thomas

Solo Cornet	Serenade Mr. Howard Reynolds	Schubert
Song	My Mother bids me bind my hair Madame Marie Duma	Haydn
Solo Bassoon	Lucy Long Mr. E. F. James	
Song	Dear Heart Mr. Ivor McKay	Tito Mattei
The Uhlans' Call		Eilenberg
Song	Loch Lomond Mrs. Van der Vere Green	Old Scottish
Song	The Soldier's Song Mr. W. A. Peterkin	Mascheroni
Valse	Amoretten Tanze	Gungl
Grand March	Les Enfants de la Garde (orchestrated by Harold Vicars) First performance	Schloesser

GRAND PIANOFORTE BY
MESSRS. S. & P. ERARD

Above the second part of this programme appeared the
following notice:

At these concerts the French Pitch (Diapason Normal) will be
exclusively used. Mr. Newman is glad to say that it will also be adopted
in future by the Philharmonic Society, the Bach Choir, the London
Symphony, Mottl, and Nikisch Concerts, and on concerts under his
direction: i.e. the Queen's Hall Choir, and the Sunday Afternoon
Concerts which begin on October 6th.

On the front page was an advertisement by a firm of London
tailors stating their willingness to make an evening dress suit
lined throughout with silk for five guineas. Refreshments could be
obtained at every Promenade concert; stalls for ices, cigars, and
flowers were on the promenade floor itself. The floral decorations were by Wills and Segar who retain the contract to this day.
The idea of having a fountain in the middle of the promenade
was Dr. Cathcart's. He said he thought it looked attractive and

that the blocks of ice which were to be placed among the flowers would keep the temperature at a reasonable level. His chief reason, however, was because the fountain would divide the crowd in the centre. Two or three seasons ago, when sitting in the grand circle listening to a rehearsal, he looked down and remarked: "Ah, well! I still have *some* asset in this hall. *That fountain is mine!*"

Both the lady vocalists in this first-night programme were Americans. They sang excellently. So, of course, did Ffrangçon-Davies who gave a memorable rendering of the *Largo al Factotum*. Peterkin (my Scots pupil) was there almost by right, it would seem. He also scored a success. The quality of his voice, his splendid rhythm and fine diction made him an instant favourite with the Promenaders. I would here like to emphasize the fact that even at this first concert we had two 'first performances'. At the end of this volume an appendix will be found which will serve to show that we began as we intended to go on.

Albert Fransella, our solo flautist, was another success, and E. F. James (bassoon) amused everyone with his inimitable rendering of *Lucy Long*. I ought also to say a word for Howard Reynolds, the cornet-player, who came specially to help us during this first season. He had retired and was living in Richmond.

Candidly, I was opposed to having a cornet solo at all; but Newman knew his public better than I did in those early days. I must admit I was impressed by Reynolds's wonderful *sostenuto*. He amazed me again, later on, by his superb playing of the *Prize Song*. In fact, his tone was the envy of every trumpeter of the day. As a matter of record I should like to set down the names of the wind section of the Queen's Hall Orchestra at this time. They were: Fransella, flute; Lalande, oboe; Manuel Gomez, clarinet; E. F. James, bassoon; Adolph Borsdorf, horn; Thomas Busby, third horn; Walter Morrow, trumpet; Colton, Davies, and Booth, trombones; Henderson, timpani; Mrs. A. Thomas, harp; and Guilmartin euphonium and tuba.

XVI

THE FIRST PROMENADE SEASON (1895)

It turned out as Robert Newman had predicted. We were educating the public by interweaving novelties with the classics. At the beginning of May he went through my proposed ten-week programme, discussing with me the drawing-power of each item.

"We must make every night so attractive that nobody will want to miss a concert," he told me.

Since those words were spoken there have been changes. Nowadays, far from being popular orchestral concerts for the people, the Promenades have become, many a night, very nearly Symphony concerts. At all events, in those early days I had to exercise care in order to keep the Promenades, the Sunday Afternoon, and the Symphony concerts as distinct in character as possible.

Newman had an extraordinary talent for popularizing an artist. He would start off someone quite unknown by giving him a couple of Promenade engagements. If successful, a contract would be given for six the following season. In the third year the artist would appear only at the Symphony and Sunday concerts—so that his drawing-power should not be diminished by his appearance in the more popular type of programme.

After the first season we decided that every unknown artist must attend an audition; we had had enough of mediocrities sent us by influential people who knew nothing about music. The first of these annual auditions took place in May, 1896. They were of an intensive nature and lasted for three weeks during which period we heard every applicant in the hall itself for at least fifteen minutes, though I actually gave an hour to those of exceptional merit. The others, I fear, had to wait.

I have kept books of these auditions. Even today I can refer to my notes for May and June, 1896, and find out the exact hour at which any artist sang or played; where he was trained and by whom; previous engagements (if any); experience, musicianship and style; and, in the last column, whether likely to be of use to Newman. The same for any year up to his death.

These auditions have always given me pleasure, and the knowledge I have gained of technique, tone, and style by listening to artists of all nationalities—sometimes from ten in the morning until six in the evening—has proved invaluable to me in forming judgments under all conditions. In one day I might hear a Japanese soprano, a solicitor from Birmingham, or a choirboy from California. I have always been carried away with enthusiasm for such work, and only wish time still permitted me to hear every would-be artist who writes asking me for an audition.

One season I shall always remember. I had spent a fruitless three weeks hearing hopeless mediocrities. Two only were marked *probable*. At ten minutes to six on a Saturday evening a charming and stylish young violinist walked on to the platform. She gave me the choice of five or six works she was prepared to play, from which I chose Lalo's *Symphonie Espagnole*. She played for forty minutes and I engaged her for two Promenade concerts. She turned out to be Réné Chemet, now known the world over and probably the most travelled lady violinist before the public.

These books of auditions contain much that now amuses me to read, the older ones especially. There are surprises everywhere: people I instantly recognized as having unusual talent, and those I knew had none at all. And there is every possible mean between those two extremes.

To return to our first Promenade season, I note that Alice Gomez made her first appearance at the second concert. She possessed the God-given gift of a lovely voice, but as is so often the case, her musicianship was not its equal.

As far back as 1891 I had been—not once but many times—to see André Wormser's charming wordless play *L'Enfant Prodigue* with the beautiful Jeanne Harding in the name part. I now gave the first concert performance of it. Incidentally, it was at one of these performances that I first met Landon Ronald. I remember I recognized the perfection of his genius in the important piano part of the work.

The piano as a percussion instrument in the orchestra is a popular device employed nowadays, but I wonder whether our young composers realize that André Wormser was one of the first to recognize its possibilities? As a young man I was deeply impressed by the wonderful tone and variety he obtained from a small orchestra using a piano as an integral part of the texture. Wormser died as recently as 1926 at the age of seventy-five. In his way he was a pioneer.

At the third concert Belle Cole appeared. She had an exceptional voice, for she could sing contralto, mezzo-soprano, and soprano with equal ease. I have rarely come across a singer with a range like hers. All the same, I must say I preferred her lowest register.

Two other singers at this same concert made a striking contrast: Jack Robertson, whose none too robust tenor voice was really more suitable for a drawing-room than for Queen's Hall but who always sang with an insight indicative of his personal charm and gentle manner; and Watkin Mills whose voice was of a penetrating quality and who sang Handel in what I call the sledge-hammer style. I found his singing rather dull and mechanical, but the Promenaders loved his Handelian runs which he executed with amazing force, each note being crystal clear. He was certainly able to give wonderful lessons in Handelian vocalization.

At the fifth concert appeared one of the greatest baritones England has ever possessed—William Ludwig, a delightful Irishman with a voice nearly as big as Edouard de Reszke's. His *Elijah* was superb. His repertory was limited, but he could reduce an audience to tears in a ballad. He was also a remarkable actor.

I shall always remember Ludwig in the *Flying Dutchman*, especially in the second act where I was so much impressed with his sudden transformation from the dour, don't-care Dutchman's style to his speechless amazement at the sight of the beautiful Senta. During those dramatic drum-taps he stood as if spellbound, holding his great black hat in front of him with both hands. On the last tap he let it fall to the ground before seemingly daring to begin *Like to a Vision seen*. One could feel a thrill throughout the house.

I remember how my father and I used to visit Ludwig at his home in Highgate where we had a sort of high tea at six o'clock. Ludwig had a large family of as mischievous little rascals as you could ever wish to see. The boys were sent to bed at six—at least, that is what was supposed to happen—but they generally managed to get into the dining-room and secrete themselves under the table. They would pull our legs and mutely beg for food as though they had never been given a meal in their lives. One evening we saw them stealing round the bushes in the garden armed with soda-water syphons. I remember my father hearing what he thought was rain on the window with a perfectly clear sky. It was, of course, these youngsters.

At the seventh, eighth, and tenth concerts I introduced three quite interesting novelties. The first was a *Largo* for four trombones by Mozart—an excellent precursor to my later production of the Beethoven *Equale* which was popular on Friday nights. Thanks to Mr. Atherley, we had a splendid trombone quartet that practised together a great deal. The second novelty was the first concert production of the *Valse and Polacca* from *Eugene Onegin* which took me back to memories of 1892 when I produced the opera in Lago's time. The third novelty was the overture to Rimsky-Korsakoff's second opera *La Nuit de Mai*.

At the eleventh concert we had a singer of whom England may be justly proud—a singer with a glorious voice and an even tone throughout a compass of well over two octaves, a singer whom I never found at fault in so much as a quaver all the years I worked with her, and who never sang out of tune—*Kirkby Lunn*. Her Brangäne in German at Covent Garden, her fine acting and singing as Kundry in America, and a marvellous rendering of Isolda's *Liebestod* at a Symphony concert in Queen's Hall are among my most cherished memories of her. As I say, a singer of whom we may well be proud.

At this same concert I introduced Mackenzie's now well-known *Benedictus*. This charming piece (one of six for violin and piano) he scored for orchestra in 1888. The delicate colour effects of the woodwind accompanying a string melody reveal the master hand. After his death in 1935 I directed an *In Memoriam* performance of this work with 60 violins at the R.A.M. students' orchestral concert in Queen's Hall, and shall ever recall the effect of their bowing, phrasing, and artistic *vibrato*. They were supported by six clarinets, four bassoons, and two horns.

I mention this because I so often read Press comments in which the writers complain that the brass of our orchestras is too strong. It never seems to occur to them that the real fact is that *the strings are too weak*. I wish they would realize this— *and say it*—because it would be helpful in furthering the cause of orchestral players now, alas, so often out of employment. For example, when Wagner is performed in a largish hall or theatre, the least number of strings required to balance the necessary wood and brass are twenty first violins, sixteen seconds, fourteen violas, twelve 'cellos, and ten basses. Nothing less will strike a balance. This is one of the worst battles a conductor has to fight. It has always been the same; even Bach complained to the Leipzig town council that the string players they gave him were 'grotesquely few'—and that was over two centuries ago!

Winifred Ludlam, a soprano pupil of mine, made quite a distinguished appearance at the seventeenth concert. Had she not joined Carl Rosa she might have achieved a more established position; but she was much too obliging. She took anybody's part when the management was in a hole. I know for a fact she sang in *Cavalleria*, *Carmen*, *Tristan* and *Maritana* in one week. That sort of thing will play havoc with anyone's voice. She still comes to Queen's Hall, often standing in the Promenade, especially on Wagner and Beethoven nights.

Another artist who sometimes comes to Queen's Hall is Lena Ashwell who, at this concert, recited Grieg's *Bergliot* with the orchestra. We had met in the old R.A.M. days when she was a piano student. We had, I remember, a common friend in

Stanley Hawley. Lena Ashwell eventually married Sir Henry Simson, the gynaecologist. Many theatre-goers must remember her remarkable performance in Tolstoi's *Resurrection*.

I have always been pleased to produce works by members of my orchestras. Although not always of first-rate quality in the composition sense, they have always been interesting and written in a practical manner. In forty-three years I have introduced many such compositions. One of these was at the nineteenth concert of this first season: a work called *The Battle of Flowers* by T. H. Frewin, one of my first violins. Frewin had trained in Ebenezer Prout's class at the R.A.M. As recently as 1935 I gave a first performance of Philip Sainton's viola concerto which was played by Bernard Shore who leads the violas in the B.B.C. Symphony Orchestra. Sainton had led this section in the old Queen's Hall Orchestra.

When Barnby brought to me a young tenor with a pretty lyrical voice we both liked everything about him except his name. The name in itself was all right—it was Lloyd—but Barnby said he felt sure it would be unwise for this young man to begin a career under that name because there was *Edward* Lloyd. After some thought Barnby hit on the name *Chandos*, and as Lloyd Chandos this tenor appeared for the first time at the twentieth concert to sing *Siegmund's Lovesong* (*Valkyries*).

Another youngster we started off in life was Richard Green who appeared at the twenty-seventh concert. He had been a great chum of mine at the Academy and a favourite pupil of Edwin Holland. Later on he studied with me. I remember working very hard with him for his part of Silvio (*Pagliacci*) which he created at Covent Garden with Melba as the Nedda. He had a fascinating way of singing though his was not a great voice; but he was popular at fashionable At Homes. He must have made a good income during his career, and I know that his people were quite well-to-do greengrocers somewhere in Kensington. Yet, many years afterwards, he came to me in rags and tatters and in great want. His end was sad: a week later he threw himself under a train. A terrible tragedy, for once he was the smartest-dressed man imaginable. In fact, his clothes always excited my admiration in those early days. Once I went so far as to tell him how much I admired his new frock suit. He wanted to give it to me there and then but, after much arguing, I persuaded him to let me buy it. That suit (made by Cooling and Lawrence of Maddox Street) must have cost a considerable sum even in those days. Yet poor Richard would have given it away.

Green and I formed two of a quartet of friends, the other two being Joseph O'Mara and Frank Broadbent, professor of singing at the Guildhall School of Music. Broadbent frequently came to my house in Elsworthy Road. In 1910 he came with a definite purpose—to persuade me to follow Dr. W. H. Cummings who had retired from his duties as Principal. On one occasion he brought with him the Secretary—Mr. Saxe Wyndham. Together they tried to persuade me to accept the position but, after much thought, I decided against it. The post was filled—with that distinction and dignity we associate with all his undertakings—by Landon Ronald who was knighted in 1922 and who only retired from the Guildhall School of Music at the end of 1937.

The name of G. H. Clutsam is by no means forgotten. Probably he will always be remembered by *I know of Two Bright Eyes*, but it is not generally known that he wrote light operas. I produced his *Carnival Scenes* at the twenty-eighth concert of this season. Clutsam was born of English parents in Australia but had spent most of his childhood in New Zealand where he appeared as a pianist prodigy at the age of five. He settled in London in 1890. I have never understood why his bigger compositions did not succeed, for this suite created an impression at the time. Still, he will be remembered for his splendid arrangement of Schubert in *Lilac-time*, produced at the Lyric Theatre in 1923.

I wonder whether we could fill Queen's Hall in these days with a Sullivan concert! I doubt it; but we did it in 1895. All the same we were progressing apace with our classical programmes. Here is the Beethoven programme for the thirtieth concert: *Egmont*, Ballet Music from *Prometheus*, *Busslied*, the *Emperor* concerto (played by Frederick Dawson), *Tremate*—Vocal Trio with orchestra—and the C minor symphony. We don't do much better in these days, do we?—or *do* we?

At the thirty-fourth concert I introduced a robust tenor— Philip Brozel—who sang the *Flower Song* (*Carmen*). Brozel modelled his singing on Jean de Reszke's with excellent results. Later I taught him his Wagner. An orchestral novelty was Baron Frédéric d'Erlanger's *Symphonic Suite*, beautifully scored and thoroughly French in mood. What a really refined musical mind is his, all his compositions give me pleasure to direct. Baron d'Erlanger and I have always been the best of friends and he has been exceedingly generous to my pet fund *The British Musicians' Pension Society* for which I have given my autograph so many times for the sum of half-a-crown. The society did not benefit as it might have done had its cause been advertised; however, the B.B.C. kindly placed slips in the Promenade concert programmes for several seasons and thus ensured a good sum for the benefit of orchestral musicians. This society, by the way, was formed to help deserving *orchestral* musicians; but its help is not withheld from others, and every penny subscribed benefits musicians, as all officials give their services to working the fund, thus avoiding overhead costs.

The public has no conception of the distress among orchestral musicians in England. Ten years ago a player could earn a living in an orchestra at a theatre or cinema; nowadays few theatres retain their orchestra and the cinemas have definitely banished them. Our musical institutions are turning out a constant stream of fully-equipped musicians—soloists who can tackle anything, so excellent is their training—and yet who are destined to swell the ranks of the unemployed.

For many years I had given my autograph willy-nilly, but I have always felt it to be a tax upon an artist to be badgered by people who never pay a ha'penny to attend a concert and are simply out to secure the signature of anyone in the limelight from a prize-fighter to the 'Quads', when they are old enough to sign their names—poor little devils! Hence my decision to refuse to give my autograph gratis any more.

If only our artists, great and small, would do this our musical charities would benefit; but it would, of course, mean some rather exacting clerical work because official receipts have to be given. Yet if artists like Melba, Caruso, Chaliapin or Kreisler had done this for twenty years, magnificent sums could have been given to less fortunate musicians. I remember one famous musician who would never sign an autograph-book—Saint-Saëns. Whenever he came to Queen's Hall the mantelshelf in the artist's room was piled high with these books. He would look at them in positive hatred and sweep the whole lot on to the floor. Few obtained *his* signature!

A Schubert concert was notable for the appearance of three artists. The first was Hilda Wilson whose lovely contralto voice seemed to have tears in it. She was a splendid oratorio-singer. Hardly a festival was without her. She was sister to H. Lane Wilson and hailed from Gloucestershire. There was also her sister Agnes, well known as a teacher of singing.

The second of these artists was David Bispham. He had been sent to me years before for an opinion on his voice which was of a real ugly, harsh quality. I told him not to attempt anything requiring beauty of tone for he simply had not got it. I suggested character-singing. Some time later I passed the Opera Comique in the Strand where a matinée was announced in aid of some charity. Attracted by the title—*The Brigands of Bluegoria*—I went in and was amazed to find Bispham was the brigand.

So completely was I convinced of his ultimate success that I wrote and advised him to go at once to Bayreuth and study under Cosima Wagner for such rôles as Beckmesser. This he did and remained in Bayreuth for some time, afterwards making a world-wide reputation as Beckmesser, Kurwenal, etcetera, both at the Metropolitan Opera House and at Covent Garden. Bispham was the first artist to sing *lieder* to really good English translations.

In 1904 I was myself in the States, directing the New York Philharmonic Society's Orchestra. On the quay, waiting to welcome me, were Bispham, Andrew Carnegie, and Professor Sanford of Harvard University. The following day Bispham arranged a remarkable reception in my honour when I seemed to be meeting all the musical people of New York. Naturally I asked him to sing. He amazed me when he sang *O Star of Eve* which I played for him.

"What have you been doing with your voice?" I asked him. "*Nothing*—except listening!"

It appeared he had heard the de Reszkes, Lasalle, Plançon, d'Andrade and others from whom he had learned much. *Another* proof of my contention that environment answers for much in musical education.

I thoroughly believe in environment. Students, in whatever branch of music, must take advantage of every opportunity to hear *beautiful musical tone*. If a mine or a mill girl is left to train musically among the mines or the mills, surrounded by the ugly sounds natural to the great industrial centres, she *may* learn to sing or play but that subtle refinement so essential to the making of a great artist will never be hers.

The third artist at this concert, Septimus Webb, had been trained at the R.A.M. and had been the chosen pupil to play to the Abbé Liszt when he visited the Academy in 1886 at the invitation of Walter Bache. Before I went under Macfarren I myself had lessons from Webb.

Dear old Sims Reeves came to us for the thirty-sixth concert. He was then nearly seventy-seven but sang like the great artist he was. His voice had nearly vanished but his diction and phrasing were as perfect as ever. Was there ever such a *caressing* voice as his—unless Vernon Rigby's or Richard Tauber's? None of

82

Caruso's overblowing and squirting out top notes! Which reminds me of Tamagno whom I remember delivering the opening phrase in *Othello* magnificently. After that—for me, he was finished.

I shall always say that if a singer can sing *one phrase* and make it linger in the hearer's mind and *recur* when someone else sings it, he has not sung in vain. So—for me—with Sims Reeves. I never hear the title of *Deeper and deeper still* (Handel) without thinking of his lovely inflection and quality. I have a vivid remembrance of his singing (at August Mann's benefit concert at the Crystal Palace) *Tom Bowling* and *Come into the garden, Maud*. He brought the house down. In *Tom Bowling* he reduced his audience to tears, but he never sacrificed tone for drama; he used tone to *express* drama. I only wish there were gramophone records of this great singer.

In the last week of the season we had arranged a programme of new works. We advertised it in every programme for a week. I refer you again to the list at the end of this volume which should do something at least to prove that we were pioneers in the production of international novelties. Amongst these will be found a recitation to music by Mackenzie. This was spoken by Charles Fry. He also spoke Edgar Allan Poe's *The Bells* to music by my old R.A.M. friend Stanley Hawley who accompanied him on the piano. Hawley had a great gift for setting poems in this way. I scored a number of them for him as he had no great knowledge of orchestral writing. Hawley, like many other young composers of the day, was a worshipper of Grieg.

Another famous name appeared in this programme—that of Foli. He sang *I'm a roamer* (Mendelssohn). He appeared again at the last concert of the season which we gave as a benefit for Robert Newman. This concert produced £400 profit, but it would have taken a much larger sum to recompense him for the hours of work and enthusiasm he put into this first season. Still, he was rewarded in another way: *he had realized his dream.*

I realized something more like a nightmare on the morning of September 30. I found an orchestra with seventy or eighty unknown faces in it. *Even my leader was missing.* Arthur Payne, the deputy-leader, told me of a certain musical festival. My regular players were all there. Moreover, they would be absent for a *week*.

I had to put up with this sort of thing for years. It was hardly fair on a young conductor to have to rehearse a week's concerts in three mornings (nine hours all told) with new and often inexperienced players. I made up my mind there and then to fight what is a bad principle, but little did I think how many years it would take me to bring about a reform.[1] The public was none the wiser because it had not yet learned to distinguish individual players. Neither could the papers tell them anything because all the critics were at the festival.

One result it did have: Fry Parker never led the Promenade concerts again. Arthur Payne took his place.

I first heard Payne at Llandudno. As a matter of fact, my father had sent me there to hear Rivière who was conducting concerts in the hall on the Esplanade. Here I sustained the shock of my life. As I took my seat I saw an elderly gentleman seated in a gilded arm-chair, *facing* the audience. He was elegantly dressed in a velvet jacket on the lapel of which reposed a huge spray of orchids more fitted for a woman's corsage. He held a bejewelled ivory baton in his hand from which dangled a massive blue tassel. This he wound round his wrist. He bowed ceremoniously to the audience and tapped loudly on his golden music-stand. Still seated, he began the overture to *Mignon*. After two bars a hoarse voice from the side of the orchestra said: "*Six* beats in a bar, please!"

I fled. I made my way to the pier concerts where Bartlett, whom I had seen billed, was conducting. Here was something very different: a packed house and quite a good orchestra ably conducted. The leader was Arthur Payne. He played the *Andante* and *Finale* from Mendelssohn's violin concerto. I was attracted by the beauty of his tone in the slow movement and made a note then and there that if I ever wanted a leader I should offer the post to him.

Many people have wondered how I managed to keep the concerts going with so little rehearsal. Nine hours' rehearsing for six concerts a week meant economy in every way; indeed, I could never have done the work had I not repeated some of the items. Out of each evening's eighteen or twenty pieces, at least five were with piano. On Beethoven nights the pianist often played a sonata rather than a concerto; thus I could avoid a concerto rehearsal. In this way I managed to squeeze everything in, especially as popular items of Wagner, Tchaikovsky, Grieg, Schubert and Mendelssohn could be repeated as often as three or four times a season. But the hours of intensive work were not in vain, for I had the satisfaction of knowing at the end of the season that I had become established as a conductor in England.

[1] See page 211.

XVII

STANFORD, HOLST AND PITT (1896)

EARLY IN 1896 I began rehearsing Stanford's *Shamus O'Brien* (libretto by Jessop) which was to be performed at the Opera Comique. The cast included my friend Joseph O'Mara, Kirkby Lunn, Maggie Davies, W. H. Stevens, and Denis O'Sullivan who sang, acted, and looked to perfection the name part.

In February, amidst all this, my mother died rather suddenly of bronchitis. I shall always remember with gratitude the kindness of O'Mara that night. I was beside myself in my agony of loss but, incongruous as it may seem, I gained comfort from his taking me out to Romano's and making me eat a few oysters.

I felt at this time somewhat like a child who is lost in a crowd, unable to explain or find its way home. My *mother* was my home —and almost my music, too; for I could discuss my plans and ideas with her, always sure of her complete understanding of my musician's mind. Her sympathetic comprehension ever gave me courage to unfold my dreams, my hopes, my fears, with the assurance that however altitudinous or unworkable they might seem she would never ridicule them nor make me feel self-conscious. Instead, her wise sweet counsel would lead me to another course by—as it were—a silken strand, so lovingly did she guide my efforts. My father and I continued our lives together with the help of a housekeeper, but the shortcomings of this system every day provided fresh evidence of the wonderful skill with which my mother had steered our ship.

I plunged again into *Shamus* which was by now in its fourth week of rehearsal. Actually the opera was to have been produced by Sir Augustus Harris, but he had badly overworked during the Covent Garden season and his own pantomime season at Drury Lane, had then been seriously ill, and since January had been away, recuperating under doctors' orders.

I rather imagine that the new producer had been roped in at the last moment; he was Richard Temple who will be remembered for his splendid singing and acting in the Savoy Operas. Stage-managing, however, was evidently not his job— or else my previous experiences with such men as Charlie Harris, Hugh Moss, von Possart, and Gordon Craig had made me over-critical. Perhaps I expected too much of Temple—at all events, he was not a success.

85

One evening I was dining alone at Pagani's when Sir Augustus Harris came in. I had known him in a casual sort of way for ten years and I knew he had a high opinion of my work. In fact, he had already approached me with regard to conducting opera during the English season at Drury Lane; but, having gained experience with pecuniary loss to myself, I did not fall at his feet to accept engagements at the ridiculous sum he offered. This evening, however, he came up to my table and began discussing *Shamus*. I told him that musically it was fairly safe but that (in my opinion) the production lacked movement. There was no sparkle, no fun in it.

"Then I shall see you at ten to-morrow morning," he told me. "I've called a full stage rehearsal."

I am not likely to forget that rehearsal. Harris began by numbering the chorus, directing them in chessboard fashion. He then worked with them until he had built up a really fine *ensemble*. From that moment the opera began to live. At times I felt positively afraid for this man who had just recovered from a serious illness. Perspiration rose from his very bald head like clouds of steam the whole day.

The next morning Stanford himself appeared, and was inclined (as was usual with him) to criticize.

"Too much movement!" he observed.

Harris turned on him.

"Who is managing this show?"

"Oh, *you* are," said Stanford, who realized he had made a tactical error. (Harris would never brook interference.)

"*Well* then!" he snapped—and the rehearsal proceeded.

Shamus was a great success. It was produced on March 2 and ran for over a hundred nights. That took us into July, but, fortunately, the Promenade concerts were not due to begin until August 29.

Stanford had queer ideas of conducting. I shall always remember him demonstrating to me (when I was still a very young man) what he termed *arsis* (rising inflection of voice) and *thesis* (falling inflection) by entirely *contradictory* gestures. He cannot have intended to do so, but he certainly conveyed to me the idea that his up-beat was stronger than his down-beat. I maintain that the point of a conductor's baton is his *emotional pencil* with which he transcribes his thoughts to his orchestra, and I cannot see the sense of allowing the strong beats of the bar to be *up*-beats.

Directing an orchestra without a baton is easier than with one, and certainly much less tiring. Safonov forgot his baton at a rehearsal one day and conducted without it. He never used one again and became known as the baton-less conductor. Had he been a last-desk player, instead of a great pianist, he would have realized how difficult it is to follow the open hand. I know this because I have sat sixty feet from a conductor and, at the start of the *Figaro* overture have not seen the baton move. The players nearest the rostrum might have *felt* the conductor begin, but the rest of us merely fell into line—and *played*. That was *with* a baton; had he used his hand only, things would have been even worse.

Thinking of Stanford reminds me of a charming letter I received from Sir Hubert Parry many years ago asking me to examine the orchestral classes at the R.C.M. "I know you are not in favour of Stanford's methods," he said, "but forget them as I have an ambition that you will, when the right time arrives, direct our orchestra."

I had to write and tell him that I could not entertain the idea as I was so busy with my work as a conductor, and that all thought of taking on any kind of scholastic work was out of the question. My hands were very full, apart from my London work, with provincial choral societies and amateur orchestras which made it impossible to devote two afternoons a week to orchestral training.

A few weeks after *Shamus O'Brien* came off Stanford called and asked me to go on tour in America with the work. He seemed upset and hurt because I did not at once appreciate his offer. I interviewed Newman but I knew he would look upon the idea as preposterous. This he did, and told me I must not even consider giving up his concerts to go to America with *Shamus* for three months. I remember showing Parry's letter about the R.C.M. to Maurice Sons who begged me to take on the work at the R.C.M. I came to the conclusion it could not be done, but had I acted on Parry's suggestion I might now have been training the R.C.M. orchestra instead of the R.A.M. I am quite satisfied as things are, but the incident goes to show how the course of one's life may be altered by the suggestions of other people.

To return to Harris.

I remember every detail of my introduction to him. It took place in Marie Roze's private sitting-room at the old Adelphi Hotel in Liverpool. "Come along!" she said to Harris after presenting me. "I want you to hear some of Mr. Wood's songs. He writes so well for the voice."

I played, and the great stage-manager stood behind me, singing the songs from sight in a very light, though not unpleasing, tenor voice. He was a splendid musician. No wonder there were such amazing performances of grand opera under his direction at Covent Garden and Drury Lane in the hey-day of Melba, Nordica, Scalchi, the dè Reszkes, and Plançon! Here was a man who understood *both* drama *and* music. To my mind, only C. B. Cochran has ever equalled Harris's insight and flair for the public taste. Who but Harris would have had the courage and initiative in *those* days—I am speaking of 1892—to bring over to Drury Lane the entire Hamburg Opera Company together with the great Klafsky and Alvarez—the most beautiful Siegfried I ever saw? Gustav Mahler, I remember, was the conductor, and my father and I did not miss one performance during the German season of the *Ring*, *Tristan*, *Der Freischütz*, etcetera. It needed pluck in those days to embark on ventures of that kind; but Harris always knew what he was about.

I had a splendid orchestra at the Opera Comique, led by Arthur Bent. My first trombonist was none other than young Gustav Holst—later to be the gifted composer of the *Planets*. I thought how delicate he looked; he was certainly not physically fitted to play a trombone. In the fourth week of the run of the opera he looked so ill that I told him to go to Margate for a week's rest. So long as he promised to spend the week in complete idleness I would pay his deputy and all expenses. I saw him off on the Sunday morning and had the satisfaction of finding him looking much better on his return. He played to the end of the run.

My next consideration was my father. Since my mother's death he had been fretting, and I knew him to be lonely. I went to Cook's and asked them to plan out a tour starting at Paris and embracing Bayreuth, the beauty-spots of Switzerland, with a return trip up the Rhine from Mainz to Cologne timed to reach home the day before the Promenades began. This would not be possible in these days because I always hold preliminary rehearsals, but in those days we began right away.

Robert Newman had been delayed in his announcements. He was determined to carry through a second season but had been unsuccessful over finance. In the end he himself took the entire project on his own shoulders. One disappointment we suffered was the loss of H. Lane Wilson as accompanist. This was because he wanted to devote all his time to composition and vocal work. I suggested that Newman should offer the post to Percy Pitt, of whose abilities we knew practically nothing, but we did know him to be a fine all-round musician and a composer of distinction. His studies in Germany had not included much organ practice and he was by no means a fluent player—indeed, he gave me some anxious moments—but we worked together many a morning from eight until a quarter to ten when the band rehearsal began. And very enjoyable I found our rehearsals together.

I had met Pitt originally in the London office of Schultz-Curtius whom I had promised at the time that I would do all I could for his young friend. Here was my chance. Pitt had just settled in London after prolonged studies with Reinecke and Jadassohn at Leipzig, and Rheinberger at Munich. It gives me much pleasure to reflect that this first musical association with him marked the beginning of an unbroken friendship during many years of music at Queen's Hall and elsewhere until his death in 1932. I had produced his Suite during the previous season when it made an excellent impression, being one of the first of annual presentations of British composers' works at the Promenades.

Percy Pitt remained organist and accompanist to the Queen's Hall orchestra until his duties as musical adviser at Covent Garden in 1902 made it impossible for him to continue. Five years later he became Musical Director for the Grand Opera Syndicate there. During his association with me I produced ten of his works. Although they never revealed any marked individuality, his orchestration was always interesting, his harmonies refined--even romantic. I missed our personal association when he left us, but as he became private accompanist to Princess Olga Ouroussoff he was often at our house. Nearly all his songs were written for and sung by her after our marriage when I had introduced her to the London public. In 1922 Pitt became Musical Director to the British Broadcasting Corporation, and I here observe that it was largely through him that I agreed in 1926 to continue the Promenade Concerts under their management.

Meanwhile things went well at Queen's Hall. The following footnote in one of the programmes of the second season gives an idea of our progress.

In consequence of the generous support given by the public and press to the season of Promenade Concerts, Mr. Newman has the pleasure to announce that on and after this Saturday evening, September 12, 1896, the orchestra will be increased to ninety performers.

Again, on Wednesday, September 23, the programme started with this heading:

MUSICAL DEVELOPMENT DURING THE REIGN OF H.M. THE QUEEN

Perhaps the greatest compliment from a musical point of view ever paid to Queen Victoria was conveyed in the dedication prefixed by Francis Hueffer to his book *Half a Century of Music in England*. This distinguished writer addressed Her Majesty as 'the friend of Mendelssohn and the first English-woman to recognize the genius of Wagner'.

To have figured in either capacity would be an enviable distinction; to have justified recognition in both is to have given proof of a catholicity of taste that might well be more widely imitated. But the liberality and discrimination here indicated have always characterized the attitude towards music, not only of Her Majesty but also of the Royal Family generally.

The Prince Consort and his 'Good little Wife' (as he affectionately called her) were themselves endowed with musical gifts which have been warmly acknowledged by no less an authority than Mendelssohn himself, who, in one of the delightful letters addressed to his mother, has described a visit which he paid to Buckingham Palace one morning in 1842, when the Queen sang to him and Prince Albert played a chorale upon the organ—'so charmingly, clearly and correctly that it would have done credit to any professional'.

It was natural that the Art so lovingly cultivated by the royal pair should receive their encouragement, and that the example thus set should be followed by their children. To this influence, so worthily exerted, is due in a great measure the enormous development and popularity of music in England at the present day. Society, following the Court, regards music with favour and its exponents flourish accordingly; while the impetus given to musical education by the foundation of the Royal College—made possible by the efforts of the Prince of Wales—is evident in all directions.

The Royal Academy of Music was founded in 1822 and granted a Royal Charter in 1830, but when Queen Victoria ascended the throne Exeter Hall was the only building available for concerts on a large scale. Things musical have changed since then, and it is peculiarly appropriate that the longest reign in British history should be commemorated in this hall named after our great Queen, and itself one of the latest and most conspicuous signs of that change.

For one concert of this season Newman formed a special choir of four hundred voices augmented by boys from the London School for Choristers. The solists were Fanny Moody and Ben Davies, the organist Walter Hedgcock of the Crystal Palace. The programme included Costa's arrangement of the National

Anthem; *Britannia*, an overture by Mackenzie; a *Coronation March* by Percy Pitt (specially commissioned by Newman); and Mendelssohn's *Hymn of Praise*.

Artists who have since won fame in music made their first appearances at this second series; these included Charles Santley, Ada Crossley, Evangeline Florence, and Lucille Hill. Dear Santley—was there ever a more devout Catholic?—stood out as a man of breezy, happy disposition, endowed with an undoubtedly fine voice and was, withal, a fine musician. On this occasion he sang a song with which his name is ever associated —*To Anthea*—in that *sostenuto marcato* style in which he excelled. He has had many imitators, but none have ever acquired the same skill in this type of singing. He never broke his vocal line but always added the words to his tone, and his *marcato*-singing was never marred by shock of diaphragm, nor aspiration.

Santley had the strongest rhythmic sense of any vocalist I ever accompanied. The technique of his Handelian vocalization was clarity itself, and the phenomenal compass of his voice, from the low bass E flat to the top baritone G, was brilliantly even throughout. His performance of Handel's great aria *Nasche il bosco* is one of my most cherished vocal memories. All his low F's told—even to the remotest corners of the largest concert-hall while his top F's were as a silver trumpet. *Oh, where has fled* —to quote the title of Tchaikovsky's lovely aria—oh, where has fled the art of singing today?

Of all the novelties we produced during this season of 1896, Tchaikovsky's *Casse Noisette Suite* was easily the most popular. We had to repeat three of its movements, so great was the ovation it received. No notice, on the other hand, was taken for years of Rimsky-Korsakoff's *Scheherazade*, even though I performed it at the Promenades, Sunday and Symphony concerts. Eventually Diaghileff adapted it for a ballet after which it became a popular repertory piece.

Thinking of the *Casse Noisette Suite* and its popularity reminds me of the overture *1812* and my introduction to it. Mackenzie Rogan, Conductor of the Coldstream Guards' Band, met me one day in the street.

"Do you know Tchaikovsky's overture *1812*?" he asked.

"No," I said. "Never heard it."

"It's fine; just been published. Would you like to hear it?"

Naturally I said I would, whereupon Rogan invited me to go down one morning to a public house near Victoria station where he was rehearsing. I seem to think my father went with me; at all events, I was sufficiently taken with what was only a military band arrangement to perform the work at the Promenade concerts; but I took good care, of course, to obtain the original version.

I have now quite lost sight of Amy Elise Horrocks whose orchestral *Légende* I performed this season. She returned to her native Brazil, where she was born of English parents, having been made a Fellow of the R.A.M. We also performed Wagner's *Das Liebesverbot* which is interesting in that it was written at the age of twenty-one. On September 23 we had a hundred and three players when we gave a work of Beethoven known as *Wellington's Victory*. An appalling work. If anybody wants to give it a second performance I will make him a present of my score and parts! Another interesting production was *Tannhauser's Pilgrimage* (Intro. Act III, original version). Jaeger, of Novello's —Elgar's great friend—discovered this version which contains sixty-four more bars than that generally played in the opera. Whenever I play this version I label it 'the original' in a programme note.

On October 9 we had the celebrated Belgian organist August Wiegand, city organist at Sydney. He gave a splendid performance of Mendelssohn's sixth sonata. Mention of Australia reminds me of Orme Darvall, a singer who had studied in Italy and had appeared at La Scala, Milan and also in Naples. He could sing *louder* than anyone I have ever heard—and that is saying something. He forced his upper notes till he sang sharp; all the same, he sang with tremendous temperament. He was so carried away that I am sure he hardly knew what he *was* singing. I remember accompanying him at St. James's Hall when he sang *Die Frist ist Um* (*Flying Duchman*). He seemed to be perpetually on tour, for he began in the curve of the piano but, as his excitement worked up, he gradually travelled round the end of it, and actually finished up *behind it*. To make matters worse, his very deep collar left the front stud and waggled above his head in a semi-circle. He was funnier still when he discovered it. As he came down the stairs from the platform he said: "Do you know, my collar came undone? Do you think anyone noticed it?" If *that's* not concentration, I give it up!

Thomas Meux also came to us during the 1896 season after his appearance with Sir Augustus Harris at Covent Garden. It gives me great pleasure frequently to meet him nowadays at the R.A.M. and to accompany many of his vocal pupils in my R.A.M. students' orchestral concerts at Queen's Hall.

Throughout this season Newman, with his business astuteness and insight (so amazing at times as to be quite uncanny), conceived the idea of showing animated pictures; indeed, I consider he anticipated the public taste for films. He entered into a contract with David Devant whereby he ran a screen production of moving photographs in the small Queen's Hall. This was easily accessible from the large hall so that many Promenaders could avail themselves of a few minutes' quietude during the interval in my programmes. At 10.30 there was another presentation, so that those who did not wish to go home at the end of the concert might, for an extra sixpence, see what was virtually the forerunner of the newsreel. The inventor was R. W. Paul, and the programme stated that the pictures were 'reproduced with all the actual movements of real life'. Here is a selection:

> Outside the Houses of Parliament
> A Wedding Procession
> Chirgwin's Comicalities
> A Peep at Paris
> Musical Hall Sports, 1896
> Bill Stickers, beware!
> Rough sea—Cornish coast
> David Devant, conjuring with rabbits
> Factory gates at dinner-time
> Mr. Maskelyne's plate-spinning
> Young ladies drilling
> A gallant Rescue
> The Coronation of the Czar at Moscow. His Imperial

Majesty and suite are seen leaving the Church after the Ceremony.

This brings me to the end of the summer season of Promenade concerts in 1896. They were followed by the Saturday Promenades which ran into April, 1897. Unfortunately, the Saturday Night Promenades only existed for the one winter season as they had to be treated as separate concerts. This means that the players received Symphony concert terms even though the price of admittance remained the same as for the summer Promenades. Thus the Saturday Proms could never be a financial success.

XVIII

DISCIPLINE (1896)

ORCHESTRAL REHEARSALS WERE now part of my daily life. I was a very young man, all the same, to take on the responsibilities of directing and training so large a body of musicians—many of them old hands who had played while I was still in my cradle. They were up to every trick of the trade —and there are many tricks.

I began my first rehearsal with a determination not to give them so much as an inch. If I ever intended to be on top I must *begin* on top. Consequently, I was not exactly loved by some of the players. During a rehearsal interval one morning I went into Tabb's library room (which was in Ridinghouse Street adjacent to door fifteen of the hall), and chanced to overhear two of the oldest hands discussing current events.

"We seem to be having a hell of a time, Teddy," said one.

"Aye. I wonder where Newman picked up this brat Wood?"

"You remember, Teddy," went on the first speaker, "how we used to stroll in at half-past ten. But this chap is on that rostrum with his big watch in his hand, and his stick—ready at *ten*."

"I know. If only half of us is there he begins. No good creeping in quietly, either, with him stopping and saying: 'Good morning! Another cab horse down?' in that nasty voice of his."

"What annoys *me*," said the other, "is that he starts the piece again. He does the same blasted trick with everyone who comes in late. I suppose there's nothing for it, Teddy: we shall *have* to get here by ten."

It was hard on them, of course; *but they had to be there by ten.* My two friends had other criticisms to pass and comparisons to make, none of which were to my greater popularity.

"And look how he works us, Teddy," continued the aggrieved musician. "Look how he works us! Why, in the old days, the conductor would say: 'Fifth symphony, Beethoven, gentlemen! We don't need to rehearse *that!* We all *know* it!'"

"Aye, and how we all yelled *No!*"

They laughed reminiscently.

"Then it would be: '*Der Freischütz*, gentlemen! *That'll* be all right.' Then: 'Suite—*The Language of Flowers* . . . Ah! . . . we had better rehearse this!'" (Laughter.)

94

"Aye . . . and at twenty-past twelve it'd be: '*Good morning, gentlemen!*'"

"Of course it would," finished the other, "and you and me, Teddy, could stroll round to the *Glue Pot* and 'ave one. Damn these youngsters, I say!"

Such was my character.

In those days the percussion department was a source of continual worry to conductors. Unless these men were actually playing in every piece one simply could not keep them on the platform. I tried every conceivable dodge at rehearsals. I would take two pieces which included the percussion-players and follow with one in which they took no part. Of course they slipped out. I then began another work requiring their attendance while one of their friends would run through the door at the back of the platform and recall them. They would troop back again, looking as though they could kill me.

This sort of thing became such a nuisance that I eventually enlisted Newman's help. He soon settled it—and in a way that gave me considerable private amusement. *He locked both orchestral entrances as soon as we were assembled.* Then, for me, the fun began. As soon as the percussion was not required, and I had begun to rehearse something else, I would see these fellows creeping up, one by one, bending double in the hope of being hidden by the music stands. They would gently push the brass bar of the exit door, following up with a good shove. They would then return, creeping along, bent double and with a puzzled expression on their faces—perhaps to watch someone else going through the same antics. I shall never forget it—but the ruse was successful. They were forced to stay in for fear Newman might lock the doors while they were *out*.

Newman was a splendid colleague. No manager in the world could have been more helpful to a conductor than he was to me. He attended every rehearsal, only going to his office when a long work was being rehearsed. He knew every single player by sight and what instrument he played, and he was the first to break the custom of employing a separate player for each percussion instrument. Many a player had earned his salary by a few taps on a triangle or by occasionally clashing the cymbals. Contracts, in future, were only to be given to players capable of playing at least three percussion instruments. There was no getting past Robert Newman!

Another nuisance came from the leader of the second violins. His name was Eayres. I looked upon him as an old remnant. He had, certainly, led the seconds under almost every great conductor. Hans Richter, however, was his god. Not that I minded that in the least, but I did resent his coming and nudging me after we had been through a work, telling me that Richter always took it a little slower or a little faster. I did my best with a few long-drawn-out "*Ohs*", but they had no effect.

One morning I had my revenge. We were rehearsing the *Flying Dutchman* overture. It is practically impossible to play it any faster than it is directed to be taken, but I took its *coda* at danger-speed, glaring at the second violins all the time. As they very nearly came to grief, I stopped.

"Second violins, play it alone!" This in a pseudo-angry tone. "Is *that* the way you played it under Richter?"

That did the trick. I rather suspect Master Eayres subsequently came in for a wigging from his colleagues; at all events, he never interfered again.

Orchestras are strange things. They will nickname anything or anybody. 'Shoolbred's Unfurnished Symphony' is one of their pet names; Hamish MacCunn's overture has been renamed 'The Land of the Mountain and Mud'; and Smetana's overture is generally known as the 'Battered Bride'. Although I refused to be dictated to by a violinist in this instance I am a great believer in a friendly spirit existing between conductor and orchestra in general, for good results cannot be obtained without it. On the other hand, I have little use for the conductor who wastes time with long dissertations. Orchestral musicians object to nursing their instruments for twenty minutes at a stretch—apart from which it is only by playing and *practising* difficult passages that the technique of them becomes familiar. Neither are orchestras interested in the type of conductor—however great he may be—who flies into tantrums, breaks batons, and strides off in a pet, any more than they are in those who explain to them the value of a dotted crotchet.

A great point of discipline with me has always been the *tuning* of an orchestra. Until as recently as 1936 I regularly supervised the tuning of every instrument in the artists' room before each concert. I have never trusted to the 'oboe A' which often proved to be 'any old A'. I have found that a fork on a resonant box tuned to the diapason normal A (435.4 at 59 deg. F.) used *night after night* has resulted in as fine an intonation as it is possible to secure in a hall of varying temperatures.

My 'tuning parade' has never been very popular with orchestras because they seem so averse to being ready to tune even only five minutes before a concert. Last year I gave it up and trusted to the B.B.C. Symphony Orchestra to tune without me. I must say every member has loyally responded.

I have tried various means of producing a good sustained A. Years ago I paid forty marks for a machine (exhibited at the German section of the Brussels Exhibition) which consisted of a fork and an electric battery; but I found the battery too weak to keep the note going for twenty minutes, and the contacts were always wearing out.

The most successful machine I ever had came out of an idea I conceived for one containing a German silver reed which varies less in changing temperature than any other. I wanted to have it blown by a three-throw crank acting on three little bellows supplying a windchest and kept at constant pressure by a spiral spring.

One day I met John Walker (the organ builder) in Elsworthy Road.

"I know exactly the sort of thing you want," he said when I had explained the idea. "I will make you one."

This he did and gave it to me. It works by turning a handle in the fashion of a hurdy-gurdy and is most effective for the purpose.

No conductor should relax his watchfulness over the tuning of his orchestra. The second woodwind will often become careless if not watched. A couple of flutes (or oboes) if asked to play a perfect fifth will often have to be *worried* into playing them so that it will pass muster. Incidentally, a guest conductor will often do an orchestra a world of good merely because his ear is fresh to their intonation.

The great thing, I have found, is to save time whenever possible. Hence my care with rehearsal lists. All the same, I remember a gross waste of twenty-three minutes one morning when Maurice Ravel came to conduct his suite *Ma Mère l'Oye.* Exactly at ten o'clock I led him to the rostrum where he received a great welcome. He opened his score, turned several pages, and then back to the first. At this he gazed for some seconds. He then turned to me in the Grand Circle.

"How many *pupitres* (desks) of first violins are there?"

"Eight, sir."

A long silence. Then (very slowly): "I will take only five *pupitres.*"

Ravel turned over more pages.

"How many *pupitres* are there of second violins?"

"Eight, sir."

"I will take only five *pupitres.*"

This went on for some time because he asked the same question about the violas, 'cellos, and basses. The orchestra behaved like angels; not a muscle was moved, not a sound uttered. *But the first note they played was at* 10.23 *by my watch!* And, I may add, I had a concerto and a symphony to rehearse.

This may be an exceptional example of absorbed deliberation, but it goes to show that composer-conductors do not always prepare and plot out beforehand. Some of them seem to me to have very little idea of what they really do want.

A conductor may know his scores by heart but his orchestra prefers him to have the copy before him. It is easier to conduct than to play from memory because if a soloist's memory fails him it is obvious to everyone; if a conductor's memory fails him the orchestra goes on playing and his plight may remain unnoticed.

Richter, who had a most reliable memory and was given to conducting without a score, once began the *alla breve* in Brahms's *Academic Festival Overture* two bars too soon. He stopped the orchestra and turned to his audience, explaining that the accident was entirely his fault. He then played the work again. Very noble and splendid of him!

I also maintain that a conductor should have good knowledge of singing and should have studied the art, for without such knowledge he cannot accompany a singer well.

Singers have to breathe, which so many conductors seem to forget. I always watch a singer's mouth, just as I watch a fiddler's bow or a pianist's hands.

Although Newman's discerning judgment always led him to do the right thing musically, he always worked with an eye on the box-office. Many continental conductors had visited us but Newman went one better in engaging Lamoureux and his Paris Symphony Orchestra for six concerts at Queen's Hall in 1896. We were all excited, I remember, at the chance of hearing forty classical works rehearsed by this great Frenchman. The way in which he had trained his strings alone was a revelation to me. Lamoureux was himself a violinist and had been educated under Gérard, Tolbecque, Leborne, and Chauvet. By the absolute unanimity of bowing, and the *exact place of the bow on the strings*, he obtained a colour and variety of tone I could not hope to achieve in those early days, having no chance of extended rehearsals.

The one blot in Lamoureux's string quality resulted from his players using modern instruments made by one firm. They were very red-looking, I remember, and *new*. It may have been that he wanted to help the French violin industry, but I was sorry about it at the time. Our English players take pride in possessing the best instruments money can buy. Those belonging to any of our great orchestras are worth thousands of pounds. On the other hand, Lamoureux's woodwind was composed of magnificent instruments—but French-made woodwind instruments are the finest in the world.

I have just heard that Bernard Shore—leader of the Violas in the B.B.C. Symphony Orchestra—has become the proud possessor of Lionel Tertis's lovely viola by Domenico Montagnana (1700).

In 1897 Lamoureux came again, this time to direct the Queen's Hall Orchestra; but Newman did not find the experiment fulfilled his expectations. He decided that the public wanted the Queen's Hall Orchestra with its own conductor. Lamoureux himself told me the same, and Fuller Maitland wrote the following in *The Times*:

It is a complete error to suppose that the concerts are in any way inferior owing to the substitution of an English for a French orchestra. It is evidently the conductor to whom the success is due; and the Englishmen proved themselves the equal of the French in those very qualities of delicacy and grace in which the latter were found to excel.

The orchestra was now increased to a hundred and three players, and the Promenade concerts were continued on Saturday evenings during the winter months. These announcements were followed a few weeks later by another proclaiming the advent of Sunday Evening Chamber Concerts, to be given in the small Queen's Hall by the Queen's Hall String Quartet under Arbos, a fine Spanish violinist. Ferdinand Weist-Hill was the quartet's second violin; Alfred Hobday the viola; W. H. Squire the 'cello; I myself the piano accompanist.

XIX

PAYING THE PIPER (1897)

THE SMALL QUEEN'S Hall is ideal for chamber concerts. It was a happy thought to have them there. Arbos was a favourite pupil of Joachim and a thoroughly charming man. He was extremely witty and could keep his friends in roars of laughter in the artists' room (or at Pagani's) with impersonations of well-known characters. His store of fun was seemingly inexhaustible, and his comic duets with Rubio the 'cellist were the funniest things I ever heard in music. I was more than sorry when the Queen of Spain, to whom Arbos was court violinist, recalled him to Madrid. A few years ago I was myself in Madrid and had the happiness of meeting him again, looking as handsome as ever. He told me he was conducting the Madrid Symphony Orchestra. I wonder what happened to him when Spain fell into such a cruel state of war!

Sarasate was a great friend of Arbos and he too a character in his way. He used to amuse the orchestra and myself over his tuning. He was inclined to tune his fiddle sharp, especially if he had harmonics to consider. I used to get the oboe to give him the A, and if I showed signs of distress at his sharp tuning he invariably smiled blandly and whispered up to me: "A leetle *flat*, yes?"

The orchestra was lighted by huge carbon arc lamps which hung above the performers. The reflected heat from these almost burned our heads sometimes, and I remember Sarasate standing beside my rostrum before his entrance in Lalo's *Symphonie Espagnole*. After the first movement he put his hand to the crown of his head, murmuring: "Oh, de heat from dhese lamps!" He then backed to the second rise and played the second movement from there, in evident distress and mopping his head. For the third movement he went back further still and stood among the 'cellos, but the heat was so intense there that he stumbled down the steep rises and came back to the side of the rostrum for the fourth and fifth movements. What the audience thought I cannot say, but I do know that the orchestra was hard put to maintain a decorum in keeping with a Symphony concert. I think it was this incident that caused Chappells to remove these terrible 'Alhambra' lamps, for which we were all grateful.

Thinking of poor Sarasate and his tour of the orchestra reminds me of seating positions in general for orchestras. I am surprised so few conductors agree with my disposition of the instruments. So many have their first violins on their left, the seconds on their right, and their 'cellos *opposite* their basses. I can never see the sense of that because so often the first and seconds are playing phrases that are at least similar, whereas the 'cellos and basses are, more often than not, actually playing the *same phrase in octaves*. It seems to me that grouping them as I do ensures a better *ensemble*.

Another point. The seating of an orchestra should be in the shape of an inverted isosceles triangle of which the conductor's stand should be the apex. The awkward disposition of having straight lines of violins each side of the conductor—and very often slightly *behind* him—is a grave error because it is only by looking into the eye of the player that a conductor establishes what I call magnetic contact and control.

One of my achievements in the world of music of which I am justly proud is the raising of the weekly wage of the orchestral musician. I know the work they have had to put in as students, and I know that every player begins his or her studies with the idea of becoming a solo artist; but there never was—there never will be—sufficient call for every instrumentalist who seeks to enter this sphere. Thus he, and she, gradually drift into the orchestras.

Newman was able to run all these musical enterprises at Queen's Hall because the rank and file of the orchestra received only 45*s*. a week for six Promenade concerts and three rehearsals, a guinea for one Symphony concert and rehearsal, and half-a-guinea for Sunday afternoon or evening concerts *without* rehearsal. In addition to this he told me that, as lessee and manager, he put down the rent of the hall during the Promenade seasons as only £120 a week. I wonder what the B.B.C. pays now!

I worried Newman year by year to raise the salary scale, if only by a shilling or two. Sometimes I was lucky and got an additional five shillings; the next year nothing—and so on until, after thirty-five years, the rank and file received £7, £8 and £9 a week. At the present time, I believe, the B.B.C. has considerably increased this figure.

I am constantly at loggerheads with various provincial and other concert-givers because I will never agree to cutting down extra players required for a work, and I am exceedingly sorry to note that many publishers are now printing in their score the heading: 'This work can be performed with the following instruments omitted.' Such a statement cannot be inserted unless the composer agrees; even so, I am very much against the practice. If a work is written for a certain number of instruments the composer should stick to his original intention, both for the sake of the orchestral musician and his own. This mistaken procedure only encourages the meanness of cheese-paring committees who frequently think nothing of spending £20 on a useless dinner but, although knowing nothing of music, will haggle for weeks over the engagement of a *cor anglais* or a bass clarinet-player for a couple of guineas. I have attended numerous committee meetings at which some old gentleman has got up and said: "Why, Sir Henry, you've got *two* flutes! what *do* you want three for?"

It is useless to explain, for they simply do not understand. It is the old, old story: they all love music very dearly so long as they are not asked for a fiver!

Some years ago, the amateur orchestral society in Hull was near to breaking up for lack of funds. Knowing they had a splendid body of very keen amateur musicians at their command, I personally interviewed a local benefactor whose name must necessarily be suppressed here. He had built a magnificent art gallery and spent thousands on pictures for it. I asked him to help place the amateur musical society of his town on a sound business basis, adding that—to further the scheme—I was willing to forgo a large part of my already reduced fee. His answer was: "No, Sir Henry! Music does not interest me."

I have paid many visits to this beautiful art gallery since and never have I seen more than half a dozen people there. Where would music be if we all made up our minds to do nothing but that which would leave behind us a tangible mark of our sojourn? We executants spend our lives in giving pleasure and (we hope) uplift to our fellow-men; yet can leave *nothing* to mark our journey but a memory which, alas, too soon must pass.

I may say that I have saved this society from an untimely death. For many seasons I have directed them and given additional rehearsals which entailed extra journeys, giving up other work to fit them in, but I could never have achieved this without the help of the great artists who answered my appeal in such a wonderful way. They have journeyed to this town for a fee only sufficient to cover their expenses and, nowadays, every concert there is given to a house packed to overflowing. I feel I must place on record the names of these dear, kind *confrères* who have given so much to help me in my endeavours. They are: Lamond, Moiseiwitsch, Solomon, Jelly d'Aranyi, Irene Scharrer, Pouishnoff, Harriet Cohen, Clifford Curzon, Cyril Smith, Leslie England, and Mark Hambourg.

Another matter—quite relevant to finance—is judgment in selecting works for performance. It is a gross act of unwisdom for amateur societies with limited funds at their disposal to attempt large modern works. There are hundreds published well within their reach, and this notion of producing the very latest is almost a fetish. I resigned a conductorship at Newcastle-on-Tyne for this very reason. I arrived for a rehearsal to find an inadequate orchestra for Vaughan Williams' *London Symphony*. When I interviewed the secretary he pointed to the publisher's note on the score: *This work may be performed without the following instruments*. We were certainly without the instruments, yet the hall was new, large, and attractive. It was a case of *not* paying the piper and consequently of not calling the *complete* tune. Nobody could form an opinion of so great a work rendered under such conditions.

The Hull Philharmonic Society is now a flourishing concern under the presidency of Judge Sir Reginald Mitchell-Banks, K.C. When I took it over it was an enthusiastic but somewhat raw society; indeed, I really think the word 'intonation' was quite foreign to some of the departments of the orchestra. The concerts were given in a fine but invariably half-filled hall. In fact, this latter condition was so depressing that I threatened to resign unless something could be done about it. Norman Dixon, who has been sub-conductor for the last five years, hit on the admirable idea of forming a ladies' committee to sell tickets. I honour Mr. Dixon for this because he slaved away for sheer love of art. When his sons are at home, three of them play in the orchestra. The Dixon family is the kind I rejoice to hear about, for it is families of this kind which help to keep the flag of music flying in the provinces of England.

Mr. Dixon's predecessor as sub-conductor was Harold Ellis who had to resign for health reasons. He not only trained the orchestra but wrote most excellent analytical programme notes. He is still the society's tympanist and does not mind being seen moving his drums to and from the hall on a hand-cart because there is no place in which to store them between rehearsals. He can do this and yet retain his dignity as one of the vice-presidents of the society.

A past chairman of the committee for many years was Mr. John Young who was indeed a good friend to the society. The present chairman is Mr. W. E. Hare who, I believe, has served on the committee longer than any other member.

When I first began to direct the Hull Philharmonic I found it had fallen into the trap I have already mentioned—that of wanting to produce works beyond its technical powers. However, everybody has been amenable to my suggestions, and now the society really flourishes and is the kind that will do much to retain musical interest in Yorkshire. One thing about it has pleased me perhaps more than anything else: to see the large gallery filled with attentive youngsters from the schools during my rehearsals, while the evening concerts are attended by parties from the boarding schools of the district.

This is all to the good. I am a strong believer in children hearing good music. We all appreciate the pioneer work that Mr. Robert Mayer has done, and is still doing, in devoting so much of his time and money to furthering the cause so dear to his heart by running Children's Concerts. He began in a small way at the Central Hall, Westminster, but the movement has extended throughout the kingdom, no less than twenty-five new centres having been started. At first Malcolm Sargent conducted them entirely, but gradually this became impossible owing to his world-wide engagements and other conductors came to his aid. Mr. Mayer has done a great work not only for the children but for adults as well, because, as a result of this movement, new choral and orchestral societies have been formed up and down the country.

I should like to add one word about the Hull Philharmonic Society. Cannot the Hull City Council find them a room for storage of instruments and stands, and for practice nights, which would not only be a kindly gesture, but surely one of foresight. Such a Society in their midst is of inestimable value—socially and educationally—and it is this paying out for hire of rooms that spells doom to such societies—which hang together by very small individual subscriptions.

I think I can say I have always felt honoured when requests to conduct amateur societies have come my way. One, however, I did not accept. A certain Captain Faithfull played second violin in an amateur orchestra. He was an imposing-looking person with a beard that covered his tail-piece, but he was very pleasant when he headed a little deputation asking me to hear this orchestra with a view to becoming its conductor.

My father and I went down to hear it. This queer little band seemed to devote most of its time to playing waltzes and was giving an exhibition at a bazaar. The standard rule was that they played through a waltz (or part of one) until the conductor tapped. Then they went on to the next. The conductor tried to prevent them repeating their first waltz—quite without effect. Nothing would stop them. Then someone reminded him to tap.

He tapped for them to go on to the next waltz.

The result was to improve the contrapuntal effect, for those who knew the secret went on but those who did not repeated. Thus we had two waltzes going at the same time, which was at least interesting. Dear Captain Faithfull, who was a little deaf, went on plonking away, until his neighbour shouted in his ear: "Stop!" and wrested his fiddle from his grasp.

After that we had tea. My father was disgusted and went home, but I was determined to see this show through to the end. I was glad I did because I was to hear a marvellous performance of Auber's *Fra Diavolo*. I think the Devil must have been there in person because in a particularly soft passage there was a loud explosion from the 'cello. The audience craned their necks to see what had happened, but I saw plainly enough. The 'cello had come unglued and the neck had fallen into the belly.

When I arrived home my father wagged a finger at me. "No, my boy," he said. "You will never conduct *that* orchestra." Neither did I.

Robert Newman was now launching out still further. He was certainly paying his pipers, for he offered them further engagements by inaugurating the Saturday Afternoon Symphony Concerts on January 30, 1897. As the birth of Schubert occurred on January 31, 1797, the first part of the programme commemorated the centenary and included the Overture and Entr'acte-music from *Rosamunde*, while three of the songs were sung by Watkin Mills: *The Erl-King*, *The Wanderer*, and *My Hawk is tired*. In the second part we gave a first performance of Glazounoff's fifth symphony.

Having had what amounted to a permanent orchestra under my control for two years, I was now in a position to present the great masterpieces as I had long conceived them. I was proud of the orchestra, for our performances were brilliant and temperamental, largely due to the band being so cosmopolitan. My string-players were drawn from all nations; my first flute Dutch; oboe French; clarinet Spanish; bassoon and trumpet English; first horn German. With such mingled temperaments it was possible to give interpretations with a *nuance* and fire that appealed to the concert-going public, even if it did not altogether meet with the approval of the more stolid academics.

I was a very fortunate young man thus to have the opportunity of being the first to direct what was virtually a permanent orchestra in London; for, up to this period, there had been only two permanent orchestras in England: that under Sir Charles Hallé in Manchester, and the Crystal Palace Orchestra under August Manns. I was now determined to take full advantage of following the tradition and example of these two great men of the day.

Speaking of Manns reminds me of a music library which was formed and given to Bournemouth by the Rev. J. B. M. Camm. I invariably met this charming amateur musician when travelling down to the Crystal Palace (now, alas, no more) to hear Manns's Saturday Afternoon Symphony Concerts to which I went as often as I could, sometimes having the privilege of sitting between Sir George Grove and Mr. W. A Barrett. Mr. Camm would travel all the way from Bournemouth to the Crystal Palace—or, indeed, to any concert where a *novelty* was being produced. He often came to my own concerts.

Mr. Camm would purchase a full score of every novelty announced, have it beautifully bound, and attend the concert with it. I remember on one occasion having an irate letter from him after he had attended a concert of mine. A novelty had been announced but could not be performed because the parts had arrived at the last moment from Russia—full of mistakes. We substituted a repertoire work and delayed the production of the novelty until there was time to make the necessary corrections. Poor Mr. Camm had thus travelled up from Bournemouth only to suffer disappointment. He imagined we had taken out the novelty on purpose; but I wrote and told him that our librarians could be relied upon to work quickly in emergency and that the work *would* be performed. A few weeks later it was given and Mr. Camm was present to hear it. Some time later I accepted his invitation to see his library. He eventually presented it to Bournemouth as a token of regard for Sir Dan Godfrey and the Municipal Orchestra.

I flatter myself we gave all these works with some *colour*. I have not been a painter all my life without realizing the value of colour. What, after all, is music but a picture? When I conduct the *St. Matthew Passion* I see in my mind's eye Rembrandt's *Descent from the Cross* from which I have learned more than even the words of the *Passion* can tell me. I may be wrong, but I do not believe in 'churchy' performances of what is called 'sacred' music. *All* music is sacred to me—at least, all *good* music. I hate to hear wonderful words such as are to be found in the Prayer Book rendered with as much feeling as though the singers were asking someone to pass the mustard. If what is misnamed 'secular' music were performed in the same colourless way *we should never have had forty-three years of Promenade concerts*.

Even dance-music can be beautiful. I am no dancer and nobody will ever see me dance the polka, much less a foxtrot; but I love the rhythm of the waltz. All the same, when I compare the American atrocities from which we suffer in these days with the dance-music of Johann Strauss, Gung'l, Lanner, Waldteufel, or Delibes, I think it is time we began once more to dance to real music. Can the beauty of the waltzes of Strauss ever be surpassed?

Dr. Eaglefield-Hull was a man of exceptional gifts as an organizer, and as a musical editor, writer, and lecturer did much fine work. His book on modern harmony (Augener) is a valuable contribution to musical theory in its recent developments. Huddersfield, his adopted city, owes him a debt of gratitude. I was asked by Dr. Hull in 1924 to write an article on the subject of orchestral colour for his *Dictionary of Modern Music and Musicians* (Dent), and I also acted as one of the editorial committee with Sir Hugh Allen, Sir Granville Bantock and Professor Edward J. Dent. The actual article is too long to quote in its entirety, but I reproduce a few of its paragraphs here. The article is entitled *Orchestral Colour and Values*.

The parallelism with painting implied by its name is incomplete. The painter's primary material consists of three colours: red, blue, and yellow. When he mixes them a thousand varieties of hue result; but, for all their variety, they result definitely and in obedience to fixed rules. The maker of orchestral music may be said to work with four primaries: the strings and harp, the woodwind instruments, the brass and percussion instruments, these last including bells. But when he blends his primaries the results are not definite. The spacing of a chord, its doubling and its distribution among the classes of instruments can be so endlessly modified that to reach a fixed result regularly is hopeless. It is well known that some of our most experienced writers for the modern orchestra cannot hear what they write with the mind's ear. Hence the so frequent remark: "I had no idea it would sound so well."

It has been suggested that orchestral colour covers a multitudinous poverty of thematic and musical ideas. This is sometimes all too true, yet it cannot be admitted that all compositions for the orchestra should stand or fall by the so-called black-and-white-test. The orchestral works of the older masters do indeed sound well on the pianoforte, which is a colourless instrument, because their significance is mainly a matter of form and design.

But it cannot be disputed that some of the most beautiful modern orchestral compositions convey nothing, or worse than nothing, when they are arranged as four-handed pieces for the pianoforte. The fact is that the colour, obtained from the orchestra but not from the piano, can entirely change harmonic ideas. Thus on the modern orchestra the most violent harmonic clashes, the juxtaposition of several keys at once, can give perfect aesthetic pleasure. Therefore the black-and-white-test is discredited. As well judge a modern painting by a pencil sketch of it! How poor and trivial, even ugly, might be the drawing of a painting that was luminous, scintillating, ethereal, by the wonder of its colour!

We want orchestral thoughts, not pianistic thoughts transcribed for orchestral instruments. We want also fewer solos for wind instruments accompanied by strings. The woodwind has been called the flower-garden of the orchestra and the clarinet the queen thereof; but in certain works, even by composers of the last twenty years, nothing palls so much as long-winded, barren and monotonous clarinet solos.

Too much stress cannot be laid on the fact that chordal spacing greatly helps variety of colour. High registers always tend to give a brilliant, luminous effect; low registers one which is heavier and gloomier. It is also important to remember that the string colour palls least of all, and the colour of the percussion instruments very quickly.

The composers of the future must not only use the orchestra in its present state of development but must expect that it will be further changed; for there is room for much improvement.

The younger composers should go on experimenting with orchestra colour. Thinking always orchestrally, they should try to put new life into the old, and create life in the new instruments and combinations of the modern orchestra. We look for the composer who will possess an orchestral colour-vision wider than any known to us hitherto, as well as a musical idiom worthy of his instrument and his material.

When I look back on the prodigious amount of work I got through during the next few years it seems impossible that a young man could have tackled all that I did and still retain a hold on the same public. It speaks well, I think, for my interest in my work that I never allowed myself to get into a rut; and, to this day, every work I direct (be it the *Messiah* or the *Pathetic Symphony*) I treat as a fresh musical experience.

I always carry in my mind a clear perception of the previous performance of a work with mental reservations that such-and-such a passage, phrase, or accent did not previously satisfy me. I am ever trying to improve on my last performance.

Perhaps I have painted my musical colours too vividly? If I have, I would rather that were said of me than that my music was pale and anaemic. In support of which I quote Ruskin (*Stones of Venice*):

The most thoughtful minds are those which love colour the most.

XX

PADEREWSKI AND CARREÑO (1897)

IT WAS INDEED a venture when Robert Newman engaged Paderewski for an orchestral concert in Queen's Hall in 1897. His fee was prohibitive. Even so, Newman plunged deeper still when he went so far as to engage him subsequently for a piano recital for which, he told me, he paid him one thousand guineas—despite which he reaped a profit of over £200.

I actually met the great pianist on April 9, 1897. I knew that the seats of the hall could have been sold twice over and was looking forward to a wonderful concert. It is over forty years since I first set eyes on this magnetic personality but I remember him coming on to the platform as well as though it were yesterday. I remember how struck I was by his quiet, forceful, and utterly dignified bearing. I had never seen such dignity before—unless when I was privileged to behold the Abbé Liszt. Unlike Pachmann, who was always aware of people and things—of his audience especially—Paderewski's whole attention was fixed on the orchestra. The moment he was seated he addressed me in the gentlest manner possible.

"Mr. Wood, will you permit me to suggest that you move your first clarinet to a position where I can see him?"

I made the requested adjustment and Paderewski appeared to devote himself to *accompanying* the flute, oboe, and clarinet solos of the Schumann concerto. I do not think these sections of that beautiful work have ever been played in *quite* the same manner since. The infinite trouble he took to obtain a perfect *ensemble* was most gratifying to me.

When he came to the Liszt concerto (E flat) he was a different man. The brilliance and force of his octave-playing were electrifying; his almost over-powering tone in the left hand was something I shall never forget. He received a tremendous ovation and among his encores played an arrangement of the *Erl-King* when, again, his left hand was almost a miracle. Then in vivid contrast he produced a lovely singing tone in Schumann's *Warum*.

Since then it has been my good fortune to meet Paderewski almost yearly (when he was in England) at Lady Cory's evening receptions. The only regret to me was that he played on his favourite Erard piano. This instrument accompanied him on all his travels, for he was devoted to it; but, to be quite candid, I thought its tone unsympathetic, although in general I am an admirer of the Erard piano.

This reminds me that Paderewski's agent was Daniel Mayer, one of the most charming men I ever met in the profession. I think I may be forgiven here for recalling an incident in connection with him that amused me greatly at the time. I called in at his office one morning to be greeted with a hoarse whisper instead of his usual kindly voice.

"Good bordig, Bister Wood!"

"You seem to have a very bad cold," I said.

"Oh, doh, Bister Wood. We Christiad Sciedtists dever have a gold!"

Of course Christian Scientists rarely make remarks of that kind. I think he must have been pulling my leg!

Lloyd Chandos reminded me, quite recently, of an incident concerning Paderewski. I cannot do better than reproduce his letter.

Your father told me that after one of the concerts at Queen's Hall in which you had conducted for Paderewski, who after saying nice things to you upon the performance, said he had been told that your father was present in the hall and that he would like to meet him. So they sent for him, and Paderewski took him by the hand and said how honoured and pleased he was to meet him, and congratulated him upon having such a son.

When telling me this, tears were in your father's eyes at the memory because, as he said, "of all the great artists appearing at Queen's Hall, possibly not one ever gave a thought or wondered whether you ever *had* a father—except Paderewski, the greatest of them all."

How true that is! It *is* the *really* great men of the world who are interested in those whom they meet. Paderewski was a man of that kind. Of such stuff are Presidents of Republics made! It is this sort of man whom one longs to meet and whom one never forgets. It is many years since this little incident took place, but I dare say Paderewski himself has not forgotten it.

Another incident in connection with Paderewski happened in Ridinghouse Street as he was leaving Queen's Hall after a concert. There was a crowd to watch him go, and two girl enthusiasts were standing together.

"Yes—go on!" said one. "Be quick!"

Her companion whipped out a pair of scissors, snipped off one of Paderewski's curls and ran away with it.

I cannot pass from thoughts of this revered name without recording how deeply impressed I was with the film *Moonlight Sonata* in which Paderewski appeared with my dear old friend Marie Tempest. I would that all young students of the piano could see this film and study the nobility of his grand playing; and all young women should certainly see the beauty and grace of Marie Tempest, and learn from her how to charm the eye as well as the ear.

I have spoken of the dignity of Paderewski. Another pianist appeared at a Symphony concert this season—Madame Carreño. She made her first appearance at a Tchaikovsky concert to play the B flat minor concerto. It is difficult to express adequately what all musicians felt about this great woman who looked a queen among pianists—and *played* like a goddess.

The instant she walked on to the platform her stately dignity held her audience who watched with riveted attention while she arranged the long train she habitually wore. Her masculine vigour of tone and touch and her marvellous precision on executing octave passages carried everyone completely away.

Carreño played with me frequently until 1916. Even though she was sixty-three on the last occasion, I never found her losing grip for one instant. Her private life was eventful enough for she married Sauret in 1872, Giovanni Tagliapietra in 1875, Eugène d'Albert in 1892, and Tagliapietra's younger brother in 1902. Evidently the matrimonial tie held no terrors for *her!*

From the conductor's point of view I must observe here that it was an absolute inspiration to look down from the rostrum into those intensely beautiful Spanish eyes as she was seated at the piano, looking what she was—complete master of her instrument.

In July, 1913, I was walking through the main street in Salzburg when the sound of a woman's voice attracted my attention.

"Why—there's Henry Wood!"

A carriage and pair drew up. There sat Carreño with Tagliapietra the younger. We chatted animatedly—mainly about the concertos she wanted to play with me at the Symphony and Sunday concerts; but, alas, I never saw her again. The following year she went to New York where she died on June 12.

I have always been sorry I never heard Carreño sing. She developed a remarkable style after a performance given under an assumed name at the insistence of Colonel Mapleson in 1872 in Edinburgh. The artist who was to have taken the part of the queen in *Les Huguenots* (Meyerbeer) fell ill at the last moment, and Mapleson persuaded Carreño to learn the part. This she did in four days and sang it with the greatest brilliancy. She appeared as an operatic soprano for some years afterwards. What is more, she actually conducted during a tour in Venezuela with Tagliapietra's opera company for three weeks during a quarrel between the official conductor and the singers. In 1889, however, she reappeared as a pianist from which time her fame increased year by year. But for her, I doubt whether her pupil Edward MacDowell would ever have attained the fame he did. She introduced his piano concertos to the public. A remarkable woman, Carreño. I never met her equal.

There were other famous people who appeared in Queen's Hall at this time. Blanche Marchesi was one. Brahms had died on April 3, and although we had announced a Grieg programme for the 24th Newman changed it to a Brahms Memorial Concert at which Marchesi sang two groups of his songs. She made a deep inpression not only by her insight into Brahms but by her amazing stage presence.

Marie Brema—a really great Wagnerian singer—came to us for a concert on May 22 (Wagner was born that day in 1813) and gave the first performance of Wagner's *Five Songs* orchestrated by Mottl, and later in the programme, her inimitable rendering of the closing scene from *Die Götterdämmerung*. At that same concert we also had the popular Dutch 'cellist Holmann who played magnificently Tchaikovsky's *Variations* for 'cello and orchestra. In addition to the Wagner, Tchaikovsky, and Brahms concerts we had programmes devoted to Liszt, Berlioz, Saint-Säens and Dvořák. Our novelties included Glazounoff's *Carnival Overture*—a great success; Tchaikovsky's overture from the opera *The Voyevode* and the third Suite (in G); and a work by Paul Gilson called *La Mer*.

The end of this second series of Symphony concerts brought me my first cessation from work and gave me a little leisure at home with my father. I appreciated—perhaps for the first time—all he did for me in attending to my correspondence which by now had grown too heavy to be left for any length of time. I went off on a sketching holiday in South Wales and, later, sent my father away on his own. I still possess sketches made on this holiday which I look upon as perhaps being some of my best work.

The third season of Promenade concerts saw some changes in the orchestra. One pleased me very much—the appointment of W. H. Squire as leader of the 'cellos in succession to Ould. Squire was, of course, a very young man in those days; but his tone and technique were superb. He was a great acquisition to the orchestra and a favourite with the audiences.

Then, again, A. E. Ferir joined our violas. He was one of the finest players of his day and enabled me to give several performances of Berlioz's *Harold in Italy*. I have not, even now, entirely lost sight of him because he leads the violas in the Los Angeles Philharmonic Orchestra and I see him when I go to the Hollywood Bowl concerts.

He introduced an interesting viola concerto by my old friend Cecil Forsyth. I have always been a warm admirer of his compositions although they are rarely performed. They have not attracted the same attention as his literary works have done. His magnificent treatise on orchestration should be on every musical student's bookshelf. He does not rhapsodize over the effect of twenty drums in the manner of Berlioz; rather does he give his readers the benefit of his own practical experience. His section dealing with strings is particularly convincing. Two other books of his are well worth study: *Music and Nationalism* (1911) and *History of Music* which he brought out in 1914 in co-operation with Stanford. I was sorry when Forsyth left England in that same year to join the publishing firm of H. W. Gray in New York. Whenever I am there I always seek him out and spend a few hours talking over old times. He is a delightful companion.

Another change in the personnel of the orchestra affected the oboe department. Lebon, a most refined French player, led for the first season, but Malsch followed him for the second. Malsch was not a success; indeed, his tone and general playing got on my nerves so much that I appointed Desiré Lalande to take his place for the third season. Lalande was, perhaps, one of the finest oboists London ever had. He was the son of a noted bassoon-player in the Hallé Orchestra.

Our euphonium and bass tuba-player, Guilmartin, had died. I had many auditions for his successor before I was satisfied, but I ended by appointing Walter Reynolds. He was very young but I felt I could trust him. My faith was not misplaced for he proved excellent and remained with us for thirty years. He actually retired in favour of his son who was definitely talented. Unfortunately, this young man died after a few seasons. The father then returned—much to my joy for I had learned to love this honest old fellow. He was a man of hobbies, and I still possess a piece of his heraldic carving.

I was delighted when Miriam Timothy came to us as harpist. She was a beautiful girl, and in those days (the wearing of black not being compulsory) she was able to express her sense of artistry in her dress. She certainly made a charming platform picture seated at her harp. I believe she could have been in the front rank of harpists had she not gone abroad after her marriage.

Miriam Timothy replaced Mrs. Apt Thomas who was not with us for long. Newman told me she was always in the hall tuning her harp and, try as he would, he could not get away from the continual twang which he could hear in his office. He also told me that he noticed the carpet on the Promenade floor near the platform on Miriam's side of the orchestra required more repairs than in any other part of the hall. Miriam undoubtedly was an attraction to the male Promenaders. Her brother-in-law, by the way, is Sir Herbert Parsons of *Phosferine* fame.

During this season a young *basso cantante* pupil of mine made his appearance. He had been in the Danish navy, but being the possessor of a beautiful voice decided to relinquish his post for art. When he came to me he was using his full name, Louis Frolich de la Cruz, but I thought this too complicated for programmes and suggested he made his *début* as Louis Frolich. This he did with much success, eventually becoming popular on the Continent. He has now settled in Geneva where he is professor of singing at the Conservatoire.

Frolich had been introduced to me by the Leversons. A few years previously Mrs. Leverson had come to me for singing lessons, indeed, she remained a pupil of mine at odd intervals for many years. She was a clever vivacious young artist of the musical comedy type and the mother of Darrell Fancourt, the well-known baritone of Gilbert-and-Sullivan fame. He, also, studied with me. This association gave to me one of the most cherished and loved friends of my life—Siegfried Schwabacher, to whom I was introduced by Mr. Leverson. Both had made fortunes as diamond merchants in South Africa. I shall speak again of dear Siegfried Schwabacher later on.

I have vivid memories of first appearances this season. Ella Russell stands out a pinnacle of brilliance and artistry. She hailed from America. Her attack on top notes was unsurpassable —right on the note every time, no scoop of feeling the way. Her wonderful top A's were so powerful that they fascinated Landon Ronald and inspired him to write the dramatic scena *Adonäis* for her. Landon tells a story of its performance. As Ella Russell came off the platform the leader of the violas was heard to remark: "It's ('ad a nice) success." Similarly, Mendelssohn is known to have had in his mind the delicious top F sharps in Jenny Lind's voice when he wrote *Hear ye, Israel*.

Speaking of *Adonäis*, which is written so wonderfully for the soprano voice, reminds me that it had fallen out of the Promenade repertoire for several years, but in 1937, when my dear friend Ronald was so ill, I suggested its inclusion in the Promenade programmes to which the B.B.C. readily consented. Stiles-Allen sang it superbly; indeed, I never remember hearing her beautiful voice to better advantage—but then, it is written so vocally, not like so much of the modern vocal writing which good musicians can just manage to *get* through but, I maintain can never be said to *sing* through.

Ella Russell studied with me for five years during which period I taught her her entire repertoire. She was one of the kindest, gentlest women I ever met, and her charm equalled her personal beauty. She died in Florence only a short while ago and in very poor circumstances. The news saddened me because I remember her lavish hospitality at her home in Hendon. Her Husband, Signor Righini, wrote to me some little time before she died, telling me of their sad plight.

Inseparable friends—two Dutchmen, Johannes Wolff and Joseph Holmann—made many appearances during this season. I first met them at Mrs. Ronald's At Homes; in fact, one could hardly go to any social function without meeting these popular society artists. The round of social excitements must have stunted the natural advancement of two such brilliant young men: no time for thought and study, with the result that, as time went on, whenever Wolff appeared with an orchestra he played a very weak violin concerto by Godard, and Holmann always trotted out *Kol Nidrei.*

At this time Robert Newman took up a very remarkable prodigy—the seven-year-old Bruno Steindel. In concerts and recitals his power, technique and musical intelligence were remarkable; but, like so many prodigies, he did not fulfil the promise of his seven years. Very different was the appearance of Adela Verne, a very young girl destined to go far in the pianistic world. Adela Verne was undoubtedly fortunate in having, in her sister Mathilde, a teacher who was always at her side. Thus the promise of youthful days did not diminish from want of supervision.

So great as to be extraordinary was the artistic difference between these sisters. Adela, for many years a deservedly popular artist, had a brilliant and very powerful technique; Mathilde, on the other hand, was a most refined and sensitive pianist of the Clara Schumann school. I always loved her performance of the Schumann concerto. Solomon is the culminating success of a long line of her pupils, amateur and professional.

Mathilde Verne had a large circle of friends and nothing delighted her more than to be with them. A few days after the publication of her memoirs—an interesting volume in which she spoke of the numerous pupils who had passed through her hands—she was present at a reception at the Savoy. Surrounded by her friends (who sincerely congratulated her on the publication of her book) she was suddenly taken ill, and died. What a wonderful and touching end to a brilliant career!

Towards the end of this season of Promenade we inaugurated a series of Sunday Afternoon Orchestral Concerts (September 19–May 22), a series of Saturday afternoon Symphony concerts (October 23–June 22), while, with the Queen's Hall Choral Society, we gave the *Messiah* on Christmas Day, *Elijah* on New Years' Day, Rossini's *Stabat Mater* on Ash Wednesday, and Gounod's *Redemption* on Good Friday—in addition to which the fourth season of Promenades was announced to begin on August 27 (1898). All these concerts drew full houses, and tickets for the choral concerts could, in many instances, have been sold twice over.

Novelties once again came in for a good share of the programmes but they were not so numerous as in either of the two previous years. The old, old story: Newman found that as soon as novelties appeared box-office receipts disappeared. For all that, we produced Liszt's amazing *Faust Symphony* which indeed marked the beginning of my determination to make his music more widely known. I even gave performances of his two oratorios *Saint Elizabeth* and *Christus* with the Nottingham Sacred Harmonic Society—a daring but entirely successful experiment.

Moussorgsky was represented by his *Night on the Bare Mountain* and the *March in A Flat*, and we produced three dances from Mackenzie's music to Barrie's *Little Minister*. Another first performance was of a work that had just won the first prize at the Irish Musical Festival (*Fies Ceoil*) of 1897. This was the *Deirdre* by Michèle Esposito, a native of Naples who had settled in Dublin. Esposito was made an honorary Mus. Doc. of Dublin University in 1917, and the Italian title of *Commendatore* was conferred on him in 1922.

David Popper made his first appearance to play his own new 'cello concerto in E Minor. His technique was phenomenal; every 'cellist will know his *bravura* solos. Percy Pitt's *Taming of the Shrew* (one of his best works) was given and greatly appreciated; and from Lenora Jackson, an American violinist who won the Mendelssohn State Prize in Berlin, we secured a splendid performance of the Vieuxtemps fourth concerto. Lamond was another new-comer this season—but not as a player of Beethoven. He played Rubinstein instead. One work we produced I thought was going to live—Parry's *Magnificat*—but it has now dropped out of the concert repertoire. I have never been able to understand why.

XXI

PRINCESS OLGA OUROUSSOFF (1898)

I HAD NOT had one day's respite from my work since the previous July when I went sketching in Wales; and now, after my last concert on June 22, I planned the greatest *private* venture of my life: my marriage with Princess Olga Ouroussoff. As it was my private life I should not mention it here but for its musical associations. As I have said before, this lady had been my pupil for some years and, as time went on, she had become a very welcome visitor and a dear friend who had helped my father and myself in the management of my home. Since my mother's death various housekeepers had worked their evil ways—undetected and unmolested—until one day when I seemed to think my weekly bill for food for my father, myself, and one maid must surely be excessive, considering the cost of a meal at any of our well-known restaurants. I asked Olga whether she considered my housekeeper could manage on less than £14 a week and learned to my surprise that half this sum would, or should suffice.

It was, however, our music that drew us together, for by this time Olga was a most accomplished singer. We were married in July, 1898, and spent a glorious six weeks at Braemar even though it rained the whole time. Our life was somewhat marred, even in those early days, by the ill-health of my dear wife resulting from a severe operation she had undergone some six years previously; but her courage and indomitable will-power were the high-lights of her character. Many a time she sang at a concert in great pain—yet she betrayed no sign of it in her singing. Hers was a true Russian soprano voice—rich, with a metallic ring; and her gift for languages made it possible for her to sing in almost any tongue.

Olga was the greatest worker ever. Every morning she spent at least a couple of hours with her accompanist, for some years Percy Pitt, and, later, Hamilton Harty. Again, later still, F. B. Kiddle. Olga made her first appearance at the Promenade concerts in 1901 when she sang *Elizabeth's Prayer* from *Tannhäuser*, her splendid *sostenuto* and even quality of voice enabling her to do full justice to this important aria. As time went on, her many engagements (coupled with my work) made it impossible for my father to cope with the ever-growing volume of correspondence, and a secretary became necessary. Our first was Miss Ward, daughter of the head of St. John's Wood Art School.

We were still in Langham Place, but had seen a house we liked better in Norfolk Crescent. When it came to the actual move my father suggested he should carry on by himself. He felt he was doing very little for us and that he could better serve us by visiting rather than by living with us and requiring thought and attention as anyone not actively engaged in so busy a household must do. Most fortunately, my pupil Ben Grove had just married. When I told him I was troubled at my father's decision he at once suggested he should live with them. To this my father readily consented.

I missed him, but I knew he was happy in his new surroundings. We liked our new home, and our days were full of happy associations with our mutual knowledge of and regard for the exigencies of our calling and complete understanding of the musical temperament. Olga never permitted anything of a domestic nature to interfere with my music; thus I was able to get through an extraordinary amount of scoring and teaching, besides studying works to be played during the coming season.

On our return from our honeymoon I plunged into my fourth Promenade season. The Sunday afternoon concerts went on as before (while the Promenades were still running) and Newman added a series of Sunday Evening Concerts as well. I want to make it clear that both these series began *four weeks before* the Promenade season closed. Six Sunday evenings in succession I directed *St. Paul*, *Messiah*, *Elijah*, *Hymn of Praise*, *Stabat Mater* and *The Golden Legend*.

The only angry words I ever had with Newman were over these Sunday Evening Concerts. I told him that no conductor could be expected to direct Promenade concerts six nights a week and perform a different oratorio each Sunday with only one chorus rehearsal—an amateur chorus at that—*and no band rehearsal*. It was all I could do to squeeze in a piano rehearsal for the soloists. He was furious with me but I stood my ground. Eventually he engaged George Riseley of Bristol to direct the Sunday Evening Concerts.

This arrangement was successful as far as it went; but Riseley found himself in trouble about the fourth week. A work down for performance the following Sunday was insufficiently rehearsed and a purely orchestral programme had to be substituted at the last moment. Choral works were rarely given after that, which did not suit Newman's plans at all.

That was the trouble with dear old Newman. No sooner had

he conceived an idea than he visualized it carried out. He himself had amazing physique and never thought for one moment that I was getting very tired or that I had no time for musical thought. His business superseded his artistic instincts—otherwise he would have seen the impossibility physically and artistically of directing and rehearsing six Promenade Concerts with the usual piano rehearsals for soloists and composers, and directing two Sunday Concerts as well, for weeks on end. I told him no human being could possibly stand up to it. In the end he dropped the Sunday Evening Concerts, retaining only those in the afternoon until April 8.

Riseley used to annoy the members of the orchestra by an unpleasant habit of spitting, in his excitement over big *sforzato* chords. One morning I happened to drop in during one of his rehearsals and was amazed to see about half-a-dozen umbrellas go up in the orchestra. Riseley was furious.

"Gentlemen, what is the meaning of this?"

A voice: "Well, sir, the rain from your mouth on the *sforzatos* reaches us here, and we had to decide between mackintoshes and umbrellas!"

That cured Riseley of the habit, but he was always trying to curry favour with the orchestra, the leaders especially. He kept a supply of perfectly dreadful cigars which he occasionally handed out. These became a joke. If anybody complained of not feeling up to the mark all he got in the way of sympathy was: "Ah! *you've* been smoking a *Flor de Riseley!*"

In addition to the concerts already enumerated, there were the Saturday Symphony Concerts which had begun on October 29 and ran until the following March. Then followed, in May, the Lamoureux concerts at which both the French and English orchestras played. There had already been three extra Wagner concerts, and Tchaikovsky concerts were down for June (1889), in addition to the usual performance on Christmas Day, New Year's Day, Ash Wednesday and Good Friday.

It was amazing that the orchestra stood it. I think I should have gone under myself (giving, as I did, every ounce of my vitality at each concert) but for the fact that Olga ran my home so perfectly. I was always sure of being given good food and good wines—and of enjoying perfect peace and comfort.

There *could* have been a perpetual round of social pleasures. The temptation to accept some of the invitations we received was indeed great, but we had to risk offending people—even to forgoing all the pleasures of parties and country house week-ends—in fact, all those delightful attractions in which we dare only participate on rare occasions. Many of our friends faded away because we neglected them in order to devote all our time to music. If we went out after concerts were over it meant late hours, so we simply cut off everything of the kind and got to bed as early as possible. Literally a life of work and sleep—but work *was* life to us.

The Lord's Day Observance Society caused Newman much anxiety at this time; indeed, while discussions were in course of progress, the continuity of the Sunday concerts was broken during the autumn of 1898 when the following notice appeared:

ROBERT NEWMAN'S QUEEN'S HALL CONCERTS

SPECIAL NOTICE

Mr. Robert Newman regrets to inform the Public that in consequence of the decision of the London County Council he is forced to

ABANDON

his

SUNDAY CONCERTS

The above appeared on my Symphony concert programme for November 26. On that for December 10 appeared a notice to the effect that the Sunday concerts would be resumed the following week, which goes to show that Newman, as usual, quickly mastered the situation.

I must remind you that Wagner in these early days failed to fill the Promenade, though every reserved seat was always sold. However, we tried to overcome that little difficulty by including a Beethoven symphony in three or four of the Monday Wagner-night programmes. This worked wonders, for Beethoven was popular. Before the inception of the Promenade, Wagner was only known to a few—chiefly through Manns at the Crystal Palace and Richter at St. James's Hall.

Obviously I had the advantage of these men because they could only present a few concerts per season in their several centres—and even then could only include a certain number of standard examples. Newman, on the other hand, was out to back me up in popularizing Wagner. He could offer the public their Wagner on Mondays at a price with which no other management could compete. Thus my early ambition was realized. However, it is a curious fact that, even now, the Wagner nights fail to attract the Promenaders as surely as those occupying higher-priced seats. I wonder why!

By delving into the complete operas, and selecting every possible excerpt that could form a concert item, I was able to introduce some forty selections. After my talks with Mottl in London and Bayreuth I added the *Bridal Procession* from Act II of *Lohengrin*, *Siegfried and the Forest Dragon*, *Wotan's Spear and the Sleeping Brünnhilde*, as well as complete acts from *Rheingold*, *Valkyries*, *Siegfried*, *Götterdämmerung*, *Tristan*, *Tannhaüser*, *Flying Dutchman*, and *Parsifal*.

One of the most delightful Wagner concerts I remember was when I gave the first and fourth scenes from *Rheingold*, my three Rhein-daughters being Lillian Blauvelt, Helen Jaxon, and Kirkby Lunn. They were perfect. No wobble, dead in tune, and all three with big voices which blended to perfection. David Bispham, I remember, was the Alberich on that occasion. Lillian Blauvelt, incidentally, made her first appearance in England at a Symphony concert on October 29 this season when she sang the Mad Scene from *Hamlet* (Thomas) and songs by Mendelssohn and Delibes. Hers was a fascinating, happy personality with a voice reminding me of Elizabeth Schumann's when she first came out.

My reputation as a Wagnerian conductor was now steadily growing.

XXII

QUEEN VICTORIA: A COMMAND PERFORMANCE (1898)

THERE WAS NO doubt about it: Wagner was becoming increasingly popular in London. Whether I was popularizing him or whether he was doing a like office for me was difficult to decide—but his name and mine were being linked together at the end of 1898. So much so that Queen Victoria commanded me to give a concert with the Queen's Hall Orchestra on Saturday November 24 of that year, Her Majesty herself choosing the programme.[1]

Naturally we were all thrilled at the prospect of going down to Windsor Castle, and I rehearsed everything with meticulous

[1] The Queen chose as follows: Good Friday Music; Prelude Act III (*Die Meistersinger*); Overture *Hänsel and Gretel*; *Le Rouet d'Omphale*; third and fourth movements *Pathetic Symphony*; *Siegfried Idyll*; Vorspiel (*Parsifal*); Overture *Die Meistersinger*.

care as I intended to take no chances. Even so, as is so often the case, the unexpected happened.

Goodwin and Tabb, our exceedingly efficient librarians, had undertaken to pack all the music and send it down to Windsor in charge of their assistant Radcliffe. He was an amusing little man and devoted to his work. The arrangement was that he was to go down by an earlier train; we, by the way, travelled in a special train due to land us at the Castle about half-past eight p.m. The concert was due to begin at half-past ten. On arrival I asked for Radcliffe and was somewhat surprised to learn he had not arrived. Neither, of course, had the scores and parts. I immediately telegraphed both Newman and Goodwin. After a delay that nearly sent me frantic a reply came to say that the lost music was on its way. Fortunately, we had time to spare, but I was glad to see Radcliffe in the flesh. It transpired that he had gone to sleep in the train and, as Windsor was a terminus, both he and the music had gone back to London. His contrition was almost comic to behold, but it was more than equalled by the jubilation of Dr. George Cathcart who was present with us.

The Doctor had made up his mind he was not going to be out of our Command Performance, but we saw no way of including him. Newman, as usual, came to the rescue. He hit on the admirable idea of making out an extra contract for another triangle-player at the enormous fee of one guinea. This he laughingly offered to Dr. Cathcart who, I believe, still treasures it.

I have never seen an orchestral platform look so exquisitely beautiful as the one I saw that night at Windsor Castle. There were masses of flowers everywhere. Special music-stands had been requisitioned, each adorned with flowers complete with little lamps so arranged that no direct light therefrom should disturb Her Majesty's vision. I had previously held a consultation with the Castle carpenters regarding the construction of this special platform. They built it according to my plan, the top rise being thirty feet from the floor level. Thus the Queen could see every player in the orchestra. I had nothing left to wish for—until I found that I had to wear white kid gloves. I felt like a bandmaster on a seaside pier.

After the last item the Queen requested that we should play the *Ride of the Valkyries*. I had taken the precaution of including scores and parts of half a dozen likely items in case of such a request, but I fear Her Majesty must have regretted her choice for the Long Gallery was rather small and the brass sounded noisy. We nearly took the roof off! However, the Queen's Hall orchestra played magnificently. It has won many laurels since but none more deservedly than on this particular night.

There were sixty guests present who bestowed their appreciation at the conclusion of every item with the most generous applause. After the concert was over I was taken to the Drawing-room and presented to Her Majesty by the Lord Chamberlain.

"Thank you very much, Mr. Wood," were the Queen's first words. "I knew Richard Wagner quite well, and I enjoyed the *Good Friday Music* so much. Unfortunately, I am too old to travel to Bayreuth now, but I do hope you will come again and play me some more *Parsifal*."

She looked at me rather closely for a moment.

"Tell me, Mr. Wood," she said . . . "are you *quite* English? Your appearance is—er—rather *un-English*!"

I assured her that I was London born of British parentage. Her Majesty then presented me with a beautiful baton inscribed with the Crown and the initials V.R.I. Bowing myself out of the great Queen's presence, the one thing uppermost in my mind was the rare beauty of her voice, the gentle sweetness of which has ever remained with me. Before leaving the Castle I was requested to sign Her Majesty's birthday-book, an honour of which I am proud. We were entertained to an excellent supper and returned to London by our special train. We arrived in the early hours of the morning, very pleased with ourselves.

The only person who was not pleased was poor old Newman. He was most upset and disappointed because he had not been presented. We learned later, however, that managers were never presented. All the same, we felt it rather hard on him because he had so enthusiastically entered into all the arrangements. However, he cheered up wonderfully a few days later when he received a diamond pin from Her Majesty. Sad to say, it was not my good fortune to play 'more *Parsifal*' for her Majesty, as she had so graciously suggested.

XXIII

THE LONDON MUSICAL FESTIVAL
(1899)

JUST AFTER CHRISTMAS, 1897, the Nottingham Sacred Harmonic Society sent me an invitation to conduct their concerts. In the season that followed I produced Mendelssohn's first

Walpurgis Night, and the third act of *Tannhaüser*. I was then able with the help of Sir Samuel Johnson, to found the Nottingham City Orchestra whose personnel consisted of about fifteen local professional players, something like fifty amateurs, and such members of the Queen's Hall Orchestra as occasion demanded.

In order to train this society and the newly-formed orchestra I went to Nottingham and took a choral practice every Wednesday evening. I frequently stayed the night as a guest of the Conservative Club, sponsored by Mr. Frank Greatorex, rehearsing the orchestra the following day. These rehearsals began at ten in the morning and went on until the same hour at night with only very brief intervals. From ten until midday I took the first and second violins; from then until two the rest of the strings; from three till five the woodwind, and from seven to ten the full orchestra. I then caught the last train back to London, arriving in the early hours of the morning. This *régime* obtained each season from November to March.

I fear this enthusiasm on my part proved a liability rather than an asset, but I did it for the advancement of choral and instrumental concerts in the Provinces. I wish still more societies could be formed in every sizeable town. They are such good fun and at the same time of such educational value, but subscriptions must necessarily be kept down to a minimum (for these young people are mainly drawn from those who live a work-a-day life) and yet do not bring in enough to purchase music and stands, much less an instrument. The few pounds interest gained from even a hundred pounds keeps the wolf from the door. It is just this annual loss of ten, twenty, or fifty pounds a year that accumulates and causes a society to close down, perhaps for ever. Nottingham was indeed fortunate when Sir Samuel Johnson saw how great was the enthusiasm amongst the members of the City Orchestra, for we were given (through his influence) a grant from the Corporation.

I cannot see why music in this form does not enter into the local budgets of town councils and municipalities, for not only is music a healthy hobby in every sense of the word, but as an educational factor it has so much to commend it. If local authorities would allot (free of all charge) the use of a suitable room wherein to hold weekly rehearsals and provide accommodation for stands and band parts, I believe we should see a great revival of real musical effort throughout the country. It must be remembered that although local authorities provide bands and other entertainments in parks and such places, the amateur musician is far more likely to take interest in them if he can 'fiddle' for himself. We must also bear in mind the fact that out-door music is impracticable for at least eight months in the year.

To return to the activities of 1899. In May came the London Musical Festival. There were two orchestras for this: Lamoureux's from Paris and the Queen's Hall. We each conducted our own except on the last day when the combined orchestras were conducted alternately by Lamoureux and myself. This was perhaps my greatest thrill of these early days, and I carry in my memory the enthusiastic interest Lamoureux displayed in this battle between *le vieux français et le jeune anglais*. I opened the festival with works by Beethoven, Wagner, Tchaikovsky, Coleridge-Taylor and Sullivan.

Lady Hallé—far and away the greatest lady violinist of the time—played the Max Bruch concerto superbly. I had heard her play solos many times at St. James's Hall but not, thus far, a concerto. I remember her telling me that her father had refused to pay for more than a dozen lessons on the violin. He told her to teach herself, and proceeded to send her to hear every great violinist of the day. The nobility of her style reminded me of Joachim but, to be quite candid, I thought her tone more musical than his; certainly her intonation was better. I remember her playing the Brahms concerto at a Symphony concert just after she had suffered a sad domestic trouble over her son. She was far from well that afternoon and I had my heart in my mouth when she clutched the rostrum rail after the first movement and whispered: "Wait a minute! I feel rather faint!" However, she recovered and played the slow movement beautifully, losing nothing of her old spirit and brilliancy in the *finale*.

Our Symphony concerts in those days were very long—far too long—and this first concert of the festival was no exception. Two and a half hours with only an interval of five minutes *is* too long.

Lamoureux produced Dukas's new work *L'Apprenti Sorcier* at the third concert on May 9. The public took to it at once, and I have performed it whenever an opportunity has occurred since. My own production at this concert was Elgar's short oratorio *Lux Christi* which had been produced three years previously at the Worcester Festival. I have just been looking at a note about Elgar in the fourth programme of the festival:

Elgar ranks in the estimation of all competent judges amongst the most able and promising of the younger generation of composers.

Most of us thought that, in time, he would give us great works, but few guessed *how* great they would prove to be.

The soloist was Paderewski. I am not likely to forget the experience of accompanying him in two concertos—the fifth of Beethoven and the second of Chopin. His unity with the orchestra was amazing. He never seemed to be listening to his own playing, his whole attention as usual being given to the orchestra—but Paderewski has ever been such an exceptionally outstanding artist that to speak of the *furore* he created is mere repetition.

At the fifth concert Newman produced for the first time in England the *Transfiguration of Christ*, an oratorio by Don Lorenzo Perosi. This was another instance of Newman's keenness to give something new to the London public.

Perosi was having a great vogue on the Continent, and Newman wanted him to come to London for the performance of the work, but was bitterly disappointed on finding that the Pope would not give him permission to leave Rome because some special services were being sung there at the time. Perosi's oratorios bored me; some of our early Victorian Mus. Docs. had produced more vital and interesting works. We had a second and a third dose of these compositions at the eighth and ninth concerts in the shape of the *Resurrection of Lazarus* and the *Resurrection of Christ*. I hardly know which I disliked the more, but was simply thankful I had not to study either as George Riseley directed them. Nothing upsets me more than to have to study for weeks a score and parts of a work never likely to be repeated.

At the sixth concert Lamoureux introduced *Fantaisie Symphonique* by his son-in-law Camille Chevillard, himself a conductor well-known to the Lamoureux Orchestra because he so often took rehearsals and conducted concerts for his distinguished father-in-law. The work was interesting, though obviously Chevillard had been influenced by both Schumann and Brahms. At this same concert Ysaÿe played the Beethoven concerto. I shall never forget his tone after the *cadenza* in the first movement, when that divine theme enters on the third string. Then Pachmann appeared at the seventh concert to play the Mendelssohn D minor concerto. He, of course, created his usual impression.

The direction of the combined orchestras was shared by Lamoureux and myself at the last concert of the festival. We had played to crowded houses all along, and on this night the hall was packed with a wonderfully enthusiastic audience. None the less, I felt that this playing-off of one conductor against another was an ordeal through which I must pass unscathed in spite of my growing reputation—that is, if I was to enhance it.

That I did justify the prediction of my friends and enhance my prestige was extremely gratifying in that I had more than held my own with a four-year-old orchestra against one of many years' standing whose great conductor was thirty-six years my senior. (Lamoureux died in 1899 at the age of sixty-five.)

Unfortunately it is a national trait to belittle our own. Perhaps less so nowadays—maybe, the natural outcome of national spirit during the Great War; at all events, I knew that many people were saying it was unfair to put Wood into such close competition with Lamoureux. However, it affected me little because I knew my own mind and intended every bar I played to *reflect* my mind. After all, I had heard every conductor of repute here and abroad; I had endeavoured to learn what not to do, and had not veered from my own line one iota since I first took up a baton. These doubting Thomases were confounded—but perhaps I cannot do better than quote Mrs. Rosa Newmarch in her book (in the *Living Masters of Music* series), for then I cannot be accused of blowing my own trumpet.

From this musical tournament the English orchestra came off with flying colours. The Lamoureux band displayed their accustomed efficiency, their polished smoothness and neatness of phrasing; but many preferred the more glowing interpretations of their younger conductor.

Lamoureux had the French vision in art—that is to say, he was greatly preoccupied with order and design. The emotion was there, but simple and symmetrical, and kept strictly within bounds.

Henry Wood's readings were fresher, more individual; and if they were sometimes overcharged with exuberant vitality and emotion, it was easy to excuse in the younger musician the fault of giving too much. The public who had hitherto regarded him as a promising conductor now began to think of him as something more. At this time some of his interpretations such as Tchaikovsky's *Pathetic* and Schubert's *Unfinished* symphonies, and the funeral March from *Siegfried* attained a level of excellence he has scarcely surpassed since.

Even so, my season's work had not yet finished, for there were still more concerts on May 15, 16, 17 and 30 and June 17 at which no less a person than Ysaÿe was again to appear.

XXIV

EUGÈNE YSAŸE (1899)

WHEN AN ARTIST of the calibre of Eugène Ysaÿe appears on the platform to rehearse a concerto there are few conductors in the world who cannot learn something from him in the art of orchestral accompaniment. I know I learned more in these early days from this great man than from all the others put together. The instant he began to rehearse I sensed his master mind and had sufficient tact to subjugate my will to his. There was nothing else to do, but I am glad to say I *thought* of doing nothing else.

We began with Bach's E major concerto. I suppose we must have spent a good two hours over it, for Ysaÿe stopped us every few bars. He turned to the strings, showed them his bowing, and gently insisted on their copying it. Every jot and tittle of phrasing was likewise illustrated and faithfully copied.

What impressed me more than anything was his marvellous singing quality and perfect *rubato*. So many artists adopt the sticky sort of *rubato* which leaves the conductor suspended in mid-air. Just when he thinks the player is about to increase his speed he does the reverse and broadens the passage. With Ysaÿe I never had that experience. I knew exactly what he was going to do and followed him naturally. His *rubato* was such that if he borrowed he faithfully paid back within four bars. It was an absolute inspiration to accompany him.

No one can imagine what agonies some soloists will cause a conductor. The pianists who seem to think that every upgoing scale should be hurried and who always arrive at the top before time; or who rush up an arpeggio with the same idea in view; or the singers who get nervous because their wind is short and who hurry a phrase in order not to pant for breath. These dear people are the trial of a conductor's life.

Ysaÿe was the first to convince me that nearly all orchestral accompaniments are too heavy, and we went over some of the more fully-orchestrated passages three or four times.

"Gentlemen, I am not a trombone—*only a solo violin.*"

In Bach's work Ysaÿe was deadly opposed to a *continuo* on the piano or harpsichord.

"It irritates me," he said. "Percussion instruments do not blend with a solo fiddle and there is no continuity of tone and they spoil my *cantilena!*"

He thereupon produced a beautifully-conceived organ part written by his friend Gevaert, Director of the Brussels Conservatoire and a great musicologist. I was so much impressed with this organ part that I begged to be allowed to copy it. Ysaÿe readily consented and I have used it ever since.

I remember so clearly the long G sharp in the slow movement of the Bach concerto as played by Ysaÿe. His control was absolute perfection, his *vibrato* sensitive and refined. Quite unlike Joachim's, or Sarasate's, or the quicker more nervous type of Kreisler. His rhythmic energy in the rondo was electrifying. The rondo tune comes over three times; he gave it with three different weights of tone. He then played Joachim's splendid *Theme and Variations in E minor*. This work is rarely played; indeed, I have only done it once since. That was a few years ago with Marie Hall, and even then I had to persuade her to learn it.

At the second concert Ysaÿe played another neglected work—the F minor concerto of Lalo. This he followed up by one for which I have always had a sneaking regard—a *Poème* for violin and orchestra by Ernest Chausson who, poor man, had only died the week previous from a cycling accident. This was the first performance in England and Ysaÿe's grief was great because his friend did not live to hear it.

The difficulty Robert Newman always experienced with Ysaÿe was getting his programme. One season—a few years later than this—he engaged him for two orchestral concerts and four recitals. He wrote several letters but received no reply. At last he became desperate.

"We go to Brussels tonight," he announced. And go we did. The next day we called on Ysaÿe who received us in his billiard-room, smoking a pipe and arrayed in a pair of woolly pyjamas. On the billiard table lay a huge pile of letters which had not even been opened.

"That accounts for it," whispered Newman, nudging me. He then tackled Ysaÿe on the subject of his programme. He was not keen on having Wieniawski or Vieuxtemps, preferring Bach and Beethoven.

Ysaÿe could not see the point. What did it matter *what* he played? All we need tell London was that *Ysaÿe was playing*. How could it matter what he played? Newman, however, would not accept that and eventually managed to prevail upon Ysaÿe to give him a programme.

"Of course, he will alter it all," he grumbled afterwards, "but I shall have something to advertise even if he doesn't play a note of it." However, we pinned him down to three concertos—the Bach No. 2, the Mozart No. 3, and the Beethoven. So that we considered our journey had not been in vain.

I can never say enough—in fact, words utterly fail me when I think of Ysaÿe's performances. The quality of his tone was so ravishingly beautiful, and it is no exaggeration to say that, having accompanied all the great violinists in the world during the past fifty years, of *all* of them Ysaÿe impressed me most. He seemed to get more colour out of a violin than any of his contemporaries and he was certainly unique as a concerto-player, especially in his use of the three positions of the bow on the strings and his intensity of tone when playing with the full hairs of the bow near the bridge. I remember his *flautando*-playing, particularly, in a work by Rimsky-Korsakoff, and still treasure the memories of this most lovable man.

The last concert of the season took us into midsummer week. We devoted ourselves to Tchaikovsky and Wagner. We opened with the *Pathetic Symphony;* Lillian Blauvelt sang the Mad Scene from *Hamlet* (Thomas), and we ended with the first act of the *Valkyries* in German with Helen Jaxon as Sieglinde, Ellison van Hoose as Siegmund, and Emil Senger as Hunding. A fine climax to a really thrilling season.

I was now more than ready for a holiday. I fear it was another busman's holiday, for I took Olga to Bayreuth. She had not experienced the atmosphere that alone belongs to the *Festspielhaus*. We stopped at Seligsburg on the way out as it gave us our only chance of meeting Olga's relatives, the de Wolkoffs, who generally sojourned in Switzerland during the summer. We spent a delightful fortnight with them in this charming little mountain retreat. There was no railway and we had a two-hour drive up from Treib pier to the village which nestled in the mountain hollow. I have been there since—as recently as 1936—but found very little change.

I still have vivid recollections of our drive up. Our driver kept falling asleep but the horses knew the road so well that they rounded the hairpin bends without his help. I did my best to keep him awake by prodding him with my stick, but he must have been the youngest of the Seven Sleepers. Nothing would keep him awake.

Old de Wolkoff was a conceited old man who fancied himself as a composer. He had studied with Rubinstein which was about all that recommended him. Olga and he argued heatedly when he declared that there was no music in England except comic songs. All the same, he managed to persuade me to produce two very slight orchestral works of his at a Promenade concert in September 1899, although it is a rule of mine never to produce a friend's work *unless* on its merits. It is one of the worst things a conductor can do and rarely honours the friendship.

I remember another occasion when I yielded. A great friend of mine pressed me to perform a work for a relative. I protested that I never did that sort of thing unless the work was good enough to stand on its own feet. I was pressed to such an extent that it was practically impossible to refuse without causing deep offence, and gave way. It was amusing to read the accounts of the performance the next day in the newspapers.

"Oh, Mr. Wood! *OH, MISTER WOOD!*"

Except for the last two, I had not missed Bayreuth for many years. So well did I know it that I felt I was showing Olga something of my own when we journeyed on there from Seligsberg. The Bayreuth atmosphere remains as ever it was—and what a lovely theatre it is! I am a great believer in the picture-frame type of proscenium, and Bayreuth has it *par excellence*, but there is a very good one at Munich, though the auditorium there is too large.

At each succeeding visit to Bayreuth I have noted improvements: in the presentation of *Lohengrin* (in which Siegfried Wagner helped so much) the device of the interstices of the trees hung right across the proscenium borders on strong netting was most effective. And again—in *Tannhäuser*—the new Paris version of the scene with the wonderful little flight of cherubs with their marvellous arrows which they shot exactly on the right chord.

In the old days Bayreuth was the Mecca of all true Wagnerians. To go there was regarded almost as a pilgrimage, for Wagner's traditions held good through the influence of both Cosima and Siegfried Wagner. All that is now gradually disappearing. Everything is commercialized. There must always be a 'star' conductor—Toscanini or Furtwängler—and this famous soprano or that famous tenor. In the old days we never knew who was singing and certainly we never knew who was conducting. The names were not advertised and we had to find out as best we could. We went there for Wagner and Wagner alone; but tradition broke down when the copyright of *Parsifal* ran out. It ought never to have been performed outside Bayreuth. One no longer thinks of Bayreuth as a pilgrimage: one just 'goes to the opera'.

I shall always remember the shock I sustained, after having heard *Parsifal* at Bayreuth (for at least the twentieth time) when I heard it again at the Metropolitan Opera House, New York, six months later, with Ternina and Burgstaller, a splendid orchestra and an excellent chorus. A fine performance—but what an atmosphere pervaded my senses when I left the theatre and went out on to Broadway among the cars with their whistles and hooters! The illuminated streets made me realize that only Bayreuth can provide the right atmosphere—Bayreuth, with its simple, peaceful, artistic existence. New York is all wrong for the sacred drama of *Parsifal;* indeed, this applies to any modern city.

Olga's musicianship rendered her deeply sensitive to Bayreuth. We both revelled in the simplicity of the daily life there; in the courtesy displayed at every turn; in our pleasant meals with the good Rhine wines; the meetings after the performances when we discussed all we had seen and heard. Everything simple, untouched by petty jealousies and wirepulling.

The American performance to which I have just referred took place in 1904—five years after this holiday. On my return I went to Manchester where I met Richter. He clutched my arm.

"You have just come back from New York? Did you hear *Parsifal?*" he queried. "Tell me—what was it like?"

"Musically good, atmospherically all wrong," I told him.

"Yes," he said thoughtfully, "you are quite right. That's my view of it. *Not like Bayreuth!*"

And few people knew more about Bayreuth than Hans Richter.

XXV

I AM HISSED IN QUEEN'S HALL
(1899)

We returned to the fifth season of the Promenade concerts which were announced to run for seven weeks—forty-two concerts for a guinea! Two rather humorous incidents occurred during the rehearsals, the second of which was the cause of my being hissed. Both came about through Newman having put down two artistes whom I had not heard at an audition.

The first was a pianist who was down to play the *Emperor* concerto. The first thing I noticed about him at rehearsal was that he was kicking the *sostenuto* pedal in his endeavour to keep time. This was more than I could endure. I stopped the band.

"You are making so much noise with the pedal that I cannot hear the orchestra," I told him. He apologized very politely and we began again. This time he kicked the pedal louder than ever. It was so bad that I went to Newman who had been watching from the balcony—no doubt with a somewhat guilty conscience. I told him I could not agree to this man playing at the concert. Newman came on to the platform and gently led the drummer-pianist away. That was the last I saw of him.

The other incident needs a little preliminary explanation. In those days very well-known arias were only given a preliminary piano rehearsal, as there was no time for orchestral rehearsals for singers; they had to make do with my piano rehearsal the previous day. Most of them found this quite sufficient for I was always careful to rehearse them well. In this instance, in which an attractive-looking blonde was involved, a dozen *orchestral* rehearsals would not have been sufficient. She was down to sing a recitative followed by an aria. The recitative began, as is so often the case, with a mere chord. In this instance it was the chord of D major; moreover, she had to begin on D. So that there was nothing very difficult and she did what was required at the rehearsal with the piano. When it came to the concert, and the chord was given, she began a third too high although I had previously warned her to let the chord die almost away and not be in a hurry to begin.

There was nothing to do but stop her. This I did after the fourth bar and she had gone beyond her compass. I then did all I possibly could to put her at her ease.

"Never mind," I whispered encouragingly. "Let's begin again. *Wait for the chord!* Don't hurry!" I then softly sang the note for her.

Now, orchestras are not kind when they scent a lack of musicianship in a singer. The usual thing happened; there was a gentle shuffling of feet. I gave the signal for a quiet chord, as before, and was met with a tremendous *fortissimo*, the note D being emphasized—particularly by the first violins who played it on two strings. It was useless for me to frown at the band; they looked as innocent as lambs.

Off the lady went again, but I knew she was utterly lost and would never be able to sing with the orchestra. More shuffling of feet. Again I stopped and this time went to the piano, gave her the chord, and accompanied her throughout the aria;

but I was hissed by some of the audience—possibly her friends.

I was hissed on another occasion: on September 3, 1912, when I produced Schönberg's *Five Orchestral Pieces*—the first note of his played in England up to that time.

There was a sequel to my blonde incident. I was somewhat surprised to receive a note from her asking me to give her lessons. I thought of all she had said to me after that concert (when she accused me of spoiling her first appearance in London) and wondered what to do. However, I felt sorry for her because she had come all the way from Australia to make a start. I hated to think she was not getting another chance; I therefore wrote and said I would give her the lessons. I had her for some little time but could make nothing of her. She was a hopeless musician.

The climax came when she turned up with the *Dream of Gerontius*.

"I have got an engagement to sing at Manchester with the Hallé Society," she announced. I gasped.

"You cannot sing *Gerontius*," I told her.

"But I have got the engagement."

"I know, but if you are wise you will get out of it."

"I can't do that."

"If you are wise you *will*. Tell them you are undergoing a slight operation—tell them anything, but do not accept that engagement."

She was furious and stalked out of the house.

I happened to be directing the *Dream* myself a few weeks later when John Coates was one of the soloists.

"I did *Gerontius* in Manchester a few weeks ago," he informed me, "and had an awful time."

"I am sorry to hear that. What happened?"

"Well, I had to sing the lady's part as well as my own. She was all over the place."

I did not ask the good John to tell me the lady's name. *I told him instead.*

Thinking of hissing, I remember an amusing incident with an orchestral attendant of ours. I had noticed a certain reluctance on his part to come on to the platform. At last I tackled him.

"Why is it that you always make a fuss if I want you on the platform?" I asked.

"Well, you see, sir, it's like this. I'm afraid I have borrowed a good many half-crowns from the members of the orchestra and I haven't been able to pay them back yet. If I come on to the platform they always hiss me and I don't like it. If you would

134

lend me some money I could pay them back and then it 'uld be all right."

We had a remarkably good season. I remember a young 'cellist named Paul Bazelaire at the very first concert. He had to come to us from a tour in France and Germany and had twice played in Berlin at the command of the Emperor. He must have created an impression because the court sculptor Degas executed a bust of him which still adorns the *Tiergarten*. He was only twelve and had already composed some fifty pieces. There again —these prodigies! Newman had him several times during the season. Then he vanished into thin air and I have never seen his name since.

Then there was a charming young Swedish pianist brought to me by Major Cuthbertson of the *Black Watch*. She showed so much promise that I could never understand why she did not make a big name for herself. As Tosta de Benici she appeared for several seasons and gathered round her a large circle of friends, including Olga and myself. I still regard her as an old friend, especially as we visited her several times in her beautiful villa at Arvica (Sweden) where, incidentally, I made sketches of the surrounding district.

The Meister Glee Singers appeared during the season. And excellent they were. Up to this time no vocal quartet had achieved anything approaching their success, probably because they rehearsed for a whole year before making an appearance in public. The four men's names were Sexton, Chilley, Fotherington, and Norcross. It was not that their voices were so good, but that their diction and *ensemble* were perfect.

Hayden Coffin was another attraction this season. He was famous at this time for his good looks and for his singing of *Queen of my Heart* (Dorothy) which he had so popularized with Marie Tempest. Antoinette Sterling also appeared. She was a ballad-singer of considerable note and possessed a fine-toned if somewhat uneven contralto voice.

Gregory Hast was another newcomer—one of the best lyrical tenors of his day. His singing was always refined; otherwise he would hardly have been principal tenor at the Temple Church for so many years. He has now retired and lives in Eastbourne where I meet him with his jolly little wife whenever I go to conduct festival concerts.

I notice that the sisters Cerasoli made their first appearance this season. These two delightful Italian ladies were actually the first to introduce to the Promenade public Bach's double concertos for two pianos and strings. That is something to be proud of! Whenever I visited Rome I never failed to lunch with them in their charming flat almost opposite the Castle of St. Angelo. On my last visit, I regret to say, only one of the sisters was there to greet me. Undoubtedly these two talented artists paved the way for Ethel Bartlett and her husband Rae Robertson, so popular in these days.

When Henri Verbrugghen, a young Belgian pupil of Hubay and Ysaÿe, played Dvořák's rarely-heard violin concerto he did a good thing for himself because his performance undoubtedly was responsible for his ultimate leadership when Arthur Payne resigned and returned to Llandudno as musical director in 1902. When Payne left us Maurice Sons was appointed leader, but not for the Promenades. Verbrugghen led the Promenades from 1902 till 1905. He had quite a career after that as conductor of the Scottish Orchestra; at Sydney where he became Principal of the Conservatoire; and, in 1918, as conductor of the first Australian State Orchestra. He finished up with the Symphony Orchestra at Minneapolis where he remained until his death.

We now congratulated ourselves on persuading that great flautist Albert Fransella to give up his work with August Manns at the Crystal Palace and join the Queen's Hall Orchestra. Cornet solos, by the way, fell out of the programmes this season as dear old Howard Reynolds had retired, but we found in Frank G. James (a name famous in the bassoon world) an excellent artist when occasion arose.

During this season Kirby Lunn, Yvonne de Treville, Fanny Moody, Alice Gomez, and Philip Brozel all made appearances. We had Lucille Hill with us many times, delighting her audiences with her warm, rich soprano voice; and Louisa Sobrino was another soprano worthy of mention. Miriam Timothy produced Niolai von Wilm's interesting *Concertstück* for harp and orchestra, and the leader of my 'cellos, W. H. Squire, made quite a hit with a charming little *Slumber Song*. He still plays with his old virtuosity. We ought to hear him more often—in fact, there ought to be more 'Billy' Squires in the 'cello world today. Such noble tone is all too scarce. He lives not far from me, and I am always pleased to see him and his charming wife.

Prices obtaining in 1899 make quite interesting reading. Here is Newman's notice concerning them:

For the 26 Sunday concerts, 3 guineas for seats in the Grand Circle; 2 guineas for unreserved seats in the Area Stalls, and 1 guinea for an unreserved seat in the Balcony. The cost of seats for the Afternoon

Concerts has been fixed as under: Orchestra 6d.; Area 1s.; Balcony 1s. 6d.; Area Stalls 2s. 6d.; Grand Circle (numbered and reserved) 3s.

For the evening Concerts the price of seats will be Area 6d.; Orchestra and Balcony 1s.; Area Stalls 1s. 6d.; Grand Circle (numbered and reserved) 2s. It is not proposed to issue Season Tickets for the series of Evening Concerts. All correspondence relating to the application for seats should be addressed to the Manager, Mr. R. Newman, at Queen's Hall. By order of the Council, Edgar F. Jacques.

It is fairly safe to predict that the prices of 1899 will never be in vogue again. Think of it! *One guinea for sixty concerts*! That is not much more than fourpence a concert.

Some idea of Newman's activities during the season of 1899–1900 may be gathered from his announcements. The following is taken from the last page of a Promenade programme:

Chevalier Recitals daily. The Sunday Concert Society's Sunday Concerts every Sunday at 3.30 and 7 p.m. Saturday Afternoon Symphony Concerts. Four Monday evening Wagner Concerts at 8.30. St. Andrew's Day Concert. Christmas Day Concert. Children's Christmas Holiday Entertainments, December 26 to January 13, every afternoon at 3. Ash Wednesday Concert; St. Patrick's Day Concert. Good Friday Concerts at 3 and 7.30. Ysaÿe Concerts and the London Musical Festival, April 30 to May 5.

On Saturday, September 16, a notice appeared on the back of the programme stating that owing to the great success of the concerts the season would be prolonged until October 21. On Tuesday, October 3, appeared a notice concerning the Sunday Concert Society.

The Council of the Sunday Concert Society begs to announce that the Sunday Concerts at Queen's Hall will be resumed on Sunday, October 15, 1899, and will be continued at 3.30 and 7 p.m. on each succeeding Sunday up to and including Sunday, April 8, 1900. The afternoon Concerts will be of the same high class as those which won so large a measure of appreciation during the seasons of 1898 and 1899. The famous Queen's Hall Orchestra will perform on each occasion under the direction of Mr. Henry J. Wood. First class soloists, vocal and instrumental, will also be engaged.[1]

[1] President: His Grace the Duke of Portland. Vice-presidents: His Grace the Duke of Newcastle, Viscount Valentia, Lord Farrer, the Rt. Hon. G. J. Shaw le Fevre, Sir Frederick Pollant, Sir Leopold Griffin, K.C.I. Council: The Rt. Hon. Lord Waldegrave, Sir J. Murray Scott, Bart., Sir W. Lawrence Young, Bart., Sir Ernest Clarke, Sir A. C. Mackenzie, Mus. Doc., Sir C.

This season the Nottingham Sacred Harmonic Society was steadily improving. We gave a splendid performance of Sullivan's *Martyr of Antioch* on February 9 with a fine cast of singers including Esther Palliser, Ada Crossley, Lloyd Chandos, W. A. Peterkin, and Robert Radford. On March 2 the City Orchestra of one hundred performers gave their fourth subscription concert.

A season's work of thirty-six weeks, based on the principle of department rehearsal,[1] brought about an excellent result. For the actual concerts we drafted in leaders from the Queen's Hall, the Hallé, and the Birmingham Orchestras. I was allowed to engage about twenty professional string-players (how wise they were to permit that!) but I took care to distribute them among the whole body of strings—in back desks particularly. Thus the weakest amateur had a professional at his side and, after several years of such training, the show they put up was really good. There must have been a noticeable improvement because dear old J. H. Ward (leader of the Queen's Hall basses) told me after a concert that he thought the Nottingham City Orchestra gave almost as good a performance of Beethoven's Fifth as the Queen's Hall players!

At this fourth subscription concert my pupil Beatrice Tattersall sang. Hers was a fine, dramatic voice, always dead in tune. She no longer sings in public but still comes—often on Wagner nights—with her brother E. Somerville Tattersall, who chats to me about Wagner. I am delighted that he has recently joined the Management Committee of the Royal Academy of Music.

The Nottingham Society rendered *Elijah* on March 23 with my old friend Ella Russell singing the soprano part. The rest of the cast included Hilda Wilson, William Green, and Andrew Black. The financial statement for the season of 1899 makes quite interesting reading.

Hubert H. Parry, Mus. Doc., Frederick Cox, Esq., Edward Cutler, Esq., Q. C., Edgar F. Jacques, Esq., Edmund Macrory, Esq., Q.C., Charles A. Russell, Esq., Q.C., Leo Schuster, Esq. Hon Treasurer: Fred Cox, Esq. Hon Secretary: Edgar F. Jacques. Manager: Robert Newman. The charities supported were: King Edward Hospital Fund; British and Foreign Musicians' Society; Charity Organization Society Church Army; Winter Relief Fund; Deep Sea Fisherman's Hospital and Dispensary Ships; Lord Mayor's Fund; Metropolitan Hospital Sunday Fund; Queen Victoria's Jubilee Institute for Nurses; *Referee* Children's Dinner Fund; Royal Society of Great Britain; Salvation Army; Soldiers' and Sailors' Families Association.

[1] See page 122.

Expenses: £280 19s. 5d.   Loss: £42 16s. 11d.

First Orchestral Concert

No loss or gain.

Messiah

Expenses: £190 5s.   Profit: £14 7s. 11d.

Martyr of Antioch

Expenses: £197 5s.   Loss: £37 6s.

Second Orchestral Concert

No loss or gain.

Elijah

Expenses: £237 4s. 6d.   Profit: £22 19s. 2d.

It will be noted that the orchestral concerts just paid for themselves, and that *Elijah* and the *Messiah* showed a small profit.

Elijah is one hundred and the *Messiah* two hundred years old, but they are still prime favourites. I tried, only this year (1938), to get seats at the last minute in the Albert Hall for the latter (under Malcolm Sargent) and failed.

I maintain that the public knows—and must be given—what it wants. For saying which I need not be deemed old-fashioned or unprogressive, for no conductor can have produced *more* contemporary works than I. Yet the older I get the more certain I become that it is necessary to regard progression cautiously, for audiences are not yet reconciled to listening to ultra-modern works which are often a mere mass of broken rhythms and atonal harmonies; neither will the average choral society face their difficulties with real interest. Both audiences and choirs look upon the great classical choral works as plums; it is the wise conductor who gives them their plums and (to change the metaphor) makes a sandwich of two classical works and one modern, thereby making the meat—the modern work—seem less tough.

As a business policy I advocate giving the public what it wants—not necessarily what I would like it to want. My long life of music has taught me that musicians are the servants of the public. If I pleased myself only, I would advocate musical festivals *entirely devoted to new works*, because I consider such Festivals should represent current thought, but I know the public far too well to advocate such a policy—which as far as choral work goes would certainly put the snuffer on a fast-guttering candle, and we must not allow the candle to burn out!

XXVI

BUSONI (1900)

ON NOVEMBER 24, 1900, musical London was thrilled at the appearance of the great Busoni of whose first visit I retain vivid memories. In every way a remarkable man, Busoni was thought by those who did not know him to be eccentric. Perhaps he was, but to younger musicians he was always courteous and intensely appreciative of their work. He possessed a delicate sense of humour and was a great letter-writer. He also expressed himself in some quite spirited pen-drawings. His two sons, by the way, are both painters.

Busoni was the son of a well-known clarinet-player, his mother (Anna Weiss) being a most accomplished pianist of German descent. He spent his boyhood in Trieste where he was giving piano recitals at the age of nine. Unlike so many prodigies, he fulfilled the promise of his early years. His improvisations were little short of marvellous and were the admiration of all serious musicians. It is strange, all the same, that he never had lessons on the piano from any great master. That may have been responsible for his remarkable style which was somewhat criticized —especially by those who admired Clara Schumann—but Busoni travelled all over the world and spent time in Bologna, Vienna, Leipzig, and other European cities. He taught for some years at the New English Conservatoire in Boston; he also arranged summer courses for advanced pianists in Berlin. In fact, he continued the work of Liszt to whose music he was ever devoted.

Busoni was a personality. We had many chats about art, and I soon discovered that his was a cultured intellect not often met with—indeed, this broad outlook seemed to pervade every note he played.

I used to tease him for sitting on a long stool at the piano.

"That's an organ stool," I told him. "What do you want to sit on a thing like that for?"

"You can tell me this, my friend," he said. "If I want to shift a couple of inches to the right when I am playing high up in the treble, or to the left when I am occupied down in the bass, who is going to stop me?"

I had no answer for that, especially as his movement was so slight that nobody in the audience could possibly have detected it. What impressed me most about him technically was his amazing use of the pedals. His pedalling was a revelation. He produced the most amazing effects with the *sostenuto* pedal—wrongly called the *loud* pedal—and could change the tone of the entire instrument, with at times almost orchestral effects.

The purists jibbed a little at his interpretations of Mozart whatever they thought about his Liszt. He evidently looked upon the solo parts of a Mozart concerto in an orchestral light because I have heard him play passages written in single notes with both hands two octaves apart. Some held up their hands in horror, but Landowska—whose harpsichord-playing has had no equal—believed that strict adherence to Mozart's notes was often contrary to his true style; and Tovey declared he claimed to be an absolute purist in *not* confining himself strictly to Mozart's written text.[1]

Personally, I am very fond of Busoni's compositions. His *Konzertstück*, his *Geharnischte Suite*, his *Turandot Suite*, *Berceuse élégiaque*, *Nocturne symphonique*, and the very fine *Indian Fantasia* for piano and orchestra show all the modern developments and contrapuntal devices which I think he effected so much better than Schönberg. I like to get my clarinet students at the R.A.M. to play his charming *Concertino* for clarinet and orchestra.

Busoni fascinated me. Whenever we drove together in one of the old-fourwheeled cabs I used to sit with my back to the horse so that I could watch the changes of expression in his face. If we passed the R.A.M. he always took hold of the brim of his hat with both hands and raised it reverently, giving the building a solemn bow as we passed. I could never get him to explain why he did this; when I asked him he simply roared with laughter. Thus I was left to form my own conclusions which, now I come to think of it, may have been fairly accurate. I think it was his derision of the antiquated methods of the Macfarren *régime*. I am afraid, if that were really what he intended to convey, there was some justification. All the same, it would have been unfair of him to have scorned the *vocal* teaching of the Academy, especially in days when I was a student; for we had people like the Garcias, Cummings, Randegger, Fred Walker, Sainton Dolby, Agnes Larcom, William Shakespeare, Duvivier and Fiori.

I could generally manage Busoni when I had him to myself, but my heart was always in my mouth if he met Sibelius. I never knew where they would get to. They would forget the time of

[1] *Vide : Essays in Musical Analysis* (Sir Donald Francis Tovey).

the concert at which they were to appear; they hardly knew the day of the week. One year I was directing the Birmingham Festival and had to commission a friend never to let these two out of his sight. He had quite an exciting time for two or three days following them about from restaurant to restaurant. He told me he never knew what time they went to bed or got up in the morning. They were like a couple of irresponsible schoolboys.

Robert Newman, I considered, was (for once) unwise in bringing Busoni and Ysaÿe together for sonata recitals, but he was as attracted by these two tremendous personalities as I was. Their temperamental differences, however, were so extreme as almost to be at variance in sonata work. Yet how different Ysaÿe was with Pugno! To hear them play the Kreutzer or the César Franck sonata was indeed an uplifting experience.

Thinking of Busoni reminds me of dear old Sullivan because, at the same concert, I opened with Wagner's *Trauermarsch* in his memory. He had died only two days previously. I was very sad because he had always been my musical mascot. He had so often dropped in for a chat during concert intervals. I remember him asking me which work of Tchaikovsky he should direct at a forthcoming Leeds festival. I suggested the fifth symphony, and still have a delightful letter from him on the subject.

"If you will promise to play this for me one night at the Promenade concerts," he wrote, "when I can come and hear it just before the Leeds Festival, I will direct it."

I arranged this just before he began his rehearsals. It was indeed a performance 'by request', but the public never knew it. After this performance he wrote me the following letter, which I greatly prize:

1, QUEEN'S MANSIONS,
VICTORIA STREET, S.W.
Sept. 4, 1898.

DEAR MR. WOOD,

I have a fairly long experience of orchestral playing and orchestral conducting, and I say quite sincerely that I have never heard a finer performance in England than that of the Tchaikovsky Symphony under your direction last Wednesday.

It was a perfect delight to listen to such accent, phrasing, delicacy and force, and I congratulate both the gifted conductor, and the splendid orchestra. And what a lovely work it is! I could see that you and the band, too, revelled in bringing out its beauties.

Forgive me this little outburst of honest admiration, and believe me.

Yours sincerely,
ARTHUR SULLIVAN.

After the festival was over he wrote to me again and told me what a success it had been, and how he wished I could have missed a concert and gone up to hear it.

Another interesting item at this concert was Saint-Saëns's *La Fiancée du timbalier* which Marie Brema introduced. I always enjoyed working with her, for not only had she a fine voice, but was able to dramatize the parts she portrayed without making gestures. Although Liverpool born, she was certainly German in style. She gave a magnificent performance of Gluck's *Orpheus* at Covent Garden in 1892 and was the first English singer to be engaged for a Bayreuth festival. In 1911 she produced *Orpheus* in English at the Savoy. How she trained that chorus to get their words over the footlights as they did is a secret I have never been able to unravel. Her daughter Tita—an enormous woman with a deep speaking voice—recited Grieg's *Bergliot*, but I did not have to subdue the orchestra to allow the audience to hear her words.

I remember lunching with them at their house in Bayswater and finding them in a hilarious mood. Some of George Bernard Shaw's plays were running at the time and Tita wanted to play a certain part in one of them at the Court Theatre. She wrote to Shaw. This was his reply—as far as I remember:

DEAR MISS BRAND,

Many thanks for your little note. I am one of the greatest admirers of your art, but I should not dream of employing a London and North Western railway engine to draw a baby carriage. Love to your mother.

GEORGE BERNARD SHAW.

By this time, of course, the sixth season (1900) of the Promenades had come and gone. Looking through the programmes I find much of interest in those eleven weeks from August 25 to November 11.

Madame von Stosch is a name that catches my eye. She made her first appearance on the opening night to play Saint-Saëns's *Rondo Capriccioso*, making such an impression that she re-appeared at no less than six Promenades during the season. She came to us with good credentials, for she was a favourite pupil of Ysaÿe; and I may say she has been a devoted friend to me. In a sense she can be said to be very much connected with Queen's Hall because when Newman became bankrupt in 1901 her second husband, Sir Edgar Speyer, formed an influential syndicate and did a great deal for the Queen's Hall Orchestra from 1902 until 1915.[1]

[1] See page 156.

143

During this season a special thanksgiving concert had been given to celebrate our victories in South Africa, the programme including the *Hymn of Praise* with Lucille Hill, Anita Sutherland, Lloyd Chandos, and a special choir of two hundred and fifty voices. This was actually the first *choral* concert ever given at the Promenades.

Of the great Ffrangçon-Davies, who sang on September 1, I shall have more to say during the course of this book, for he was a most remarkable artist. Whether he sang oratorio, or the Prologue from *Pagliacci*, or the ballad *Edward* (which I scored for him), or merely the *Men of Harlech*, the splendour of his voice and his original outlook on everything he sang places him quite alone.

Another newcomer was Evelyn Suart, a delightful pianist whose grace and charm, as well as technical qualities, were displayed in her playing of the second concerto of Saint-Saëns.

At a Wagner concert in September of this year I was asked to play the festival march called *Philadelphia*. I wonder what has happened to it? It must have gone 'off to Philadelphia in the morning' for I have never heard of it since.

On September 25, Jessie Goldsack made her first appearance at a Promenade concert. She was a young contralto with a very beautiful voice. Her teacher, Hilda Wilson, first brought her to me. She afterwards became one of my best pupils, but eventually gave up her musical career and married John Linton, a young engineer who did splendid work in France during the war (rising to field rank in less than six months) and who was awarded the Military Cross. She was indeed a loss to the singing world. I shall always remember her beautiful singing of *Have Mercy, Lord* when I directed the *Matthew Passion* at Sheffield Festival in 1908. Another quite remarkable singer who appeared this season was Florence Schmidt whose truly brilliant soprano voice created a deep impression. She did exactly the same thing. She married the sculptor Derwent Wood. Thus two singers who might have continued splendid careers gave them up to enter the bonds of matrimony.

Here is a landmark in the history of the Promenade concerts! *On October 23, 1900, we gave our first Brahms concert.* Moreover, we produced for the first time the double concerto for violin, 'cello and orchestra which two members of the band played admirably: Philip Lewis and Purcell Jones.

Another performance well worth recording is Landon Ronald's first orchestral composition which we produced as a novelty on November 3. He was only twenty-seven at the time, but the themes and orchestration showed him to be a highly cultivated musician. His songs and piano works had already attracted attention. He tells a story in connection with this, his first essay in orchestral form, which I reproduce from a letter he wrote me a few weeks ago (1938):

In 1899 I was conducting comic opera at the Lyric Theatre, Shaftesbury Avenue, getting very bored with the monotony of listening to the same poor music every night, and suddenly determined to try my hand at writing a work for concert orchestra in my spare hours. This I did, calling it a *Suite de Ballet*. I sent it to Henry J. Wood, a complete stranger, and begged him to produce it at one of his famous 'Proms'. Within a week I got a reply from him accepting the work, giving me the date of performance and time of rehearsal.

Shall I ever forget the thrill? But I was yet to learn that Henry Wood was not only a genius as a conductor but a very severe taskmaster. On the eve of the production of my first orchestral work, I was indolently conducting at the theatre when a telegram was handed to me. It was from Wood and read: 'YOUR SCORE AND PARTS ARE LACKING ALL MARKS OF EXPRESSION, ALL MARKS OF BOWING AND PHRASING. IMPOSSIBLE TO REHEARSE TOMORROW MORNING OR PRODUCE TOMORROW NIGHT UNLESS YOU CAN RECTIFY.'

I handed my baton to the principal violin, left my seat as if I had been stung, and within five minutes was in a hansom cab on my way to Queen's Hall. With a beating heart, I asked the librarian for the score and parts of my *Suite de Ballet*. He gave it me, and I reached my desk at home about 10.30. I sat up all night, marking score and parts with every imaginable mark of expression, and at eight o'clock the next morning duly delivered them at Queen's Hall. I attended the rehearsal and marvelled at the grasp Wood had of my work, and the infinite pains he took over every bar of it. He was very cordial afterwards but (as a parting shot) said: "*Let it be a warning to you never to be careless over your work.*"

I thanked him from my heart, and to this day have never forgotten his advice.

I always enjoy evenings spent with Landon Ronald. He still tells me I drove him out of England when we were both very young men. He badly wanted to conduct in London but says he found there was no chance for anyone except myself. However, he scored great successes on the Continent in 1909, directing concerts in Rome, Bremen, Leipzig, and Vienna, but his association with Sir Augustus Harris at Covent Garden established him as a director of opera and, in any other country, he would have been acclaimed a great director of Opera. Elgar always appreciated his great talent and told me on several occasions of his admiration for his conducting of his works. With this I heartily agree, for no one, in my judgment, has ever approached the ideal Elgar as has Landon Ronald.

It is always a delight to me to be with him for he has a store of most amusing stories and anecdotes. As an after-dinner speaker I have rarely met his equal.

XXVII

ALBANI, MARCHESI, BACKHAUS, WEINGARTNER, AND SIBELIUS
(1900–1)

I WAS NOW A kind of commercial traveller as my numerous choral rehearsals kept me from home at least four nights a week for years. This was because it has always been my rule never to direct choral concerts without plenty of rehearsals. The average amateur choralist is not a trained musician, and as the time between each concert is short (the rehearsals last under two hours) there is little time to become acquainted with the music, words and rhythm. Choir-training calls for a true knowledge of singing.

I make a point of *resting* my choirs for a few minutes every quarter of an hour, and give them a little talk about voices and singing. I do this because I have noticed the bad effect on choirs whose master has made them sing for two hours without rest. No trained solo-singer would think of singing full force for two hours. The same thing applies to the orchestras. Violinists are glad to be allowed to drop their right arm for a few minutes. When allowed to do so they attack with renewed vigour a few moments later.

Olga and I inaugurated a series of 'Mr. and Mrs. Henry J. Wood's Vocal Recitals' which proved attractive both in London and in the Provinces. I thoroughly enjoyed accompanying for these recitals especially as the little-known charming duets by Schumann, Goring Thomas, Tchaikovsky and Saint-Saëns were exquisitely rendered by Olga and Gregory Hast, whose voices blended perfectly. The rest of the programme was made up of the best classical *lieder* sung in the original language in all cases— English, French, German, Italian, Russian. Olga assisted at many of Rosa Newmarch's lectures on the part-songs of Russia, introducing to the London public at Steinway Hall songs by Glinka, Dargomijsky, Rubinstein, Balakireff, Borodin, Cui,

Moussorgsky, and Rimsky-Korsakoff. These recitals continued until her death.

Altogether the season seemed to pass quickly enough. Looking back over the years, memories come to me of many great artists whose friendship I enjoyed and with whom I worked. I remember Albani giving her farewell concert, assisted by Ada Crossley, Edward Lloyd, Santley, and the Royal Choral Society—six hundred strong. This was actually the first appearance of the Queen's Hall Orchestra in the Albert Hall. I had the greatest admiration for Albani's singing. She had a truly noble, dramatic soprano voice of immense range and power, yet—in spite of the size of her voice—her *coloratura* was excellent, no matter what she sang.

On November 22 I had been up to Nottingham for a concert at which we performed the first two acts of *Tannhäuser* (without cuts) introducing the Paris version of the *Venusberg* scene for the first time in England. My singers were Watkin-Mills, William Green, Fischer Sobell, Henry Turnpenny, Robert Radford, Faithful Pearce, Thomas Seadon, and Ella Russell.

On Sunday afternoon, December 2, the Queen's Hall Orchestra made its first public appearance with the National Sunday League. The President (Alderman Sir P. Treloar, J.P.) made a memorable little speech on behalf of the charities for which the concert was being given. My admiration for the work of the League still remains unabated. I have directed for them for thirty-six years and still direct some of their Sunday afternoon concerts at the Palladium. I may here observe that the great kindness shown me by the late Henry Mills, the League's secretary, has been continued by the present secretary Mr. Austin.

I had also been busy with Newman's fifth season of Saturday Afternoon Symphony Concerts which had begun on October 27 when Blanche Marchesi sang Beethoven's great aria *Abscheulicher*, from *Fidelio*. Then there were the concerts at the Crystal Palace which ran alternately with those at Queen's Hall on these Saturday afternoons. Our orchestra numbered a hundred and ten players. We seemed to attract the gossipy type of women season-ticket holders whom one sees at seaside orchestral concerts and who knit, sew, and talk the whole time. Many stories are told of them, but I may be forgiven for this chestnut as it actually happened when I was conducting Tchaikovsky's fifth symphony. The long, sudden silence before the final coda took the dear ladies by surprise and a voice reverberated through the hall: "Oh, no! *We always fry ours in drippin'*."

The Sunday afternoon concerts had begun on October 7 and had gone on continuously; we never missed a Sunday. Londoners knew there was always a good programme and formed the habit of attending these concerts. Hence their success for over thirty years.

Olga made her first appearance at the Saturday 'Pops' at St. James's Hall on December 1, 1900, singing songs by Tchaikovsky, Glinka, Grieg, Dvořák and Basil Harwood. Borwick was the solo pianist and Lady Hallé led the Brahms *Sextet in G*.

We opened the new year of 1901 with a Wagner-Tchaikovsky concert at which Blanche Marchesi sangs songs by Handel and Horatio Parker. Her mother, Mathilde Marchesi, was a famous teacher and a favourite pupil of Manuel Garcia. She taught in London from 1849 to 1854. After seven years in Vienna she went to Paris where her book *École de Chant* created quite a sensation. Rossini admired her intensely, and it must not be forgotten that she trained Melba.

Blanche Marchesi, however, was first trained as a violinist, but from 1881 devoted her life to singing, appearing for the first time in Queen's Hall in 1896. Hers was an extraordinary personality. She was full of life and energy, and even if she did not actually possess a great voice her interpretative ability was of the first order. She sang fluently in four languages. She, like her mother, was a teacher and produced a number of fine young singers of whom perhaps Muriel Brunskill and Astra Desmond are the best known to present-day audiences.

The Tchaikovsky B flat minor piano concerto must now be one of the greatest favourites with the public. Most pianists like playing it. There was one, however, who hated it—Busoni. "Too much *tempo di valse* about it for my liking," he told me. He played it at our seventh Symphony concert, but I rather fancy that was the only time.

On January 26, 1901, we gave a memorial concert for Queen Victoria. The programme was prefaced by one of Jacques's articles entitled *Musical Development during the Victorian Era* in which the following appeared:

It is pleasant to remember that the amazing developments of public taste in the direction of high-class orchestral music that marks the last five years of the late Queen Victoria's reign is contemporaneous with the establishment and growth of the Queen's Hall Orchestra and the various concert enterprises associated with Mr. Robert Newman's name. Real recognition of the fact came in November, 1898, when the Queen's Hall Orchestra appeared by command at Windsor Castle, performing selections from Wagner's *Parsifal* and in the presence of its distinguished chief, Mr. Henry J. Wood, received the hallmark of Her Majesty's approval.

Although we had Busoni again for our Symphony concert on March 2, he only played one work—Weber's *Konzertstück*. The second part of the programme was occupied with a long selection from *Parsifal* (*Verwandlungsmusik*, Act I). I remember this performance so well because for many months I had been visiting the well-known Shoreditch bell-founders, Mears and Stainbank, supervising the casting of four very large hemispherical bells—C. G. A. E. Up to this time we had played the important *Parsifal* bell-motive on some miserable tube bells supplemented by a grand piano. Later on Mears and Stainbank completed an octave of these hemispherical bells. Their tone was magnificent; they were in tune and of the utmost value for all works containing any important bell parts. I still use them—in fact, the B.B.C. purchased them. They stand permanently in the alcove at the right hand side of the organ in Queen's Hall.

On March 16 we gave a performance of Beethoven's ninth symphony when the Wolverhampton Festival Choral Society was invited to sing the choral *finale*. This they certainly did magnificently. Their verve, energy, and the brilliance with which they threw off the high *tessitura* were most thrilling. We had a fine quartet of solo singers: Lillian Blauvelt, Kirby Lunn, Lloyd Chandos and Daniel Price. They had attended ten piano rehearsals. Thus the *ensemble* was well-nigh perfect.

Bach's *Brandenburg Concertos* are now a household word among Promenaders; but I am reminded that Ysaÿe produced the fourth of them (in G) for solo violin, two flutes and strings, for the first time in England in 1901. Fransella and Borlé, my first and second flautists, played with him and created a deep impression. Ysaÿe, by the way, conducted one of the London Musical Festival concerts of this season, the other conductors being Saint-Saëns, Colonne, Weingartner, and myself. The artists make quite a fine show of names: Marchesi, Busoni, Maric Brema, Lady Hallé, Ysaÿe, Van Rooy, Hugo Becker, Joachim, and Olga.

Undoubtedly we had all the great artists of the day, even in the orchestra, and Payne and Ferir could give a fine performance of Mozart's *Sinfonia Concertante* for violin and viola. As for Robert Newman, he was indefatigable. He would welcome

149

anything out of the ordinary so long as it was up to standard. For example, on Good Friday of this year I recall some impressive recitations by the actress Mrs. Brown Potter. As the London season did not end until after mid-summer, Newman announced extra Symphony concerts for June. We began with a Wagner concert, with Mdlle. de Laronviére as the soloist; we then gave a Verdi Memorial Concert in conjunction with both Ysaÿe and Busoni. Ysaÿe appeared again at the last of these concerts to play the Tchaikovsky concerto for the first time, and Olga sang some of the lesser-known arias of Tchaikovsky in their native Russian. I am not likely to forget Ysaÿe's visit on this occasion for his cuts were so drastic that my score and band-parts never recovered from them!

The great philanthropist Andrew Carnegie attended these extra concerts and came to see me on several occasions. He did his best to entice me to America to direct the Pittsburg orchestral concerts, but Newman always came down on offers of that kind. Although I had a secret desire to accept his pressing and generous offers I felt my loyalty to Newman to be the first call upon me.

The seventh season of the Promenades opened on August 24. Here is the notice which appeared on the first programme:

SIXTY-SIX PROMENADE CONCERTS. *Eleven weeks' season from August 24 to November* 8. Season Tickets (transferable) 1 guinea; Grand Circle, 3 guineas; numbered seats, 5 guineas front row.

From the back of the same programme:

The Small and Large Halls may be engaged for concerts, cinderellas, banquets, wedding receptions, public meetings (non-political), conversaziones, dinners, suppers, lectures and social gatherings.

The cost of hiring:

Large Hall: afternoon concerts 20 guineas; evening concerts 25 guineas; dances, balls, and banquets 45 guineas, including use of organ, light warming, and numbering of seats, but not attendants and pianoforte. Small Hall: afternoon concerts 4 guineas; evening ditto. Dances, balls and banquets, 10 guineas.

One of the immediate successes of the seventh season of Promenades was Backhaus. He played Mendelssohn's G minor piano concerto at his first appearance and, later, the Paganini-Brahms variations. We were still in early days, and it was not an invariable rule that a pianist should play a concerto.

This remarkable young pianist was first brought to me by Otto Kling, at that time manager of the London branch of Breitkopf and Härtel, I remember him bringing this fair-headed, shy boy to my home in Langham Place. As it happened, I was not able to offer him an engagement at once as all our arrangements were made for some time ahead, but I promised Kling I would do all I could for him at the earliest opportunity. I had noted the purity of his tone and that his technique was of a high order, and I foretold that he would become a virtuoso. I remember his playing in Strauss's *Burlesque* and the delightfully picturesque and rarely-played *Sortilegi* by Pick-Mangiagalli, both for piano and orchestra.

How seldom we hear Backhaus in England these days! Years ago he was playing in London and everywhere in the Provinces. I regret this, for Backhaus is a great player.

Thomas Meux sang Wolfram's aria *Gazing round* (*Tannhäuser*) on September 2. He is now the well-known professor of singing at the R.A.M. During the following week we gave an evening to Sullivan's music—both parts of the programme. Our list of works included a *Processional March*, overture *In Memoriam*, incidental music to the *Tempest*, overture *Di Ballo*, incidental music to *Henry VIII*, overture *Macbeth*, masque music from the *Merchant of Venice*, and the *Fantasia* from *H.M.S. Pinafore*. Such a programme makes strange reading in these days when Sullivan is chiefly remembered by the Savoy Operas. As a matter of fact we did include a few solos from *Ivanhoe* and the light operas, not even disdaining a couple of quartets from the *Mikado* and one from the *Yeomen of the Guard*. Our four singers, by the way, were Florence Schmidt, Lloyd Chandos, Kirby Lunn and W. A. Peterkin.

A popular lady violinist, Beatrice Langley, who used to appear at every important At Home or *soirée*, played at a Promenade concert this season; and we made much of Liapounoff's *Ouverture Solennelle*. Liapounoff was one of the protégés of the Moscow Conservatoire and was considered to be the foremost living representative of the National tendencies. He was actually a great friend of the instigator, Balakireff. He collected many Russian folksongs, but I much preferred his piano composition to anything he wrote orchestrally.

Weingartner's second symphony was our great novelty on September 24. He and I had always been good friends, especially in his young days; but I must say his conducting interests me more now than his compositions. Perhaps his great orchestral technique, though it must naturally be responsible for his clever scoring, was his undoing; at all events, the inspiration of the composer did not always seem to be there.

Weingartner never remained in one post for long, and I have a feeling he is disappointed because his compositions have not had world-wide recognition. He is charming and genial in character and the greatest living exponent of Beethoven. I have heard his performances of all the nine symphonies many times during my life and have thought them magnificent. I still consider his direction of the ninth supreme. His literary achievements are also great; his *Uber das Dirigiren* must have been of enormous benefit to conductors all over the world. His book on conducting the Beethoven symphonies has probably influenced most of the young conductors who have, perhaps naturally, taken it as gospel. Landon Ronald once told me he was almost sorry the book had been written for that very reason. There is no questioning Weingartner's knowledge of Beethoven. For years he virtually lived with those nine symphonies. Latterly his conducting has been criticized for its economy of movement. Only those who sit facing him can really see much movement at all; but Weingartner has an amazing faculty for conducting with his eyes. He seems to get everything he wants by that means. His is a great personality. Olga introduced many of his songs to the English public and he often played her accompaniments himself. His orchestration of Weber's *Invitation à la Valse* I consider superior to that of Berlioz—but (in my opinion) he made one mistake: he divided some arpeggios between three solo bassoons. I found they did not get through, but after putting all three instruments on to the entire passage the effect was quite different. What looks well on paper does not always *sound* so well. How often do composers discover that! Tchaikovsky never made that mistake: he doubled and redoubled his instruments on important themes.

Transcriptions are not to everybody's taste. Personally I feel when (for instance) an organ work is transcribed for orchestra, the transcriber should forget the organ and think only of the orchestra. Otherwise why transcribe? That was what Elgar did when he published his orchestral version of Bach's C minor Fantasia and Fugue. He used percussion instruments, three-part shakes for the trumpets, and *glissandi* for the harps. He did the job thoroughly while he was about it.

Stokowski, the famous conductor of Philadelphia, has made several beautiful transcriptions of Bach's organ works and chorales. If I criticize them, it is to say that I always seem to find the organist peeping out—which is against all I have ever believed about transcriptions.

I had great pleasure this season in performing W. H. Reed's *Rondo Caprice*, written for and played by Manuel Gomez. Reed was a member of my orchestra for years, and I have always been interested in his compositions. He was for a long period leader of the London Symphony Orchestra. He certainly did well in listening to George Bernard Shaw who told him to write a book on Elgar. All music-lovers should read *Elgar as I knew him;* it is delightful.

We tried another work of the Russian Nationalist School—this time a symphony by Balakireff, but the Promenade public did not take kindly to it. They were much better pleased years later with *Tamara* and *Russia*.

A new Swedish soprano, Jenny Norelli, made an excellent impression, and a new Canadian composer, Clarence Lucas, scored a decided success on a Saturday evening with his overture *Macbeth*. Then there was a young Italian composer, Nicoló Celega, who appeared with a new symphonic poem called the *The Heart of Fingal*. This young man was a pupil of Mazzucato at the Milan Conservatoire; which reminds me, I took the valuable opportunity of studying Verdi's *Requiem* with Mazzucato when he happened to be in London on a short visit in 1901, as I knew him to be a great friend and intimate of Verdi, and thus able to give me the true tradition of the work.

I feel I must mention the appearance of Marie Roze at a Promenade concert, for I owed so much to her in the early days of my career. Her voice was not what it was when I first knew her, but her style and delivery—certainly her perfect diction—were as good as ever and won for her appreciation from the Promenaders.

On October 14 we produced a work of old Ebenezer Prout—a *Triumphal March*. It really was a dreadful work—part of a cantata called *King Alfred*. When Edward German and I were students together at the R.A.M. we used to play a trick on poor old Ebenezer. Whenever he came up the stairs one of us played a bit of this march. He was delighted and his usually grave face wore a smile.

"Ah!" he would observe. "I see you know my *King Alfred*." As a matter of fact, we knew nothing about the work but I had bought a copy of the march, and out of sheer devilment,

German and I used to play it whenever he was within earshot.

The woodwind section of the orchestra was amazingly good at this time. I took the chance of performing works like Mozart's *Serenades* and *Divertimenti*, Beethoven's *Septet*, or the Schubert *Octet*, but I found they did not go down at all well with the public. My young stalwarts who will stand stock still for forty or fifty minutes for Beethoven or Tchaikovsky symphonies will not do the same thing for seven or eight players. I suppose they feel they are not getting their money's worth! And Queen's Hall is not the ideal hall for chamber music.

What *did* go down well was the first performance of Elgar's *Pomp and Circumstance* marches. I shall never forget the scene at the close of the first of them—the one in D major. The people simply rose and yelled. I had to play it again—with the same result; in fact, they refused to let me go on with the programme. After considerable delay, while the audience roared its applause, I went off and fetched Harry Dearth who was to sing *Hiawatha's Vision* (Coleridge-Taylor); but they would not listen. Merely to restore order, I played the march a third time. And that, I may say, was the one and only time in the history of the Promenade concerts that an orchestral item was accorded a double encore. Little did I think then that the lovely, broad melody of the *trio* would one day develop into our second national anthem—*Land of Hope and Glory*.

The next item of interest that comes back to me now is the production of MacDowell's *Indian Suite*. I remember an amusing incident which occurred during a dinner given by John Lane to MacDowell. Lane, though he knew much about publishing, evidently knew little about music.

"I suppose," he said, "you don't happen to want a magnificent old Broadwood grand? It must be hundreds of years old and is getting better and more valuable each year. It must be worth a large sum of money by now."

We all laughed.

"Well, what are you laughing at?" asked Lane, who saw nothing funny in what he had said.

"Old Broadwoods are not like Strad violins," I told him. "They don't improve by age or playing on them for years."

"I can't see that," said Lane. We did our best, but I fear we left him entirely unconvinced.

Three Englishmen are worthy of mention here: Norman O'Neill, whose overture *In Autumn* (which he dedicated to me)

I produced this season; W. H. Bell, whose symphonic prelude *A Song of Morning* (originally produced at the Gloucester Festival) we performed for the first time in London; and John Coates, the now well-known tenor.

O'Neill's works have always appealed to me—indeed, I have produced most of those he wrote. Bell I met again at his home in Cape Town; he was one of the greatest talkers I ever met, but he had plenty of wit and humour. I produced his *Song of Greeting* at the R.A.M. Centenary Concert in 1922.

John Coates I chiefly remember as a newcomer because his wife was so anxious on his behalf. She could not make up her mind whether or not he had chosen the right songs. She need not have worried because he was an instant success—less on account of his voice than of his great artistry.

Incidentally, I see my name is on this programme as acting in three capacities: pianist, organist, and conductor. It was, however, very nearly my last appearance as organist. I played my own arrangement of Handel's G minor organ concerto which Arthur Payne conducted. The fact inspired Newman again: nothing would do but that I must give an organ recital on November 13. This *was* my last appearance, and this is what I played:

Fantasia	Tours
Ave Maria	Arcadelt
Prelude and Fugue in D	Bach
Bell Rondo	Morandi
Toccata (Sym. No. 5)	Widor

Olga was the singer, and Percy Pitt accompanied.

Newman seemed more than ever inclined to work me hard. He could not even let the Promenade season finish on Saturday evening November 9—how late that seems compared with the first week in October in these days!—in the ordinary way. He wanted to begin the Saturday Afternoon Symphony Concerts. He did—*on that very afternoon!* I wonder what the B.B.C. Symphony Orchestra would say to rehearsing from 10 till 1; playing for a Symphony concert from 3 till 5.30, and taking on the last night of the Proms from 8 till 10.45—*on top of a ten weeks' season!* But that is how we did things in those days.

Even so, on November 22 we gave a memorial concert to Sullivan (whose death had occurred on that date the previous year) with a programme including the *Golden Legend* with Blauvelt, Kirkby Lunn, John Coates, and Ffrangçon-Davies, bringing up the Wolverhampton Choral Society for the choral parts. Then, on December 2, we gave *Elijah* with Blauvelt, Ada Crossley, Lloyd Chandos and Ffrangçon-Davies, this time bringing up the Nottingham Sacred Harmonic Society for the choral parts.

Newman had not even yet finished with me. He arranged three special orchestral concerts at the Albert Hall on Saturday afternoons, November 16 and 30, and December 14, when we augumented the orchestra to 200 performers, the extra players being recruited from former members. They were all Wagner concerts, but a Beethoven symphony was given at each. The soloists were Marie Brema, Kirkby Lunn, Philip Brozel, Ffrangçon-Davies, and Olga. And yet Frank H. Bedells, secretary of the Nottingham Society, could announce that

Mr. Henry J. Wood will hold 65 rehearsals for the chorus and orchestra in Nottingham, thus enabling us to present our programmes to the Nottingham public in the most complete and artistic manner. The chorus will consist of 280 picked voices, the orchestra of 80 performers, and two orchestral concerts of 160 performers.

It had certainly been a year of work. Olga had made her *début* at the Promenades on October 7 when she sang most beautifully Elizabeth's Prayer from *Tannhäuser*. Two nights later I turned pianist and played the fourth piano part in Bach's A minor concerto for strings and four pianos which we now regularly perform each season on one or other of the Bach nights. My colleagues that night were the sisters Cerasoli and Percy Pitt.

On the 26th no less a person than Sibelius appeared for the first time at the Promenades when I performed his suite *King Christian II*. Granville Bantock and I have always been the champions of Sibelius, but now that I have performed all his seven symphonies in one season (1937) I look back with pride and satisfaction when I remember I was the first to have helped popularize the music of this deep and original thinker. Since those days we have been able to devote whole concerts to his works and be sure of large appreciative audiences.

Unfortunately, at the end of this season of 1901 Newman found himself unable to carry on the financial burden of mantaining the Queen's Hall Orchestra. Several bodies were anxious to take over the management of the concerts, but we had to steer a clear course; otherwise we might have found ourselves in the hands of a firm of publishers and have had to study their interests; or, again, some composer. That would have been disastrous. Fortunately, my friend Sir Edgar Speyer intervened and formed a small syndicate to take over the whole organization, Newman retaining the management of the Queen's Hall. About the same time Chappell's became its lessees.

The great thing was to keep up the standard of the concerts, and it was here that I found Speyer a true friend. Both he and his wife took a deep interest in everything we produced, and, as I shall show later, Speyer himself was most generous to the cause of good music. However many rehearsals I asked for in order to ensure a perfect performance of a work, he agreed without a murmur. On one occasion—for Strauss's *Ein Heldenleben*—I had as many as seventeen. Above all, I was allowed *sectional* rehearsals. For his *Don Quixote* I had six with the strings, three with the wind, and two full rehearsals.

Another characteristic about Speyer that won my gratitude was his willingness to have any great composer of foreign nationality over here to conduct his own works. Speyer, it must be remembered, was by birth a German; but he was more than willing to have Claude Debussy at Queen's Hall—and Germans did not look so kindly on Frenchmen in those days.

The story of how I went to Paris to persuade the great Debussy to come to London really belongs to 1907. He actually came in 1908 and again in 1909, but as the story is so much connected with Speyer it may as well be told here. The point was that we wanted Debussy and wondered how to set about getting him.

"You must go to Paris," said Speyer. Then he wondered whether Debussy was anything of a conductor but concluded that, whether he was or not, London wanted him and London must have him.

"You must go to Paris next week," insisted Speyer, "and you must make him promise to come next year. You will be given a cheque for your expenses. Tell Debussy what you like, *but make him come over.*"

This was a delicate mission. Even though Speyer told me to say that his house was at Debussy's disposal and that he would be entertained royally, I was none too comfortable about it. I thought of the lovely Italian garden at 46, Grosvenor Street (knowing that Debussy would have his own suite of rooms there) and summoned up all my diplomatic powers to persuade the great French composer to make his first visit to London.

Speyer and I had a good talk about the fee we were to offer. We had paid conductor-composers such fees as thirty or forty guineas but such sums hardly seemed to suit the present situation. At last we decided on a hundred guineas, and off I went to Paris. How to break it to him, knowing he was reputed to be of a very retiring disposition and averse to appearing in public, I really was not quite sure. However, I made up my mind to tackle him through Madame Debussy who, as it happened, spoke perfect English. With the fee in my mind I thought of how so many English composers had spoilt things by conducting for next to nothing. Elgar told me he often conducted with hardly so much as his railway fare being paid. I tactfully approached Madame Debussy and revealed my mission. When she told her husband and mentioned the fee he jumped up, furious.

"What? A hundred guineas . . . for *me?* And yet you pay Caruso four hundred guineas?"

I corrected this immediately. "We never engage Caruso or any other singer at such a fee," I told him. Debussy calmed down and offered to think it over. I felt things were not too good, all the same; so I went out after lunch and wired to Speyer, suggesting two hundred guineas. Speyer wired back his agreement, repeating his assertion that we must have Debussy whatever the cost.

Fortunately, it did happen: Debussy agreed to come. He seemed quite unable to realize that the London public wanted him at all, even though he was inclined to think his music was more popular with us than in Paris. He certainly never regretted coming for he loved London and thoroughly enjoyed both his visits. The story of his actual conducting, however, can remain until I come to the concerts at which he appeared. I have told this story somewhat unchronologically because it at least gives an idea of how delightful I found Sepyer to work with. He was so sincere in his outlook, a lover of art willing to spend any amount of money to advance the cause of good music. He once told me it had cost him many thousands of pounds to make Richard Strauss's Symphonic Poems known to England!

We had no really great solo oboe-player at this time. When I suggested we might remedy this he immediately set about getting the best artist available. "I have written to the Paris Conservatoire," he told me a few days afterwards. "Come on! We will go over there next week and hear their best players. We will stay at the Ritz and enjoy ourselves."

We heard six and chose Henri de Busscher, a truly superb player. I still meet him when I go to direct the Hollywood Bowl concerts; he leads the oboes in the Los Angeles Philharmonic Orchestra. Incidentally, while we were in Paris I met Lorée, the great instrument maker. He made me two *oboi d'amorés* and two *oboi da caccias*.

Looking back over this season I find I conducted one hundred and thirty concerts and gave five hundred lessons. No wonder we never had time to accept the invitations showered on us for dinners, dances, and parties! Indeed I often wonder whether, as a young man with a charming and vivacious wife, we ought not to have had our friends round us instead of giving up our lives entirely to musical work.

XXVIII

SAINT-SAËNS, NIKISCH, STRAUSS, AND KREISLER (1902-3)

THE SEAL WAS set on the success of the Sunday concerts when King Edward and Queen Alexandra honoured us by their presence on Sunday afternoon, February 2, 1902. I gave virtually the same programme as at Windsor Castle in 1898 at the command of Queen Victoria. Music had advanced in England during the latter part of her reign, for she was a great lover of the art; thus it augured well for music that Royal recognition should come so early in the reign of King Edward and his beautiful Queen. This was indeed a proud day for Newman, the orchestra, and myself.

During the London Festival of 1902 I came to know Saint-Saëns very well as he was in London for some considerable time. I remember how regularly he would go over to Queen's Hall as early as 8.30 in the morning to enjoy an hour on the organ before the orchestral rehearsals began. I often went there myself in order to listen, unseen, to his unique extemporization.

A very hilarious lunch we had when Saint-Saëns and Ysaÿe came to us at Elsworthy Road. Saint-Saëns was in a vocal mood and declared he ought to have been a *tenore robusto* instead of a composer. He insisted on displaying his stentorian voice in all kinds of *solfeggi*. He made grand opera of everything that day. When Olga apologized because the drawing-room curtains had not come back from the cleaners he dashed to the piano and proceeded to improvise a free *fantasia* to express the horror of his feelings at being asked into a drawing-room without curtains. He laughed heartily at what was extremely clever musical fun (had he not written his '*Le Carneval des Animaux*', which is so full of fun?).

Newman decided to run four extra concerts in May and June. The first two were the usual type of Wagner and Tchaikovsky concert, but those on June 16 and 20 were conducted by no less a person than the great Nikisch. As he had already created an enormous following, Newman showed his wisdom in engaging him for two extra concerts without soloists. He felt the public wanted Nikisch, and Nikisch only.

Artur Nikisch! What a magical name his was to all young conductors between 1890 and 1922! To my mind, no other conductor has ever been so endowed with musical gifts as he. I remember his dapper little figure—he was always so neatly dressed—and his deep white cuffs and flowing tie, his very long baton controlled with the supple wrist of a great violinist, his mellow, dreamy speaking voice which he maintained even when he stopped an orchestra at rehearsals in the most exciting and strenuous passages, and his marvellous way of listening so intently to every phrase he directed.

When rehearsing a melody, he invariably sang it to the orchestra with great emotional feeling—and then would say: "Now play it as *you* feel it." No conductor that I have heard has ever surpassed his emotional feeling and dramatic intensity. And who will ever forget his spear-thrust gestures for big accentuated chords? He told me he always devoted his attention to the inflection and apex of *every* phrase he directed. He was certainly the greatest master of emotional expression I ever met.

Nikisch almost hypnotized his orchestras. I remember him rehearsing the slow movement in Tchaikovsky's fifth symphony and how marvellously he drew the melodic line of the horn solo from Borsdorf. He fixed his wonderfully expressive eyes on him the whole time. Then:

"Thank you, Mr. Borsdorf! Let us do that again, and this time I want you to play it exactly as *you* feel it."

Borsdorf played it again, more beautifully than before, *but there was something of Nikisch in every note of it.*

We young conductors, both on the Continent and in England, adored this amazing man whose name resounded throughout France, Germany, Italy, and America. It thrilled me to hear other conductors talk about him. Landon Ronald, I know, worshipped his every movement. In the words of Fritz Reiner when he visited me in 1936: "Ah! Nikisch was a miracle!"

I remember (on one of the last occasions on which Nikisch lunched at Elsworthy Road) I told him that some of the Press were 'going for' me for my too-free *rubato*.

"Don't you worry about that!" said Nikisch. "We feel music differently. If they get enjoyment out of it, let them stick to their square four beats in a bar. All the same, a metronome would do it much better."

And I still think of his last words to me (already quoted):
Let everything be a grand improvisation!

Nikisch's friendliness was amazing. If you met him after ten years he always gave you the impression he had been thinking of you in the meantime and that you were the one person in the world he wanted to meet again. A little disconcerting to the less demonstrative Englishman, but he soon made it clear that your work and doings in the interim *were* known to him.

It was the same when he came in contact with members of orchestras. He would secure a list of their names, memorize them, and saunter round greeting the second clarinet or the third horn-player, calling them by name. Even though he used the list for the purpose I admired him for taking the trouble to learn the names by heart, and you can imagine how his action was appreciated. A wonderful artist and a wonderful friend.

Once every season the Countess of Stafford used to engage about forty players from the Queen's Hall Orchestra to give a private orchestral concert at Chandos House. Arthur Payne had now left us and gone to Llandudno and our leader was Maurice Sons. I remember how I laughed when Sons presented himself at the front door of the house and the butler took his violin-case and told him the band used the side entrance. Sons was a Dutchman of hypersensitive temperament who could be easily upset, and his fury at what he considered was a flagrant insult was most amusing. He objected to being called 'one of the band' in the first place, and he strongly resented being told to go down the steps, under a portico, and in through the tradesmen's entrance. As it happened, I had just come in and was standing in the hall. This put matters right. Even though the others had accepted the side entrance without a murmur, I am certain Sons would have gone home rather than use it.

However, we gave some very delightful programmes including chamber-music and works like the *Siegfried Idyll*, the Brahms *Serenades*, and some of the lesser-played Mozart symphonies. The Countess on one occasion introduced me to Baron de Rothschild who informed me he had an orchestra of his own which he seemed to infer was superior to mine. "It is only composed of sixteen players," he told me, "but they are *artists*, every one of them."

The eighth season of the Promenades provides a few interesting memories. We began on August 23 and gave sixty-six concerts. We found Edgar Jacques had become slack over the preparation of his analytical notes. Sometimes he kept the scores of novelties until a few hours before the final rehearsal which gave me no chance to study them properly. Consequently there were often blank spaces in the programmes where notes should have appeared. This was a dodge of Newman's—to 'buck up old man Jacques', as he put it. It had no effect in moving Jacques to more prompt work, and only made him furious.

"Baines and Scarsbrook refuse to take my notes unless they get them two days before the concert," he told me. "I can't make out why."

I could have told him that Newman was at the back of it all, and that he was paying Percy Pitt a weekly salary to look after Jacques. Any notice he failed to furnish Pitt had to write, in future.

This season was marked by the playing of Schubert's eight and Tchaikovsky's six symphonies. Only the last three of Tchaikovsky's really attracted the public, and only two of Schubert's, although the latter's fifth has a following now. We gave no less than *twenty-nine* first performances, of which the more important will be found in the Appendix at the end of this volume.

In spite of my seemingly unending work it had been suggested that, as we had such fine woodwind players, it would be delightful to form a quintet and play the less-known works written for wind instruments, particularly those of Mozart and Beethoven. I gave many lectures on the woodwind instruments of the orchestra which my colleagues illustrated, I playing the piano.[1]

A very finished and beautiful rendering of Beethoven's G major piano concerto (with Clara Schumann's *cadenzas*) was given by Fanny Davies who had become a favourite with our audiences. What a funny little nervous way she had of walking on to the platform with her head on one side! She and Maurice Sons—this is some years after—were advertised to play sonatas together in Scotland. Sons was generally referred to as 'Herr Sons', but it was rather unfortunate that, on the back of a programme, appeared a notice to the effect that 'At the next concert Miss Fanny Davies will appear, assisted by Her Sons.'

Another name worthy of mention is that of Muriel Foster who appeared for the first time on September 15. A richer, warmer mezzo-soprano voice I have rarely heard, and her musicianship was of the highest. I am quite sure that Elgar conceived all his mezzo-soprano parts in *Gerontius* and later

---

[1] Fransella (flute); Lalande (oboe); Gomez (clarinet); E. F. James (bassoon); Borsdorf (horn).

oratorios with Muriel Foster in his mind. I do know that no other mezzo-soprano or contralto ever extracted a word of praise from him over the interpretations of his parts.

Richard Strauss came over to conduct *Ein Heldenleben*—the first performance in England of this wonderfully beautiful tone-poem which he dedicated to the Concert-Gebouw, Amsterdam —at the Saturday Symphony concert on December 16, the solo violin part (at his own special request) being played by Zimmermann of Amsterdam.

In appearance Strauss did not give one the impression he was a musician at all—much less the great one he was. Tall, and with a nobility of bearing that attracted immediate attention, one would say: "Whoever this man is, or *whatever* he is, he is a man of distinction."

I had the delightful task of preparing the work for his coming and was extremely gratified when, after the first of his rehearsals, he turned to me with "Bravo! Splendid!" It was evidently no undeserved approbation, for he gave his performance with only two short rehearsals. There was not an inch of room to spare in Queen's Hall that afternoon, and Strauss was given a tremendous reception at the conclusion of the work.

Newman, ever watchful to follow up a success, suggested that *Ein Heldenleben* should have a second performance at the earliest possible moment, with the result that I was fortunate in directing this performance not quite four weeks after Strauss had presented it to the London public. We performed it on New Year's Day, 1903, when the Queen's Hall Orchestra gave a splendid account of themselves, Zimmermann again playing the violin *obbligato*.

The production of *Ein Heldenleben* was the beginning of my lasting friendship with Strauss and his wife. Edgar Speyer had been an intimate friend of theirs for years, knowing them in Berlin and Munich; and in this way we frequently met at 46, Grosvenor Street. As I came to know them more intimately I realized that Strauss always played second fiddle where his vivacious and somewhat overbearing wife was concerned; but he adored her and would watch (with a smile of pride and pleasure from the other end of a dining table) the effect on the other guests of her brilliant and ready repartee. I remember one occasion when Speyer at his own hospitable table raised his glass to drink the health of "our distinguished guest Dr. Richard Strauss". Before another glass could be raised Madame Strauss excitedly lifted her own. "No, no!" she said, pointing to herself with her left hand—"No, no! *To Strauss de Ahna*". Everyone laughed—we just had to, for the dear man himself laughed more than any of us and seemed to enjoy his wife claiming the precedence.

Many a time Madame Strauss would ask me to take her on a shopping expedition; or to drive with her, for Lady Speyer always placed a car at her disposal for such expeditions. One morning, when Olga was away singing in the Provinces, Madame Strauss arrived to collect me to go shopping. She had evidently given instructions beforehand because we drove straight down Regent Street and stopped at Dickins and Jones. I said I would wait, but she insisted I should go in with her. We were met at the door by a young man who appeared to be washing his hands.

"What can I do for you, Madame?"

To my utter consternation one word only was snapped out by 'Strauss de Anna'.

"*Trawers!*"

The young man bowed.

"Oh, yes, Madame! This way to the *lingerie* department."

I lagged behind, hoping to get a chance of making a retreat, but we were already at the counter which was only a few steps away. A charming young lady came forward.

"What may I show you, Madame?"

"*Trawers!*"

I feel hot, even now, when I think of those nether garments being displayed for Madame's approval. After a moment's consideration:

"I vill take dis von."

"Only one, Madame? We usually supply at least *two*. They require *washing*."

"No, no! Dis von only!"

Once in the car, I registered a vow never to shop with a lady again. We proceeded up Regent Street when our car grazed a passing carriage. A crowd collected, and so angry was the coachman that we got out to ascertain the actual damage done. It was nothing much, but you know how a crowd will stand and gape and gather every type from a policeman to an errand boy. There was one of the latter leaning on his bicycle, sucking an orange. He was quite a youngster of cherubic countenance and he attracted Madame's eye. Going up to him, she chucked him under the chin.

"Ach, you dear leetle *Bube!*"

The *Bube's* cherubic expression changed into one of menace. In the twinkling of an eye the crowd's attention was transferred from chauffeur and coachman to Madame and *Bube*. I hurriedly explained that errand boys were not used to being called a *booby* without provocation, and told her what the word sounded to mean in English. After that we made a hurried retreat into the car—and home!

As I have said, Sir Edgar and Lady Speyer were lavish in their entertainments at Grosvenor Street. Had it been anyone but 'Strauss de Anna' (whom one accepted as law unto herself) I should have defended my host in no uncertain manner when, with this beautifully gowned woman of perfect figure on my arm and about to descend the broad staircase into the dining-room, she let forth: "Do you t'ink it is anyt'ing for me to stay in a house like dis, Henry? My chimney smoke, and dey gif me ze gold of ze egg for my breakfast. Ach! No! It is nossing for me, Henry!"

Thank goodness the dining-room was reached before I had 'ze gold of ze egg' explained to me and the conversation could turn to generalities in the genial and charming presence of our host and hostess. I am sure I may be forgiven for these little reminiscences, for those who knew her were aware that Madame Strauss just said what came into her mind without a trace of unkindness, and certainly with no idea of the effect conveyed to the less demonstrative English mind. An elaborate sweet was served during this dinner—Strauss coined a phrase in appreciation of it: "This is well orchestrated," he told our hostess.

At the conclusion of the London Musical Festival this year Hugo Gurlitz ran what he called a *Grand Musical and Lyric Festival* for which he engaged Richard Strauss and Ernst von Possart. The great feature was a complete performance of Byron's *Manfred* with Schumann's music. Possart was a great producer. He was at this time Intendant to the Royal Bavarian Theatre and the Munich Wagner Festival Plays. He recited this dramatic poem, impersonating Manfred, in a way that deeply impressed me. Strauss prepared both the Queen's Hall Orchestra and the Choral Society with minute care and secured a memorable performance. At the second concert Possart recited *Enoch Arden* (Tennyson) to which Strauss had written music which he accompanied most beautifully on the piano. At the third concert Strauss conducted his *Don Juan, Tod und Verklärung* and *Till Eulenspiegel*, while between them Possart, in a most charming manner, recited a selection of Heine's poems. At the fourth concert he recited excerpts from both Goethe and Schiller to some of which Strauss played accompaniments.

As a conductor, I always liked his Mozart better than anything else and am happy to possess a score of the G minor symphony with the *nuances* most carefully marked in his very fine handwriting. I have always modelled my Strauss on Strauss himself as I was fortunate in hearing him rehearse and produce all his important works for a period of years. He was always most complimentary to me over my direction of his tone-poems which he heard me conduct on several occasions as a member of the audience. I was chatting with him one day about music in general, *tempi* in particular, when he ended our exchange of views with: "My dear Mr. Wood, do whatever you like in music, but never be *dull*."

The enormous strain of my work was by this time sadly undermining my health, and Dr. Cathcart insisted on my going for a cruise to Morocco. This I did, even though it meant being away from the Promenade concerts from October 13 to November 8. Arthur Payne conducted in my absence.

Olga remained at home when I set off on my rest cure journey to Morocco—as it was decided by my doctor that if we travelled together I should never leave music altogether—and this they decreed was necessary. As events turned out I am thankful that my dear wife remained in England, for although my father was in good health when I left London, he was taken ill very suddenly, and died as unexpectedly. Olga cabled me, advising me to continue with my prescribed programme, as it was of course too late to be of use. Dr. Cathcart and Siegfried stood by Olga during this sad time, and Ben Grove—with whom it will be remembered my father was living—took all my responsibilities on his kindly shoulders. So passed my father—my friend.

It was a great disappointment to miss the visit of the Meiningen Orchestra, so famous for its rendering of Bach and Brahms. Up to this time we in England thought Richter was the only conductor imbued with the true Brahms tradition, but Steinbach's interpretations proved a revelation to London. Well they might, for it was Brahms himself who recommended Steinbach as successor to von Bülow as *Hofkapellmeister* to the Meiningen Orchestra; and when it is remembered that the great man had all his later symphonies played over by this orchestra (while in manuscript prior to publication) it will be seen that London in 1902 heard Brahms as never before.

Some time later, when visiting Cologne, I was introduced to Franz Wüllner (among other musicians and *littérateurs*) by the well-known Cologne critic Professor Nietzel. Wüllner was very kind and gave me much of his time, taking me with him to see Steinbach.

"I was very sad at missing your London Festival," I told him.

"Then why not come as my guest? I am just off on a three weeks' tour with my orchestra?"

I readily accepted his wonderful invitation and heard, during those three memorable weeks, Brahms's works played many times over—as it were by Brahms's own orchestra and Brahms's chosen director of it. From that day to this I do not think my interpretation of Brahms has varied one iota. I remember Newman giving me a cutting from *The Times* after Steinbach's festival in which Fuller Maitland had written: *Steinbach plays Brahms like Wood plays Tchaikovsky*. That was praise for one or both of us; but the fact must remain that, praise or otherwise, I moulded my Brahms on Steinbach and the Meiningen Orchestra.

During that three weeks' tour we visited Wiesbaden and Freiburg among many other places; and often—even to this day—while conducting a Brahms symphony I visualize the scenes of those festivals. The leader of their 'cellos was Karl Piening, a distinguished artist with whom I found much in common. I shall always remember with gratitude his many kindnesses to me during that tour. It was he who brought to my notice a new 'cello concerto by Strässer, an influential professor of harmony and counterpoint at Cologne Conservatoire.

Looking back over the year 1902, I notice a few items of interest. I imagine, for example, that Brahms's first symphony is not exactly a novelty with Brahms Promenaders in these days, but I should like to record the fact that I introduced it to the Promenade public on September 9, 1902. I remember, too, the eminent English 'cellist Bertie Withers who made several appearances this season. He was a favourite pupil of Hugo Becker, and I still recall a certain cutting quality of his tone. He has done wonderful work during the past few years at the R.A.M. with the chamber-music class, including the production of the entire range of the chamber-music of Dvořák.

Ethel Smyth's name and music appeared for the first time on October 7 when we gave the first concert performance of a dance from her opera *Der Wald* which had just been produced at Covent Garden. It had previously been performed in Berlin. It was indeed an event of importance for a British composer to get an opera performed both in Berlin *and* London in those days—and a woman at that! I did not meet Ethel Smyth until much later as she was not in England when this work was played.

While I was on holiday Newman engaged Colonne. Anton van Rooy was the singer and the pianist Adela Verne. I remember my disappointment at not being able to get back for this particular concert because van Rooy was such a fine Wagnerian singer and more so because I had met him several times and had accompanied him at Edward Speyer's house at Elstree when he sang Brahms *lieder* to perfection.

One memory of this year 1902 is connected with George Moore of whom I had seen a good deal the previous summer. Early in the year we produced Elgar's incidental music to Moore's *Grania and Diarmid*. This was the only work Elgar ever dedicated to me. He did so in this instance, I think, because in a sense I was responsible for his writing it at all. Moore had tried to persuade me to write it—in fact, he used to come to my room early in the morning and wake me up to hear the latest section as he wrote it. I told him I was not a composer and never intended to compose again, but he was not to be put off. I made all kinds of suggestions, but nothing seemed to satisfy him. One day he asked me whether I knew Elgar. I told him I knew him very well. As he seemed to think Elgar was the man to write the music to his play, I gave him a letter of introduction.

We were at Bayreuth for the festival when all this took place. After the performances we naturally congregated together in the one and only restaurant there, and discussed what we had seen and heard. We never got to bed until the early hours of the morning; thus I did not exactly welcome Mr. Moore at my bedside soon after it was light. However, the letter to Elgar settled the matter.

A strange, quiet Irishman, Moore! I always think his character is portrayed to a nicety in Henry Tonk's picture of him in the Tate Gallery. Moore is seated at a table surrounded by some of his painter-friends. He himself studied the art at one time in Paris. I have often read his impressions on modern painting which I have found helpful. His novels I admire, too —especially *Evelyn Innes* which is a story connected with musical life.

Jacques Thibaud was one of our important visitors in the Symphony concert season of 1903 when he came over to play the third Saint-Saëns violin concerto. A delightful, fascinating man. No matter in what part of the world one comes across him he seems to be surrounded by an enormous circle of friends. I think it was entirely owing to him that the French conferred on me the coveted *Officier du Légion d'Honneur* in 1926.

Some years later, I had been conducting concerts in Monte Carlo and found Cortot was giving a recital with Thibaud. Cortot invited us (with Thibaud) to lunch. There was a large bottle of champagne on the sideboard but during the meal we only drank red wine. Thibaud kept eyeing this champagne. At last he could endure it no longer. . . .

"What about that champagne, Cortot?" he asked. "You have forgotten it."

Cortot murmured: "So I have!"

"I am good at opening champagne bottles," announced Thibaud. He then proceeded to prove the assertion. When I saw him later in the evening he dug me in the ribs. "I wasn't going to have that champagne standing there and then put back in the cellar!"

I met those two again in Edinburgh at the house of Methven Simpson after one of his concerts. Simpson was a true friend to art in Edinburgh. He had a music-shop in Princes Street. His wife was French and, like most of her compatriots, was skilled in the art of cooking—a fact which both Thibaud and Cortot appreciated. For that matter, I did myself, and enjoyed many a delightful dinner with them. Thibaud was playing at a Symphony concert at Queen's Hall soon after this happy meeting in Edinburgh. During the interval a quietly-spoken distinguished-looking man asked permission to see M. Thibaud. "No you can't," snapped Newman—who was guarding the artist's room door—"come after the concert if you like." The visitor returned after the concert to be greeted by Thibaud: "Ah, your Majesty, you did then come to hear me play," and then introduced us to the King of Portugal.

The ninth season of Promenades ran for nine weeks only—fifty-five concerts as against sixty-six of the previous year. Cyril Scott made his first appearance when I played his first symphony in A minor. He had already written a suite for orchestra which Richter had performed in Manchester in 1892, but Scott's output (although he was then only twenty-four) had included a *Symphonic Fantasy*, a quartet, a *Magnificat*, a 'cello concerto, five overtures, and about two dozen songs. I think he was actually the first to announce that his main intention regarding the symphonic form was to secure continuous flow without a cadence from beginning to end of a movement. In those days he was considered rather remarkable for the number of parts into which he divided his strings. He is the only composer I know who does not sing when playing over his compositions: he always whistles.

I remember, too, the first appearance of Rose A. Fyleman. She ultimately gave up singing to devote herself to literature, poetry in particular. I still meet her occasionally and well remember my introduction to her (and her mother) at Nottingham. I imagine she must now be known the world over for her children's poems. Who does not know *There are fairies at the bottom of our garden?*

Josef Holbrooke's first appearance to play his piano concerto I well remember. I have cause to, for a high old time I had correcting his band parts. Later on Lamond played his concerto in F minor (*The Song of Gwyn ap Nudd*) giving a marvellous performance of this deeply interesting work. I have introduced many of Holbrooke's compositions since those early days, including the variations on 'Three Blind Mice'—always a popular item—and, at the Symphony concerts, his tone-poem *Ulalume* and the suite *Les Hommages*.

A British composer who, I feel, has never taken the position he deserves is York Bowen. His symphonic poem *The Lament of Tasso* was performed this season with the greatest success. Bowen wrote *par excellence* for his instrument and I have produced all his concertos with him as soloist.

William Wallace wrote a charming orchestral suite which I produced this season. Wallace will perhaps be best remembered by his rollicking *Freebooter Songs* of which *Son of Mine* scored the greatest success, being sung by every baritone up and down the country. Later on I produced his symphonic poems *Villon* and *Wallace*. I still meet him in connection with the Royal Academy of Music. Wallace is a man of many parts. It is not only in music he is so well versed: art takes a place in his life, and with great distinction. In addition he is, I believe, an M.D. of Glasgow.

That delightful man and artist Gerwase Elwes came to us for the first time on September 10; also Howard-Jones, the friend and pupil of Eugène d'Albert. Another Englishman was Frederick Austin who sang the *Pilgrim Song* (Tchaikovsky) which I scored specially for him. He is indeed a fine singer and a musician of the first rank. How masterly was his scoring and arranging of the music of the *Beggar's Opera* which seemed to run for ever at Hammersmith! I believe there were well over a thousand performances.

Many Promenaders will remember with affection the name of F. B. Kiddle—so long organist accompanist for the concerts. I find that he made his first appearance to play Guilmant's symphony in D minor for organ and orchestra in which there is one of the longest and best-written pedal passages in the whole range of organ literature. Kiddle succeeded Percy Pitt when the latter went to Covent Garden.

Some months before this Ffrangçon-Davies brought me a symphonic poem called *Into the Everlasting* by another English composer—Rutland Boughton. I at once put it down for performance and secured a success with it, but did not dream at the time that Boughton would turn his attention to writing opera and establish a kind of Bayreuth at Glastonbury just as Christie has given us a Mozart Bayreuth at Glyndebourne.

What talent is Boughton's! *The Immortal Hour*—easily the most popular of his works—was performed at Glastonbury in 1914 and then again by the same company at Bournemouth the following year. The Glastonbury company brought it to the Old Vic in 1920, and Sir Barry Jackson (of one of whose water-colour sketches I am the proud possessor) brought up the Birmingham Repertory Company and staged it at the Regent Theatre which used to stand opposite St. Pancras station. A friend of mine told me she had seen it fifty times, and I am sure she was not the only one who could say that. Rarely has an opera been more popular. I never hear that lovely little trifle for tenor voice and harp (*The Fairy Song*) without remembering the charm with which Frank Mullings sang it.

It is always pleasing to secure really beautiful renderings of Mozart. Two stand out in my memory, both occurring during this season. The first was when Mathilde Verne and her sister Adela played the concerto in E flat for two pianos, and the other was when Lionel Tertis—that superb artist with the golden tone—took part in the performance of the *Sinfonia Concertante* in the same key for violin, viola, and orchestra. The violin part was played by Hans Wessely who had been a professor at the R.A.M. since 1889, some of our most distinguished violinists being his pupils.

Kreisler made his first appearance with us at a Symphony concert on November 14, 1903, playing the Brahms concerto. A few days later he sent me a delightful photograph of himself thus inscribed: *To Mr. Henry Wood in grateful remembrance of his glorious conductorship of the Brahms violin concerto. Most cordially yours, FRITZ KREISLER. Nov. 16, 1903.*

To say my conducting was 'glorious' was praise indeed, but I know that whatever I accomplished was but a natural response to Kreisler's lofty appeal. His reading was so pure, so utterly untrammelled, and the unaffected dignity of his playing was but the reflection of the calm dignity of his manner. To this first meeting I can now look back with gratitude for a friendship thus begun—one that it has been my good fortune to retain throughout the years although, alas, we do not have opportunities of meeting because he comes to London for recitals only.

It will be remembered that Kreisler gave the first performance of Elgar's only violin concerto which the composer directed at the Philharmonic Society's concert in November 1910; after this I was privileged to direct the first of eight successive performances of what is the loveliest concerto ever written for a violin—and with the man who made it his own; for, to my mind, no one has even approached his wonderful performances of it.

I recall how, in a lecture he gave soon after the production of his first symphony in Manchester by Richter, Elgar made the unfortunate remark that the centre of music was not in London but 'further north', but this was no doubt inspired by his friendship with Richter. Little did Elgar think that when Kreisler suggested giving the first performance of his violin concerto *outside London* the Hallé Concert Society would reply to the effect that they 'could not engage Mr. Kreisler until the following season'. This was not good enough, for Kreisler had put much thought and study into this work and was naturally disposed to give *first performances* only. Had he waited until 'the following season' he would undoubtedly have been forestalled. He therefore determined to take the Queen's Hall Orchestra and me to Manchester. This he did, but the attendance was very disappointing. Manchester stayed at home that night.

Now that I look back on this incident over the years I cannot avoid the feeling that it was a case of 'Manchester for the Mancunians!'—for the Hallé Orchestra, in other words. I know I am no longer quite so popular in Manchester because I identified myself with the Brand Lane concerts, for although Brand Lane engaged part of the Hallé Orchestra they remembered that he had butted in on their stronghold and, what is more, made a success of it.

Some years before Kreisler's experience Newman had taken the Lamoureux Orchestra to Manchester under the impression that Manchester was musical but—again—*Manchester stayed at home*.

I had the pleasure of meeting Kreisler as recently as 1937 at Lady Cory's. I would that his parting words might materialize: "I wish we could make music together again, my friend. I must try to bring it about."

At our fourth Symphony concert the great Schumann-Heink sang *Non più di fior* of Mozart. During the past fifty years I have taught this aria to many pupils—in fact to any who had the range and breath-control to sing it—but up to now I have only once heard it interpreted to perfection—and that was by Schumann-Heink. I had heard her at her *début* in London as far back as 1892, and again at Bayreuth four years later. Her physique and vitality were phenomenal and for several years she undertook tours embracing hundreds of concerts, singing as many as a hundred and fifty operatic *rôles*. She created Clytemnestra in Strauss's *Elektra*.

I remember, after one of the Bayreuth performances, going to her rooms with Siegfried Schwabacher. She thought nothing of cooking quite an elaborate supper for ten of us, running in and out all the time, talking and laughing and even singing. We could hear her warbling in the kitchen. It must have been half-past one in the morning when she began giving us a demonstration of various dances she had seen on her travels. Felix Mottl accompanied her on the piano. What great fun it was.

We had Carreño at this concert to play the Grieg concerto. Every seat had been booked weeks before. Fancy two such phenomenal women appearing at the same concert! They did indeed sing and play as well as they looked. (I always divide artists into two classes: those who look better than they play or sing, and those who play or sing better than they look. When you get both, you have the world-successful artist.)

This season Emil Pauer gave a concert with Emil Sauer. Pauer had a big reputation as a conductor—in fact, he succeeded Nikisch with the Boston Symphony Orchestra. This concert naturally went by the name of the Pauer-Sauer concert. Two other jangling names are, strangely enough, those of two distinguished accompanists—Kiddle and Liddle, the latter famous for his many beautiful songs, nearly all of which were sung by Clara Butt—notably *Abide with me*.

Pauer was never a favourite conductor of mine. In this very concert there was nearly a catastrophe in *Francesca da Rimini*, largely owning to the uncertainty of Pauer's beat. He seemed to suffer from a general baton vibrato and the orchestra could not follow him when he became excited.

Sauer was one of the greatest pianists of his time. He studied under Nicholas Rubinstein and, later, the Abbé Liszt. He and the Speyers were great friends. Sauer could keep us in fits of laughter with his views on art and even politics and finance. His autobiography, by the way, which appeared in 1901 under the title of *My World*, is well worth reading. I note with interest that I performed Gustav Mahler's first symphony in 1903 which I think must have been the first note of his music to be played in England. The memory of it takes me back to **very** early days, for I met him in 1892 when he came over with the Hamburg Opera Company. I shall speak of Mahler again later on.

Thinking of British composers—and I may say I am always thinking of them—I am sure I was wise at our Sunday Afternoon Concerts in devoting our main interests to the finest classical orchestral music and sandwiching *one work* by a British composer at *every concert* in between these classical items. I thought it a grave error to attempt a whole concert of works by British composers, whereas if I slipped one in at every concert the public would *have* to listen to it; but I knew only too well that a complete programme of native works would mean a very poor audience. Vaughan Williams entirely agrees with my view.

Edgar L. Bainton is a composer who should have taken a more prominent position than he has. I thought so well of his *Pompilia* which portrayed so admirably the fundamental idea underlying the narrative in *The Ring and the Book*. I have often met Bainton at Newcastle-on-Tyne where he was Principal of the School of Music. He was a friend of my own friends Sir Archibald and Lady Ross with whom I spent so many happy times at their home outside Newcastle—Heddon Hall.

As there are not too many contraltos with voices of even quality, I mention one here who possessed such a voice—Mrs. Harriet Foster who sang at a Promenade concert on October 14. On many visits to New York she and her husband (a clever reporter of baseball and general sporting events) have been kind in entertaining me.

On October 15 I produced Bruckner's seventh symphony. This was its first and last performance at the Promenades. The public would not have it then; neither will they now. Perhaps Bruckner is only appreciated in Austria? The length of his symphonies alone is prejudicial to their success, but I often play his delightful overture in G. minor and am always sure of a ready response. The same thing applies to Carl Nielsen, a Danish composer (to my mind of great distinction) whose works are rarely heard outside his own country. I feel he is too Danish—too *local*, too cold, as it were—and that his idiom is only completely understood by his own countrymen. Yet look at Puccini and Mascagni—Italians of the Italians, surely? —whose operas, notwithstanding, appeal to the whole world! The reason is because their *theme* and idiom—Love—is understood by the whole world.

Incomprehensible to me is the fact that Elgar's works fail to make a real appeal on the continent. Is he too English? Is

Gustav Holst the same? Bax, too, who to my mind is one of the strongest, most original and most romantic of British Composers. I have performed his works in America, France and Italy. I played his third Symphony at the Augusteo (Rome) in 1935 only to be met with decided hostility from a packed house. The audience hissed the work for three minutes after which they applauded for five. It was explained to me that the hisses were for Bax's work and the applause for my conducting of it, but I was deeply resentful and tried hard not to go on to take personal recalls. I had chosen Bax as a representative British composer and deeply resented the attitude of the audience and if I go again to Rome I shall give it them again.

I had also taken the trouble to learn enough Italian to make a speech to the orchestra after the final rehearsal. That little speech took some preparation but it was received with cheers. For the most part my baton had been my tongue.

So far as Bax is concerned I think it is true to say that musicians abroad have appreciated his originality and orchestral technique, but that seems to be all. Yet he is not English—at least, not in the sense that Elgar is. Then there is Delius, who is perhaps less English than either Bax or Elgar but who is definitely appreciated. Perhaps his name does not look English? But, then, neither does Holst's. It is difficult to assign a cause for this apathy abroad where our music is concerned, but I still hope to see the day dawn when British music is recognized in foreign lands as much as in England—for, after all, music is a universal language.

XXIX

WE GO TO AMERICA (1904)

IT WAS A great event in my life when Olga, Dr. Cathcart and I set sail for America on December 23, 1903. We sailed on the *Majestic*. I had had a great deal of trouble with Robert Newman who was averse to letting me off for a whole month. However, I wheedled and coaxed him and at last he gave way. I was released until January 23, 1904.

The visit of Richard Arnold, Felix Leifels, and Henry Schmidt was really responsible for my going at all. They had been in London since the beginning of September and we had had several pleasant interviews, all of which had disturbed me not a little. I badly wanted to go to New York. I introduced them to Newman in rather a doubting frame of mind, but that little lunch we had at Pagani's worked wonders—together with their persuasive powers. At all events, he gave his consent.

Behind their visit was Andrew Carnegie. He had attended those extra concerts of mine at Queen's Hall during June and July of the previous year, as has already been related. All the same, we had to play our cards carefully with Newman. We told him it would be a good thing for me to go to New York to conduct the Philharmonic Society because, up to this time, no British-born conductor had ever been invited to direct this world-renowned orchestra now entering upon its sixty-second season.

That we enjoyed our visit goes almost without saying. Only those who have experienced American hospitality can form a judgment of it. If we could have stood up to it we could have had two breakfasts, two lunches, and at least three dinners every day; a fleet of cars was always at our disposal.

On our arrival in New York harbour we were deeply touched when Andrew Carnegie came on board to welcome us. Subsequently we paid several visits to his wonderful and lovely house; he also arranged with his private organist that we should hear the organ of which he was so proud. Surely he must have been the only man who ever engaged an organist to awaken him every morning with the sound of an organ prelude? This, it appeared, was his invariable rule.

My concerts in Carnegie Hall were indeed a success and my reception by the New York public was something I shall never forget. I never received *longer* applause after orchestral items nor so many recalls at the end of my concerts. All sorts of suggestions were hinted at by the leading people in New York, and I was asked to make an annual visit of three months to the States. It was a temptation and I turned the whole matter over in my mind very seriously at the time. Why not conduct the Promenade and Symphony concerts, etcetera, in England from August to December and go to America from January till April? It was certainly worth considering.

On the other hand, I was devoted to Robert Newman and the Queen's Hall Orchestra. I felt they had made me and that I must continue to make them. I confess I thought wistfully of America at Christmas-time for a season or two afterwards, but when the War came I was thankful I had decided to remain in England. Queen's Hall (and its orchestra) was my first love after all.

Professor Sanford of Yale, one of the most delightful Americans I ever had the pleasure of meeting, visited London every year in September. He was a rich man and a pianist of real distinction who had worked seriously with Rubinstein, Batiste, and Ritter. Unfortunately, nervousness (and probably a natural diffidence together with the possession of a large fortune) prevented him from becoming what Rubinstein was of opinion he would become —one of the greatest artists of the century. Sanford did make a few public appearances with the Theodore Thomas Orchestra and was actually invited by Elgar, with whom he was intimate, to take part in one of the Worcester Festivals. What such a friend as Professor Sanford meant to us on our first to New York can readily be imagined. He knew everybody and introduced us to everybody, and his charming house was the Mecca of musical and artistic New York during our visit.

While we were there an unfortunate incident occurred in connection with Dr. Cathcart. He had a habit of dropping off to sleep at odd moments, particularly after meals. On the one and only occasion we did not accompany him to a restaurant he went to sleep and found, on waking, that a valuable diamond pin was missing from his scarf. He made inquiries but it was never recovered.

I remember meeting Hermann Wetzler, a German composer who possessed almost as great a faculty for telling witty stories as Landon Ronald. I never set eyes on him again until I met him in 1937 at the house of Adila Fachiri. I invited him to dinner and was thus able to return his hospitality to Olga and myself— after thirty-three years!

I still recall my first impressions of the wonderful Carnegie Hall, with its tiers of shallow boxes—a delightful sight when viewed from the rostrum. I also remember a lunch—probably at the Waldorf, but I forget; at all events, I know that when the band stopped playing canaries in cages began a vocal concert and the strength of their *fortissimi* was so great that we had to retire to the lounge in order to be able to talk in peace. The only other thing I can remember of this visit (it is thirty-four years ago) is a press notice which said something about a wonderful *crescendo* I produced in the *tremolo* in the *Freischültz* overture.

After a month of amazing excitement and pleasure I had a terrific rush to get back to London. When the *Celtic* entered the Mersey a fog prevented our approaching Liverpool. I was dreadfully worried when we were told we could not land that night, for I was due to take an orchestral rehearsal at Queen's Hall at ten o'clock the following morning for Marie Hall's concert the same day. I appealed to Captain (H. St. George

Lindsay) explaining my difficulties. I asked him whether he would requisition a tug for which I was willing to pay. He demurred at this—quite reasonably because, as he said, the whole ship would want the tug.

"But just keep quiet and say nothing, and I will see what I can do," he continued, "though neither your wife nor Dr. Cathcart must accompany you or I shall have trouble with the other passengers."

While everything was wrapped in fog and stillness I was taken ashore (shortly after midnight) in the pilot's cutter. I will confess that when I was confronted with a rope ladder in order to descend to the waiting cutter I very nearly withdrew my request. A horrifying experience, this descent in pitch darkness—as it were, into the sea! However, I caught what I think was the 2.30 from Lime Street, arrived at Euston about seven o'clock, and walked into Queen's Hall for my rehearsal at ten, nobody being aware of the near thing it had been.

During the season 1903–4 I directed many Sunday evening concerts for the National Sunday League, known as 'Sunday Evenings for the People'. The audiences I found most appreciative. I gave them a good selection of classical works and was quite proud of the fact that I introduced to them the *Brandenburg Concertos*.

Kreisler gave a concert with us early in the season, playing three concertos: Brahms, d'Erlanger, and Vieuxtemps. I am surprised the d'Erlanger work has not been more popular with violinists, for it is splendidly written from the solo point of view and well orchestrated; I directed it again, some years later, with Ysaÿe as the soloist—I hope to do it again.

While in Edinburgh on a tour with Percy Harrison I dined with Mrs. George Towry White, a delightful old lady who had invited me many times to visit her at her home in Oban. She and her daughter had travelled to Edinburgh to hear the Queen's Hall Orchestra and to have a talk with me. I shall always remember the daughter because, a few years before this, she had inquired at Weekes's for a music teacher. They had recommended me—probably because I bought a Bord pianette from them as a youngster.

Shortly afterwards Mrs. White wrote to me from a hotel in Bayswater and told me she wished her daughter to have lessons. I went to the hotel and was somewhat taken aback on finding they were to be *violin* lessons. I was not too keen on trying to teach the violin to someone whose technique might prove superior to my own. However, I took Miss White's fiddle, plucked the strings in a professional manner, and tactfully suggested she should play me something. She began on the *Intermezzo* from *Cavalleria*. I thought I could manage that, even though I had let my violin-practice slide for some years. I took a few lessons myself, and with the help of good old Spohr's *Violin Tutor*, we got on famously and Mrs. White was delighted with her daughter's progress.

I saw them again some years afterwards when the daughter was writing plays. Since then I have lost sight of them, but should Miss Towry White ever chance to read this she can rest assured she was the one and only violin pupil I ever had—or am ever likely to have.

The season of 1904 was very full for me. Fortunately there was time for a little diversion. I enjoyed many dinners given to Elgar by his friend Leo Schuster at his delightful home in Old Queen Street. The Elgar festival at Covent Garden was due to begin in March and, three days before, Schuster gave a wonderful dinner party to Elgar. He had even conceived a series of emblematic decorations on the panels of his dining-room referring to various phases of Elgar's works.

Elgar, however, was in one of his very silent and standoffish moods. In fact, his manner was so noticeable that Lady Maud Warrender, who was sitting next to me, drew my attention to it. "What's the matter with Elgar tonight?" she whispered. "He seems far away from us all. I suppose it is because he doesn't like this sort of homage."

We all felt rather uncomfortable when Schuster rose and asked us to drink the health of his illustrious friend. We obeyed, and when we resumed our seats we naturally expected Elgar to make a suitable reply. Instead he went on talking to an old friend and probably had no idea his health had been drunk at all.

I now had a new interest. I had formed a 'Select Choir' which I rehearsed in a beautiful room at Erard's piano galleries in Great Marlborough Street, managed by Daniel Mayer. This little choir numbered about a hundred and was entirely financed by Siegfred Schwabacher who, as my most intimate friend and companion for so many years, took a deep interest in my work as a teacher of singing, particularly as a choral trainer. His ideal was that I should train a perfectly-balanced choir that could sing for an hour without accompaniment, without loss of pitch, especially in old glees and madrigals and the sacred works of Palestrina.

This choir cost Schwabacher about £300 a year to run. I gave my services, naturally; even so, among other expenses there was that of a paid secretary. This was C. W. James who was a kind of 'devil' to Kalisch and a very charming man. All my pupils, old and new, were members of the choir, among the most distinguished of whom were Lady Maud Warrender and Lady Speyer.

The vocal test for membership was quite severe: applicants had to have a respectable voice, no tremolo, to sing in tune, and be fair readers. I did not lay too much stress on the reading at sight because my idea was to get people with voices. We had plenty of time to memorize what we sang. The rehearsals were on Tuesday evenings: ladies from 5.30 till 7; men from 8.30 till 10. Once a month only we had full practices.

After a few seasons this choir had to be given up. I was very sorry about it, but with my work at Queen's Hall, as well as with four or five choral societies in the Provinces, it was impossible for me to carry on. Neither could we find anyone to take my place because the choir was really a sort of school for choral singing. Nearly all its members had been trained privately by me: they all tried to breathe alike, to phrase alike, and to adopt the same style of expression. Schwabacher, rather than let it go on as an ordinary choral society, eventually decided to give up the entire project. However, a few months later I found that Kennedy Scott was starting a choir in London and was happy to give him the names and addresses of those who had been in my Select Choir. He still says I thereby laid the foundation of the Philharmonic Choir—now one of the most distinguished choral bodies in the world. Kennedy Scott has been responsible for this, for he possesses a wide knowledge of choral training.

I enjoyed those days very much. I remember that we used to have delightful little informal dinners between the two Tuesday rehearsals at Bellini's in Mill Street. We talked 'shop' to our hearts' content, often being joined by Major Cuthbertson, Freddy Ashton Jonson and Willie Grey, all great musical enthusiasts.

In spite of so much other work, I managed to do a little lecturing at this period. I have always been interested in elocution and studied it with several exponents of the art including Rosina Phillipi and Ian Forbes-Robertson, brother of Sir Johnstone. I always read through my lectures with Ian Forbes-Robertson who took the trouble to hear me rehearse at St. James's Hall. He declared that his own voice, with its intense depth of quality, was a *made* voice. We might call it 'stagey' in these days, but its tone was magnificent.

One of the finest voices I ever heard was Gladstone's. I sat in the thirtieth row at the side of a large tent at the Wrexham Eisteddfod—a tent must surely be the worst place in the world to speak in—and heard every word. Gladstone's tone, and the beauty of his inflection, made a deep impression on me at the time. *He* needed no microphone, and the memory of him that day has left me wondering whether elocution is becoming a lost art in England in these days when electrical means of amplifying voices would seem to do away with the need for it, and how often one has to strain one's ear to catch the confidential tones of some actors and actresses!

Whatever might have been said against my little choir, nobody could reasonably have said it was composed of poor voices. I often think modern composers have done much to ruin voices. They seem to overlook the fact that whereas orchestral instruments can play any interval (no matter how difficult or even how ugly) and come to no harm, the same does not apply to the voice. A choir studying a very modern work is so occupied with getting the right notes and difficult cross-rhythms that there is no time to think *how* they are singing.

Even after months of rehearsals, although they may sing the *notes*, the right colour is missing. I have proved it by turning to a classical work after rehearsing something very modern: the choir sounds entirely different. It is amazing what the human voice can do; but if trained soloists can merely manage to scrape through some of these ultra-modern works, a chorus of amateurs can hardly be expected to give pleasure to an audience. They are uncomfortable, and all joy and spontaneity suffer in consequence.

How beautiful the human voice can be! I shall never forget *three* speaking-voices: Queen Victoria's, Gladstone's, and Lewis Waller's. And—thinking of that last named—what an untimely death!

I deplore the fact that our voices are getting smaller and smaller and that we may in future generations require the help of a microphone in even a small hall. If that ever comes about it will be largely through microphone laziness! I fear we are becoming lazy listeners, speakers, and singers—simply because no effort is required to perfect our delivery with a microphone in front of us. Labour-saving devices are all to be desired in these days of domestic service problems, but they must not curtail the necessity for serious education in the art of speech or song. To my mind, training is at a discount—a tiny voice of no quality or distinction can be reinforced by mechanical means, and made to serve for that which went for years of thought and study in the days before the advent of this marvellous invention, and when a LISTENER was in the same hall and quick to tell you if he did not hear all *you* had to say. Nowadays our theatres are small enough, yet often how difficult it is to catch every word. Perhaps in some way it is this craze for naturalness, which seems to pervade our theatres; they are all, seemingly, afraid of ACTING, just as our singers are afraid of being dramatic, hence they become tame and dull, and unconvincing. Our speakers, too, rely on the microphone, or we should not get the after-dinner speeches to which we have to listen nowadays, for the mere necessity of training one's voice bred consciousness of what one had to say in the days of Gladstone.

XXX

MELBA, AND JOACHIM (1904)

In 1885, when I was playing Wedlake's organ at the Inventions Exhibition, I remember attending a reception given by the directors at which was a Mrs. Armstrong. She was on a visit to London with her father who had just taken up a Government appointment, and I was deeply impressed by the beauty of her voice when she sang in response to a request 'to oblige with a song'; but her name meant little or nothing to me at the time. I certainly did not dream that she was to be the great *Melba* or that she would one day give a concert with the Queen's Hall Orchestra on May 4, 1904.

In the meantime she had studied in Paris under Mathilde Marchesi. I consider it a tribute to Marchesi's powers as a teacher that Melba's voice was the same in quality after she had studied with her as it was before, though, of course, her artistry had developed enormously. I always maintain that a good teacher does not try to take out a pupil's voice, clean it, and put it back again with its natural character changed: it is the business of the teacher to show the pupil how to use his or her voice, to discover faults and correct them.

When Melba made her *début* in 1887 she was already a matured singer. I realized that at her first performance at Covent Garden when she appeared as Lucia. She always retained that peculiar silvery tone (her voice was almost that of a boy soprano) even in quality throughout its compass without a trace of breathiness or *vibrato ;* and I am quite sure she never forced a note in her life. That is why her voice lasted fresh and bright to the very end. How different from those unwise singers who seek first and foremost to assure themselves of an enormous voice and who lose all beauty of tone in a few years by constant endeavour to force that tone! I often wonder what pleasure they derive from shouting louder than someone else.

In 1894 I often played for Melba's rehearsals at her house in Great Cumberland Place when she was preparing the part of Nedda in *Pagliacci.* I look back over the years now and marvel at the infinite pains to which she went in the duet with Richard Green. Her scale and arpeggio technique, I remember, was perfect. Her notes were like a string of pearls—touching, yet separate, strung on a continuous vocal line of tone that was never marred nor distorted by laryngeal jerks, jaw-oscillations, or diaphragmatic shocks.

I remember one particular concert with the Queen's Hall Orchestra, when she sang the Mad Scene from *Hamlet* (Ambroise Thomas) which she interpreted ideally. Her other solo was the much-despised Bach-Gounod *Ave Maria* for which Arthur Payne played the violin part, I the organ, while the conducting was in the hands of Landon Ronald.

Ternina, the great Croatian Wagnerian soprano, sang at this same concert. She was a wonderful-looking woman. I always remember the beauty of her arms (so often mere appendages) when she appeared in Wagner's operas. *Her* gestures gave colour to everything she sang. I heard her many times in Munich and am not likely to forget her marvellous Isolda, both singing and acting. I remember her as Kundry in Bayreuth in 1899 and again as an ideal Leonore. She succeeded Klafsky at Bremen in 1886.

The outstanding event of the 1904 season was the diamond jubilee of Joseph Joachim. A wonderful reception was given for him in Queen's Hall on Monday, May 16. The president was Arthur James Balfour whom, for the first time, I had the honour of meeting. On the programme appeared a delightful poem by Robert Bridges and, on the second page, a reproduction of a pencil drawing by Frau Moritz Hauptmann; also a recently-taken photograph.

I opened the concert with Mendelssohn's *Hebrides* Overture. I may say that, in those early days of my conducting, Mendelssohn was not a great favourite of mine: I was more devoted to Bach, Beethoven, Brahms, and Wagner. Joachim, on the other hand, had known Mendelssohn personally—indeed, he had played with him. He was naturally devoted to Mendelssohn's works. I was therefore not a little proud of the result of my conducting of the *Hebrides* overture, for it brought nothing but words of praise from Joachim.

Later, that amazing personality Sir Hubert Parry read, and Balfour presented an illuminated address to Joachim together with his portrait by Sargent. The second item on the programme was announced as 'solo violin', and someone went into the artists' room and brought Joachim's fiddle-case which he opened amid tremendous applause and enthusiasm. I began the introduction to Beethoven's violin concerto and Joachim gave a memorable performance of it with his own *cadenza*. This was followed by his arrangement of Schumann's *Abendlied* for violin and orchestra. The musical part of the programme closed with Joachim conducting his own overture to Shakespeare's *King Henry IV* (written in 1885) and also the Brahms *Academic Festival Overture*.

In his address Balfour referred to Joachim's association with Mendelssohn and told us how the composer conducted the concerto we had just heard when Joachim played it at the Philharmonic concert of May 27, 1844. He then addressed Joachim thus:

"Learning from Mendelssohn and working with Brahms and in the comradeship of life-long friends, you have devoted your whole energies as executant and composer to continuing the tradition and maintaining the ideal of classical music. We now hold it that the sixtieth anniversary of your first appearance in London should not pass without greeting. Your first thoughts as a performer have ever been for the composer, not for yourself."

The list of the committee and subscribers numbered six hundred and three and contained all the greatest names in music, literature, painting, and even politics.

Of Joachim I always felt that one was in the presence of a Hungarian gentleman of great intellect, and although his playing lacked the emotional depth of that of dear Ysaÿe, his was a quiet classical serenity free from any trace of exaggeration and always musical and scholarly. Joachim was always conscious of his dignity; one could never have the fun out of him that was possible with Ysaÿe. He was a great friend and always a welcome guest at the house of Edward Speyer in Elstree—generally known as the 'Elstree Speyer', and cousin to Sir Edgar. Those two did not quite hit it musically: Edgar was all out for the modern in music, Edward for the strictly classical.

On May 31 May Harrison made her first appearance with the Queen's Hall Orchestra at St. James's Hall. She played the Bach *concerto in E*, the Mendelssohn concerto, the *Chaconne* of Bach, and the *Introduction and Rondo Capriccioso* of Saint-Saëns.

There were four Harrison sisters of whom May and Beatrice are the best-known now; but the other two were talented—Margaret especially. She made her *début* as a violinist in 1918. They were born in Roorkee, in North-West India, but were brought to England by their parents when very young. Both May and Beatrice won the Gold Medal of the Associated Board for violin and 'cello respectively, and May took Kreisler's place at a Mendelssohn festival in Helsingfors. I shall never forget the scene of enthusiasm at the end of her first orchestral concert. The audience, instead of handing up bouquets of flowers to this very pretty little girl of twelve, presented her with a collection of toys and other gifts. The platform looked like Hamley's toy shop at Christmas.

Beatrice appeared in 1921. Hugo Becker had already told me about her amazing talent as a 'cellist. Since then I have had the pleasure of accompanying these two talented sisters in the Brahms and Delius double concertos. The latter was actually written for them and they were the first to introduce it to the London public.

The season finished in June with a charity concert for the Life Boat Fund. Lady Maud Warrender was one of the artists. Also Holmann, an amusing Dutch 'cellist (already mentioned) whose playing was delightful—unless one sat near him. In moments of intensity he was apt to grunt audibly and this habit became worse as he grew older. What he would have done had there been broadcasting in those days, I do not know. A microphone is not kind to people with such queer habits.

The season had been a brilliant one for me. Plançon, the loveliest bass I ever heard, had sung, also Melba and Caruso; Kreisler had played, and last (but not least) Saint-Saëns had been over to play his fantasy for piano and orchestra called *Africa*.

Early in the tenth season of the Promenades I introduced to the London public the name of Claude Debussy. His *L'Après Midi d'un Faune* had been written in 1892 and published ten years later. I shall never forget the riveted attention of the

Promenade when we first performed it. The beauty of the harmonies, the exquisitely beautiful orchestration, the atmosphere so fresh and original, created the deepest impression. In fact I received more letters asking for a repetition than I had ever received before on the production of a novelty. I gave four performances of the work and followed it up with others including *La Mer*, *Images*, *Printemps* and *Le Martyre de St. Sébastien*.

Maurice Sons took up the leadership of the Queen's Hall Orchestra this season though, as I have already pointed out, he never actually led the Promenade concerts. I had met him when I was guest conductor to the Scottish Orchestra (of which he was leader for something like sixteen years) and was happy to be able to offer him the leadership of the Queen's Hall Orchestra which, combined with a Professorship at the R.C.M. made it worth his while to come to London. The Professorship was really the reason why he never led the Promenades: he felt he must take his holiday during the Long Vacation.

Sons had been something of a prodigy. appearing for the first time as a soloist with orchestra at the age of eleven. He afterwards studied under Wieniawski until the late King of Holland sent him for further study to Dresden. His tone was enormous. I used to tease the first violins and tell them that when Sons left off it sounded as though at least four players were missing. Many of his pupils became members of the orchestra but he never allowed any of them to come to my auditions until he was perfectly satisfied with their playing. He was so honest about it too; he never hinted that any of the applicants had been pupils of his. One of them, by the way, is very well known to present-day Promenaders—Marie Wilson. Of her part in the Promenade concerts I shall speak later.

Spencer Dyke, an old friend of mine at the R.A.M., played a violin concerto by Stewart Macpherson this season. Macpherson founded the Music Teachers' Society in 1908 and indeed was among the first to advocate aural training as a basis of musical education. His works on harmony, counterpoint, form, aural culture, etcetera, are now well known. Dyke's work as a teacher of violin I have always admired. Many of his pupils have been through my hands. I appreciate teachers who study the best literature on their subject, and have little patience with those who consider their own particular method the one and only. Teachers of singing generally deem it wise to say they teach the 'Italian method'—whatever that may mean. If it is the *modern* Italian yelling, heaven help their pupils! Method can only be founded on long and wide experience coupled with a definitely analytical ear.

During this season I made the acquaintance of Percy Grainger. I remember Grieg speaking to me about him; he was very much taken with this promising young pianist. On August 17 Grainger played the Tchaikovsky concerto but I must say I preferred him to play Grieg even though his playing of the Tchaikovsky was energetic and clean-fingered.

Balfour Gardiner gave quite a remarkable concert with my orchestra some years later in which he introduced an entirely British programme, including some of Grainger's now popular works. Grainger collected a number of British folk-tunes, many of which he used as a basis for works like *Molly on the Shore, Shepherd's Hey, Handel in the Strand,* and others. The clog-dance *Handel in the Strand* was originally written for violin, 'cello and piano, but I scored it for full orchestra as a popular piece for the Promenade concerts. When Grainger heard it he asked me whether Schott's might publish it, a compliment I very much appreciated.

The next-comer of note was Egon Petri, the pupil and friend of Busoni. If his idea was to show England how Liszt should be played he certainly succeeded. After him Donald Francis Tovey (now Sir Donald) in whom Joachim took such lively interest. Tovey's knowledge is encyclopaedic; there seems to be nothing he does not know about old manuscripts.

At this particular concert we had rather an amusing incident with him. In the first half he played a Mozart concerto with his own improvised *cadenza.* At the rehearsal, of course, we did not stop for the *cadenza,* but I was rather fearful of it because I never knew whether Tovey's *cadenzas* were going to last five minutes or fifty. Once he began improvising he lost count of time—in fact, he temporarily left this world altogether. I never met a man with such powers of concentration. When not actually playing during a concerto he would listen intently to the orchestra but with his arms on the top of the piano, elbows out, and tips of his fingers together, his head on his hands. There he would remain, motionless, as though he were saying his prayers. I used to look down at him in apprehension, feeling certain he would never come in on his cue; but sure enough, about four crotchets beforehand, his head would go up and he would be in at the exact moment.

When he was actually playing I think he scared me more still because he *would* place his right foot on the *sostenuto* pedal and his left behind the stool leg. As his excitement worked up this left leg would stretch out further and further until I was certain the next instant he would fall off the seat and crash his nose on the keys. But he always managed to avoid accidents.

In the second half of this programme he was down to play the Brahms variations on a theme by Paganini, *Book I*. The promenaders crowded round the platform to watch his fingers and gave him a tremendous reception. He came off and asked me whether he should merely return and bow, or play an encore. I thought it might be quicker if he played the encore. "Yes," I said. "Go on and play them a short piece."

He went on, but I did not think he would sit down and play *Book II* of the variations—yet that is what he proceeded to do. At ten minutes past eleven I sent the band home and told Percy Pitt to play the national anthem on the organ as soon as Tovey had finished.

Later Tovey gave an orchestral concert with me when I produced his piano concerto in A. He was a great writer of programme notes but hardly the kind one can quickly read at a concert. They require study if they are to be appreciated. Hubert Foss eventually persuaded the Oxford University Press to publish them in five volumes under the title: *Essays in Musical Analysis*, and a masterly work it is.

I produced a work of Napier Miles this season. It had a strong west-country flavour about it—indeed, it was called *From the West Country* and was written in overture form. Miles is a Bristolian and I have paid pleasurable visits to his home. He was the man who helped Marie Hall at the beginning of her career, and is the composer of a cantata *Hymn before Sunrise*, produced at the Bristol Festival of 1896, and also of several operas.

I now felt it was high time I began to popularize the works of Liszt. My first effort was with the *Dante* symphony of which we gave a splendid performance with the help of Smallwood Metcalfe's choir. We also gave the *Faust Symphony* with the same choir later; but my idea was to get the public to know and like the twelve symphonic poems, and I pegged away at them in face of Press criticism and in spite of opposition of the Schumannites and Joachimites that almost amounted to malice, but I stuck to my determination to popularize Liszt at whatever cost. I look back on those years with satisfaction, for we are now able to give programmes devoted to Liszt's works and be sure of an appreciative audience. There is always a danger with a composer who has been famous as a performer or a conductor:

Liszt, Rubinstein, Busoni, d'Albert, and Dohnányi, have all suffered because the public is slow to acknowledge artists in two branches of music. As for Liszt, the *Faust Symphony* alone is enough to stamp him as a great composer.

Raoul Pugno played at the season's opening Symphony concert. I shall always see him in my mind's eye—a huge person with a flowing beard; but I reverence above all others his Mozart and César Franck. I liked his solo recitals but always felt that— to hear Pugno at his best—one had to hear him with an orchestra.

He was a strange creature, very particular in money matters. His petty cash account was the bane of his existence. I found him one night during the interval, when tea was brought to him, poring over a sheet of figures.

"What's the matter?" I asked. "You seem very worried."

"I am twopence out in my accounts. Whether I gave a tip or bought a paper, I cannot remember. But I must get it right. It will worry me all night if I don't."

I had visions of him playing wrong notes in César Franck's *Les Djinns* and thought I had better do something about it. I offered the twopence so that the accounts could be balanced, but Pugno would not hear of it. That was not the same thing. However, I think he must have suddenly remembered how he spent those two pennies, for he played magnificently.

From February 1 to 12 we were off touring with Percy Harrison. This was the first visit to the Provinces of the Queen's Hall Orchestra. We visited Birmingham, Leeds, Aberdeen, Dundee, Glasgow, Edinburgh, Newcastle, Bradford, Manchester, Liverpool, and Sheffield. Olga was the singer, and 'Daddy' Harrison looked after us all as only he knew how. He was a good-humoured soul who spent his days touring Great Britain with the world's greatest artists—and was making *young* artists too, for he always engaged a young oncoming singer and pianist on all his Prima Donna tours. He was the real old type of concert manager. He would run three or four tours a season, losing heavily on the swings but occasionally making a good thing out of the roundabouts. I must say he did the thing handsomely and I never heard an artist murmur a word against him. He was a fresh-looking, dapper little fellow of uncertain age. We used to try to get to know how old he was but he never would tell us. He died in Birmingham somewhat in obscurity; I did not even hear of his death until some months after it occurred.

XXXI

THE TRAFALGAR DAY CENTENARY
(1905)

ROBERT NEWMAN, AS I have said before, always had an eye on the main chance. If there was ever a possible excuse for arranging a concert he always took advantage of it. Naturally he was not inclined to miss the Nelson Centenary on October 21, 1905. It was one hundred years since the battle of Trafalgar. Nothing would satisfy him but that I must go the whole hog on a 'sea-business' programme, as he called it.

I thought of everything that could be said to be remotely connected with the sea or to reflect British seamanship. I put down a programme beginning with Mackenzie's *Britannia* overture and followed it with *The Bay of Biscay*, *Hearts of Oak*, Tchaikovsky's *1812* overture, *The Death of Nelson*, Chopin's *Funeral March*, *Rocked in the Cradle of the Deep*, and the *Flying Dutchman* overture.

This seemed to be all I could think of, but we both felt we ought to have a real popular climax to a programme of this kind. Three weeks before the concert I conceived the idea of orchestrating and arranging a *fantasia* on British sea-songs. I collected everything I could find and put down the titles. I visited Besson's, Boosey's, Potter's, Hawkes', and Rudal Carte's in order to obtain the correct naval 'calls' and to find their proper order. Through the kindness of various members of these firms I was able to do this and to make my *fanfares* authentic. I then set to work on my score and in due course the *fantasia* was put into rehearsal. When it came to printing the programmes we set the thing out in fine style. It came out like this:

NEW FANTASIA FOR ORCHESTRA ON BRITISH SEA-SONGS

I.   Bugle Calls:
        (a) Admiral's Salute
        (b) Action
        (c) General Assembly
        (d) Landing Party
        (e) Prepare to Ram
        (f) Quick, Double, Extend and Close

II.	The Anchor's Weighed	
	Solo Trumpet	Mr. F. L. Gyp
	Solo Trombone	Mr. Arthur Falkner

| III. | The Saucy Arethusa | |
| | Solo Euphonium | Mr. Walter Reynolds |

| IV. | Tom Bowling | |
| | Solo Violoncello | Mr. Jacques Renard |

V.	Jack's the Lad (Hornpipe)	
	Solo Violin	Mr. Henri Verbrugghen
	Solo Flute	Mr. Albert Fransella
	Solo Piccolo	Mr. C. A. Souper

VI.	Farewell and Adieu, Ye Spanish Ladies	
	Quartet of Solo Trombones	
	Mr. Arthur Falkner	Mr. T. A. Guttridge
	Mr. A. J. Pearse	Mr. H. Herring

VII.	Home, Sweet Home	
	Solo Clarinet	Mr. C. W. Fawcett
	Solo Oboe	Mr. H. de Busscher

VIII.	See the Conquering Hero Comes	
	Solo Horns	Mr. E. Priegnitz
		and
		Mr. F. Salkeld

| IX. | Rule, Britannia! | |
| | Organ and Full Orchestra | |

Lewis Waller recited Kipling's *Ballad of the Camperdown* and the singers were Lloyd Chandos and Robert Radford.

I little dreamed when I arranged this item—merely to finish a programme for a special occasion—that the Promenade public would demand its repetition on the last night of the season for ever afterwards. As it had proved a success at the original centenary concert I put it down for the last night of the season following—just to see how it would go. One year I thought we had had enough of it and left it out, but on the Monday morning I received so many letters of protest and disappointment that I resolved never to omit it again.

And now that it has been played for more than thirty seasons I look back over the years and reflect a little. I seem to realize that, in a sense, this *fantasia* on British sea-songs epitomizes the Promenades. Where else in the whole world could we see such sights as we see in Queen's Hall during the months of August and September each year? Hundreds of young men and girls—have you ever noticed the preponderance of young people in the Promenade?—who wander during the interval to sit on the steps of All Souls' Church, and discuss the concerto or the quality of some soprano's high C; who will stand stock still for forty minutes at a stretch in a hall with the thermometer high in the eighties; who will applaud generously and whole-heartedly those whose artistry they appreciate?

As for the *fantasia*, the younger Promenaders thoroughly enjoy their own part in it. They stamp their feet in time to the hornpipe—that is until I whip up the orchestra in a fierce *accelerando* which leaves behind all those whose stamping technique is not of the very first quality. I like to win by two bars, if possible; but sometimes have to be content with a bar-and-a-half. It is good fun, and I enjoy it as much as they. When it comes to the singing of *Rule, Britannia!* we reach a climax that only Britons *can* reach, and I realize I can be nowhere in the world but in my native England. It is then that I realize that Queen's Hall is indeed my spiritual home, and my mind goes back over sixty years to that little cottage not half a mile away in Oxford Street.

I think of the days of the Great War when *Rule, Britannia!* was sung with a depth of feeling that brought tears to the eyes. Britain's navy meant something to us all in those days, for on it did our safety depend—and still *does* depend.

The ritual of the 'Last Prom of the Season' is now established. It is a gala night and the young Promenader is determined not to take his music too seriously. Even so, he listens as intently as ever to the first part of the programme. As each leader of the various orchestra sections takes his place he is greeted with a round of applause; even the attendant who opens the lid of the piano is recognized and similarly applauded. The Principal Violin, that night, receives almost as much applause as I do on other nights, whereas my own welcome is something I can never quite get used to, even after all these years. The scenes at the end must strike any one witnessing them for the first time as being unique. Yet, when I look back over the many demonstrations it has been my joy to witness, I realize more than ever how well worth while it has been to slave all these years. It is a far cry to that morning in 1895, when I was only a youngster myself, and I listened to Robert Newman telling me he wanted to create a public to listen to good music.

And now they *have* listened all these forty-odd years! How

still they have stood! How they have loved their Bach, their Beethoven, their Brahms, and their Wagner! More than I ever hoped they would in my wildest dreams.

And as each Last Night of the Season has come round and I have been almost mobbed and my car pushed out into Langham Place by a crowd of jolly young men and girls, I have realized increasingly with the years that music is a great power in England; that there are hundreds of young people who have discovered what their fathers discovered—*that the best melodies are in the best music.*

It is strange how the words of *Rule, Britannia!* have become distorted in the course of time. James Thompson's original read—

Rule, Britannia! Britannia rule (not rules) the waves!
For Britons never shall be slaves.

Dr. Arne wrote the music in 1740 as one of the numbers in a masque for the Prince of Wales, given as part of an entertainment to commemorate the accession of the House of Hanover, and also to commemorate Princess Augusta's birthday. Originally there were six stanzas for tenor solo, taken by an actor impersonating King Alfred which, indeed, was the title of the masque.

Nobody in Queen's Hall, I imagine, thinks of that on the last night of the Promenade season. Neither do I, but when I look down on that sea of faces before me and conduct my great, amateur, untrained choir, I know that I am British, I know that I am in my native London, and I know that in *them* the spirit of Horatio Nelson still lives and will never die.

After the Sunday concerts were over (1905) I had a pressing invitation from Strauss to pay a visit to Heidelberg to hear the *Domestic Symphony* under his personal direction. I remember how much impressed I was with the old-world place and with the students—hundreds of them with their heroic little scars on their cheeks. I was also much taken with the new concert hall, especially as I had never seen one in which the entire orchestral platform could be raised and lowered by hydraulic lifts. The performance of the *Domestica* with the Heidelberg orchestra was in no way comparable with that which Strauss had already directed in London with the Queen's Hall Orchestra, but it was an excellent performance all the same.

Strauss and his wife, I remember, had to hurry off early the next morning for another performance of the work. I laugh even now when I think of how I went to their rooms just before breakfast. The bedroom door was open and all I could see was Strauss with his head buried in a large trunk, presenting an imposing rear elevation.

"Why don't you let your wife do the packing?" I asked.

Strauss looked up and smiled knowingly.

"No, my friend," he said. "I always do the packing. Much more satisfactory. We do then not lose our train!"

Looking back over the earlier part of 1905, I am reminded that in April the Queen's Hall Orchestra made its first appearance at the Alexandra Palace to begin a series of popular concerts on Saturday evenings. I know I wondered what sort of impression a mere hundred players would make in a hall whose acoustics I immediately likened to those of St. Pancras railway station. We could have quadrupled the personnel of the orchestra and not have overdone it.

At that time Allen Gill was conducting the Alexandra Palace Choral and Orchestral Society. I first met him at the R.A.M. where he was studying the 'cello, and well remember his performance of Bach's *Mass* at the Palace with a colossal chorus of 600 voices.

During the eleventh season of the Promenades I notice the name of Irene Scharrer who was then a newcomer. She might not have been except for her own persistency. I remember her calling at my house in Norfolk Crescent on one of my busiest teaching days. Olga interviewed her and told her that she was afraid I should not be able to see her. However, she was not to be put off so easily. Olga fetched me and I interviewed Miss Scharrer for a moment. I explained that I had singing lessons to give every half-hour until half-past six that evening, and suggested making an appointment for another day.

No; even that would not do. Miss Scharrer would wait. Olga came to me at lunch-time and told me she was still walking up and down outside.

"Do hear her play—just for ten minutes!" pleaded Olga whose heart always went out to people who wanted to make a start in music. "I will put off lunch," she added, which made me feel there was nothing else to be done. I bowed to her better judgment and went to the door and called to Miss Scharrer.

My first impression as she came in was: "What a pretty child!" but as soon as she touched the piano I recognized an artist of distinction, the beauty of tone, and the *finesse* of her phrasing interested me so greatly that I heard her play for nearly an hour and promised her a Promenade engagement. All this time lunch was still waiting and Olga had to make excuses to my two o'clock pupil. That is how Irene Scharrer came to appear at the Promenades.

Since then I have conducted for her many times and have noted the extraordinary fascination she holds over her audiences.

Mischa Elman also made his first bow this season, playing Glazounoff's A minor concerto. His talent—he was then very much the pretty boy, of course—was remarkable. He played with such emotional warmth in those days that I have actually seen tears in the eyes of some of the string players in the orchestra. Not even Ysaÿe himself brought out all the passion in the themes of the Tchaikovsky violin concerto as did this mere child. Elman has grown up long since those days, but my best memories of him belong to his youth. Incidentally, a good story is told of him—how true I cannot say—when he sat next to the great pianist Godowsky in a box at the Carnegie Hall in New York. Heifetz had just played two movements of a concerto. Elman seemed a little bored. Stifling a yawn, he is reported to have turned to Godowsky who was evidently much impressed by Heifetz's playing. . . .

"Whew! It's fearfully hot in this hall!"

"*Only for violinists,*" answered Godowsky.

I frequently met the Viennese sculptor Emil Fuchs at Pagani's at this time when I so often lunched there with Percy Pitt. A very talented man. I remember how much his bust of Forbes-Robertson was admired, but executing busts of famous people was not a particularly paying concern. Fuchs, I know, was impressed with Sargent's success as a popular portrait painter—so much so that he himself decided to become one.

Fuchs lived with his sister at Abbey Lodge, Regent's Park—a charming place now the site of a block of flats—where he built a large studio in a corner of the garden to accommodate his work as a sculptor. King Edward took a personal interest in him which resulted in his being invited to design His Majesty's likeness for the Mint. Even so, I am not at all sure it did Fuchs any good. There was a definite feeling against a foreigner being asked to design English coins; at all events, after that commission Fuchs began to lose his former popularity.

He was an amazing man and worked like a black. It was, however, in rather a weak moment after an extremely good lunch at Pagani's that I consented to sit for him to paint my portrait. The trouble was to find the time.

"Come at eight in the morning," was Fuchs' first cheerful suggestion. As I hesitated he offered an alternative.

"I tell you what," he said with an air of a man who had settled a difficult problem, "I'll put my fencing-lesson back to 5.30. I shall be ready for you at six if I do that."

Fuchs never wasted a second. While he painted he would interview business men. The next sitter after myself, I remember, was none other than Baden-Powell, then Major.

I recall an amusing incident about Fuchs just before he gave an exhibition of his oil paintings at the Grafton Galleries. He booked the galleries and announced the date. His idea was eventually to take the whole collection over to New York for a similar show there. One morning a representative of Willing's called. The conversation between him and Fuchs was as follows:

"I am about to give the most marvellous exhibition of portraiture ever seen in London."

"Yes, sir!"

"Now, you understand, everybody who is anybody in London *must* be there. I want this exhibition thoroughly advertised. No half measures."

"If you will state your requirements, sir, I will have an estimate prepared."

"Very good. I want bills posted over the whole of London, on every hoarding, on every railway station, the underground, buses, trams—in fact, everywhere you can think of."

The man departed and the estimate was duly prepared. I was lucky enough to be with Fuchs when it arrived. I will not repeat what he said. It can be imagined. The estimate was for something just under *ten thousand pounds*.

Merely as a matter of record I should like to mention that at the New Year concert (January 2) I directed the first, and I hope the only performance of three of Wagner's very early overtures: *Polonia*, *Columbus*, and *Rule, Britannia!* Had Robert Newman listened to me he would never have had them produced at all. His idea was to increase our Wagner repertory, but we never repeated any of these overtures. Fortunately the *Casse Noisette Suite* and the *Pathetic Symphony* were included in the programme. They saved the whole concert.

XXXII

GRIEG (1906)

THE IMPORTANT EVENT of 1906 was a visit from Grieg to London for a concert at which Johanne Stockmarr played his piano concerto. He came over at the invitation of Sir Edgar Speyer with whom he stayed at 46, Grosvenor Street, in that delightful suite of rooms which were always placed at the disposal of his distinguished visitors. Grieg especially enjoyed the charming Italian garden.

As was Speyer's custom, there was a dinner party on the night of a guest's arrival. Speyer was always anxious for his famous guests to meet the right people. We were all so taken with this shy, refined, delicate little man whose wife spoke such excellent English. After dinner we went into the library for some music. Speyer was very fond of tigerskin rugs and possessed some fine specimens, one of which, unfortunately, was the cause of a minor but quite unpleasant accident to Grieg himself. Madame Grieg had been asked to sing some of her husband's songs. Grieg, going over to the piano, tripped over the head of one of these rugs and fell. We were all very much distressed and our host immediately got him some brandy. He was too shaken to play though there were no serious consequences. I played for Madame Grieg but was sorry not to have heard them together for, although her voice was not great, there was a beautiful understanding between these two which was evident to us all.

The songs I played were *Ein Schwann*, *Von Montepincio* and *Ein Traume*. The first of these had already been scored for orchestra but the other two had never been sung except with piano. Grieg told Speyer he wished he had scored them, and added: "I wonder whether I dare ask Wood to score them for me?"

Dare ask me? I felt deeply honoured that he should even think of entrusting such work to my care! I told him I should be only too pleased to score them for him. This I actually did and sent them out to Bergen, where the Griegs lived a secluded life in their wonderful country house with its superb views, and was delighted at receiving a charming letter from Madame Grieg in acknowledgment.

Grieg first visited London in 1888 when he came for a Philharmonic concert. Madame Grieg came with him and sang several of his songs in private. Her amazing insight into his music was so remarkable that husband and wife were persuaded to give a joint recital of songs a fortnight later, and also to appear at the Popular Concerts. They were here again the following year, and in 1894 Grieg received the honorary degree of Mus. Doc. Cambridge. As far as I remember, the only other visit was in 1896.

This visit in 1906, when he directed *Bergliot* and the *Lyric Suite*, was the last I saw of him, for he died in an hotel in Bergen while on his way to Christiania. A composer of great charm and originality was lost to the world! He will never be forgotten in England where his songs, and piano concerto, and the music to *Peer Gynt* are established in the affections of all music-lovers.

Madame Grieg died only a short while ago at an advanced age. I recollect conducting concerts at Copenhagen in 1933 after the last of which a wonderful banquet was arranged. This did not begin until a quarter before midnight and it must have been well after one o'clock when Madame Grieg rose and made a remarkable speech in English—she must have been considerably over eighty—in which she said how kind I had been to her husband and what he thought of me. That speech is one of the really touching memories of my life of music.

Looking through the programmes for 1906, I note the name of Camilla Landi, the Milanese mezzo-soprano. She could sing arias covering a wide range with equal ease. At a concert on January 20 she sang two colossal arias: Borodin's *Cavatine de Kontchakovna* (*Prince Igor*) and *Chanson Circassienne* by Cui. She lived in London for several years and her mother taught there a great deal between 1895 and 1898.

On February 3 Maurice Sons and Hugo Becker played Brahms's double concerto. Never shall I forget my piano rehearsals with them. Sons was always touchy, and Becker was a handsome Strasburgian who knew the Brahms tradition probably as no one else in the world did. Sons thought he knew as much or even more, and a high old time I had of it between them. Becker pulled Sons up about every third bar, illustrating on his 'cello how he wanted him to play the violin part. Sons contradicted everything Becker said. However, by dint of exerting considerable tact and telling more lies in one hour than I ever told before or since, I managed to prevent these two coming to blows in my drawing-room. They were both, of course, first-rate artists.

I had to be most diplomatic with Sons at orchestral rehearsals.

To tell the truth, if there was ever any squabbling it was generally amongst the Dutch members of the orchestra. I shall always remember a rehearsal of *Don Quixote*. I was trying to get a perfect *ensemble* between Sons who was playing the solo violin part, and Fransella who was the solo flautist. They sat some considerable distance apart.

"Listen to *each other !*" I counselled them.

"How can I follow *that ?*" snapped Fransella, pointing with his flute to Sons. Now it happened that Sons was so concentrated on the work that he missed what Fransella said, which perhaps was as well.

"*What's* he saying?" demanded Sons, red with anger.

"He says how splendidly you and he are playing together," I said. "Let us try it over again!" Thus the storm was averted.

Looking further through the programmes, I see the name of Ethel Leginska, a pianist of considerable power. She was an artistic person and undoubtedly talented. Her playing of a concerto by Henselt in F minor, which was quite unknown in England at this time, and has remained so, I thought a pleasing work. Later on Leginska went to America, and the last I heard of her was that she was conducting a ladies' orchestra in New York. Her name must have been more or less well-known in that city for she produced quite a stream of talented pupils.

Another newcomer was an admirable soprano named Eve Simony who came over from the Theâtre de la Monnaie in Brussels. She had a superb technique and created a deep impression with an aria by David. I wonder why we never hear of her now?

The next newcomer whose name catches my eye is one better known than either of the foregoing—Edward Isaacs. He came to us on August 24 to play Beethoven's first concerto. The logical clarity of his playing impressed everyone. It is sad that he has practically lost his sight for he is an excellent player. He has given much of his time—most successfully—to teaching in Manchester.

I see that I gave a first performance of Busoni's new orchestral suite *Turandot* on August 21, which was warmly received.

On August 27 we gave a first performance of *Isolde's Narration to Brangäne*—that is to say, the first *concert* version. I arranged the prelude and ending to it. It was only a matter of making use of forty bars or so of other matter in Act I in either case. I always made use of the original Wagner, never so much as writing in a chord of my own. Occasionally it meant a little transposition to suit the key of the vocal extract; other than that I have never touched or even re-touched a bar of Wagner in all the concert versions I have edited. I may add that all these concert versions are unpublished.

Herbert Witherspoon, whom I have already mentioned as a pupil of mine, appeared at a Promenade concert this season. He had a fine bass voice. He afterwards went to New York to become Director of the Metropolitan Opera House. He was also Principal of the School of Music in Chicago.

I remember that he once offered me a sum in dollars that represented £14 an hour to hold master classes in singing, but when he told me that there would be three lessons in each hour and also that there would be a further batch of students on the floor of the teaching room (entrance fee five dollars per head) seated on chairs all round me, I refused point-blank. Had he offered me £400 an hour my answer would have been the same. It is absolutely unfair for any pupil to be expected to pay a fee for a lesson lasting twenty minutes. By the time the pupil has sung a few vocal exercises for, say, ten minutes and then sung part of a song for the other ten, the lesson has gone and nothing has been done. If I give a lesson I like to take at least forty minutes over it so that I *can* teach the pupil something. The American method of living at top speed and white heat cannot be successfully applied to art.

Lady flautists are not common but we had an uncommonly good one in Marguerite de Forest Andersen. She went down remarkably well with the Promenaders in a work by Chaminade. She did not, however, gain quite such a success with the members of the orchestra—with Albert Fransella in particular. He said as much—none too politely—to Robert Newman.

"If there are any more of them, I shall resign," he announced. Fransella was a great player and Newman took the hint. He engaged no more lady flautists!

Our 'cellos at this time were led by Warwick Evans, a lively young man with an amazing tone. I think he is the only 'cellist who ever managed to get through Boellman's absurdly-scored *Variations Symphoniques*. Tone on the 'cello is not easily come by; far from it. I have been deeply concerned about present-day students whose tone seems to me to be so small, and of little carrying power, and have been forced to conclude that 'cello tone is a gift and can rarely be imparted.

The name of Alfred Bruneau is forgotten in these days. Undeservedly so because he was a composer of considerable ingenuity. Bruneau was a music critic and wrote for *Figaro* and *Le Matin*. He left behind him three volumes of criticisms which show him to have had great musical insight and to have been possessed of a fine literary style. We hear little of him in these days though I still play his interesting suite from the opera *L'Attaque du Moulin* which Sir Augustus Harris produced so successfully at Covent Garden in 1894.

Robert Newman frequently invited celebrated organists to appear at our concerts. There was an organist in Jamaica who was something—a very *little* something of a composer. His particular vice was tone-poems. He insisted on sending me these perpetrations as soon as he had got them out of his system, but I regret to say I regarded them as one of his misfortunes and could never discover one good enough to produce. But still they came. Whether I was feeling a little guilty or not I cannot now remember, but as I knew he was playing almost nightly in New York I must have thought he was fairly good as an organist. At all events, I suggested his name to Newman.

"Very well," he said cheerfully. "Got his address?"

"I have!" I told him. "On dozens of his orchestral scores." Newman took down the name and address and the organist was engaged. In due course he arrived. Playing for safety first, I suggested he should perform the St. Anne's fugue of Bach. I thought I was safe because there is very little pedalling and it is not difficult in any other way. Indeed, one section is for manuals only. The next I heard was that the gentleman was at Queen's Hall at eight o'clock every morning in order to practise this fugue, and it was not long before Newman confronted me. I always knew the state of the barometer with Newman from the habit he had of looking out of the corner of his eye while his moustache bristled fiercely.

"Have you heard him?"

My heart sank. As a matter of fact I had not. I took an early opportunity of doing so and found his playing to be dull in the extreme. Moreover, I was punished for my sins by being regularly written to each season for years afterwards. However, I never advocated his being engaged again.

Perhaps St. Cecilia was angry with me for this! I think she must have been because, when I went for a quiet cruise to Norway and Sweden—after taking particular care to ask not to be put near anyone who knew anything about me *or* music— I was punished by being brought face to face with this very organist and his wife on the companion-way. I dodged as best I could but it was no good.

"How nice to see you again, Mr. Wood! I am *very* pleased. *We are to sit next to you at table.*"

I said how delighted I was and then sneaked off into a corner to do some sketching. But they always discovered me—and they *would* discuss music and talk about Reinecke. They completely ruined that cruise for me. It is said that St. Cecilia watches over all earnest organists. I think she might have remembered there was an earnest and also a very tired conductor who wanted nothing more than to get away from everything and do a little daubing!

Talking of St. Cecilia, I have always wished her day could be celebrated each year. Had I had the time in past years I should have made an effort to institute such an event. I hope one of my younger colleagues will think about the suggestion. Why should not music be honoured, as is the sister art, that of painting, by a representative banquet every year? This reminds me of a letter I received from the Rev. Arthur Farr, Rector of Coningsby in Lincolnshire. He told me that he had been instructing children in his church and, as it was St. Cecilia's day, had told them the story of her life and how she became the patron saint of music and musicians. After he had finished he examined his young scholars.

"Now, *who* is the patron saint of music?"

Bright boy: "Please, sir, I know. *Sir Henry Wood.*"

The Rector concluded his letter by saying: "I thought you would be pleased to know that at least one boy had put you in the calendar."

I notice the name of Zděnek Fibich in the Promenade programmes for this season. He came to us on September 21 when we performed his overture, *Une Nuit à Carlstein*, a beautiful work with a strong breeze from his native Bohemia blowing through it. Fibich is now forgotten whereas Dvořák and Smetana are still remembered, but all three were prominent representatives of the Bohemian Renaissance of the nineteenth century. I have always kept an eye on the works of Fibich, which appeal to me greatly.

We had a Scottish baritone named Robert Burnett with us for the first time. He had a rich quality rather on the bass side. We can always do with deep baritones and I was personally sorry when this particular one gave up singing in public and retired to Edinburgh to teach, for I well remember his spirited singing of *The Pipes of Pan.*

I produced Norman O'Neill's overture *In Springtime* during this season. He is best remembered for his music to the *Blue Bird* and *Mary Rose*, both produced at the Haymarket theatre, and how charming are both! O'Neill was the son of G. B. O'Neill the painter, and the husband of Adine Rückert (a pupil of Clara Schumann); she also appeared at the Promenade concerts this season as Mrs. Norman O'Neill.

I note too the name of George Halford in the programmes. We performed his excellent overture called *In Memoriam*. Halford's name may not mean much to London concert-goers now but I am glad to record it here even if only out of admiration for the work he did for Birmingham where, for years, he ran concerts introducing music that otherwise might never have been heard there. Birmingham has always taken pride in its music ever since the days when Mendelssohn conducted the first performance of *Elijah* in its town hall, and when the full history of its activities comes to be written the name of George Halford should not be overlooked. Birmingham owes him a great deal.

On October 16 Arthur Catterall made his first appearance as a soloist to play Joachim's *Hungarian Concerto*. I remember my first meeting with him very well; it was in a room at the back of a shop in Kendal whose proprietor was an oboe-player. This man asked me to hear a 'violinist friend' of his and offered to telegraph to Manchester for him to come over to Kendal. As soon as I heard Catterall play I knew him to be a first-rate artist and marked him down for future reference, considering he would make a splendid leader. Some years later I was glad to suggest his name to Robert Newman as a leader for the Promenades in Sons' absence. He led them for two years, eventually being appointed leader for the Symphony concerts after the B.B.C. took them over.

Catterall was a pupil of Willy Hess and Adolph Brodsky, and led the Hallé Orchestra from 1912 till 1925. He recently resigned his leadership of the B.B.C. Symphony Orchestra and has since been devoting himself to solo work and chamber-music, and is a professor at the R.A.M.

I am glad to notice some of the *Divertimenti* and *Serenades* for wind instruments by Mozart finding their way into concert programmes. As I have already pointed out, I was one of the first to introduce both pieces for strings alone and woodwind alone, being exceptionally fortunate in having so fine a combination of wind instruments in the Queen's Hall Orchestra by means of which I could give performances of real merit.

I remember rehearsing Mozart's *Theme, Variations, and Rondo in B flat* with Busoni in the hall. Busoni knew most things—indeed, it was not often that one could catch him out. He was like Liszt in that respect: there was little he did not know or could not play. However, on this occasion Busoni was taken by surprise. He came on to the platform, climbed up into my rostrum and followed every note while I conducted. The effect of the clarinets and *corni di bassetti* seemed to take his fancy. He was most enthusiastic over them.

"Those *legato arpeggi* are wonderful," he said. "Some of our younger composers can afford to learn much from Mozart."

Busoni came to the hall two or three days later to hear his *Eine Lustspiel-ouvertüre* which is one of two of a merry nature: it has buoyant themes and a particularly lovely second subject for the clarinet.

We also made quite a hit with some variations for strings by Arensky on the theme of that song by Tchaikovsky in which he sets the pretty legend of Christ playing with His brothers and cousins. They gathered roses, you remember, but only gave Him the thorns. These variations brought me so many letters that we gave a repeat performance. This was a *real* request performance, I may add—not one merely engineered by the management as is so often the case.

Another production this season was an *Episode* for orchestra (*Ausfahrt in Schiffbruch*) by a young German composer named Ernst Boehe. Nobody had heard of him until then, but the piece received such an ovation that Newman was all for doing it again at a Symphony concert and getting young Boehe to come over and conduct it—which is another proof that if a work is beautiful and attractively scored the concert-going public is not slow to recognize the fact.

We also had Marie Hall with us. In my mind's eye I can still see that frail, delicate girl coming on to the platform and can hear her faultless intonation and pure technique. Her father, I know, wanted her to take up the harp as he himself had done (he was harpist in the Carl Rosa Company) but his daughter was determined to be a violinist. A local teacher taught her until she was nine when Émile Sauret heard her play. He begged her parents to send her to the R.A.M. but this was not done. On the other hand, everybody of note heard her play and gave her advice. Elgar taught her in Malvern, Wilhelmj in London, Max Mossel in Birmingham. It was Kubelik, however, who really decided her career, for he told her to go to Prague and study under Sevçik. Unfortunately we do not hear much of Marie Hall these days; she is now Mrs. Edward Baring and lives in Cheltenham, but in her day she was among the fine women violinists.

I note among our novelties for this season three works of Sibelius. *En Saga* was one. A haunting work. That subject running throughout in the violas always attracts me. Whenever I direct this poem, I see the picture that wonderful theme so vividly portrays—I love the work, so thoroughly national—as of course is *Finlandia*. What a furore *that* created! It was a revelation to London.

The third work was *Karelia* which I am inclined to class with works like the *Casse-Noisette Suite* or *Peer Gynt*, but it never quite caught on with London concert-goers.

With all our activities we occasionally found time to perform outside London, especially as we had an invitation from Henry C. Embleton, a great benefactor to musical Leeds. He lavished money on the Choral Union and was a deep admirer of Elgar. I directed a performance this season of the *Dream of Gerontius* with Kirkby Lunn, John Coates, and Ffrangçon-Davies. Our reputation was now thoroughly established, for the Promenades had been running for over ten years. Looking back over forty odd years this does not seem long, but we thought differently then.

A final glance at the programmes for the year 1906 brings to my mind a Commemoration Concert given by the Concert-goers' Club to celebrate the 150th anniversary of the birth of Mozart. Edgar Speyer was in the chair and W. H. Hadow gave an interesting explanatory talk between the items. We began (as was fitting) with Mozart's first symphony, and ended with his symphony in G minor.

On April 3, I gave a first performance of the suite *Pelléas et Mélisande* by Sibelius, and on May 1 conducted a Bach concert in aid of the fund for the purchase of Bach's house at Eisenach and the endowment of a Bach museum. Madame von Stosch (Lady Speyer, or, more correctly *then*, Mrs. Speyer) played the *Chaconne* and Maria Philippi sang *Schlage doch* (from a secular cantata for contralto with *campanella obbligato*) and also an aria from the humorous cantata *Phoebus and Pan*. One of the programmes printed on silk now hangs in the Bach museum at Eisenach.

Our first performance of Borodin's opera ballet *Mlada* created a profound impression—sufficient to make it what it is now— a regular piece in our repertoire.

The proceeds of our last concert were usually devoted to the Queen's Hall Orchestra's Endowment Fund when Robert Newman gave the hall free of charge. When Chappell's took over the management members were paid out according to their contributions. Strangely enough—the season ended on a Friday instead of a Saturday with a concert at which the singers were Olga and Ffrangçon-Davies.

XXXIII

SOLEMN TRIBUTE (1907)

ONLY THRICE IN the history of the Promenade concerts have we played Chopin's *Funeral March* as an act of solemn tribute to the memory of distinguished musicians. Two of these occurred during the season of 1907—for Joachim and Grieg respectively—and the third the following year for Sarasate.

Joachim died two days before the season opened. I had not seen him since that happy day in 1904 when we had honoured him in Queen's Hall and he had played the Beethoven concerto so memorably.

On looking at the score of an arrangement of the march published by Breitkopf and Härtel, in the key of C minor, I was not impressed by it and, although there was very little time, sat up all night and scored it afresh. The Breitkopf arrangement transposed the movement up a whole tone. I transposed mine only a semitone—into B minor—but I directed the 'cellos to lower their fourth string from C down to B natural. Thus, with the help of four tympani (two players) I was able to bring out the full solemnity of the reiterating B and D in the bass. I also had a third drum tuned to F sharp. The melody of the trio section I gave to the solo violin with an accompaniment of harp and organ; for the repeats of both sections I had the melody played in octaves by strings over a woodwind accompaniment.

Having rejected Breitkopf's arrangement so unceremoniously, I was more than surprised, and certainly much gratified, when they asked me to let them publish it. This I did, though I realized that there would only be a limited demand for it in the concert world. However, the Italian composer Mancinelli, who conducted for so many years at Covent Garden, wrote to me and said that he had played it as a concert piece in America and that he never used any other arrangement. I was rather pleased about this for I had respect for Mancinelli whose superb performance of the *Meistersinger* (with Paul Plançon and the de Reszkes) I had by no means forgotten.

I was indeed sad at the passing of Joachim and felt equally the death of the gentle Grieg to whom we paid our tribute before the season was over.

Among the distinguished names of those who, fortunately, are still with us, is that of Walford Davies whose charming *Holiday*

Tunes I produced on August 29. Two days later I gave a first performance of Sibelius's *Danse Intermezzo No. 2*. Early in September we presented a new work by Ravel in the form of his *Introduction and Allegro for Harp and Strings*, the solo part being played by Alfred Kastner, a fine artist who left us to settle in Los Angeles as principal harpist in the Symphony Orchestra.

I notice another instance of Newman's promptitude over a novelty. Although we had a big repertoire of Mozart, he had heard of a first performance in Germany of a concerto for three pianos (not scheduled in Köchel's list) and nothing would satisfy him but that we must do it. On this occasion Verbrugghen conducted and the three solo pianists were York Bowen, F. B. Kiddle, and myself.

Verbrugghen, I note, was soloist when, on October 1, I produced Sibelius's violin concerto.

The next item of interest came two days later when I introduced Frank Bridge's splendid and dramatic song *Isobel* which stirred the Promenaders to enthusiastic applause. How beautifully written for the voice! as are also his songs *Love went a' riding* and *Oh, that it were so* among others.

Another name—rather a neglected one in England, I fear—is that of Max Reger, one of the greatest contrapuntists of modern times. I produced his *Serenade* but, owing to its length —it took seventy minutes—was compelled to perform it in two sections at two different concerts.

Reger himself came over to hear it and naturally we asked him up to lunch. Knowing nothing in the way of his likes and dislikes, I took the precaution of ringing up the German Club. They told me I must order in at least a couple of dozen bottles of beer.

Never shall I forget the appearance of our dining-room with all these bottles in a row. The lunch began at one—as lunches did in those days—but it did not end until half-past three when we retired to the drawing-room. Although the good Reger had lived up to his reputation and had consumed most of the beer without the slightest inconvenience to himself, I thought the poor fellow might be thirsty so I offered him a whisky and soda. He was so pleased with the first that he had three more. He did not, however, remain to tea. He drove down to the German Club after leaving us. I told Olga I thought he had gone down there to get a drink.

Walford Davies was at that lunch. I think he hardly knew what to make of this huge German, even though he must have known most of his music. Perhaps he thought, as I did, that Reger's output was almost, but not *quite*, as colossal as his intake.

We loved having Reger, of course, but I think Olga was glad he was not staying the week-end.

Other programme items of interest this very full season were Elgar's new suite—afterwards to be called the *Wand of Youth* (No. 1); the C minor piano concerto of Delius played by Théodor Szántó (to whom it was dedicated); and Vincent d'Indy's *Symphonie Montagnarde* for piano and orchestra played by Carlos Sobrino and since popularized by Cortot.

On the last night of the season Agnes Nicholls sang two novelties: Hamilton Harty's *Ode to a Nightingale* and Granville Bantock's aria *Christ in the Wilderness*. This closed the season— which reminds me that, four days previously, we had said farewell to Kreisler at a Symphony Concert on the eve of his first American tour. He played a *Rhapsodie* by Leone Sinigaglia whom, later, I was to meet in Rome.

XXXIV

THE SHEFFIELD AND NORWICH FESTIVALS (1908)

THE SHEFFIELD MUSICAL Festival originated in quite a modest way—by a performance of Mendelssohn's *Elijah* in 1895 under Henry Coward whose Choral Union undoubtedly contained the nucleus of the fine choir that was subsequently established. In 1896 there was a two-day festival, and in 1899 the first of the three-day festivals, both conducted by August Manns. At the next meeting, in 1902, I was asked to undertake the work of conducting. Naturally I was keen to do this as I had heard of the excellent choral singing in Sheffield.

On my arrival I became acquainted with several charming people all of whom I found to be devoted workers. First and foremost there was Mr. T. Walter Hall, chairman of the executive committee; after him, Mr. E. Willoughby Firth, J.P., and Mr. Noel Burbidge who shared the duties of honorary secretary; J. B. Marrison, the chairman of the chorus committee: Mr. and Mrs. J. H. Lawson who acted as secretaries to the same committee; and also the dear old organist, J. W. Phillips, of whom I became very fond.

Phillips was rather deaf and was unable to hear me tap on my desk when I wanted to stop, so I bought a bell which I rang instead of tapping, which, by the way, gave me the idea of using this means at Queen's Hall. My leader conducts for me and this bell is useful for attracting his attention at so great a distance. The first time I used it in Queen's Hall one of the members of the orchestra convulsed the others by saying: "Hot water for No. 10, please!"

Another excellent use to which I put this bell is when I have a composer sitting in the body of the hall listening to one of his own works in rehearsal. The only composer whom I have never been able to persuade to use it is Vaughan Williams who said his courage always failed him.

In Sheffield I also met Mr. and Mrs. J. A. Rodgers. He was music critic to the *Sheffield Daily Telegraph* and she often sang small parts at these festivals. Rodgers was an energetic, widely-read musician and a conductor (both chorally and orchestrally) of distinction. As chorus master of the Sheffield Amateur Musical Society he took the utmost trouble with his choir. Moreover, he actually conducted an experimental series of Promenade concerts in Sheffield for some years. Unfortunately, he died all too early.

Owing to the genius of Henry Coward as chorus master the choir sang with a snap and a verve with which no other choirs could hope to compete. Consequently, with a fine orchestra to accompany, I fancied I saw another of my dreams on the point of being realized: there seemed every chance of first-rate performances with real perfection of *ensemble* between soloists, chorus and orchestra. So often had choirs known their job and sung with fine interpretation—only to be let down by the orchestra.

It is not surprising when one thinks of the conditions—of the rough-and-ready method of 'running through' the works on the afternoon of the day of the concert. The brass, as a very good example, consisted chiefly of local theatre players. I do not wish to be unkind to any such players, but I am not exaggerating when I say I have rehearsed for two hours and literally have not heard one single chord in tune. No one who has not gone through it can even begin to imagine what some brass-players can be like.

There are people, I know, who consider these festivals to be valueless—at least in these days. I am of another opinion. We have a world-wide reputation for choral singing to keep up, and now that we have great orchestral organizations (which are virtually permanent orchestras) there is no reason why we should not keep it up. It is only at these festivals that choirs and orchestras meet.

It has been my personal rule to devote two entire days to rehearsing them *together*. Many a time I have directed rehearsals from 2 till 10 or 10.30 p.m. I have never wasted time in those rehearsals by asking the choir to sit down while I go over the solo parts. I do all that in London before I ever set foot in the festival town. I take both piano *and* orchestral preliminary rehearsals with principals so that the entire rehearsal in the festival town may be devoted to those who need it most—the choir and orchestra. As recently as 1936 I devoted four hours to a rehearsal for chorus and orchestra of Rachmaninoff's *Bells*, a work lasting only thirty-eight minutes. (This, of course, *in addition to* my previous rehearsals in London.) I may add that I instituted this system, which, I believe, has been followed by other conductors.

The 1902 festival opened with *Elijah*. The principals were Ella Russell, Ada Crossley, Ben Davies and Ffrangçon-Davies. Elgar conducted his *Dream of Gerontius* with Marie Brema, John Coates amd Ffrangçon-Davies, closing with his *Coronation Ode* after Ysaÿe had played the Beethoven concerto. Cowen conducted his *Ode to the Passions* and we followed with a selection from *Israel in Egypt*, Coleridge-Taylor's *Meg Blane* (which he had written specially), and Brahms's rarely-heard *Triumphlied* with an eight-part chorus and a solo baritone part sung by David Bispham. The *Triumphlied* is a mighty work but perhaps not highly inspired; it is rarely if ever performed in England now. Another novelty was Strauss's early work. *The Wanderer's Song to the Storm*, the words of which were Goethe's; and we closed the whole festival with the *Hymn of Praise*.

I recall the rehearsal in London for *Elijah*, as I had a slight difference of opinion with dear old Ffrangçon-Davies who could really be exasperating when the mood took him. He began *It is enough* with what was no more than a very quiet *falsetto*. I considered that this would not carry over four wood-wind instruments and the strings.

"Do you intend to sing it *falsetto pianissimo*?" I asked. "Because if you want to sing it that way I must cut out the two clarinets and the two bassoons, and *mute* the strings. Otherwise you won't be heard."

"I wasn't singing *falsetto*," said Ffrangçon.

"Excuse me, you were."

"I wasn't."

We tried it again to prove the point but the result was just the same. Neither would Ffrangçon admit he was singing *falsetto*. I left it at that, but at the concert he sang the phrase in a proper *mezza-voce*. He might just as well have sung it that way at the rehearsal—but singers are like that sometimes!

I feel I must mention Miss Marie Foxon, a member of the

executive committee, because she has done so much for the music of Sheffield. Not only as a teacher has she turned out quite a number of singers but she has been the means of bringing artists in the chamber-music world to Sheffield. Her sister is a well-known piano teacher in the north who has produced pianists who have played with me at the Promenades. Which reminds me that my chief concern over the Sheffield Festival was that it clashed with the Promenades. Robert Newman was averse to letting me off—in fact, he told me that money was being lost. Consequently, when the next invitation came in 1905 I was doubtful as to what I ought to do.

Olga and I discussed the whole question. We came to the conclusion that if I left the Promenade Concerts to go to Sheffield I should be doing the very thing I objected to my orchestral musicians doing. I had been fighting this deputy question for years. I could hardly have said all I did say and then calmly leave a deputy-conductor in my place. So there was nothing else for it: I had in very honesty to give up the whole project. It was disappointing but I asked to be released and was in turn asked to suggest a suitable conductor to take my place in Sheffield for the 1905 festival. I immediately thought of Weingartner who was an old friend for whom I had the deepest respect musically. He was duly approached and agreed to come on condition he might bring his own leader.

Having already spoken of this question of deputies in Chapter XVIII, it might be of interest if I explained the whole situation and how it was eventually dealt with. The members of the Queen's Hall Orchestra had accepted their individual contracts for a hundred and fifty concerts per season but had the right to send deputies in case of illness or when they were offered outside engagements. The former was reasonable enough; but the latter simply meant that when they were offered jobs at a higher fee than that which they received for being at Queen's Hall they took these jobs, sent a deputy at a lower figure, and 'kept the change'. It obviously paid them.

Had it only occurred in one or two isolated cases nothing might have been said; but to find on a Monday morning that my orchestra contained seventy or eighty new faces—people I had never seen before in many instances—was beyond a joke. I had to endure the same thing during the run of *The Lady Slavey*. I appointed a double-bass player whom I never saw again after the opening—and yet the show ran for a hundred nights.

So that it is not surprising that in 1904 I took up a definite position, Robert Newman (as usual) backing me up. The way he dealt with the situation was thoroughly characteristic. As I have already pointed out, he was a man of few words. Neither would he ever go on to the platform and make a speech to the orchestra. Instead he wrote down on a piece of paper what he wanted to say, never wasting a word, and proceeded to *read* what he had written. On this occasion he strode on to the platform in his customary business-like manner, halted, held up the paper, and read thus:

"Gentlemen, in future there will be *no* deputies! . . . *Good* morning!" With which he strode off.

There was no argument about it. Nothing was said to either of us, we simply found that about forty members had resigned and that we were faced with the task of replacing them. This we quickly did. Those forty players then formed an orchestra of their own which they called the *London Symphony Orchestra*. So that I was directly the cause of the formation of that well-known body of musicians who gave their first concert on June 9, 1904, Richter being their principal conductor until 1911. Everybody seems to have conducted them: Nikisch, Safonov, Arbos, Koussevitsky, Steinbach, Mengelberg, Furtwangler, Coates. My action may have seemed high-handed at the time, but it at least provided London with two permanent orchestras of first-rate quality instead of only one.

The autumn of 1908 was a busy one for me. The Sheffield Festival began on October 5, again clashing with the Promenades. This time, however, Newman sent for Colonne who came over to conduct the 'New Symphony Orchestra' while I was away and having taken the Queen's Hall Orchestra with me to Sheffield. For this festival there were no specially-written works, but I produced Delius's *Sea Drift* for the first time in England, and Debussy re-scored *L'Enfant Prodigue* for the occasion. Bach was represented by the *Matthew Passion;* Beethoven by the *Choral Symphony;* Berlioz by his *Te Deum;* César Franck by his *Beatitudes,* and Walford Davies by *Everyman.*

Apart from musicians, few people had heard anything of Delius or his music in those days and the committee was not at all in love with the idea of producing *Sea Drift.* I was rather hurt, to be candid, when they turned it down. I determined to produce it if possible, and wrote asking that I might meet the committee personally and play and sing the work to them. It was the subsequent enthusiasm of Walter Hall that brought about its inclusion in the programme. For all that, the chorus did not take kindly to it. They thought it an impossible work and although Dr. Coward himself was not really in sympathy with it he managed to bring it off. I purposely asked for Frederic Austin to sing the solo part because I knew of no one else who could be trusted to sing it *con amore*.

The *Beatitudes* we all found to be a lovely work, even if too long; at all events, by comparison with some of the works from which we suffer in these days it was by no means *dull*.

L'Enfant Prodigue was re-scored by Debussy at his own suggestion. He played it through to me on that memorable occasion when I went to Paris to persuade him to come over to England. I told him at the time I thought it would be a splendid work for the Sheffield Festival, especially as the choir was over-worked. As it demands no chorus I thought it would provide a convenient rest for the choir; moreover, it was new to this country. Debussy won the *Grand Prix de Rome* with it in 1884. The soloists we had were Agnes Nicholls, Felix Senius, and Frederic Austin. Senius had a beautiful tenor voice and an artistic delivery. He once sang *Gerontius* with me. Unfortunately, he died quite young.

Incidentally, we rather startled Yorkshire by singing *L'Enfant Prodigue* in French. That was a very new departure for Sheffield in those days. We also gave a first performance in England of a suite from the opera *Christmas Eve* by Rimsky-Korsakov, with Kirkby Lunn and Francis Harford, who was a *real* bass. On the Wednesday evening we opened with an overture in G minor by York Bowen.

Looking back on this splendid festival now, we had the pick of the artists of the day: Agnes Nicholls, Jennie Taggart, Edna Thornton, Perceval Allen, Madame de Vere Sapio, Mrs. Henry J. Wood, Jessie Goldsack, Kirkby Lunn, and Gwladys Roberts were our sopranos and contraltos, while for tenors and basses we had Lloyd Chandos, Felix Senius, Webster Millar, Frederic Austin, Dalton Baker, Herbert Brown, Robert Charlesworth, Francis Harford, Joseph Lycett and Herbert Witherspoon. Our instrumentalists were Teresa Carreño and Fritz Kreisler.

The Norwich Festival, when I took over its conductorship, claimed the dignity of nearly a hundred and forty years establishment. Festivals were held in Norwich as far back as 1770. They recurred in 1802, 1809, 1811, 1813, 1814, and 1817. These were hardly more than miscellaneous concerts held either in St. Andrew's Hall, the theatre, or else in the church of St. Peter Mancroft; and the orchestras had always been composed of local players, professional and amateur. In 1824, however, the first of the real triennial festivals took place, the chorus of a hundred and fifty voices and an orchestra of a hundred and ten

213

being conducted by Sir George Smart. Over ten thousand people attended that festival which showed a profit of more than £2,000. Sir Julius Benedict conducted from 1842 until 1878, and Randegger from 1881 until 1905. In 1839 Spohr came over from Germany specially to conduct his *Calvary*. So that this was a well-established festival.

Randegger, however, was no longer young and the committee felt that a young conductor was necessary. I knew, when I accepted the invitation to conduct, that the quality of the singing would not compare, tonally or interpretatively, with that of the northern choirs; but I was delighted with the work of Haydon Hare, organist of St. Nicholas, Great Yarmouth, for the splendid way in which he trained the chorus. He had no outstanding material to handle but the choir knew its job. We had a magnificent array of twenty-five soloists[1] and we also had Kreisler to play the Beethoven concerto and Carreño Tchaikovsky. We performed the *Dream of Gerontius* with Julia Culp as the Angel and Gervase Elwes as Gerontius. He, of course, interpreted it as only he could. We drew heavily on our soloists for a performance of *Phoebus and Pan* and our Wagner concert was made the more interesting by my employing four Wagner tubas made specially for me by Messrs. Mahillon of Brussels.

This innovation added to my work because the four players I employed lived at Kettering. There was nothing else for it except to get out of the train there on my way up north and rehearse these men for two hours. I had done this, on and off, for the past two years; but it repaid me. I obtained the effect Wagner wanted, which was the main thing.

We produced Bach's *Magnificat* with Kirkby Lunn, Gervase Elwes and Herbert Witherspoon; we also gave Elgar's *King Olaf* and Debussy's *Blessed Damozel* for the first time in England. Another novelty was *Christmas Night*, a choral work by Hugo Wolf.

I persuaded the committee to offer a prize for a *libretto* suitable for a cantata lasting forty to fifty minutes. I did this because I thought that by this means some new British composer might be induced to write something worth hearing, especially as I felt that our festival novelties had sunk rather into a groove. We seemed always to be having the same set of composers.

[1] Perceval Allen, Hattie Molineaux, Elsie Nicholl, Agnes Nicholls, Lenira Sparkes, Jennie Taggart, Mrs. Henry J. Wood, Julia Culp, Molly Deane, Jessie Goldsack, Kirkby Lunn, Gwladys Roberts, Dorothy Webster, Lloyd Chandos, Gervase Elwes, Noel Fleming, Webster Millar, Frederic Austin, Dalton Baker, Herbert Brown, Ward Cowdray, David Evans, Frederic Ranalow, and Herbert Witherspoon.

Gerald Cumberland won the *libretto* prize with his *Cleopatra* and the winning musical setting was Julius Harrison's. The solo parts were taken by Perceval Allen, Jessie Goldsack, Edna Thornton, and Lloyd Chandos who made a most excellent Anthony.

I had difficulty with the hidden chorus—but one always does. However, by dint of leaving doors and windows open, and also by having three harmoniums each tuned four vibrations sharp to its neighbour, I managed to avoid the inevitable flatness distant choruses always produce. The further away the singers were, the higher the pitch to which they sang. There is nothing like a little science in these matters!

We closed the festival with *Elijah* and I remember with pleasure that instead of having to put up with a local organist (who might have been good but who might have been superlatively bad) F. B. Kiddle was with me as organist for the whole festival.

Earlier in this chapter I mentioned that I prepared a Festival performing edition of the Bach *Matthew Passion*. In the next I give my reasons for so doing and a few examples.

XXXV

BACH'S *MATTHEW PASSION*

EVEN AS A BOY I was always fascinated by paintings of religious subjects. I have spent days in the various art galleries of Europe studying them. Now that I am approaching my three-score years and ten, I find the fascination as strong as ever. My first impression of Bach's *Matthew Passion* convinced me that he had the greatest reverence for the Passion of Christ; now that I know every note in that wonderful work I am still more certain of it.

Owing to my long association with the Promenade Concerts, and to the fact that the British public will never credit a musician with knowing anything except what they *think* he knows, I am regarded as the 'Conductor of the Promenade Concerts' and that only. I often wonder what they think I do with myself for the other ten months of the year! Perhaps this book will do something towards telling them.

My point in making this observation here is that it is a conductor's job to obtain complete mastery over his art, to regard it from the viewpoint of the times in which he lives, and to produce his performances as near to perfection as his material will allow. You will perhaps hear people say that of *course* they would rather go to a Symphony concert than to one of the Promenades because the standard of performance is likely to be higher. I entirely agree with them. So would I. The preparation for a Symphony concert is at least a degree more leisurely, and therefore more thoughtful than it can ever be for a Promenade concert. Four or five rehearsals for a single Symphony concert is one thing; a morning of rehearsal for tonight's Promenade *plus* a new work down for tomorrow night as well as a bit of the programme for the Strauss concert next week, is quite another. That is, if some composer-conductor does not expect me to give half an hour of my time to let him rehearse a work of his own lasting ten minutes! That sort of thing happens only too frequently. Rehearsing with your watch in your hand—every minute precious—is no joke either for conductor or orchestra. I have had forty odd years of it, so I am entitled to speak.

I do as much work in my own study as I do at Queen's Hall. Probably every other conductor does the same, but the fact remains that it *is* done.

It has been in those quiet hours of study that I have gone through so many of Bach's works note by note. Now Bach wrote the *Matthew Passion* for performance in a church. It was sung for the first time in his own church at Leipzig on Good Friday, 1752. His choir and orchestra were small and the condition under which he produced it were those prevailing in Germany in the mid-eighteenth century. Such conditions are not comparable with twentieth century, much less a Twentieth Century Musical Festival.

Busoni was never tired of reminding me of this. "If you are out to give an historical performance of a work like the *Matthew Passion*, all well and good," he said. "I'll be there to hear it. But you must do it in a church or else in a very small hall seating not more than three hundred people. You must use Bach's original instruments and instrumentation and with an Orchestra of twenty-eight, and Chorus of forty; but this would be absurd, in a large hall—in a modern Festival."

"But what about all this fuss over the use of Bach's instruments?"

"No good nowadays, unless used under his conditions," decided Busoni.

He was a clear-thinking man. Beyond his undoubted genius he preserved a sane outlook on life. He knew what he was talking about. So that when I came to carry out my intention of giving a festival performance of the *Matthew Passion* at Sheffield in 1908 I pondered over the question of the orchestra I should need to balance this choir of over three hundred voices—and a Yorkshire choir at that.

I suppose I could have saved myself eighteen months' hard work by using the performing edition of Robert Franz, so general in Germany. Franz added trumpets, trombones, and drums to balance the weight of a large choir. This I refused to consider because Bach had not used them. I intended to amplify Bach's own instrumentation but by keeping strictly to his score. For instance, take that dramatic and demoniacal shout:

EXAMPLE I. No. 54.

where the terrifying crash of the organ does not, in my opinion, require the addition of brass, as in the Franz edition.

That was why I determined to prepare a performing edition of the *Matthew Passion* for festival use. My 'performing' edition was based on that of Breitkopf and Härtel whose London Manager at that time was Otto Kling. He was a good friend to me, being always so helpful about foreign orchestral material. I told him how deeply interested I was in endeavouring to present a performance of the *Matthew Passion* at a forthcoming Sheffield Festival, but that I did not like the only English edition available From my point of view a great opportunity had been missed when it was translated from the German by not following more faithfully the Biblical text. We had several meetings and chats and finally through Otto Kling's influence Breitkopf and Härtel published a version made by Claude Aveling from the Book of St. Matthew. From this, I worked. I purchased four hundred vocal scores, marked them with breath and expression marks, and placed them in my Library for use with the Sheffield Choir of three hundred and elsewhere. In addition to a full—a very full—complement of strings I retained the *oboi d'amore* and *oboi da caccia* as before, but I reinforced my woodwind to *eight* flutes,

217

eight oboes, and *eight* bassoons. The bassoons, admittedly, were not used by Bach, but their tone blends with the other wind and they form a fine addition to the bass in the Choruses.

So that all I did was to *amplify* Bach's *original* orchestra. I imagine, had he lived to produce it at a twentieth-century festival performance of the work, Bach would have done the same.

He rarely used marks of expression; it was not the custom in his day. Probably he *told* his choirs what he wanted. I have always made it a rule to mark what I want sung as did Elgar because it saves so much time in rehearsal. In the original, the opening sentence of the chorus appears thus:

EXAMPLE II. No. 1

Come——— ye daughters, share my mourn——— ing, share my mourning

This is a three-bar phrase with a natural musical apex on the top G. Any great solo singer or instrumentalist would feel it as I have marked it thus:

EXAMPLE III

Come——— ye daughters, share my mourn——— ing, share my mourning

Again, at the entry of the Chorale *O Lamb of God Beloved* in the first Chorus, surely Bach meant this noble Chorale to dominate the whole? It is the *canto fermo*, standing by itself against the other counterpoints. Bach used boys' voices, and so have I faithfully followed, but I have found that unless a vast number of boys is used, they do not stand out above the texture of the mixed adult chorus. I have directed the Chorales as Bach intended for his church performances with the congregation joining the choristers, but have found this congregational singing in a large concert hall not only detracted from the spirit of reverence, but that a great deal of his masterly harmonization was lost. The only exception was on March 31, 1927, when I directed a performance in Queen's Hall rendered by the

Royal Academy of Music's Chorus and Orchestra, when the Chorales were sung by the audience and Chorus with beautiful effect. But then, the 'audience' was composed of eight hundred professors and students, each with a marked copy!

The amazement and terror of the villagers who ask How? Whom? What? and Where? can only be expressed by a *fortissimo* chordal ejaculation. I have so often heard it rendered meaningless and insincere by being rendered *mezzo-forte* or even *piano*. I have marked my score thus:

EXAMPLE IV

I noted a low E for the first basses in the last chord. How difficult it is to get a low bass note through! I marked it with a good many *forte*-signs and left it to those who could drive it through.

Then came the question of the Chorales. Some could be accompanied, some not. Some could be sung seated, some standing. There is nothing very original in that; but I did make an attempt to govern the length of the pauses. These Chorales make convenient punctuations in the Gospel narrative, but that is no reason why a ponderous slow *tempo* should be employed for them. Surely they represent the sentiments of a crowd of simple worshippers—villagers and peasants, most of them? The worst thing I know about a long pause is that it begets another— a long breath. Bach used the pause-sign as a convenient method of indicating the end of the line. Compare these two versions of half of the first chorale:

Bach's:

EXAMPLE V. No. 3

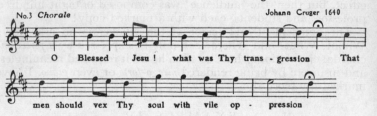

As I have marked it:

EXAMPLE VI

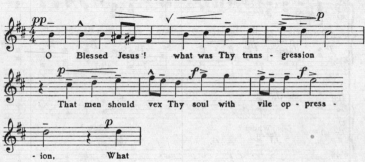

The effect is much the same in either case, but the crotchet rests in my version guide the eye and tend to make the rendering simple and natural. Another reason I would have the Chorales represent the expression of simple villagers is because their tunes are not Bach's at all. They actually *were* the sentiments of the peasantry and virtually folktunes. Johann Crüger (1640), for example, wrote the original melody of No. 3 (*O Blessed Jesu*) which is also used for No. 55. Heinrich Issac (who died in 1517) wrote that of No. 16 (*All mine the sin that bound Thee*) which is also used for No. 44. Hans Leo Hassler (1601) wrote that of No. 21 (*O gentle Shepherd, tend me*) which tune is repeated in four other Chorales, Nos. 23, 53, 63, and 72, with different text. This emphasizes my point regarding the congregational singing of them, as all would inevitably be sung with the same intonation —the same expression—or none!

I gave a great deal of thought to the accompanying chords of the recitatives. A harpsichord may be the traditional instrument—but how horrible this is today, in a large concert hall—and for that matter, horrible under any conditions. Indeed, to my way of thinking, the jingle-jangle of tinny sound from a harpsichord—especially after the majesty of a chorus or the simple sentiment of a Chorale—is not only inartistic but unmusical. The harpsichord is in itself a sweetly-toned instrument, fitted ideally for little Mozart and Bach pieces, in a drawing-room, but when used with a voice or in an orchestra, it produces a jarring effect—in fact we might just as well use mandolines and banjoes.

To use a piano does not help matters. The only instrument to use is the instrument of the church—the organ: just a quiet chord on the swell diapason with the box closed, and no pedals. Nothing could surely be more fitting.

In some instances I varied the organ chords, giving them over to four 'cellos and one bass, with beautiful effect. This, to my ear, gave a tenderness appropriate to certain sentences sung by the narrator. Bach scored reverently, for when Jesus Himself is heard the accompaniments are for Strings only. I went a little further still: I *muted* those Strings. Just a musical gesture; but it produces that *tonal hush* (if I may use such an expression) which alone should accompany the sayings of Christ in a Passion work.

How the accents matter in Bach's choral writing! and although he wrote to the German text, the following example which I have marked is I feel sure what he intended:

EXAMPLE VII. No. 5

Another—this time to emphasize the quarrelsome, cantankerous mood of the crowd:

EXAMPLE VIII. No. 7

I find that many editions do not differentiate between a *recitativo* and an *arioso*. There is a great difference: one is free in rhythm and the other rhythmic. This, for example, is marked wrongly as *recitativo*; it should be marked *arioso*:

EXAMPLE IX. No. 9

How Bach grasped the mood of the Apostles in the scene where they asked *Lord, is it I?* They began eagerly to deny that any of them should betray his Master; *murmuring* the question as here:

EXAMPLE X. No. 15

One of them must have been more anxious than the others. Perhaps it was Judas. Notice how Judas—if it is really he—insists as much as he dare on the A flat in the tenor part in bar three. He encourages the others and they all clamour together in the last two bars. That is how I look at it, at all events; hence my marking. One of the most difficult passages to interpret successfully is the following. I can only see one way of expressing its musical intention which surely must be taken to portray the footsteps of Our Saviour. I play the scale as marked—but *adagio*. Such steps would be very slow and laboured.

EXAMPLE XI. No. 20

In No. 25 the Lamentations of the Daughters of Zion sound like a distant, murmured prayer if taken *largo espressivo* and with *eight beats* in a bar:

EXAMPLE XII. No. 25

Though not nearly as frequently as Wagner, Bach nearly always employed a definite motif to suggest a definite emotion in his accompaniments.[1] What might be called the *Motif* of

---

[1] See Dr. Schweitzer's two volumes on Bach, translated by Ernest Newman.

Humility has a beautiful effect on the strings, bowed thus:

EXAMPLE XIII. No. 28

The words *Leave Him, bind Him not*! must surely have been spoken *quietly* and pleadingly—"No, *don't* bind Him." Therefore, surely, it is a mistake to render the passage other than as I have marked it:

EXAMPLE XIV. No. 33

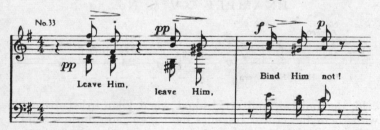

At the third repetition one surely sees the awe-stricken crowd and hears them raising their voices in the extremity of their emotions:

EXAMPLE XV. No. 33

The derision in *This fellow said "I am able to destroy the Temple of God and build it again in three days"* is obvious. A Temple could be destroyed and rebuilt in *time*, but in three days!— I therefore see that the three days are the words that convicted Our Lord, and on which great stress must be laid.

EXAMPLE XVI. No. 39

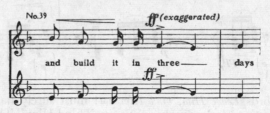

The two fugal choruses *Let Him be crucified!* I see thus:— first:

EXAMPLE XVII. No. 54

cold, demoniacal, and cruel—and when Pilate tried to reason with them the crowd becomes more and more furious, and I feel that Bach expressed this, by repeating the chorus a tone higher the second time. The A minor version I restrict to an ordinary *allegro*, but the second time I have it much louder and *allegro furioso*:

EXAMPLE XVIII. No. 59

In the entire score I have not tampered with so much as a single chord of Bach. I have never inverted, much less *invented*

one. My only deliberate alterations have been to restore Nos. 50 and 51 to their original positions in the score, and I have omitted *one* note. This, the bass B at the opening of the beautiful Contralto Aria: "*Thy Mercy show, O God.*" It always jarred on me, for it sounded as if the 'cellos and basses had come in a quaver too soon, and to my mind spoiled the entrance of the violin *obbligato*. This note I deliberately omitted:

EXAMPLE XIX. No. 47

Several years ago I had a good many chats with Gordon Craig who was running the Goldoni Theatre in Florence. He had taken it over as a dramatic school for training young producers. His great ambition, he told me, was to dramatize the Bach *Matthew Passion*. No doubt if he could have carried out his intentions he would have produced a marvellous result. He explained many of the scenes he had thought out, and drew many sketches—and what an artist he is—of what he had in mind. If Craig's ambition had materialized, we might have established an Oberammergau Passion Play in England. I knew Gordon Craig very well, and how idealistic are his productions. We all know how, after rehearsing *Hamlet* for months in Russia, he scrapped the production and began all over again! I am afraid that the beautiful vision he saw of this greatest of all dramas proved too costly to be carried out. He was very anxious that I should collaborate—for he knew how much I loved the *Passion* music.

XXXVI

THE DEATH OF OLGA.
DEBUSSY AND ROSA NEWMARCH (1909)

IN A PREVIOUS chapter I described how I went to Paris to persuade the great French composer Debussy to come to London to conduct some of his own works at Queen's Hall. On February 1, 1908, he came and a crowded audience was present to give him a real English welcome. I recall most vividly my first impressions of that dark, bearded Frenchman: his deep, soulful eyes; his quiet and rather grating voice; most of all, his enormous head. I have never seen such a head on a man of his stature; it reminded me of heads of the early Egyptians.

Debussy seemed delighted—almost like a child—because he thought that we in London appreciated his music more than his own countrymen in his beloved Paris. It may be that the French capital has always been hard on its composers. Berlioz, you remember, suffered agonies of mind because his popularity was greater outside France than in it, and César Franck complained bitterly because recognition was so slow in coming.

Debussy certainly had nothing of which to complain regarding the reception accorded to him in London that afternoon; for not even Strauss had received a warmer welcome. Moreover, I had thoroughly rehearsed *L'Après-Midi d'un Faune* and *La Mer* with the orchestra, paying the greatest attention to the fine, gossamer-like effects which pervade both works. At the rehearsal Maurice Sons acted as interpreter, for Debussy spoke very little English. Sons was useful in that way, being a most accomplished linguist.

In fact, nothing could have been happier for all of us; we liked him and he liked us. So that when Newman suggested a return visit to Queen's Hall on February 27, 1909, he was more than willing to come. We repeated *L'Après-Midi* because of the ovation it had received the previous year, but instead of *La Mer* we produced the three *Nocturnes*, Smallwood Metcalfe's Eastbourne choir undertaking the choral part in *Sirènes*.

Again, I had rehearsed the orchestra until there was practically nothing left for Debussy to do. The rehearsal went off smoothly enough but at the concert there was a peculiar accident. I do not remember ever witnessing anything quite like it. In the second of the *Nocturnes* (a movement called *Fêtes*) the time changes a good deal. To the surprise of all of us, Debussy (who, quite candidly, was not a good conductor even of his own works) suddenly lost his head, and his beat! Realizing what he had done, he evidently felt the best thing was to stop and begin the movement over again. He tapped the desk, and tapped again.

Then the most extraordinary thing happened. *The orchestra refused to stop*. It really was an amazing situation. Here was a famous composer directing a work of his own and, having got into difficulties, was asking the orchestra to stop and was being met with refusal. They obviously did not intend to stop: they knew that the audience would think the fault was theirs. Moreover, the work (which they liked immensely) was going beautifully and they meant to give a first-rate performance of it; which they proceeded to do and succeeded in doing. I never knew them more unanimous.

The audience by no means missed the fact that something had gone wrong because it was so evident that he had tried to stop the orchestra. At the end, in truly English fashion, they recorded their appreciation to such an extent that he was compelled to repeat the movement. This time nothing went wrong and the ovation was even greater than before. Debussy was non-plussed and certainly did not understand the English mind; but I was proud of my orchestra that afternoon and had the satisfaction of seeing that he had been proud to conduct it.

"They *wouldn't* stop!" he told me in the artist's room afterwards; I fancy he went back to Paris with something to think about.

I retain very pleasant memories of this great man and also of his wife who spoke English so fluently. I remember, too, Chou-Chou, his little daughter who, I seem to think, died early in life. Debussy died in 1918 and his wife some years after. He was a retiring, sensitive man who really disliked appearing in public; thus I felt I had indeed done something for musical London in getting him over at all. And all thanks, too, to Sir Edgar Speyer.

He was just an original thinker who contented himself with his music and his deep, intellectual criticisms. He was devoted to the whole-tone scale, the wide intervals of which appealed to his ear. He first heard the scale in Russia and ever afterwards it pervaded his own work, the delicacy of which reflects his own finely-constructed mind. It was an honour and a very deep pleasure to have known him personally, to have enjoyed his friendship, and to have been the recipient of a signed photograph of himself—a rare present for him to make to anyone.

Late in the season of 1908 we had another distinguished visitor in the person of Jan Kubelik. He was already known to me for I had met him when he made his *début* eight years previously at a concert under Richter in St. James's Hall. What a *furore* there was that night! London concert-goers were not slow to realize that he was capable of the most dangerous flights in virtuosity; in fact, people were saying that here was a second Paganini. The purity of his tone, his faultless intonation and technique, and his amazing facility in playing double harmonics took everyone's breath away. So that he now came to us with an established reputation, for we had all heard of his successes abroad, not only in America but throughout Europe where he had received all sorts of decorations and had been accorded the rare honour of an audition by the Pope.

Kubelik looked every inch a violinist. That far-away expression in his eyes, his dark hair, his slim figure, so well proportioned. This last characteristic I fear he has now lost, for I found it hard to reconcile his somewhat Chestertonian proportions, when I last saw him, with his erstwhile youthful grace. In his playing of the Paganini concerto he used Sauret's superlatively difficult *cadenzas*, and the more receptive of the audience must indeed have felt that the mantle of the great Paganini had fallen round these young shoulders. He proved his power again in Saint-Saëns's *Havanaise*.

Kubelik agreed with me when I remarked on the ineffective scoring of the Paganini concerto. "You don't want trumpet and drums in the middle of your fireworks," I told him.

"Why don't you re-score it? If you will, I'll play it."

I did so, but was not quite so reverent towards it as I had been towards the *Matthew Passion*. There were one or two spots (where tonic chords were held down in the accompaniment) which I took leave to embellish a little. I wrote in a few nicely-moving basses. Some considerable time afterwards Kubelik played the concerto again at the Albert Hall and we used my re-scored version. He was delighted and begged me to play it through. Instead of playing his own part he sat and listened. At the conclusion he professed himself satisfied; which was more than Maurice Sons was.

"Isn't he going to *play* it through?" asked Sons who was in quite a fever over it. I asked Kubelik whether he wanted to do this.

"No," said Kubelik. "I've heard it. That's quite enough."

230

I was surprised myself because these new harmonies were quite enough to put any soloist off, hearing them for the first time. Not so Kubelik. He sailed through the work with complete indifference and gave a remarkable performance.

Kubelik married Countess Czaky Szell in 1903 and has now retired from public work. His son Raphael, however, appeared in London as recently as October, 1937, to conduct the Prague Orchestra. He possesses all the elegance and grace his famous father once had; and we welcomed him here. I rather doubt the wisdom of the management of the Prague Orchestra sending *any* guest conductor over with that admirable body of musicians, which is so associated with its permanent conductor—Talich.

One of the really *treasured* women friends of my life has been Mrs. Rosa Newmarch. I first met her in this very year 1908— on the steps of Queen's Hall. Perhaps it would be more accurate to say that Mrs. Newmarch met me, for she actually made herself known to me as I was about to enter the hall for a concert.

"You will not know me, Mr. Wood," she said by way of introduction. "My name is Rosa Newmarch; I am deeply interested in what you are doing for Russian music. I have been living in Russia."

"Then you must meet my wife," I replied. "She is Russian by birth."

I have had cause to thank the day that gave me so dear a friend—one whom I meet continually. Even though she has passed her eighty-first birthday she can still hold her own at a dinner-table with most amusing conversation and sparkling repartee.

Though she was the daughter of Samuel Jefferson, M.D., and the granddaughter of James Kenney the dramatist (from whom she may have inherited the power of her pen), Mrs. Newmarch has always written under her married name. For some years she worked under Stassov at the Imperial Public Library in St. Petersburg, and the result of her labours there is reflected in articles and lectures which have done much to further the interest—in those days only just awakening—in Tchaikovsky. Our meeting had an important sequel, for it led to Mrs. Newmarch's becoming official programme annotator to the Queen's Hall Orchestra, a position she held from 1908 to 1920. Further than this she translated from the German a life of Brahms, from the French one of César Franck; she wrote biographies of Borodin and Liszt; of Tchaikovsky whose letters she translated from the Russian; she wrote a work on Russian Opera and edited books of Russian songs; she translated the *libretto* of Moussorgsky's *Boris Godounov*, Tchaikovsky's *Queen of Spades*, and Rimsky-Korsakoff's *Ivan the Terrible*. Last—but not least for me personally—she edited the *Living Masters of Music*, one volume of which is devoted to myself.

Mrs. Newmarch's analytical notes still attract me, for they are not merely a synopsis of the works she treats, but are beautiful specimens of English literature. I owe her something else; she was directly responsible for my interest in Sibelius. She had told me so much about him. She knows him intimately and is, I believe, at the present time writing his life.

It is not too much to say that Rosa Newmarch has been a rock upon which I have leaned often enough. She seemed always to understand my troubles, so to speak, at a distance. It has not been even necessary for me to discuss them with her, *for she was always at hand*, with real understanding. In paying her this little tribute, which I do in all sincerity, I can only add that I have never witnessed greater devotion in a daughter than in hers—Elsie Newmarch.

Present-day Promenaders will be interested to know that the first appearance of their favourite Myra Hess at these concerts also belongs to this season of 1908 when she played Liszt's E flat concerto—not the type of music with which she is generally associated in these days. Curiously enough, I was rather long in securing her for a Promenade. Not that Robert Newman was disinterested—quite the contrary; he knew that she had made an impression the previous year with a Beethoven concerto in a concert of her own at Queen's Hall. It just happened that we had been inundated with pianists; there was nothing more in it than that. However, once Newman did engage Miss Hess, he re-engaged her as many as five or six times in a single season.

Myra Hess has never lost the fascination she exerted over her audience then. She is perhaps best known for her rich, romantic interpretation of the Schumann concerto, but she displays no less musical style—which is often intense—when she plays the Brahms concerto in B flat. She still seems to me the dark-haired girl she was in 1908. She is more fortunate than a good many of us in that she has changed very little in appearance with the years. Her musicianship has matured— whose does not in thirty years?—but she *was* the great artist, even then. Incidentally, I may remark here that I have given my services for charity many times in the course of my long career, but only *once* for a solo artist's concert and that was for —Myra Hess.

Benno Moiseiwitsch is now one of the foremost of the world's pianists. He played to me this same year 1909 when he had just completed his studies under Leschetizky. I was deeply impressed and it was not long before Newman had introduced him to the Promenade public. We were very glad to have him with us during the War when so many artists were not available. I treasure the memory of a Saturday night dinner at the Savage Club in 1936 when 'Brother Benno' took the chair and introduced his great friend Rachmaninoff. I think every pianist of note in London must have been there that night. At this dinner George Baker spoke about my work and what I stood for, musically, in London. It was all rather embarrassing but I felt myself greatly honoured when, at the end of what I can only describe as an oration, he announced that it was the unanimous wish of the club that I should be made a life member.

Another pianist for whom I had the profoundest respect was Moriz Rosenthal who came to us in 1909 to play the Chopin E minor and the Liszt E flat major concertos. He had an extraordinary technique and always fascinated me whenever I looked at his hands. He held them in such a position that even his clear octaves *looked* as though he were striking chords; and yet nothing except the octaves sounded, for his playing was always crystal-clear. I accompanied the same Chopin concerto for him at Huddersfield three years ago and again noticed the same characteristic.

I always persuaded Rosenthal to play his arrangement of Johann Strauss's waltzes, which were really paraphrases but most masterly and ingenious. I admire their cleverness, for Rosenthal brings out the melody of one of them with his left hand somewhere in the tenor register and superimposes the melody of *another* up in the treble. He ought to publish these extremely clever arrangements.

A strange personality, his. He hated noise of any kind. Whenever he went to an hotel he would take stock of his surroundings with the greatest care. Perhaps he would see a pair of child's shoes outside the next bedroom to his. "That won't do!" he would say to himself. "I can't have children next to me." Off he would go to the manager and demand that his room be changed forthwith. He has even been known to preserve a perfect asylum in this respect by taking four rooms beside his own. He was very smart in this because he made his own the central one, taking those above, below, and on either side. Modern fl℘t life, I fear, would not suit Mr. Rosenthal!

At one time he had a mania for taking his own supply of drinking water which he carried about in a huge leathern bag of sufficient size to take at least two gallons.

Looking back over 1908 again, I note an item in a concert which gave me extreme pleasure at the time. Franz von Vecsey played a beautiful concerto by Jenö Hubay who was originally known as Eugen Huber. Hubay's success as a violinist lay less in his solo-playing than in his quartet leadership; at least that was Brahms's opinion. He thought most highly of Hubay's powers as a chamber-music artist. In addition, Hubay was a very great teacher, Vecsey being one of his pupils. Thus it was particularly interesting to me to hear both master and pupil in the double violin concerto of Bach which they played to perfection. Incidentally, other pupils of Hubay well known to concert-goers in these days are Telmanyi, Szigeti, and Jelly d'Aranyi.

Montague Phillips is a name well remembered, for his songs are still popular. He came to us this season with a new song with orchestral accompaniment which his wife, Clara Butterworth, sang for him. I always regarded Phillips as a fluent writer both for orchestra and voice, though the accompaniments to his songs are rather difficult for the ordinary accompanist. I have a feeling that they never sounded quite the same as when he played them and, perhaps, as when his wife sang them. This occasion, by the way, marks the first appearance of these two artists together at a Promenade concert.

I had the pleasure of producing his latest overture *Charles II* at a Liverpool Philharmonic Concert on March 22, 1938, and a real success it proved.

Last year I read of the death of Henry Hadley, a very well-known American composer and conductor. I was the first to play his orchestral works in England and produced his tone-poem *Salomé* in August, 1909. It made such a good impression that it enabled me to introduce nearly all he wrote for orchestra.

Here is an item of interest to present-day Promenaders who will not have forgotten Sir Walford Davies's *Solemn Melody* for strings. It has been played so repeatedly that it can hardly have been missed. I have found the date of its first performance in Queen's Hall, which was September 8, 1909. I note that, two days later, Rowsby Woof made his first appearance to play the E flat concerto by Mozart, the authenticity óf which has been gravely doubted. Woof is now a well-known professor at the R.A.M.

Strangely enough, out of all the hundreds of people I can clearly remember—in some cases in quite close detail—one has slipped my memory entirely. Although I have produced many of Moszkowski's works, and can clearly remember Dora Bright playing his concerto this season, I cannot recall ever having seen Moszkowski in person. I have no recollection of him beyond his photographs, yet it is a fact that he was at Queen's Hall in 1908. I *must* have met him in that case—but there it is: I have completely forgotten him. I have played the ballet-music from his opera *Boabdil* many times and like it for its fullness of character. It is very Moorish, as the Americans say—but I *mean Moor*. Poor Moszkowski! He was reduced to great want in Paris after the War. His is a very sad story. He died in absolute poverty in 1925.

On New Year's day, 1909, Marie Hall played the Tchaikovsky concerto and we also gave our first performance of Elgar's symphony in A flat—another instance of Robert Newman's quickness where a notable novelty was concerned. Richter had only just produced it in Manchester. That was Newman's way: either he was the first to produce a work at all or else the first to produce it in London. He never demurred when I made a suggestion regarding a novelty; rather was he eager to put it down for performance at an early date. Elgar, by the way, appeared this season to conduct his second *Wand of Youth* suite and wound up the concert with his overture *In the South*, so rarely played now.

There are a few choral items of interest in this season. I have directed Berlioz's *Faust* on many occasions, but I do not remember a performance pleasing me more than that given by the Hanley Glee and Madrigal Society which gave a really dramatic interpretation of the choral part of the work. The orchestra was thoroughly prepared with their own part because we had given it at Hanley only three weeks previously. The singing made such an impression in London that the choir stayed up in order to sing at Windsor Castle.

Another choral concert of note was when we brought up the Sheffield Amateur Musical Society which had been running for forty years before I took over the conductorship of it in 1904. On this occasion we celebrated the centenary of the birth of Mendelssohn by a performance of *Elijah*. We also had the Norwich Festival Chorus for the *Dream of Gerontius* and, once again, I noted the splendid training by Haydon Hare. As usual,

Muriel Foster made the perfect 'Angel'. She retired from public life some few years ago. Her husband was Ludovic Goetz who adopted his wife's name of Foster. He is a man who has greatly patronized the arts and is now a director of the R.A.M. I was indeed sorry to read of the death of Muriel Foster two days before Christmas, 1937.

My provincial activities this year took quite a goodly portion of my time. For one thing, Hans Richter decided to give up his conductorship of the Manchester Gentlemen's Concerts. I never found out exactly why he wanted to drop them; but it may have been that he did not like conducting a small orchestra. At all events, I remember him calling on me and asking me whether I would take on the work.

Richter seemed in very good spirits that morning. He had been to a concert of mine the night before and pleased me very much by his kindly remarks about my conducting; evidently he strongly approved of my decisive manner, in down beats especially. "Ach!" he said in his German way. "You haf dis *von* . . . *two* . . . *l'ree* . . . *four*," and proceeded to illustrate. I loved old Richter; he was always so downright.

I enjoyed, too, conducting the Gentlemen's Concerts. It was a great pity they were ever given up. The audience was a purely subscription audience which may or may not have accounted for the fact that it was so cold. I think that was really the coldest audience I ever encountered. Ysaÿe thought the same thing.

"Well," he remarked of one of their concerts, "that's the only time I've ever walked on to a platform to the sound of my own feet."

Yet that was by no means true of all Manchester audiences. Certainly not of those at the Free Trade Hall for the Brand Lane concerts, of which I speak again later.

Among my other journeys into the Provinces I included a visit to Exeter where I gave a matinée concert with part of the Queen's Hall Orchestra at the Hippodrome. I remember how we all assembled for rehearsal at twelve o'clock. There was much arranging of the seats for the orchestra as there always is in a place of this kind. We wanted to have a run through the symphony. During the rehearsal I noticed an appalling smell of fish and remarked on it to Maurice Sons. We wondered where it was coming from. As the rehearsal proceeded it became definitely worse, and when we disbanded at one o'clock I went in search of the manager to make inquiries about it.

"Oh, yes!" he said cheerfully. "That's the sea-lion."

"Sea-lion? What sea-lion? Where is it?"

"In a tank under your stage."

"That accounts for it," I said. "I thought I heard some splashing, but I never knew sea-lions smelt like that."

"Oh, *he* doesn't smell," said the manager. "It's the fish we feed him on. But come downstairs and have a look at him."

On the way down he explained that we had 'bought out' a menagerie for the afternoon, but that the sea-lion could not be moved. He had been left in his tank under the stage.

"Unless we keep feeding him," said the manager, "he will bark and spoil your music."

With which knowledge I had to be content. All through that concert, especially when the hall became warmer, the smell of fish was really beyond a joke. Indeed, I was quite sorry for people who had paid to sit in the front rows. During the soft passages I could hear that sea-lion splashing about in his tank and expected every moment to hear his bark; but he was so busy eating that he kept silence. And that, for all I know to the contrary, is the one and only time I ever 'performed on a sea-lion'.

London's music-lovers were thrilled at the first appearance of Sibelius on February 13, 1909, for the performance of *En Saga* and the ever-popular *Finlandia*. He had a fine reception and was thoroughly pleased with his visit. I notice also that I gave Granville Bantock's comedy overture *The Pierrot of the Minute* its first performance this season. An intensely beautiful though difficult work, it ought to have become more widely-known than it has. Had Ravel or Debussy written it, there would have been no question: it would have been played the world over. Other novelties of outstanding interest include the first performance of the second of Haydn's violin concertos by Marjorie Hayward, and a concerto for four solo violins and orchestra by L. W. Maurer.

Maurer was interesting. He was born at Potsdam and toured northern Europe as a *virtuoso* violinist, eventually settling in Moscow. He wrote several operas and concertos, but this particular work was first performed in Paris in 1838, the four soloists being himself, Spohr, Müller and Wich. For our own performance of it, four members of the Queen's Hall Orchestra undertook the solo parts: Arthur Beckwith, Sutherland Mackay, Frederick Stock, and Harold Lock. Maurer died in St. Petersburg in October, 1878.

Another novelty was a work in four movements by the well-known American composer G. W. Chadwick, Professor of harmony and composition at the New England Conservatory in Boston. The work was given under the title of *Symphonic Sketches* (the several movements being called *Jubilee*, *Noël*, *Hobgoblin*, and *A Vagrom Ballad*), and was dedicated to Frederick J. Converse of whose orchestral pieces I have given so many performances at Queen's Hall and with whom, as I think I have already mentioned, I have spent so many happy times in Boston.

Two days later I produced my own scoring of a piece that has gone the round of the world—Dvořák's famous *Humoresque*. It was Kreisler who first suggested I should score it for small orchestra; later he himself made his own arrangement of it for violin and piano, now so well-known. My orchestral version has remained a popular item at the Promenade concerts for many years.

On September 28, Miss Christian Carpenter made her first appearance to play Paderewski's new *Polish Fantasia* (op. 19) which had then only just been produced by the Philharmonic Society under the direction of Sir Alexander Mackenzie. I was interested in Miss Carpenter because she was brought to me by John Walker of the firm of celebrated organ-builders. He was a neighbour of mine in Elsworthy Road and, as he was a practical scientist and a keen inventor of organ mechanism, I always enjoyed his society. He had a workshop in the garden where a few men were always at work, and in his house was quite a large organ which actually went through the drawing-room floor into the basement. Miss Carpenter, by the way, afterwards settled down in Bath as principal teacher of the piano at the Royal School, so ably directed by Miss Steel.

Sibelius's suite *Svanehvit* was produced for the first time on September 29 and at the same concert Frederick Kiddle played Bossi's new organ concerto. We concluded the concert with the first performance of young Oskar Borsdorf's *Concert Overture* in D. He was the son of the great horn-player whom I mentioned in connection with Nikisch, and was a pupil of the R.A.M. under McEwen and A. E. Izard. This overture—a brisk, breezy work full of energy and high spirits—made a great success with the public. Oskar Borsdorf later settled in New York where we have since often met. He has been successful with his light operatic and other works.

What a delightful person that Roman aristocrat Don Roffredo Caetani turned out to be! His full title was *Principe di Bassano* he was the son of the ducal house of Sermoneta, though his mother was English. Dear old Elgar brought him to me and I looked over his orchestral compositions (he was a pupil of Sgambati) and became so much interested in his *Prélude Symphonique* that I produced it on October 5. This work was one of a set of five, lyrical and charming in character, showing great imagination and excellent workmanship. I am sorry no opportunity has occurred of introducing more of this highly-cultured and keenly intelligent musician's works.

We seemed to have quite a run on works for four solo instruments and orchestra this season, for on October 7 I produced another concerto for four violins by Leonardo Leo, the old Brindisi composer born in 1694. Needless to say, it was very different in character from Maurer's; neither do we know who played it at its first production; but we do know that poor Leo died suddenly in 1744 while seated at his harpsichord. Our own soloists were again members of the orchestra: this time they were S. Abbas, H. Koenig, E. Groell (a nephew of Arthur Nikisch) and D. Weinberger.

On the following evening we produced a work for four solo horns for the first time in England. This was a very difficult *Concertstück* by Schumann (op. 86). The soloists—all our own men—were A. E. Brain, Brain Senior, Oskar Borsdorf and G. W. Smith. This work was written in one of Schumann's most prolific years (1849) and is not heard nearly enough. It was a favourite with Schumann himself and is contemporary with *Manfred*. It certainly does require four fine and even horn-players: but these we had in 1909.

Another novelty of a most intriguing character was Walford Davies's *Songs of Nature* written for a chorus of treble voices, piano, flute, horn and strings, in seven movements. I suppose this work must have been repeated, but I cannot remember when. One of the most interesting of all the novelties this season came fairly early (August 31). It was a musical satire by Moussorgsky called *The Musician's Peepshow*. The easiest way of describing it is to reproduce Mrs. Newmarch's analytical notes. She says the work "was undertaken at the suggestion of Stassov, was often sung at his house, and was enjoyed long after the death of the composer by those who remembered the individuals it characterized. A showman invited a crowd to walk into his booth and take a look at his collection of puppets. The musical parody of the *scena* is obvious; there are no attempts at elaborate joking, and the mood is, on the whole, that of healthy and good-tempered raillery. Moussorgsky laughs at a silly order of things that deserved laughter; but we never find him sneering at the tendencies of his great contemporaries merely because he was out of sympathy with them.''

I scored *The Musician's Peepshow* specially for the Queen's Hall Orchestra. I did so because I was always keen to add to a singer's repertoire, and this work suited Thorpe Bates, then at the zenith of his career. The words were translated by Mrs. Newmarch and required the perfect diction Bates was capable of giving them. They began like this:

> ' Walk up, please, and see the show,
> Gents and ladies, one and all;
> Pay your penny—come and see
> All the wonders of the show!'

The last concert of the season, October 23, 1909, proved, alas, to be the last time my dear wife was to sing in public. She had been down to Birmingham earlier in the year (March 25) when she sang three of Delius's songs.[1] On this last occasion she sang two new songs by Stanford which he had specially orchestrated for her: *I think that we were Children* and *O Flames of Passion*. The poems were gleaned from a manuscript cycle called *Songs of the Triumph of Love* by Edmund Holmes. The first was of a dreamy nature, charmingly orchestrated and in great contrast with the second which was fiery and scored for a very full orchestra including trumpets, trombones, and harp. The accompaniment of this song interested me. Over sustained chords for bass and woodwind the strings and drum had *staccato* chords on the second and third beats of the bar, suggestive of the rhythmic pulsation of flames. The song ended with a triumphant outburst of sonority for the last line: *In Love's White Flame, in Love's Transcendent Light!* I remember how well both songs suited Olga's voice and what an ovation she received.

Although these ten weeks of arduous work were at an end I had no respite from concerts and rehearsals, for there were still the Symphony concerts on October 30, November 13 and 27, and December 11 as well as Newman's benefit concert on November 21, while the Sunday concerts (which had begun while the Promenades were still running) continued from September 26 weekly until the spring of 1910. I had very little time to devote to anything other than work and had been, in addition, sadly torn with anxiety during the past few weeks, for my dear wife had sung at that last concert in great pain. She had steadily grown worse and was removed to a nursing

[1] *Das Veilchen, Abendstimmung, and Eine Vogelweise.*

home either on December 3 or 4—I cannot remember which; but there was a Sunday concert on the 5th and I am certain that I did not direct well that day, for I wanted to stay at the nursing home, and decided to go on with my work only on persuasion from my dear friends Dr. Cathcart and Siegfried Schwabacher, for the surgeon's verdict, "This is very grave," was with me subconsciously every moment.

The kindness of the Speyers during the next few weeks I cannot recall without a lump in my throat. They left me at perfect freedom to take meals in their house at any hour, and their kindly advice to go on with my work was coupled with that of Robert Newman and my dear old friends Cathcart and Schwabacher. I felt the strain intensely, for I visited the nursing home three times a day and always went there shortly before midnight to bid my dear one good night.

Olga died on December 20. Her passing left a greater blank than that of even my dear mother in that I had now lost a comrade and the love of my life. What I should have done without the comfort of my friends I dread to think, for I know I felt that life, for me, was now devoid of all meaning. Dr. Cathcart did for me all that I should have done myself and, after her burial, took me home and comforted me a little with the knowledge that, had she lived, she would never have been able to enjoy the fullness of life again. I remember him taking me away to Folkestone for a few days but I am not sure when this actually was because I notice from programmes that I directed a concert on Boxing Day and another on New Year's Day.

To Schwabacher I owe my ultimate recovery from the great shock I had received for he helped me to regain my normal stride. He never taxed me with his presence but he was always there when I needed him and always ready with his kindly advice. On reflecting I wish I had acted on some of it, but when one is young one has one's own way. Schwabacher helped me in my musical life, my private life, and as far as I was able to command, my financial affairs. He was ever my great and privileged friend.

It is not often given man and woman to find such a perfect union as ours had been, for Olga was so much the embodiment of all I ever wanted musically and artistically, coupled with a worldly sophistication with which her upbringing had endowed her (and which was so lacking in me) that she was able to help me form plans for a future I could never have conjured up for myself at that time. It is quaint that, in thinking of her now,

I should recall so many stories and incidents of her childhood in Russia and England. I recount one only here as it is connected with music.

Anton Rubinstein was a devoted friend of Olga's mother, Princess Sofie Ouroussoff (*née* Narishkin). One day during a visit to her, Rubinstein took the small Olga on his knee and fed her with pieces of sugar dipped in his after-luncheon coffee. Although such luncheons in Russia often lasted from 12.30 to 4, Olga always looked forward to Rubinstein's visits. When was 'her Anton' coming again to give her more coffee-sugar . . .?

So ended the happiest, the dearest years of my life. . . .

. . . In Love's White Flame . . . in Love's Transcendent Light. . . .

XXXVII

I WORK ON ALONE (1910)

Work was the only thing for me now. Fortunately I had plenty of it, but although it brought me in contact with literally hundreds of people I was very much alone. I drowned at least part of my sorrow in painting and now took regular lessons from Edward King, sketching a good deal from nature.

Then there was my teaching. I think nearly every pupil who has since made a name must have passed through my hands this year. I had the Gentlemen's Concerts in Manchester, as well as my choral rehearsals in preparation for the festivals of 1911.

I remember going with Schwabacher to St. James's theatre to see *The Importance of being Earnest* in which Sir George Alexander was playing lead. I was to meet him often later on when he lived near to me; in fact I was with him only the week before he died. We enjoyed many chats about art.

On April 3 I directed a memorial concert to Colonne for the Sunday Concert Society. I always felt Colonne had been over-shadowed to a degree by Lamoureux—at any rate, so far as Queen's Hall was concerned. I know that Newman was always inclined to push Lamoureux rather than Colonne, and yet I always thought Colonne the more talented of the two; certainly his readings were broader—more German—even though he was not the trainer Lamoureux was. I recall how anxious I was for poor Colonne for he looked far from well when he arrived from Paris to take my place at Queen's Hall in 1908 during my absence in Sheffield for the festival. He told me then he thought this would be his last visit to London. Incidentally, we all knew him as *Edouard* Colonne but his baptismal name was—*Judas*! One is left wondering what can have been in the minds of his parents to give him such a name. Colonne died in Paris on March 28; he was nearly seventy-two.

On July 10 I accepted an invitation to conduct the *Dream of Gerontius* at Arundel Castle, the seat of the Duke of Norfolk. For this Henry Coward's Sheffield Musical Union provided the chorus.

I remember how deeply impressed I was by the wonderful old castle, founded in the tenth century, with its magnificent Norman keep (over a hundred feet high) and its deer park of 1,200 acres. The Duke and Duchess of Norfolk were great patrons of music; indeed, it would be difficult to estimate what they have done for Sheffield's festivals. We gave a perfect performance of *Gerontius* in their lovely ballroom and in the presence of distinguished guests.

I retain pleasing memories of that visit. For one thing, it was a lovely July day and I much enjoyed listening, out on the grass terrace, to the choir singing madrigals and part-songs conducted by Dr. Coward. It was once again brought home to me that Henry Coward was indeed the master choir trainer of England. Another point which I have never forgotten was the beautifully finished singing of Herbert Heyner in the parts of the Priest and the Angel of the Agony.

The Duke of Norfolk was very friendly. I had already met him in connection with the Sheffield Festivals. We strolled together in the beautiful grounds and, as we walked, he drew my attention to a notice *Please keep off the Grass* and told me that he happened to be in the grounds on one of the 'public days' and passed a party of trippers, disregarding his own notice by walking across the grass. One of the party shouted to him:

"Hi! Can't you read what it says there? It's the likes o' you that gets us into trouble."

The Duke then inquired where I was sleeping. I described the situation of the bedroom which had been allotted to me.

"Ah yes!" he said. "I have slept in that room. I hope you won't find it too light."

The remark referred to the presence of a round window set in a recess in the thick wall, for which reason it could not be curtained.

"But if you find it too light—do what I always do," he counselled me. *"Stuff your trousers in it!"*

That was on July 14. I was in York on the 18th for the four-day orchestral festival (18–21). After that I began seriously to think about a holiday which I sadly needed after all I had gone through the previous Christmas. I went down to Hindhead for ten days—from July 30 until August 8. After which—nothing but work for the rest of the year.

The sixteenth season of the Promenades began on August 23 when I produced Moussorgsky's now famous *Song of the Flea* which was sung by Robert Burnett. I orchestrated it for the occasion and the words again were translated by Rosa Newmarch. I need hardly say it was a tremendous success—as, indeed, it has been ever since.

I produced Arnold Bax's *Opus One* this season. It was a tone-poem called *In the Faery Hills*. In a programme note he described what he meant by it. "I have attempted here to suggest the revelries of the 'Hidden People' often at the twilight hour in the shadowy depths of the hollow hills of Ireland."

I like Bax in this mood. I feel it is the true Bax—that dear, kind man of the shy smile, I have known so well for so many years. He is *really* unpretentious—but then great men are.

I also produced not exactly an *Opus One*, but an *Opus Three* of Busoni's on October 8. Looking back, it seems quaint to think that he was quite unknown in those days as a composer. He was regarded entirely as a pianist. The work in question is known as the *Lustspiel-Ouverture*. The following year I produced a work which present-day Wagner-lovers would hardly believe ever existed. Who knows Wagner's *Symphony in C*? He wrote one, and I produced it in 1911.

On September 24 I was with the Queen's Hall Orchestra at the Crystal Palace conducting a concert at which the singer was Tetrazzini. She sang *Caro Nome* and *Carnevale di Venezia*.

I remember her coming along to my house for a piano rehearsal. No trying to get out of attending my piano rehearsal here, as do some of our younger and less renowned artists of to-day! A plump, cheery little woman always ready to chat about singers past and present in the most animated fashion. After we had finished our rehearsal I asked her to sing me the Polacca from *Mignon*! (*Io son Titania.*)

Tetrazzini shook her head.

"I am sorry but I am not singing it this season," she said.

"Not singing it? I don't understand."

"No; I am not singing it *this season*," she repeated. "I never try to keep up more than three *coloratura* arias at once. I just practise those three. But I promise to sing it for you the next time I come to England."

That is the way with these really great artists. I have noted it in others. Gerhardt, Patti, Nordica, Ackté, and Melba in similar circumstances would have returned the same answer. They decided upon their season's repertoire, and devoted their whole attention to perfecting every detail. How different from the procedure of artists of lesser degree who accept engagements to sing *anything*—no matter what or whether they have ever seen it or not! Conversely, how shortsighted the policy of engaging artists at the last moment and confronting them with something they may manage to get through but cannot possibly *build into their voices* in the time allowed them! The voices of Tetrazzini and Melba were unscratched, highly-polished surfaces which lasted fresh and bright long after the age when so many voices become hard and dull.

Even Artur Nikisch told me I did more work in a month than he did in a year because circumstances compelled me to tackle everything as it came (whether I actually wanted to or not), whereas he himself could plan a tour and repeat his programme wherever he went.

Referring to Tetrazzini again, I remember the vivid account Percy Pitt gave me of her *début* at Covent Garden, when she appeared as Violetta in *La Traviata* on November 2, 1907. Neil Forsyth, the manager, was not particularly interested in her—at least, it would seem so because he did not even trouble to go down to the Opera House that night. At the end of the first act Tetrazzini received twenty recalls and the excitement of the audience was intense—so much so that Pitt telephoned Forsyth.

"For heaven's sake come down," he said. "This woman's a terrific success. You *must* hear her!"

Forsyth arrived during the second act, and saw and heard for himself. At the end of the opera the audience expressed the wildest enthusiasm and Forsyth immediately offered Tetrazzini a contract.

By the end of 1910 I was more or less prepared for the very full year that was to follow—a year that was destined to be perhaps the busiest of my life, for, apart from my usual activities, it seems to have been a year of festivals.

XXXVIII

ELGAR, CASALS, CARL FLESCH, SEVÇIK, AND RACHMANINOFF (1911)

1910 HAD GONE. Its months might have been only weeks for I had seen to it that I had no idle moment to remind me of my loneliness; yet, strangely enough, the results of some of my working hours are a lasting reminder for I made many sketches during this year.

1911 contained a red-letter day for me—February 23. On that day I was knighted by His Majesty King George V. That I appreciated such an honour goes without saying for it set the seal upon my work. But I remember how grateful I felt to my wonderful public who had supported me so splendidly for the past sixteen years and from this support had brought about this Royal recognition, and for the way in which they had entered into the spirit of my determination to help them to learn and love the great classical masterpieces. I would say here that this determination has not diminished with the years of routine (such as the Promenade concerts have necessarily to be), and also that I have always given of my best, no matter what school of thought I have been called upon to interpret.

A concert on New Year's Day was the beginning of a gigantic year of work, a summary of which is worth recording. There were twenty-nine Sunday afternoon concerts; thirty-eight of various artists in London and of certain provincial societies; sixty-one Promenade concerts; twelve Symphony concerts. That makes a total of one hundred and forty concerts. In addition there were the festivals at Sheffield and Norwich; also the Empire Festival in the Crystal Palace at which I directed four out of the six concerts as well as the London Musical Festival. Besides the necessary rehearsals for these London concerts, I directed some forty chorus rehearsals in the Provinces. So that I filled practically every moment.

On March 18 Casals made his acquaintance with the Queen's Hall Orchestra and myself. His is an interesting if somewhat curious personality. There is no outward show of virtuosity to attract the public, yet his technique, tone, and musicianship positively command riveted attention with the first stroke of his bow.

At this concert he played what is to my mind the finest of all 'cello concertos—Dvořák's in B minor. As usual, I used my own band-parts and whenever the solo 'cello entered I reduced the accompaniments to a double quartet of strings and two basses, only allowing the full strings to play the *tuttis*. I found this worked admirably because there was no danger of swamping the soloist—so easily done owing to the depth of the 'cello's register.

Any conductor who has accompanied Casals knows how fidgety he can be over a concerto. He has a habit at rehearsals of turning round to the orchestra and hissing them down if they dare to make too strong a *crescendo*, but I flatter myself I have always given Casals entire satisfaction. Before he arrives I always make a little speech to the orchestra.

"Now, Gentlemen! Casals will be with us in a few minutes. You know what an intensely light orchestral accompaniment he demands—no colour at all. So I beg of you Strings to try to play on one hair of your bow; perhaps two—sometimes three—but never more. Thus you will save endless stoppages and many scowlings and hisses." This always has the right effect and I think I am pretty safe in saying that I am the only conductor in the world with whom Casals has risked playing the Boccherini concerto *without a rehearsal*. There is no doubt that the Queen's Hall orchestra *did* accompany concertos and arias in faultless style.

On October 21 that marvellous dramatic singer and actress Aïno Ackté appeared. Her temperament was like quicksilver. In the aria *Herbstabend* (Sibelius) and the closing scene from *Salomé* (Strauss) she simply electrified the audience. Hers was one of clearest and brightest soprano voices I ever heard. During the course of my continental travels I was privileged to see her in no less than five performances of *Salomé*. Rarely has a woman been endowed with the full equipment that goes to make what a really great opera-singer needs—looks, figure, voice and brains. She had all these, added to which she was a great and really convincing actress. I believe I am right in saying she was the only *singer* who ever actually danced that voluptuous Dance of the Seven Veils, the usual procedure being to engage a *danseuse* for the purpose. I persuaded the Birmingham Festival Committee to engage her for Verdi's *Requiem*, the other artists being Muriel Foster, John McCormack, and Clarence Whitehill—and a truly dramatic performance, in the Italian tradition, resulted!

An outstanding event during this season's Symphony concerts was the production of Ravel's *Pavane pour une Infante défunte*. I had previously given the actual *first* performance of this little gem at the Gentlemen's Concerts in Manchester on February 27.

The Sheffield Festival of 1911 was held from April 26 to 28. To me this was of importance because, for the first time, I was my own chorus-master, directing the entire festival. I remember telling Artur Nikisch this (some time after) and recall his reply in that soft voice which I had learned to revere:

"Ah! That is the ideal way of giving a *real* musical festival because the chorus really learns your method and beat."

Bach was represented by his B minor *Mass* and a repeat of the 1908 performance (without cuts) of the *Matthew Passion*. The only unknown work of the festival was a cantata by George Schumann (born 1866) of the Berlin *Singakademie*. Although George Schumann is not a very original composer, this work is excellently written for both chorus and orchestra. It delighted the Sheffield public. I am inclined to think, however, that it has not been repeated in England—which is a pity, for its broad, fine phrases and excellent *libretto* appealed to the chorus who really loved it, and how wonderfully our choruses *can* sing if they *enjoy* the work in hand.

I also gave what was probably the first concert performance in England of the *Ring*, and our last concert was devoted to a splendidly-rehearsed and finished rendering of part of Granville Bantock's *Omar Khayyàm* as well as the Grail scene from *Parsifal*.

When I look back on those days I realize what a great choral festival Sheffield's was. I shall always remember the quality of the contraltos—who were *real* contraltos, not merely rows of light mezzo-sopranos—while the balance of the four parts of the chorus was irreproachable. And what enthusiasm—local and county—from the Duke of Norfolk to the school children! Not a seat vacant in the hall at any one of the performances!

I deeply deplore the fact that the fine, proud spirit with which the city entered into those festivals has gradually faded into a kind of apology when patrons are asked to support it nowadays. The attitude appears to be 'please support this festival which, it seems, we have *got* to give because one or two of the old-time enthusiasts seem to consider it our duty'.

How different it used to be! In those days we were fêted and feasted. House parties were the rule, not the exception. Sheffield was as famous for its festivals as for its steel. Of the 'props' of those days, Colonel Herbert Hughes and Mr. Willoughby Firth have passed away though Mr. Walter Hall and Mr. Noël Burbidge are still alive; but what are a few idealists in a multitude of differing factions mostly out for self-aggrandisement? In those days the whole community was out for Sheffield's glory.

The London Musical Festival comprised six concerts given between May 22 and 27. We opened the first evening with the *Dream of Gerontius* followed by the first performance in England of Reger's *Hundredth Psalm*.

Gerontius ought to have created a far deeper impression when it was originally performed at the Birmingham Festival (in October, 1900) than it did. I know how anxious Richter was over it. I can see him now, pacing up and down his bedroom with the score on the mantelpiece, but I shall never believe he was to blame for its failure. I do blame him, however, for not postponing its performance when it became evident that the copies would not leave the printers' hands until a few months before the production. The choral idiom was so new, so strange and so excessively difficult for a chorus brought up on the *Elijah* style of writing that at least another six months of choral preparation would not have been too much.

I seized an opportunity of going to the Lower Rhine Festival at Düsseldorf early in May of 1902 with my friend Alfred Kalisch to hear the work under Professor Buths who had translated the *libretto* into German. He had rehearsed the chorus for nearly two years and had gathered together a special orchestra of a hundred and thirty players. The three soloists were Muriel Foster (the creator of the Angel's part), Ludwig Wüllner, and Johannes Messchaert. The astounding impression the performance made on everyone has remained in my memory ever since. It is quite impossible to describe the ovation dear Elgar received; he was recalled twenty times after the end of the first part. I have never seen an audience so excited nor a composer so spontaneously acclaimed; certainly not an Englishman—unless, perhaps, Sullivan after the first performance of the *Golden Legend* at the Leeds Festival in 1886. I am proud to remember that I was present at the great banquet given by the town council of Düsseldorf in honour of my compatriot whereat were gathered all the foremost critics and musicians of Germany. Strauss delivered an oration couched in the warmest terms. I fear I cannot reproduce its text but I remember how he eulogized Elgar, greeting him in the name of German musicians as 'this new and great English genius'.

As a Choral Work *Gerontius* is now supreme in England, and should be likewise the world over. Cardinal Newman's poem is one of the masterpieces in our language. This alone, I should have thought, was enough to open the doors of a Catholic world of music; yet how rarely is the *Dream* given on the Continent— and dear Elgar himself such a devout Catholic!

Our own performance on May 22 (London Festival) was remarkable for the first appearance of the fine Dutch mezzo-soprano, Julia Culp, whom I had been coaching for the part of the Angel, on and off, for three months past. Her devout delivery, her repose, the lovely even quality of her voice, her diction (her English was perfect) seemed to bring the Catholic Church into Queen's Hall. I shall always feel, too, that Gervase Elwes established his reputation at this performance and became at once the greatest exponent of the name part. As for the Norwich Festival Chorus, it covered itself with glory.

Robert Newman was greatly disappointed because Elgar did not attend this performance. For my part, I was more surprised than disappointed because Elgar knew I had made the journey to Düsseldorf to learn all I could from the festival performance there, especially as it was virtually directed by himself. Elgar was a curiously shy man; on the other hand, I think he only believed in performances he himself conducted. At all events, I never remember him attending a performance of his own works under the direction of another conductor. It was therefore all the more surprising to me that he came to that lecture I gave in St. James's Hall.[1]

Reverting to the London Festival (at Queen's Hall) the afternoon of May 23 was a whole Festival in itself, for the Brahms double concerto was in the hands of two geniuses—Kreisler and Casals, the concert closing with the first performance in England of Debussy's *Rondes de Printemps* (No. 3 of *Images*). The following day we gave the first performance of Elgar's newly-written *Symphony No. 2* in E flat, dedicated to the memory of King Edward VII.

It was my experience that several performances of this important work were necessary before the public really came to understand it. The appeal is by no means instant as with a more commonplace idiom; yet this symphony undoubtedly grows on one. It is the same with his *Falstaff* which I purposely played twice during the season for years, once under the composer's direction and once under my own. Yet it has never really taken hold of the British public, nor does it draw a full house.

The emotional basis of Elgar's second symphony is different from that of the first. The great contrast of light and shade which helped towards the success of the A flat symphony are here subservient to a lower colour-scheme altogether—at least, in three of the movements. Incidentally, it was about this time that Mahillon made the four valve trombones of which I have already spoken. Elgar, I remember, was delighted with the beautiful *legato* these instruments produced in the finale but I did not care for the horn-like quality of them. They now repose in my library at the R.A.M.—probably silenced for ever.

Elgar was very much upset and disappointed because the

[1] A lecture on woodwind instruments.

250

public did not receive his second symphony with more warmth. He received three or four recalls, but I shall never forget his face when I opened the curtains at the side of the platform.

"Henry," he said disconsolately, "they don't like it. They don't like it!"

Nevertheless, I cheered him up for I knew, what the public was slow to understand, that it was a great symphony. I patted him on the shoulder, and persuaded him to go on to take his call; but he left the hall later, sad and disappointed. I felt very sorry for him, but he only needed to bide time, and now as we know No. 2 has taken its rightful place.

The concert finished with the first performance of a Poem for orchestra called *Dante and Beatrice* by Granville Bantock who himself conducted. He was more fortunate than poor, dear Elgar, for the work was very well received.

For the concert on May 25 Strauss had been engaged to conduct a programme of four of his own works and two by Mozart. Unfortunately, a sudden indisposition prevented him from coming and I had to take his place at a few hours' notice. This might have been a trial had not it been for the fact that I had taken all the preliminary rehearsals. Harold Bauer was the pianist and gave a remarkably fine performance of Mozart's eighth concerto and Strauss's *Burlesque*. This latter work gave the tympanist, Mr. Dix, a fine chance to display the powers of the chromatic tympani which, as I have mentioned before, I was the first to introduce into England. Ackté repeated her performance of the closing scene from *Salomé* with which the concert closed. The Friday evening was devoted to Bach's B minor *Mass* for which the Sheffield chorus paid London a special visit, this being their only appearance unconnected with their own festival. Their singing of the *Mass* has probably never been surpassed, but we knew each other well and I had so recently directed the work in Sheffield. Besides which, I had run up to Sheffield several times for rehearsals in the interim.

The climax came on the Saturday morning with the *Matthew Passion*. We had ten solo singers. Agnes Nicholls, whose beautiful voice seemed to have been made for Bach's arias, sang faultlessly and with a reverence that was most touching. (But then, she was a *great artist* gifted with a lovely voice.) The Leeds Choral Union, trained by Mr. A Farrer Briggs, undertook the choral work.

There have been many London Musical Festivals since 1911, but I deplore the fact that they have gradually assumed the appearance of being merely a well-advertised series of Symphony concerts. Yet look at our lists of artists then!

Ackté	Thorpe Bates	Robert Radford
Ellen Beck	Herbert Brown	Harold Bauer
Julia Culp	Ben Davies	Kreisler
Agnes Nicholls	Gervase Elwes	Casals
Edna Thornton	Herbert Heyner	

The choirs were those of Norwich and Sheffield Festivals and the Leeds Choral Union. The conductors were Strauss, Granville Bantock, Walford Davies, Percy Pitt and myself.

The Norwich Festival of 1911 was the thirtieth, and it was pleasurable to me to meet Mr. F. Oddin Taylor, Mr. P. Hansell, and the honorary secretary, Mr. Edmund Reeve, when I went there to begin work. I really think that without these three indefatigable workers the festival could not have been pulled through. They had engaged the best singers of the day, and for instrumentalists they had Moriz Rosenthal and Eugène Ysaÿe. I remember how much impressed I was when we performed Bach's *Mass* in that lovely Gothic St. Andrew's Hall, originally the nave of a monastic church. More ideal surroundings could hardly have been conceived.

Robert Newman went to meet Ysaÿe at the station on the morning of the day of his concert. The first thing Ysaÿe said was: "*Don't tell Henry* but I've been fishing at Godine for the last two months and haven't taken my fiddle out of its case."

Ysaÿe started off with an organ rehearsal with Haydon Hare for the Vivaldi concerto which he played that evening as well as the Beethoven, his performance of which was easily the worst I ever directed. In the slow movement his memory went to pieces—indeed, I do not know what he would have done had not Maurice Sons prompted him as he went along, playing the solo part on his own violin. Ysaÿe managed to get through but, fond as I was of him, I did think he walked away with two hundred and fifty guineas that night at the expense of much anxiety on my part. Fortunately the Norwich audience did not know its Beethoven well enough to appreciate what had happened.

Among our various productions were Enesco's *Humoresque* on themes by Johann Strauss; Mozart's *Requiem; The Kingdom* (Elgar); *Hymn of Praise, Messiah*, and Walford Davies's *Everyman*. These we interspersed with classical items.

As at Sheffield, this was a real festive season with invitations to lunches and dinners everywhere. The Misses Colman, who took particular interest in these festivals, threw open the Guildhall for a general invitation lunch for members of the chorus, the orchestra, and friends. I shall always remember their kind hospitality and am only too sorry they have ceased to take active interest in the festival since I gave up conducting it. However, I still hear from them with news of what is going on musically in Norwich. I devised a plan to create a real festival atmosphere. Each morning four trumpeters and four trombones played a *fanfare* in a corner of the square outside St. Andrew's Hall. This *fanfare* was always founded on the main theme of the work about to be performed, so that it was changed each day and was played at 11.20 and again at 11.25, the quartet being directed by Francis G. Sanders, organist of St. Peter, Cranleigh Gardens. The idea was a great success and proved excellent for gathering in our audience.

I remember how we all laughed one morning during the festival of 1914 when the work down for performance was Vaughan Williams's *Sea Symphony* which he himself was to conduct. He told me he was walking through the town on his way to the hall when, to his horror, he heard the opening theme of his symphony. He thought his watch must have stopped and that he was late.

"Good heavens!" he said to himself. "Wood's started without me!" He began to run and arrived in the square somewhat out of breath, only to be met with the second *fanfare*—greatly to our amusement, and his relief!

Two great violinists created a sensation in London during the season of 1911. Carl Flesch made his first appearance in England on November 15. His playing of the Beethoven and Brahms concertos showed us all that he was a violinist of the very first rank. He proved it again in his masterly rendering of the *Adagio and Fugue* from an unaccompanied sonata of Bach. This great Hungarian artist had taught in various European centres as well as in America where (to use their own expression) he was considered the violin 'pedagogue' of the day. He made a second appearance a fortnight later to give the first performance of Josef Suk's *Fantasia* for violin and orchestra, a work which was received well by Press and public alike. Curiously enough after meeting Flesch in 1911 I never set eyes on him again for twenty-five years—until 1936. Early in 1937 he sent me a copy of his splendid work *Problems of Tone-production in Violin-playing* on the title-page of which he wrote, *To Sir Henry Wood, one of the greatest and most complete musicians of our time. From Carl Flesch. London, 2–1–37.*

The other violinist was Sevçik who gave a concert with his pupils and drew an audience that must have embraced most violinists of the day, for the teacher of Kubelik and Marie Hall had attained a unique position in the musical world. I remember how deeply impressed I was with Sevçik's method—so much so that I paid a visit to Prague later on in order to learn more about it. I was interested to find that every five minutes during a lesson Sevçik called upon his pupils to test the truth of their fifths. If only a fraction out of pitch they were made to re-tune. I appreciated the enormous advantages of his semitonal system of fingering and had the pleasure of playing for several of his pupils during their lessons. Thus I studied the method thoroughly.

A very distinguished pupil of Sevçik was Daisy Kennedy who has been associated with so many of our concerts since. My earliest impressions of her are of her beautiful rendering of Max Bruch's Scottish *Fantasia*—and her auburn hair! She so impressed me, that I advised Robert Newman to engage her for a Promenade Concert to repeat the Scottish *Fantasia*.

She met with immediate approbation; which set her among the popular favourites of London Concerts.

At one of these Concerts her memory played tricks and at the end of the Brahms Concerto she addressed the audience. "This has happened because I have not had a rehearsal," she declared. I cannot say how sorry I was about this happening for, apart from being a charming artist, Daisy Kennedy is also a charming woman. She loved to be with her friends and to have them round her, and her *salons* before the death of her husband (John Drinkwater) were always crowded with people who sincerely admired her.

So far as failing memory is concerned, she is not the only artist who has suffered from it by a long way. I have had 'frights' on many occasions—not least with Joachim who nearly always 'fluffed' something. My long experience has taught me that nobody is really safe; lapses of memory may attack even the most experienced artist at any time.

Robert Newman, active as usual, instituted a series of orchestral concerts on alternate Saturday nights, six of which carried us up to April of 1912. On December 12 Sevçik paid London another visit when he engaged the Queen's Hall Orchestra for another pupils' concert.

Early in the Promenade season of 1911 that charming soprano Carrie Tubb made her first appearance.

She was already an experienced singer, having done much work in the Provinces. Not only had her voice a great brilliance but she had the power to dominate an orchestra whether she sang an aria from the *Messiah* or a scene from *Götterdämmerung*. Her conscientiousness was remarkable. She sang *Isolda's Death-song* at this concert, but not until she had had twenty lessons from me. In fact, she was a continuous pupil for she left nothing to chance and went through everything she sang, bar by bar, with me beforehand. That was even in the hey-day of her success. How different from many of the present-day singers who are anxious to accept a twenty-guinea engagement and net £20 19s. 6d. out of it!

On August 23 we interested our public in a first performance of the waltz from *Der Rosenkavalier* which had been produced the previous January in Dresden. We all thought it a strange, lovely mixture of Mozart-like episodes, folk tunes, and even romanticism of fifty years ago; and those who knew their Strauss well must have detected touches of *Till Eulenspiegel*, *Don Quixote*, and *Ein Heldenleben* mingled with the strains of older Viennese waltzes.

Margaret Balfour was another *débutante* this season. She sang Rossi's aria *Ah, rendimi!* Hers was a lovely voice then and has remained lovely. I remember she was introduced to me by her teachers Miss Gambogi and Miss Holding, the latter being an old pupil of mine. I realized that Margaret Balfour had been splendidly taught; there was no fluff in her voice and she sang dead in tune. I do dislike fluffy, draughty voices—'confidential' voices I call them because they seem big to the singer (owing to waste of breath) but never come through in a hall to express joy or happiness; rather are they lugubrious and sad. There is nothing of this about Margaret Balfour's clear tones. Her voice is as good today as ever it was.

In these days Hamilton Harty was not known as a conductor though he was considered a great accompanist and a talented composer. Both his *Irish Symphony* and his violin concerto deserve to be more widely known than they are. This season we produced three charming pieces which he wrote for our great oboist Henri de Busscher called *Orientale*, *Chansonette*, and *À la Campagne*.

He has written some lovely songs, and we conductors are so grateful to him for his splendid arrangement of Handel's *Water* and *Fire* music.

As a conductor his subtle musical insight gives grace and charm to anything he may direct. His many years of fine work for the Hallé Orchestra, carrying on the tradition of Hans Richter, and adding still further laurels to the reputation of this famous body of musicians, is well known to us all—and I am sure Manchester must acknowledge to the full the value of his sojourn among them, and equally regret his departure.

A distinguished composer devoted to the lighter forms was Eric Coates whose entire orchestral output must have been played at some time or other by the Queen's Hall Orchestra. He dedicated to me his *Miniature Suite* which we performed on October 17. It is a pity Coates did not discover some librettist such as Sullivan found in Gilbert, for I am sure he might have carried on the Sullivan and Edward German traditions and have produced excellent English light operas and operettas.

During this season of 1911 we had no less than seventy-eight soloists, which is five more than for 1910. Of these forty *were newcomers*, twenty-three women and seventeen men. There were twenty-four pianists and six violinists—and all, with very few exceptions, were of *British origin*.

An advertisement in one of the programmes for this season serves to remind me of my activities in painting. I reproduce it here as a matter of interest.

PICCADILLY ARCADE GALLERY
PICCADILLY, W.

(Opposite Burlington House)

AN EXHIBITION

of

FIFTY SKETCHES IN OIL

by

SIR HENRY WOOD

will be held on

MONDAY MAY 22

to

SATURDAY JUNE 3
(10 a.m. to 7 p.m.)

FOR THE BENEFIT OF THE QUEEN'S HALL
ORCHESTRA ENDOWMENT FUND

Admission One Shilling

Catalogue, with prefatory note by Mrs. Rosa Newmarch, Sixpence

The Queen's Hall Orchestra Endowment Fund, which bene-fited by the sum of £200 from this Exhibition, as has been referred to elsewhere, was 'To provide for the endowment of members when they retire from the Queen's Hall Orchestra by subscriptions of members with the aid of donations'. The trustees were The Rt. Hon. Sir Edgar Speyer, Bart., H. Egan Hill, Esq., and myself. The Treasurer was Walter Reynolds, and the Hon. Sec. Fred J. Winterbottom. This excellent scheme was warmly sup-ported by my friends and, of course, by Sir Edgar Speyer himself. I think I have already said that when Chappell's took over, the members were paid out according to their individual investments.

I have come across a letter from King George V's Private Secretary which is yet another reminder of the willingness of our Royal House to patronize music. When I think of what a man like Speyer spent in furthering good music in this country I feel increasingly that Royal patronage has so often played a part in putting England where it now is in the musical world. The occasion of this letter was a Concert at the Crystal Palace which I was directing. It read:

Dear Sir,
I am desired by the Earl of Plymouth to say that the King desires that you should be presented to him and the Queen in his tea room immediately after the Concert tomorrow, Friday afternoon.

The letter is dated May 11, 1911.

Sheffield did not resume its festivals after the war until 1933; the hard-headed business men of the north were not so venture-some as the music-lovers of Norwich. We opened this festival with Mahler's *Eighth Symphony* which I had originally produced for the B.B.C. in 1930 and which I again conducted for them this year 1938. Some people are inclined to run Mahler down but I admire this great work.

Delius was represented by his lovely *Song of the High Hills* the solo parts in which were sung most beautifully by Elsie Suddaby and Frank Titterton.

The Festival of 1936 was a stupendous achievement. The loss on this gigantic programme was £1,000, but in the same year Leeds Festival faced a loss of £600, and if one compares the two, it will be readily seen that the artists' fees alone for Sheffield would easily double those of Leeds. I must say although my programme was ambitious, the Committee, headed by that very kind dear man— A. J. Ward as Chairman—who died only recently, and who must be a great loss to Sheffield's artistic coterie—upheld my views, and decided an all-or-nothing policy. Look at the programme.

Te Deum (Berlioz)	Isobel Baillie
Violin Concerto (Brahms)	Eva Turner
The Bells (Rachmaninoff)	Jo Vincent
Magnificat (Bach)	Muriel Brunskill
Piano Concerto No. 2 (Rachmaninoff)	Mary Jarred
Tod and Verklärung (Strauss)	Jessie King
A Sea Symphony (Vaughan Williams)	Parry Jones
Manzoni Requiem (Verdi)	Walter Widdop
Haffner Symphony (Mozart)	Keith Falkner
Cello Concerto (Haydn)	Roy Henderson
Belshazzar's Feast (Walton)	Alexander Kipnis
Missa Solemnis (Beethoven)	Harold Williams
Piano Concerto in B Flat Minor	Rachmaninoff
(Tchaikovsky)	Solomon
Brigg Fair (Delius)	Busch
The King shall Rejoice (Handel)	Suggia

As usual, the Duchess of Norfolk patronized, and took great interest in the Festival, and the Duke of Kent accompanied her one evening to hear Vaughan Williams's *Sea Symphony*, and Walton's *Belshazzar's Feast*.

Rachmaninoff came to England to supervise the performance of *The Bells* which I had originally introduced to England with the Liverpool Philharmonic Society in 1921, and had repeated at the Norwich Festival of 1927. For the Sheffield performance Rachmaninoff remodelled the choral parts of the third movement as it was found in previous performances that there were too many notes and words to be chorally effective. I was most grateful to him for going to the trouble and expense of having the movement re-engraved specially for Sheffield. Isobel Baillie, Parry Jones and Harold Williams were the soloists; they excelled themselves (as did the chorus) no doubt inspired by the presence of Rachmaninoff. I hope I may hear again, one day, Harold Williams's beautiful quality intoning *Hear the tolling of the Bells, mournful Bells!*

As I have decided that this is the last Festival I intend directing for Sheffield, I can look back on the years with the knowledge and satisfaction that this city perhaps more than any other in England has had of my best, my most unstinted care, but never— even in the hey-day of their pride in their Festivals, have they been given a programme so magnificent, nor carried out with greater success than this of 1936.

At the first Norwich Festival I conducted the chorus master was Dr. Mann of King's College, Cambridge. He afterwards resigned owing to pressure of work and Haydon Hare took his place. I remember him so well, a very downright man—a spade was a spade with him. He caused me great amusement at a committee meeting by the way he handled the members. They never seemed to resent his sharp manner even when he told the chairman to put away his watch as he would not catch his usual train. "I'm going to settle this programme today."

One member ventured a remark about Spohr's *Last Judgment*.

"Now, what do *you* know about Spohr *or* the *Last Judgment?*" said Mann. "My dear sir, you may be an excellent solicitor but you don't know B from a bull's foot." He treated them to any amount of this sort of thing but they never took offence.

One of my outstanding memories of the 1924 Norwich Festival is Maggie Teyte's interpretation of the soprano part in *Elijah*. When I first approached her about it she was doubtful about taking it on.

"I am an opera-singer," she told me. "I don't think I want to sing oratorio. But if you will teach me the part I will see what I can do."

Her performance was a triumph and proved my contention that oratorio is *sacred drama*. Her rendering of the Widow's part was a lesson in interpretation. I wish every oratorio singer could have heard her performance. What a lesson too, for the Contralto, whose duplicate parts of the Angel and Queen are so often sung with the same stodgy delivery; what a chance there is for varying colour of tone, and expression—that of the Angel so very beautiful, and full of feeling, and that of the Queen —a virago, calling forth all the drama that Maggie Teyte knew so well how to portray. I shall never forget the pleading tone of her voice when she asked the man of God to help her: *My son is sick. Help my son! there is no breath left in him.*

At the 1927 festival I produced *Morning Heroes* which Arthur Bliss wrote specially for the occasion. A work of great moments and one which plainly reflected the composer's wartime service. The orator's part was spoken by Basil Maine with great effect. Another memory of this festival was Leos Janáček's *Slavonic Festival Mass*. This also was a new work. Janáček had visited me the previous year (with Mrs. Newmarch) to discuss the possibility of my including it in the programme.

Queen Mary and the Duchess of York (as she then was) came over from Sandringham to this festival to hear Vaughan Williams's *Sea Symphony*. Between the morning and afternoon performances a luncheon was given by the Bishop of Norwich at which both the Queen and Duchess were present. I remember how the Queen made us all feel at ease in the drawing-room afterwards by lighting her cigarette, thus giving us permission to smoke.

XXXIX

BRAND LANE OF MANCHESTER

BRAND LANE WAS born in London in 1854. In 1875, at the age of twenty one, he settled in Manchester as a teacher of singing. Always interested in choirs and choral conducting, he founded the Manchester Philharmonic Choir in 1880 and started the first of a long series of concerts at the Free Trade Hall the following year.

In 1912, the Gentlemen's Concerts having been given up, Brand Lane called on me and asked me to direct his own. We began with a Wagner concert with the Queen's Hall Orchestra and followed with another of a miscellaneous character with Solomon and Marchesi. I remember we gave three first performances of works by Dohnányi, Percy Grainger, and Ethel Smyth.

I was now permanent conductor to what might be described as concerts run on Promenade lines with Symphony-concert artists of the very first rank. To engage such artists naturally meant paying high fees, but Brand Lane never objected to doing that so long as he secured the right people. So quick was he to do so that he often had them at his own concerts before they appeared at those of the Hallé Concert Society. While the Hallé people were negotiating Brand Lane was actually presenting.

All the same, he could never have made purely orchestral concerts pay, even with the additional attraction of a well-known artist; but he regarded his concerts *with a big orchestra* as the swings on which he occasionally lost, while the roundabouts were his alternate concerts *without* orchestra. As he had an enormous subscription list he sold out before the doors were even opened. I do not remember ever seeing a vacant seat in the Free Trade Hall for a Brand Lane concert all the years I directed them.

As a concert manager I consider Brand Lane second to none; indeed, I have always considered him the Robert Newman of the North. He was artistic but a wonderful man of business, and perfectly delightful to work with. My relations with him were always of the happiest.

When I took over these concerts I had already had some experience of Manchester audiences, to whom I was by no means unknown, through having directed the Gentlemen's Concerts for so many years as well as, on occasions, the Hallé. Moreover, as the Queen's Hall Orchestra was undertaking provincial tours at that time Newman was able to arrange to be fairly near Manchester and to work in our dates round those for which Brand Lane engaged us. Thus Newman and he readily came to terms.

For all the experience I had had of Manchester, I must admit I had no idea that an audience of Mancunians could be as demonstrative as they proved to be at these concerts.

Excellent as he was in every way, Brand Lane occasionally committed errors of judgment. One, I have good cause to remember. I arrived in Manchester for the final rehearsal of *Elijah* to find a huge poster advertising the concert confronting me outside the hall. Some of the lettering could be read at a considerable distance. I noted the name of the work, and two others: one of these was that of Madame and the other my own.

"What about the other artists?" was my thought as I crossed the road to get a closer view. There I found, in very much smaller lettering, the names of Phyllis Lett, Gerwase Elwes, and Robert Radford. I doubted the wisdom of this uneven distribution because there was that lovely singer Agnes Nicholls and indeed, half a dozen names occurred to me as being just as suitable. However, I proceeded to the hall in time for the two o'clock rehearsal, determined to have a word with Brand Lane about that poster at the first opportunity. I made up my mind to tell him I thought he had been indiscreet.

I was not greatly surprised to find the three artists whose names appeared in small letters looking somewhat resentful. The atmosphere was not exactly cheerful, but I said nothing and the rehearsal began. Madame was a trifle shaky in the scene between Elijah and the Widow of Zarephath, but that might have passed more or less unnoticed had she not come to grief in *Cast thy burden*. She went off the rails in the first line and I had to stop. She apologized and asked me to go over it again. The second time she was no better. Again she asked me to go over the passage. Again she made mistakes. Suddenly, Gervase Elwes (normally the sweetest-tempered of men) banged down into his chair in disgust.

"I don't know whether you expect us to stop here all afternoon rehearsing a mere hymn-tune, Sir Henry," he said indignantly. "Madame does not appear to know much about it."

At that remark the tension became so great that I dared not risk further trouble. After rehearsing all that was necessary I tactfully suggested that the three other artists should go to the hotel (the Midland) and rest before the concert. Madame remained with me and as we were discussing this rather delicate matter one of the violinists approached us and said that if he could help Madame by playing her part or the top line of the accompaniment on his violin he would be only too pleased to offer his services. The offer was gratefully accepted and it relieved me considerably for, having the responsibility of a heavy oratorio on my shoulders, I did not feel disposed to rehearse for another hour or so.

Madame was a great artist, and was not alone in this weakness of being well acquainted with the solos in a work, but neglecting to study properly the *concerted* music. I well remember the trouble with another famous singer at a Queen's Hall Symphony Concert one Saturday afternoon. She was down for the Recitative and Aria, *O ma Lyre Immortelle*, and at the morning rehearsal Mr. Fransella played the introduction, most beautifully. I looked at her to start on the F sharp—there was a long silence —we smiled at each other, and finally I said, "Do start, Madame."

She answered, "I am sorry, but I never sing the Recitative as I can never get my first note."

"Oh," I said, "don't bother, I will hum it to you this afternoon", but she replied, "No, thank you, I could not risk it in public."

My favourite 'conducting meal' is a lightly-boiled egg, toast and a pot of China tea. A few years ago I ordered this slight meal when staying at the Adelphi Hotel in Liverpool (which, next to the Langham Hotel in London is my favourite English hotel, no better food anywhere!) before going to the Philharmonic Hall to conduct a concert. I ordered it for half-past five, changed and rested before the concert, after which I was glad to get to bed. I was not so pleased, however, on the following morning at 5.30 when a young waiter entered my room with a trolley on which was an exact replica of my meal of the previous evening.

"What are you doing?"

"I have brought your tea, sir."

"Tea? What for? What is the time?"

"Half-past five, sir. You ordered it for half-past five. And

I've walked four miles to get you this tea, sir." (This very ruefully.)

"I am very sorry," I said, "but I don't want it. That's the meal I ordered, and had, yesterday afternoon. Please take it away and don't call me for another three hours."

"Very good, sir."

With that he disappeared. I found out afterwards that he was new to the job and that the other waiters had played a trick on him as a freshman. They had repeated my order, marking it a.m. instead of p.m.

Not all conductors direct their concerts after so light a meal. Safonov, the celebrated Russian conductor, was a case in point—at least I surmise so from my experience with him the last time he was in London. He invited me to lunch with him at the Piccadilly Hotel. His first words were: "Do you like oysters?"

I admitted I did.

He took my arm and we walked over to Driver's where we tucked away three dozen each. As a matter of fact, I thought this an excellent, sustaining meal and I knew Safonov had a concert that evening. But no; we marched back to the Piccadilly and went through a long *table d'hôte* accompanied by a generous supply of good wines. I realized that Safonov's methods and mine differed but I was somewhat taken aback at half-past three (after coffee and liqueurs) when he suddenly said: "Do you like *pâtisserie*?"

Again I said: "Yes."

I little thought I was going to be hurled off to a pastrycook's then and there, but there was no gainsaying him. A taxi was called and off we drove to a Belgian *pâtisserie* in Oxford Street where we ate some delicious éclairs. After that I dropped him at his hotel. This proved to be our last meeting, for he died in 1918.

Safonov evidently liked good food and plenty of it.

While on the subject of food, I call to mind the elegant Stokowski, whom I had invited to my house for lunch, and after exchanging greetings—for we had not met for some time—he surprised me by saying: "I hope you haven't prepared any special dishes for me. I can eat just *anything* you know."

I admit I like a good meal *after* a concert but would never think of eating much *before* one. I put my good health down to the exercise of discipline; my habits of life have always served my work. Rest, massage, and a rub-down with spirit after a rehearsal or concert is my rule, and I never allow myself to become over-tired by sight-seeing. *Undisturbed concentration* has been the invariable rule of life, for music's sake.

I frequently receive notes from secretaries of societies informing me that I can catch a train *ten minutes* after a concert is over. It never seems to occur to them that it would be suicidal to start on a journey without a change and rub down.

I perspire profusely but I believe Albert Coates suffers even more than I do, which reminds me of a joke played on him at one of the Leeds Festivals. During rehearsals he hung up various under-garments on a string across the general artists' room. There were shouts of laughter when he came in and found that one of the orchestra had used a rubber stamp belonging to one of the gramophone companies and had stamped every garment *TESTED AND REJECTED*.

To return to Brand Lane.

For the engagement of these well-known artists Brand Lane had an excellent arrangement with various agents with all of whom he appeared to be on good terms. If an artist such as Melba or Clara Butt happened to be touring the Northern Provinces he so arranged it that they did not appear in Manchester. Thus neither he nor the agent suffered from having an artist twice in a season, possibly with only a little space of time in between. This plan worked admirably.

Another point about Brand Lane was that he never grumbled at the fee he was expected to pay. He wrote to an artist, asked what his or her fee was, and paid without demur if their reputation justified it. Only once did I ever find him grumbling and that was over a pupil of mine, named Tamaki Miura. This young Japanese possessed a splendid voice, clear and penetrating though perhaps not highly colourful. She had already sung at Covent Garden and I happened to say something about her to Brand Lane during the interval of one of the concerts.

"Is she any good?" he asked. I told him I thought she might be very useful to him, and he took her name and address. He wrote to her, mentioning a date, and inquired what fee she would expect.

I must explain that whenever Tamaki Miura appeared at a concert she wore native dress. These dresses were really very beautiful and were extremely costly. When she came to me for her lessons her husband always came with her. The ritual and ceremony always amused me, but it never varied an iota! He'd fumble with the key of her music-case which was always kept locked. The process of unlocking it and locking it up again was quite elaborate and took two or three minutes.

As soon as the lesson began he retired to the far end of the room, turned a chair round and sat facing the wall with his back turned to us, holding his wife's expensive furs over his arm. There he remained motionless during the forty minutes' lesson. After that came the performance of locking up the music again. He said he always locked everything up. Judging by the time he wasted, he might have been locking up the Crown jewels instead of three pieces of music.

The next time I saw Brand Lane he had heard from Tamaki Miura.

"How much do you think she asks?"

I said I hadn't the faintest idea.

"Four hundred guineas—*and a new umbrella.*"

We had a good laugh over it and I tackled her the next time she came for a lesson.

"Your fees are absurdly high," I told her. "Melba or Patti would sing for four hundred guineas."

"But if they get four hundred guineas, why can't I?"

There was an obvious answer to that and I gave it her.

"But my dress costs two hundred and forty guineas."

"Even so, you can't expect Brand Lane to pay that sum for a singer quite unknown to the Manchester public. It would be different if you were well-known there. I suggest you reduce your fees considerably."

I was a bit curious about that new umbrella. "What do you want the new umbrella for? What has that got to do with it?"

Her answer was illuminating.

"My friends tell me it always rains in Manchester."

One would have thought she could have bought the umbrella out of her fee—but that was far too simple for this Japanese mind. At all events, the next I heard was that she would go for a hundred guineas on condition a carpet was put down for her on the platform. In the end she sang for fifty guineas, and there was *no* carpet. *But there was a new umbrella!*

This story has quite a good ending. I asked Mrs. Miura whether she knew *Madame Butterfly* for I felt she would make a wonderful *Butterfly.* I told her the work had a Japanese setting and she agreed to study it. I wrote to Judson, the American agent, with the result that he offered her an engagement to sing the part of *Butterfly* at the Metropolitan Opera House. Later I received a charming letter from her thanking me for all I had done. They ought to have had her in the part at Covent Garden. She would have been a great success.

As time went on Brand Lane seemed to engage everyone with a name, including such world-famous artists as Melba, Tetrazzini, Ackté, Suggia, Lady Tree, Mrs. Langtry, Heifetz, Strauss, Sibelius, Clara Butt, Sapellnikoff, Pachmann, Madame Donalda, Busoni, Ysaÿe, Gervase Elwes, Kubelik, Nikisch, etcetera. An American soprano, I remember, introduced to this country by Oscar Hammerstein, appeared at one of the concerts, and I know I went to a good deal of trouble over a rehearsal with her in Queen's Hall. The frequent stoppages, unfortunately, were misinterpreted by her mother who was sitting just within the little curtains at the side of the platform. She seemed to think I was interfering with her daughter's interpretation; at all events, she came on to the platform. She then made a little speech in which she expressed her opinions rather definitely. I explained that I was doing everything I could for her daughter. Then she began to argue which was more than I could endure. To the intense amusement of the orchestra I dismissed the lady by saying: "In any case, Madam, *I don't conduct mothers!*" It was a few minutes before they quietened down and we could proceed with the rehearsal.

I used to look forward to the Brand Lane concerts. I was always sure of some first-rank artist even though we did not go in for the production of novelties. One of my most vivid memories is of the Peace Celebration Concert in 1919. We had two great French artists with us: Cortot and Sarah Bernhardt. And the full Hallé Orchestra; so that this was really a sensational concert. Single tickets were a guinea, and the hall was packed.

After Brand Lane's death these concerts were given up— much to my sorrow, for conducting them had. been among the pleasantest of my long life of music. I shall always consider myself fortunate in having worked with two such splendid managers as Robert Newman and Brand Lane.

XL

SCHÖNBERG AND SCRIABIN
(1912, 1913, and part of 1914)

WHAT GREAT SEASONS these two of 1912 and 1913 were—
the last two of the good old peaceful times! What a galaxy of
stars illuminated the musical firmament of London! Read their
names and think back to musical seasons when we had with us,
among others:

Ackté	Flesch
Blauvelt	Godowsky
Busoni	Kreisler
Carreño	Lamond
Casals	Mysz-Gmeiner
d'Albert	Pugno
Dohnányi	Thibaud
Elman	

so that you may realize what those two seasons meant to London
music-lovers. We certainly had the pick of the artists.

I think I can say I remember in clear detail not only these
but literally hundreds of artists of all kinds. I have already
confessed, however, that Moszkowski had eluded my memory;
but there is another—much greater than he—who just remains,
as it were, a shadow of memory. This is Tchaikovsky.

It is forty-five years since I last set eyes on him so perhaps it
is excusable, but I can see him sitting and listening to Madame
Svaitlovski, a somewhat rotund little woman with an excellent
voice, while she sang arias from *Eugène Onegin*. She had actually
played the part of the Nurse in the opera during Lago's season
at the Olympic under my direction.

She gave a reception at the Grafton Galleries in honour of
Tchaikovsky, and sang several of his songs in the original
Russian. As a matter of fact, Tchaikovsky was to have played
for her but he told her he was too nervous. I cannot remember
accurately what happened or how I came to play instead, but
I do remember being asked to do so, and also have a very faint
recollection of receiving a telegram in French which said something like 'Too nervous to play this afternoon; please play for
me'. Whether it came from Tchaikovsky himself or his agent is
more than I can be certain of now. However, I do remember

him sitting there with an expression of great sadness on his face. He was—and looked—the man who was to compose the *Pathetic Symphony*. He said very little but bowed with great courtesy every time he was addressed. The only other memory I have of him must date back a year or two previously when I met him in a crowded artists' room at St. James's Hall after a performance of his fourth symphony. At the final rehearsal I remember how staggered we were when Tchaikovsky, failing to get the reckless Russian spirit he wanted in the *finale*, eventually obtained it by exclaiming "Vodka—more Vodka!!"

There was an exhibition at Earl's Court in 1912. Mrs. George Cornwallis-West, a great musical enthusiast, had conceived the idea of presenting a series of twelve concerts under the title of *Shakespeare's England*. The programmes were to consist of music of various composers which had any reference to Shakespeare's plays, but there was no suggestion of keeping it to *actual* Tudor music. Without wishing to damp Mrs. Cornwallis-West's enthusiasm, I told her I thought that side-shows of this nature in a large exhibition would not be a success, but she assured me that *Shakespeare's England* would be a great draw. At all events, she engaged the Queen's Hall Orchestra and me for these twelve concerts.

The next job was to find the music. Such works as Tchaikovsky's *Romeo and Juliet*—and Gounod's and Berlioz's came to my mind at once. There were also Shakespearian settings of various kinds by Eric Coates and Roger Quilter as well as works by Svendsen, Henry Hugo Pierson, and others. For the rest, I spent hours in the British Museum—what a wonderful place it is!—and found musical works relative to *Othello*, *Hamlet*, *Macbeth*, *King Lear*, *The Tempest* and *Antony and Cleopatra*. I found dances and ballet-music—in fact, everything that had been written for the comedies, the historical plays, and the tragedies.

Evidently there had been some misgivings after my warning, for Mr. Cornwallis-West interviewed Robert Newman and me after the third concert. I reminded him that I had already expressed my opinion, and also that contracts with the Queen's Hall Orchestra could not be broken. Neither, by the terms of the contract, could the orchestra give performances in the open air; nor could it in any way be divided up. He saw the point and there was no ill-feeling about it in any way whatsoever.

The orchestra was accommodated in a shell built in a vast hall. The opening was packed with a vastly representative audience—all of whom had received an invitation—but alas, we did not again see such a crowded hall! Gerwase Elwes was our vocalist and was going to sing a group of Shakespearian songs at the third concert, but *there was not one single person to be seen in that enormous hall!*

At 3.15 the orchestra showed signs of becoming excited, and it was whispered that one man had come in. He walked all round the orchestral stand. I should not even have known that, had not the leader of the second violins whispered: "There is an audience of one man, and he is walking round studying orchestration!"

That is the only time I have ever played before so select an audience. I did not know it at the time, but we might have had two more, for a small boy was outside with his uncle.

"Now come along!" said the uncle. "We are going to hear Mr. Wood and his lovely orchestra."

"But I don't want to hear Mr. Wood. I want to go on the scenic railway!"

That little boy's name was L. Gurney Parrott. He is now Secretary to the Royal Academy of Music. Thus he sometimes *has* to listen to 'Mr. Wood and his lovely orchestra'! (Mr. Parrott recently told me this little episode.)

The proceeds from these concerts given in the Empress Theatre, had there been any, would have gone to the Shakespeare Memorial Fund. They were really under the general director-ship of Dr. Charles Harris who founded the Imperial Choir which he culled from various choral organizations in the environs of London. We shared the conducting.

On Sunday, January 21, at Queen's Hall I produced a work in manuscript—a miniature suite for woodwind instruments—by Madame Poldowski. I see the programme says she was a distinguished young Polish composer who had been a pupil of Vincent d'Indy. More interesting still, I think, is the fact that she was the daughter of Wieniawski, the master of Ysaÿe and Sons. I knew her first as Miss Wieniawski, then as Madame Poldowski, and finally as Lady Dean Paul. As a composer she had exceptional talent. Her settings of the poems of Paul Verlaine were introduced by Gervase Elwes: *L'Heure Exquise* is a very beautiful song. Poldowski's compositions had a great vogue in Paris and this particular suite made a deep impression.

On March 25 I directed a somewhat unusual type of concert consisting of four piano concertos played by students of the Imperial and Royal Academy of Music in Vienna. What was called *The Master School of Pianoforte* was under the direction of

Godowsky who was present. In the first half of the programme a Beethoven concerto was played by Theodore Henrion, and the Schumann by Becky Davison; in the second a Rachmaninoff concerto was played by Jacques Richinsky and one by Saint-Saëns was played by Antonie Geiger. I had never heard of these pianists until then; neither have I seen any of their names since.

April 15, 1912, will ever be remembered as one of the most tragic days in the history of British seamanship, for the White Star liner *Titanic* struck a submerged iceberg and foundered on her maiden voyage with a loss of over 1,500 lives. On May 24 there was a Titanic Band Memorial Concert in the Albert Hall organized by Fergesson McConnell in memory of the eight musicians of the ship's band who perished, playing to the last.

No less than seven orchestras, combined, took part and numbered six hundred performers. I remember the magnificent array of twelve trombones. Ada Crossley was the singer and the concert closed with Dyke's *Nearer, my God, to Thee* scored for the full orchestra.

Years later I was conversing with a young engineer in Manchester who was on the *Titanic* with his mother. He was a boy of ten at the time. He described how, when the terrible order to jump overboard was given, his mother could not pluck up enough courage to obey it. He took her by the legs and pushed her over, following himself the next instant. In the water he felt his mother clinging to him and has never forgotten the horror of that awful moment when he was called upon to make the decision that saved both their lives.

There was a tenseness in the Albert Hall at that concert which reflected the national horror at the disaster. I am thankful that I took part in its direction but more thankful still that such awful disasters are rare.

On April 20 I came into contact with a deeply attractive personality in Juan Manén, a Spanish violinist who, in those days, rivalled even the great Sarasate. Manén was certainly one of the most wonderful-looking men I ever set eyes on. He was dark and bearded, with an aesthetic expression that made me think he would have been an ideal sitter for the sixteenth-century painter Velasquez. He had a marvellous technique and was a composer of considerable distinction, being the author of two operas, a symphony, a violin concerto, and many other pieces for the instrument. He also edited the complete works of Paganini. He played again only a year or two ago, but I think he has lost some of his fascination, or perhaps it is that so many violinists of distinction have appeared in the meantime.

During this season my old friend Lamond gave a joint orchestra concert with Szigeti, then only a lad of twenty. I remember Szigeti's remarkable rendering of the Brahms violin concerto and also Lamond's playing of the Beethoven G major, and the Tchaikovsky B flat minor concertos. Between these items we played Lamond's own symphony in A (Op. 3) which he had written in 1889 and which August Manns had produced for him. It was a classical work as regards form and themes but trombones were not used.

I always maintain it is a pity Lamond looks so much like Beethoven—with the unfortunate result that the average concert-goer believes that he cannot play any other composer's works. This is the greatest error—for his interpretation of Liszt, Rubin-stein and Tchaikovsky concertos equals that with which his name is associated, *The Emperor* of Beethoven. A case in point—a few weeks ago I was to direct the New Symphony Orchestra at a Sunday Afternoon Concert at the Palladium, and suggested he should play the Tchaikovsky—but the management would have none of it! Beethoven it must be, and Beethoven it was—(and of course rendered in his inimitable style). It is so extra-ordinary that, in spite of his long residence in Germany, no one can doubt his Scottish birth—for in spite of a certain German accent, his speech proclaims the city from whence he came, and that which has recently honoured him, by conferring upon its renowned son the degree of Mus. Doc., Glasgow University. I believe now, as is the custom abroad, Lamond prefers to be addressed as Dr. Lamond.

The eighteenth season of the Promenades opened on August 17 and ran until October 26. I note the name of Sinigaglia for the first time when we produced his new suite called *Piemonte*. Sinigaglia's orchestral works have always been thought well of in England for their delicacy and for their Piedmontese atmo-sphere. He was friendly with both Dvořák and Goldmark, who considerably influenced his work. I remember Nikisch being full of the overture to Goldini's comedy *La Baruffe Chiozzote* which he liked because it was so lively. "Nothing gloomy about it," he told me.

On August 22 we gave the first performance of Georges Enesco's second *Rumanian Rhapsody in D*. Enesco first came to us in 1909. He was then the uncontested leader of a true Rumanian school of violin-playing. In opposition to Kubelik's over-taut bow, his was so loose that I wonder the wood did not touch the string. His romantic style is very much reflected in his remarkable pupil Menuhin. I produced the first of his

Rumanian Rhapsodies and found that the London public appreciated the strong national flavour of his music. I believe the only other Rumanian composer whose music I ever introduced was Stan Golestan. He also wrote a Rumanian Rhapsody which I produced in September 1919. Enesco, by the way, was a great friend of Sir Edgar Speyer.

Frederick Kiddle introduced a *Fantaisie Triomphale* for organ and orchestra by the brilliant French organist and composer Théodore Dubois whose playing attracted Paris musicians so much in 1877 when he succeeded Saint-Saëns at the Madeleine. Dubois became Director of the Paris Conservatoire in 1896.

On August 29 we performed for the first time the *Prelude* and *Serenade* from Erik Korngold's pantomime *The Snowman*. This created a deep impression especially as it was known that when the work was written Korngold was only eleven. At the time of this performance he was fifteen. Since then he has written at least three operas and much orchestral music.

September 3 was a real red-letter day in our history for we introduced an extremely important novelty and a name appeared that has since become famous—that of Arnold Schönberg. Even at this time he was the most talked-of composer of the day. The work was the Five Orchestral Pieces which, you will remember, I have already mentioned as having been hissed. This, I think, goes to refute the popular idea that the Promenaders accord acclamation to every work played, no matter what. My opinion is that they always show themselves capable of expressing opinions of their own, in no uncertain manner.

Early in January 1914 we repeated these Orchestral Pieces at a Symphony concert with Schönberg conducting. The performance drew a large and appreciative audience who may or may not have been surprised to read the following notice in the programmes:

Herr Arnold Schönberg has promised his co-operation at today's concert on condition that during the performance of his Orchestral Pieces perfect silence is maintained.

Schönberg was so delighted with the performance and its reception that he sent the following letter to Robert Newman from Berlin. It was published in the *Daily Telegraph* on Friday, January 23, 1914—only a little over six months before the outbreak of war with Germany. The last sentence, in view of this, looks significant. The letter was addressed to the members of the Queen's Hall Orchestra.

DEAR SIRS,

I wish to tell you that you have given me great pleasure. By that I mean not only the numerous manifestations of sympathy with which you have honoured me, and which gave me such a pleasant feeling at the rehearsals, but also the careful way with which you played in my rehearsals and the performances.

Such achievements are in absolute harmony with your artistic qualities. These are such as appeal mostly to the artist who can look ahead. I mean your present mastership in your performances and the unexcelled qualities of your 'ensemble', the precision, beauty of sound, and noble taste and careful thoroughness of every detail, which are the merit of every single one of you and the success of all of you together. I must tell you that on the Continent, as far as my knowledge goes, there are only at the most two orchestras which would be compared with you—the Amsterdam Orchestra and the Viennese Philharmonic.

I must say it was the first time since Gustav Mahler that I heard such music played again as a musician of culture demands. I presume that this letter will be published, and that is the reason I mention this fact, so that it should be taken note of by some of our German orchestras, who have too much false pride to learn what is expected of them at the present time.

They may learn what is required of them by modern composers, and they may learn how easily an artistic predominance is lost if untiring energy and a most essential sense of duty are not constantly at work, as well as renewal of technical knowledge.

It was a great pleasure to me to find your orchestra a confirmation of the fact that the last technical acquirements of the instrumental soloists in concerts, not only in playing soli, but also in full orchestra, can be made use of. This I have long known, it is true, but have not heard anything about it for a long time. That it is possible to play in tune the quickest movements distinctly, clearly, and the same in *pianissimo;* that difficult parts can also be rendered purely and sonorously; that—but need I tell you all I understand, but which to many a famous orchestra appears to be an unjust demand? That is indeed the praise I have for you. One must always aim higher, as you know: therefore, in conclusion I say once more that I experienced a great pleasure, which has only been troubled by the sad knowledge that with us things are not everywhere as they should be. With kindest regards, yours most sincerely,

ARNOLD SCHÖNBERG.

On September 10 we gave two quite noteworthy perform-ances: Glazounoff's Introduction and Dance (*Salomé*) and a first concert-performance of Wolf-Ferrari's Introductions to Acts II and III of the *Jewels of the Madonna*. The following night we introduced Francis Korbay's *Hungarian Overture*. Korbay was a charming man and a well-known teacher of singing who lived in London for many years. His Hungarian

273

songs must be known the world over by now. Quite an interesting fact about him is that the Abbé Liszt stood sponsor for him at his christening. The programme ended with the first concert performance of Elgar's new *Coronation March* specially written for the coronation of King George V and Queen Mary on June 22, 1911. It is a fine march and yet I never seem to see it in programmes nowadays. Elgar had a great talent for writing marches but only the five of the *Pomp and Circumstance* series seem to remain in the concert repertoire. Four days later we gave a first concert performance of his *Crown of India* suite originally produced at the Coliseum on March 11, 1912—so that we were not long in securing it for our own programmes.

On September 19 we gave the first performance in London of Enrico Bossi's *Intermezzi Goldoniani* for strings. Bossi was organist of Como cathedral and later became a professor at the Naples Conservatoire. In 1895 he moved to Venice and became Director of the Music School at Bologna. At this time he was considered a modern among Italian composers but his music reflected German influence. His *Song of Songs* was produced at Leipzig in 1900 and his oratorio *Paradise Lost* at Augsburg three years later.

Another production of ours was Frank Bridge's splendid suite *The Sea*, a great favourite of mine. I have played it in France, Germany, Italy, Holland, South Africa, and America with the greatest success. Why is it an invariable rule that composers are inclined to lose interest in their earlier works; it is always the latest from their pen of which they think most, and for which they have most affection. Unfortunately the public does not always see eye to eye with them. Frank Bridge is no exception—and always appears uninterested when I tell him how well his lovely work has gone at so and so—and will remark: "Oh, that. It's such an old work, why do you play it?"

Elgar on the other hand *was* an exception. I remember when visiting him at his home in Hereford, how he played through on the piano his cantata—*King Olaf*—which he had written some twenty-five years previous, exclaiming: "By Jove, Henry, what jolly fine tunes! I couldn't write them today!"

On September 25 we produced Benjamin Dale's *Concert Piece* for organ and orchestra with Kiddle at the organ. This is a really fine work. I little thought at the time that I should have the pleasure of seeing the composer almost daily at the R.A.M. when, twenty-four years after this, he became Warden. His music has a melodic charm and beauty all its own, and its workmanship is excellent. I wish Dale's output were larger because I so admire the viola suite he wrote specially for Tertis. It is a work of the first rank, the solo part being beautifully laid out and the scoring perfect. His little choral work—*Before the paling of the stars*—is a great favourite of mine—a little choral gem, which should be heard more often.

The fairy play *Where the Rainbow Ends* is now a classic comparable with *The Blue Bird* and *Peter Pan*. On September 26 we produced Roger Quilter's new suite taken from the music to the play—and very delightful we found it.

I was so pleased with Poldowski's *Miniature Suite* for woodwind instruments, which we had given with such success at a Sunday concert the previous season, that I prevailed upon her to write something else. She responded with a *Nocturne* which created the deepest impression on all musicians present, not only for its beauty as music but because it was a real novelty in every way. If the musical reader will glance at the constitution of the orchestra required for this piece he will not be surprised that it produced such a novel effect. The strings employed were the usual, but the wind instruments were most *unusual*. They comprised:

Two Piccolos
Three Flutes
Alto Flute in G
Three Oboes
Oboe d'Amore
Cor Anglais
Hecklephone (Bass Oboe)
Three Clarinets
Corno di Bassetto
Contra Bass Clarinet
Two Bassoons
Two double Bassoons
Three Horns
Two Trumpets
Tympani
Bass Drum
Harps

The Promenades were now drawing to a close, but there was still time for half a dozen more interesting novelties. On the 8th Arthur Catterall played a new violin concerto by Coleridge-Taylor; on the 9th we introduced an English Dance by Cyril Scott; on the 10th we gave Edgar Bainton's *Celtic Sketches* and, at the same concert, Théodor Szántó played the second edition of Delius's very beautiful piano concerto in C minor which

Delius had dedicated to him; and on the 16th Guiomar Novaës played Mozart's eighth piano concerto in D minor. This charming woman had made a tremendous name for herself in America but I do not think she has played in London since she played with me at this particular Promenade and, again, at a Sunday concert.

That is the way with these people. They appear in London, create a little following for themselves, disappear to America, and come back again after twenty years and wonder why they are forgotten. However, if Guiomar Novaës ever comes back to London she can rest assured I have not forgotten her, even after a quarter of a century! I am always telling our British artists not to leave the country for any length of time because someone else slips in and on their return they find their niche occupied, and may never quite regain their position.

Our last novelty of note this season was Julius Harrison's clever variations on *Down among the Dead Men* which nobody who heard it could forget.

Unless you call three days at Brighton and one long walk over Hampstead Heath a *holiday*, I had none this year. I remember the walk over the Heath with Dr. Cathcart very well. At first I thought he had an attack of lumbago because he was walking bent forward like an old man. He assured me, however, that he was quite well but was working out a method recently put forward of a new theory regarding the spine.

"The spine being curved is all wrong, according to a correspondent," he told me. "It should be *straight*, they say. When you lie down it should touch whatever you are lying on *everywhere*, and I'm trying to demonstrate their method to you, and for my satisfaction."

As we walked he enlarged on the theme at considerable length. When we came near Jack Straw's Castle he stretched himself on the grass and told me more about the *correct* position of the spine. There was a seat close by, and nothing would do but that I must lie flat upon it and endeavour to make my spine touch everywhere. The natural curvature of it seemed to offer resistance to this, but I did my best. Now that I come to think of it, we were rather too *near* the famous hostelry Jack Straw's Castle for demonstrations of this nature which *might* have been misinterpreted!

I spent a good deal of my spare time with Dr. Cathcart and Siegfried Schwabacher this summer, but my actual holiday amounted to no more than those three days at Brighton and the 'spine-walk' over Hampstead Heath.

I have cause to remember the Promenade Concert on October 11. There was a fog in Hampstead that night. I left home, as usual, in a taxi at 7.20, but at the corner of Fitzroy Road the driver ran into a wall with the result that my head came into sharp contact with a window. I was rather badly cut and had to return home. Robert Newman was telephoned and told that I would come as soon as my wounds were dressed. I suggested that the concert should begin without me but Newman said he would wait. I arrived at twenty minutes past eight—the only time in my whole career I have been late for a concert—and walked on to the platform with my head bound up, to receive a tremendous welcome from the waiting audience.

Most inconveniently for me, the Birmingham Festival clashed with the Promenades this season and I had to say I was afraid I could not find freedom to conduct it on that account, pointing out that if the Festival had been at the end of October instead of at the beginning, I should have been delighted to accept. I received a reply saying that the Promenade concerts did not spread uniformly over the same period each year and that some seasons they ended much earlier than others. This was true. I discussed it with Newman as the deputy question was in my mind, and I felt I must abide by the decision for which I had fought so hard in the past. However, he took another view.

"That question has been settled a long time now," he said. "I do not see any reason why you should give up the Birmingham Festival if I can get a good conductor to take your place. What about George Henschel?"

Henschel, by the way, was an old friend of Speyer's and, as everybody concerned seemed quite satisfied, I went to Birmingham with an easy conscience.

We opened the festival (as was quite natural in Birmingham) with *Elijah*. Birmingham does not forget that Mendelssohn wrote this great work for its festival in 1846 and came over from Germany to conduct it. It was a memorable performance not least because the part of the prophet was taken by the great American bass Clarence Whitehill, assisted by Carrie Tubb, Clara Butt, and John McCormack.

In the evening Sibelius appeared and directed for the first time his new symphony (No. 4) in A minor, and Elgar conducted the first performance of *The Music-makers*. How wonderfully Muriel Foster sang the solo part.

On the second day Walford Davies conducted the first performance of *The Song of St. Francis* and Casals played the Haydn concerto, also taking the solo 'cello part in *Don Quixote*, giving to the part of the Chivalrous Knight quite a new interpretation and an added value to this unique piece of writing.

The happiest and certainly the truest Italian rendering of Verdi's *Requiem* I ever directed was at the third concert of this same festival when we had a quartet of soloists absolutely made for the work; Ackté, Muriel Foster, John McCormack, and Clarence Whitehill. I doubt whether I shall ever hear another quartet of singers who will let themselves go and dominate a whole performance as these four did. As for Ackté, her voice, style, and diction simply carried us off our feet. She was magnificent.

On the last day of the festival I directed Brahms's *Requiem* which I followed with Scriabin's *Prometheus* and the closing scene from Strauss's *Salomé*, sung as only Ackté could sing it. We finished the concert with Bach's fourth motet, *Be not afraid*, and the whole festival ended with Elgar directing a properly-rehearsed performance of his great oratorio *The Apostles*.

So I thoroughly enjoyed my change from conducting at Queen's Hall. Thinking of my admirable deputy Dr. George Henschel, as he was then, reminds me that during my holiday in Scotland last year (1937) I went to Aviemore to visit his grave. He lies buried in a corner of a truly old-world churchyard, high up on a promontory overlooking Loch Alvie, which in Gaelic means the Lake of Waterlilies. Facing the grave is a seat in just such a spot as he often sought to rest and meditate and think musically. Inside the little church, which looks like a private chapel, there are two monuments, one to Henschel and the other to his wife. The inscription on his reads:

1850 1934

In Memory of

GEORGE HENSCHEL

Kt. Mus.Doc.

O Love that will not let me go,
I rest my weary soul in Thee;
I give thee back the life I owe,
That in Thine ocean depths its flow
May richer, fuller be.

This Tablet was erected by residents and friends in grateful remembrance of his love and constant help in the district.

I know Henschel learned to love Scotland during his conductorship of the Scottish Orchestra. Remembering he was not of British birth, and the names of the various foreign conductors who have directed the Scottish Orchestra it occurs to me that the Scots' temperament inclines towards a foreign name. On one occasion, when a permanent conductor was sought, Richter recommended a certain Wilhelm Bruch. He could not speak a word of English, and hated the cramped life of Glasgow—no cafés—no lager—everything closed at night —and deadly dull on Sundays! The band nicknamed him Sleepy Billy, as he evinced excessive boredom. After the first month, the first English he spoke was to express a longing to go home. Home he went after a season in Scotland.

Yet the Scottish Orchestra still seems to prefer a foreign name—anyway I think it was a pity they let Barbirolli go to America.

The Sunday concerts were going on as usual. There is nothing of note to record regarding them because we rarely performed novelties as the concerts had to be given without rehearsal and therefore contained repertoire material. However, the Sunday Concert Society was always ready and willing to give to charity. I see that the proceeds of a concert on October 26, as a good example, were sent to the relief fund for the stricken in South Wales after the shocking colliery disaster of 1913.

It is really quite diverting to look through these old programmes and to note how Robert Newman always took advantage not only of a centenary but the demise of any public personage. It was amazing how Chopin's *Funeral March*, as we played it, attracted an audience. I have just been looking at a note in one of the programmes to the effect that the March would be played as a tribute to George I, King of the Hellenes.

I have spoken of Carrie Tubb and her careful study with me of whatever she was going to sing. Another pupil who did the same thing was Ada Forest. She eventually married Cherry Kearton whom I occasionally meet nowadays. Whenever that happens I always want other conversation to cease in order to allow him to talk about birds and beasts. Last time we dined together I remember him telling me about his wonderful intrusion into Penguin Island. His screen pictures of animal life are easily the most beautiful I have seen.

We had Scriabin with us in 1913; a distinguished-looking man with a heavy moustache and small pointed beard, and very dreamy eyes. I thought he looked far from well and seemed to be a mass of nerves. After he had rehearsed his piano concerto

(Op. 20) he played through *Prometheus*. This he described with exotic enthusiasm.

This work created an innovation in concert programmes. I felt it so involved, and difficult as well as interesting, that I persuaded Newman to allow me to put it into the programme twice during the same concert—first and last. I noted that very few people left the hall, which proved the experiment quite worth while. The work is scored for full orchestra—piano, organ, chorus and what was known as a Colour Organ. Arthur Cook was the pianist and Stanley Marchant (who was organist of St. Paul's Cathedral at that time, and is now Professor Marchant, Principal of the Royal Academy of Music), the organist. Kreisler was directly answerable for my interest in Scriabin. "You should introduce his works, for he is by far the most interesting of the modern Russian school."

Scriabin's own piano-playing was really lovely. His touch was delicate, coupled with perfect technique.

He was one of Safonov's pupils but his earlier works were definitely influenced by Chopin and later by Liszt—perhaps even to some extent by Wagner. Latterly—and this is the point about him and his Light Organ—he became aesthetically-minded, musically transcendental, and even a little neurotic. *Prometheus* shows him to be a student of theosophy and that his musical mind was for ever striving after visionary themes and yearnings for Life in the highest sense. A paean of ecstasy. He became convinced there was a correlation between sound and colour, that certain harmonic combinations possessed luminous affinities. I discussed all this with him and some Anglo-Russian friends, but I fear he left me unconvinced. You cannot tell me that middle C produces a definite colour when it is struck. If so, what pitch are you going by? The one we use now, or the one in use in England before Dr. Cathcart persuaded Newman to have it lowered? I am afraid it does not work in practice.

However, Scriabin was convinced that sound and colour were closely related and because of that belief he invented the so-called Keyboard of Light. As soon as his views were made known in London a wealthy man named Rivington spent something like £20,000 over a period of years on this Light Organ which threw combinations of various shades on to a screen. The whole thing was operated from the keys of a silent piano and I seem to think the lights were electric arc lamps. As the notes changed, so the colours altered. The part for the colour Organ is seriously set down in the score on the top line, and resembles the part one might give to the right hand for a harmonium.

Even though I could not agree with his views I could see what was in Scriabin's mind. His ultimate scheme was to unite all the arts in the service of what he considered to be the Perfect Rite. When he died, two years after this, he was actually engaged on a colossal work called *Mystery* in which the secondary arts were to serve the primary. The Perfect Symphony, in his view, would unite sound with colour and even perfume. This last idea appeared to me alarming to a degree. I cannot imagine a symphony being made more perfect by a perfume-laden atmosphere. Even though I appreciate the use of incense in a church, to have it in a concert hall would remind me of the days when small boys came round in cinemas and sprayed everyone with vile smelling disinfectant.

However, one must give Scriabin his due: he was sincere in his efforts to do away with all barriers dividing the performer and listener. All, in his view, should experience the whole evolution of the creative spirit. *Prometheus*, by the way, was not inspired by, nor had it any connection with, the story of the Titan in Greek mythology.

I remember how disappointed Scriabin was because we did not give him the chorus to sing on changing vowels to re-inforce the closing section. That, in a measure, was his own fault because he had marked it *ad lib* in the score. As the introduction of the chorus made a difficult production still more difficult, Robert Newman decided to do without it.

A splendid Bach and Beethoven programme for the Symphony Concert, on April 5, opened with *In dulci jubilo* and continued with the motet *Be not Afraid* and the *Actus Tragicus* from *God's Time is Best*. In the second half we did the *Choral Symphony*, with the 1912 Birmingham Festival Chorus. With them came their admirable trainer R. H. Wilson (who also trained the Hallé Chorus) and C. W. Perkins, organist to the Corporation of Birmingham.

I used to cycle in those days. Indeed, I was very keen—at least, keen enough to ride from Nottingham to London, a distance of a hundred and twenty five miles, in one day. I started at four in the morning and arrived home at eight in the evening.

I remember some time during this year, when I was still living in Norfolk Crescent, that something went wrong with my machine. A shop in Edgware Road had been telephoned and a man was expected to call. I gave particular instructions to the maid not to let him go without seeing me as I wanted to explain what I required done. The maid came to my studio, which was on the ground floor, and told me the man had called and was waiting upstairs in the drawing room. I went up and saw him leaning over the piano and looking out of the window. He had his back to me and I noted his wide breeches which were not unlike our present-day plus-fours.

"Thank you for calling so promptly," I began. "I want you to look at my bicycle and . . ."

The figure at the piano turned round.

"Bicycle? *I am Ethel Smyth!*"

That was my introduction to Dame Ethel. She was, of course, *not* Dame Ethel in those days. What I had taken for breeches were—*bloomers!* She, like myself, was a cyclist.

I think I must have played practically everything Dame Ethel has written—certainly everything that can be performed in a concert-hall. I remember her conducting one of her own works at Queen's Hall one night at a Promenade concert. She went up to my rostrum, took up my baton and surveyed its length critically. Deciding that it was more than she could manage, she calmly snapped it in two, threw away one half and conducted with the other.

Dame Ethel is law unto herself and given, like many composers, to making last-minute suggestions. On one occasion she left a note for me after the final morning rehearsal. It read: "For heaven's sake no *ritard* and the woodwind chord *too soon* rather than an eyelash too late." After that admonition Robert Murchie's eyelashes seemed to dominate the whole performance, but his flute was certainly *not* an 'eyelash too late'.

Sometimes Dame Ethel goes further than last-minute suggestions: she makes last-minute *alterations*. I remember going with Lady Speyer and Lady Maud Warrender to hear *The Wreckers* at His Majesty's. We arrived at 2.15 for the 2.30 matinée. I said: "Where's Ethel Smyth? I don't see her anywhere. It's a wonder she hasn't been down into the orchestral pit by now to make a few alterations in the band parts."

"She would never do that as late as this," said Lady Speyer. "It is nearly twenty-past two."

"I don't care," I said. "She will be there with her little slips to pin on."

"I don't believe it."

"All right. I'll bet you a pound she does."

"Done!"

We waited.

Sure enough, at 2.25 the composer appeared, stealing in through the iron door, and proceeded to affix alterations over certain brass parts.

I was jubilant.

"I don't suppose she has told the conductor, either," I said. "He will wonder what on earth is happening when he comes to the passage. Now what about that pound you owe me?"

Lady Speyer paid up.

Dame Ethel wrote a book some time ago in which she referred to me as 'Henry Wood who was once my friend'. I have never thought of Dame Ethel with anything other than deep admiration for her talents as a composer, and her friendship in the past has been productive of great pleasure to me. However, I recently heard from her, atoning for past differences—differences of which she alone was conscious.

During the Promenade season a young singer appeared with an excellent voice and plenty of intelligence to sing *Senta's Ballad*. This was Jessie Brett-Young whose name must be familiar to most people on account of the success of her husband's novels. At this time, however, he was practising as a doctor in Brixham. Shortly afterwards he paid me a visit and told me that life in the medical profession was proving too strenuous as his health was not robust. He told me he was musical and asked me whether I thought he could work up and become a professional accompanist. I told him I thought it would take five years at least and advised him against it.

Some time later I met his wife again. "What do you think my husband has done?" she asked. "He has written a novel which is so successful that his publishers want others to follow it. He has sold his practice and we are leaving England for good and are going to live in Capri." Brett-Young's novels are now famous, and I rather flatter myself that readers of fiction might have lost many hours of very interesting reading, but for my advice.

Among the novelties that scored a success this season was Vaughan Williams's incidental music to *The Wasps*, a Greek play. A splendid work, of which the overture has now taken a permanent place in the general repertoire, I play it whenever I get the chance and the public love it. Dohnányi's suite in F sharp minor received such a warm reception that it was repeated a few weeks later; and Stravinsky's now well-known *L'Oiseau de Feu* (The Bird of Fire) received a like compliment.

A newcomer this season was Phyllis Lett whose vigorous contralto voice was heard to advantage in Beethoven's *Creation's Hymn* and Frank Bridge's splendid setting of the Riemann melody *A Joyous Easter Hymn*. Miss Lett's style—both in dress and song—always created an impression at the Promenades.

Another excellent singer—a dramatic soprano this time—was Ellen Beck who appeared regularly for several seasons. Her voice was of such power that she could easily dominate an orchestra, and I shall always feel grateful to her for undertaking the principal part in Liszt's oratorio *St. Elizabeth* when I produced it with the Nottingham Sacred Harmonic Society. I have enjoyed many visits to her, and many happy lunches with her at her home in Copenhagen, in company with our mutual friend Johanne Stockmarr.

The production of *Variations on a Chinese Theme* by Eugène Goossens created an impression, too. I think everyone predicted then that he would make for himself a great position. I was personally sorry when he left England and went to America, but he never fails to seek me out in the artists' room at Queen's Hall whenever he visits London.

Looking back over the Promenade season of 1913, I see we gave sixty-one concerts in all, with eighty-four artists, fifty-three of whom were singers and thirty-one instrumentalists. Out of these latter eighteen were pianists. Again, twenty-eight of these artists appeared for the first time in the proportion of twenty singers to eight instrumentalists. Nowadays the tendency is to have more instrumentalists than singers. There were, by the way, twenty-four novelties; thirteen were British and eleven foreign.

In May of this year a holiday had been planned in Italy. While in Rome a very curious coincidence occurred. I was walking in the Colosseum when a pageboy came from my hotel with a telegram. It was from Sir Oswald Stoll, of the *London Coliseum!*

It read:

WOULD YOU ENTERTAIN CONDUCTING SOME
PARSIFAL TABLEAUX FOR ME FOR A PERIOD
OF NOT LESS THAN A MONTH WIRE TERMS.

I wired that I would consider, and would write. The result was that I agreed to accept this interesting engagement, even though I must admit I felt rather sceptical and timorous of a presentation of this sacred drama under such conditions.

By the time I reached London it was near the date of the production. I found that Mr. Dove, Sir Oswald's musical director, was anxious lest I should not be back in time. The first thing I did was to call on the artist, Mr. Byam Shaw, who had undertaken to paint the scenes. When I saw his beautiful watercolour sketches I no longer felt afraid that *Parsifal* would suffer desecration by being thus unconventionally produced.

The Coliseum was, I believe, the only theatre at this time possessing a revolving stage. By means of it three or four tableaux could be set and presented in quick succession. We had hard work to time the scenes and I had to sit up many nights after my usual day's work in order to make a separate score from Wagner's original.

I cannot quite remember how many scenes there were but I rather think there were twelve, lasting forty minutes. Unfortunately the Coliseum orchestra was not at all suited to this class of music, although the players were splendid musicians for the work they were usually called upon to do. Sir Oswald Stoll, however, was determined to present *Parsifal* in the most perfect way possible and augmented the orchestra, engaging an excellent leader, Mr. E. Groell—a nephew of Arthur Nikisch. Despite this, I was not musically satisfied for I had to boil down the orchestration considerably. I still have my manuscript score of this forty minutes' *pastiche*, and although it seemed curious that such a deeply devotional work as this should form a turn in a London music-hall—and be so successful—I cannot recall ever having played to a more reverent or attentive audience. But then, the tableaux were the most artistic and beautiful things imaginable. The lighting effects, too, were superb. As for the dressing of the models, they made me wish that presentations of grand opera could be as beautiful. *The Flower Maidens'* scene was a riot of rapturous colour—so beautiful that one did not miss the vocal parts.

I cannot praise Sir Oswald Stoll sufficiently for his reverent treatment of the drama. Two shows a day for five weeks brought to an end one of the most pleasurable engagements of my long career. I should enjoy doing it again, but I wonder how it would appeal in these days! I have often thought that if Sullivan's beautiful work *The Golden Legend* were similarly presented, it would be a great success.

As I have said elsewhere, it was my custom to hold annual auditions both for orchestral players and other artists, and I now set to work to deal with the evergrowing number of applicants for orchestral work. These auditions provided me with more and more food for thought as time went on, for each year the number of women who presented themselves proved a problem. For some years many of these had equalled or even surpassed the men players until I felt it was unfair that they should study and gain such musicianship, only to slide back into a necessarily disappointed existence.

I discussed this several times with Robert Newman, but he could never see eye to eye with me. Yet Ysaÿe had remarked on the subject to me a year previously.

"You do not seem to employ women in your orchestras in England," he observed. "I have them in mine in Brussels and find their work equal to that of the men."

I pressed this view upon Newman, and I think it did eventually strengthen my plea, for he offered to try them out during the autumn Symphony season of 1913. I tried hard to get them into the Promenade season that year, but his argument was that they would never stand the racket of nightly concerts for ten weeks.

As soon as the rumour had spread that I was proposing to take women players, I received applications to hear a hundred and thirty seven of them to fill six vacancies. The chosen six took their seats in the Queen's Hall Orchestra for the first time at a Symphony concert on October 18, 1913, and let me say now that I have never regretted my decision. The names of the six are worthy of record: The Misses J. Grimson, M. Dudding, D. Garland, J. C. Stewart, S. Maturin, and D. Clarke.

I will say that our men took kindly to the innovation, but there were many people who criticized us on the grounds that the women would undercut the men. But, from the very first, Newman paid the same rates and they were given the same status. A separate bandroom was provided for them for Newman—once he had decided on a course of action—would allow nothing to stand in his way, either in the matter of expense or trouble to perfect it. So that, dear Ladies of the Orchestras, you have the excellence of the playing of these six young women of 1913 to thank for the established position you hold today and, incidentally, you owe just a little to Henry J. Wood.

I was anxious to produce Schönberg's *Gurre-Lieder*, a vast work for soli, chorus, and orchestra which, in some ways, reminds me of Mahler's eighth symphony. On hearing of a performance of it under Schönberg's personal direction at the Alberthalle in Leipzig, I immediately rushed over there. I was very impressed by the work but, alas, never found a chance of producing it. As a colossal festival production it would have been ideal, but there was difficulty in getting the words translated into English, particularly the woman's spoken part. Besides, I could never get a committee to take interest in a work of Schönberg at that time (We were not then fortunate enough to have a B.B.C. to produce contemporary works.) Some idea of its proportions may be gathered from the fact that it is scored for five solo voices, three male four-part choirs, a mixed chorus of eight parts, and a very full orchestra.

I met Schönberg while I was in Leipzig. He was a lively little man with a very round head. We found much in common because he was not only interested in music but in painting. Indeed, he actually gave an exhibition of his own works in Vienna in 1901. His portraits and what he called his 'visions' were most interesting but I did not care at all for his self-portrait.

Schönberg's knowledge of harmony was naturally profound. I studied his manual on the subject in 1922. I advise all young composers to do the same.

Thinking of modernity, we did rather a daring thing in January 1913: we produced Mahler's *Song of the Earth* (*Das Lied von der Erde*). Apart from being difficult this work was excessively modern but very beautiful. It is written in symphonic form for tenor and contralto solo and full orchestra. Gerwase Elwes took the tenor part and Doris Woodall that of the contralto. The words of the solos—there are three for either voice—are settings of six of Hans Bethge's poems called *The Chinese Flute*.

We risked it again with Scriabin's *The Divine Poem* but we took care of the box office by engaging Casals to play Dvořák's 'cello concerto at the same concert. A work taking fifty-five minutes without a break needs such a plum. *The Divine Poem* was another excursion into the realms of philosophy; it was a 'poem of self-assertion'. Scriabin may have been striving to find himself; my opinion is that he did so in his third symphony.

From early May, 1914, to the end of June, I had planned a rest, and I really wanted to spend my time painting in Scotland or else the Lake District, but I was persuaded to go abroad. I now realize the unwisdom of so doing for I undertook far too many unhealthy journeys in hot climates for the good of my health and the rest that I needed. However, I allowed myself to be persuaded—not even without misgiving. Nowadays I am a prisoner, though a very willing one, until the middle of June when I have my Royal Academy Students' Orchestral Concert at Queen's Hall, which I would not miss for worlds.

In 1914 I arrived back in England somewhat travel-weary, in time to conduct a rehearsal—rather a melancholy one, I fear—for the *Empress of Ireland* concert at the Albert Hall on June 29, to be followed by the pleasure of meeting once again Delius and his wife with the latter of whom I discussed our mutual hobby of painting in oils. Madame Delius told me she was considering a re-arrangement of her pictures which I had so admired when I visited them in Grez-sur-Loing. She even suggested my going to help her. This I should have greatly enjoyed but, also, my plans were frustrated.

Speyer, as Strauss's great friend, suggested a special concert of his works on June 26. Strauss came over and directed four of his tone poems, and Elena Gerhardt sang three of his songs with orchestra. Strauss then finished up by conducting his beloved Mozart symphony in G minor.

And this, be it noted, was only just a little over six weeks before the outbreak of war with his own country.

XLI

THE WAR YEARS

I HAD EARMARKED a week to spend at Bayreuth in order to hear *Parsifal* on August 4, 1914, as a kind of refresher prior to directing my own concert performance at the Norwich Festival in the autumn; but Newman begged me not to leave England on account of the unrest everywhere on the Continent. I must admit I disagreed with him, but I gave in to what proved to be wise counsel.

I fear I have never read my morning paper with the diligence of the average Englishman; and when war was declared, so far as I was concerned, it came as a bolt from the blue. I interviewed Speyer and Newman regarding the season's Promenade concerts, and discussed the question of whether they were to be run at all.

"Not *run* them?" snapped Newman. "Why not? The war can't last three months and the public will need its music and, incidentally, our orchestra its salaries."

So we opened on August 15. Public feeling had not then reached boiling-point, but it was getting dangerous. I remember how intensely unhappy I was during those early days. I felt so deeply for my friends the Speyers who were, as I have pointed out, of German birth. Yet they had done so much for the furtherance of music in London. Despite this they were not spared little slights and veiled insults, both of Press and public.

We opened our first concert with the national anthem and *La Marseillaise* to a crowded house in whose demeanour one could trace no signs of war or thoughts of war. For all that, the lesser Press was demanding that all German music should be deleted from our published programmes; and a large number of letters had reached Newman. The following Sunday we had a long meeting of the Queen's Hall directors and decided to withdraw the usual Wagner programme on the morrow, substituting a programme of Russian, French, and British composers, preceded by the national anthem and ending with *La Marseillaise*. This slip appeared in the programmes:

Sir Henry Wood begs the kind indulgence of those members of his audience who may be disappointed at the non-performance of the customary Monday Evening Wagner programme, the postponement of which has been rendered necessary by a variety of circumstances. He confidently hopes for a continuance of their valued support.

On the following Friday this appeared:

The Directors of the Queen's Hall Orchestra think that some explanation of the change of programme on Monday evening, August 17, is due to their Subscribers and to all those who have so loyally supported the Promenade Concerts in the past. The substitution of a mixed programme in place of a wholly Wagnerian one was not dictated by any narrow-minded intolerant policy, but was the result of outside pressure brought to bear upon them at the eleventh hour by the Lessees of the Queen's Hall.

With regard to the future, the Directors hope—with the broadminded co-operation of their audience—to carry through as nearly as possible the original scheme of the Concerts as set forth in their Prospectus.

They take this opportunity of emphatically contradicting the statements that German music will be boycotted during the present season. The greatest examples of Music and Art are world possessions and unassailable even by the prejudices and passions of the hour.

For the Directors of the Queen's Hall Orchestra,

ROBERT NEWMAN,
Manager.

The usual Wagner programme was reinstated on August 24, not to be disturbed again during the four years of the War.

Ever watchful, Newman had placed (just under my rostrum) a fine bust of King George with the acknowledgment 'The bust of H.M. the King is kindly lent by Mr. Alfred Drury, R.A.' heading every programme. Another proof of Newman's perspicacity appeared in a footnote which stated that the full programme of each evening's concert would be found in the daily papers, as follows:

Saturdays:	*Daily Telegraph*
Mondays:	*The Times*
Tuesdays:	*Standard*
Wednesdays:	*Morning Post*
Thursdays:	*Daily Express*
Fridays:	*Daily Chronicle*

By this means he prepared the way for any emergency change of programme, allocating his advertisements evenly.

From the very first the National Anthems of the Allies, as they ranged themselves with us, were played every night and, one by one, flags were added to the three which already hung over the organ on the opening night, until, in 1918, there were eight.

I scored every national anthem we played because none were arranged for a large orchestra, but I must admit that the monotony of these repetitions nightly during 1914 and 1915 for over two months at a stretch—they were discontinued afterwards unless by special request any particular one was repeated—resulted in untold boredom for me, even though some nights an allied victory would bring forth frantic enthusiasm.

While I was scoring the French and Belgian national anthems I decided to re-score our own noble tune. I had done this already—as far back as the opening of the Promenades in 1895—because I had never liked Costa's arrangement; the clashing of the bass drum and cymbals on every note got on my nerves. Moreover, it was useless from a pitch point of view to ask an audience to sing it in the key of B flat so I lowered it to G major. The note G, in my opinion, is the *station note* in the male and female voice, by which I mean it is the most easily-produced note. It has been the reciting note in our churches and cathedrals for centuries.

Curwen's publish my two versions in G. Version A is for orchestra alone; version B is for chorus and orchestra. There is only *one* clash of cymbals—at the apex of the melody in the last line, and the harmonization is very nearly the same in both

290

versions—just simple, diatonic harmonies without any modern innovations in the way of passing notes. The choral version has the usual descending scale in the bass as an introduction which gives the singers a chance of gathering themselves together for a good attack on the first note (the word *God*). It is most important that the first note should be declaimed. Nothing sounds worse than an uncertain beginning followed by a crescendo. Surely a national anthem should be treated like a great chorale!

The management had no straightforward task before them now. Everyone who lived through those dreadful years will remember how either cheering or depressing news affected the mind of the public. Day in, day out, we received hundreds of letters; some were kind and grateful, others resentful because men should remain to make music, while the foolish few who tried from the first to banish all music written by a German gave Newman endless anxiety even though he was strengthened in his determination to prove that art was beyond any national limits and that the classics were the world's possessions.

I cannot say I could look round and find the hall crowded every night as I had formerly done, but the fact that the concerts went on provides further evidence of Speyer's generosity. Eventually, owing to pressure of public opinion, he left England; but he left it richer in music than he found it—at a cost of over £30,000, to himself.

Just before they left this country I was walking with Lady Speyer in Hyde Park. We watched one of the many units of young men marching and drilling. I remember Lady Speyer turning to me and saying: "My dear Henry how can these young, untrained boys hope to conquer our armies of trained soldiers? It is dreadful."

When Chappell's took over the Queen's Hall Orchestra from Speyer, William Boosey failed to come to terms with him regarding the established title of the orchestra. Eventually, however, a way was found out of the difficulty by slipping in the word 'New'. Thus it was christened the New Queen's Hall Orchestra. Speyer presented me with the old title deeds before he went to America. I still hold them.

We were indeed fortunate in having the boy Solomon and the very young Moiseiwitsch living in London at this time, for they were both popular favourites. We were especially glad of Moiseiwitsch because, as the war progressed, it became increasingly difficult to secure artists and, incidentally, novelties from abroad; and he so readily undertook any new work for piano and orchestra.

I shall always remember little Solomon's first appearance at the Promenades on August 24, 1914. This child of eleven appealed tremendously to the audience with his winning, soulful eyes, his little silk shirt and short knickers. The piano seemed too large for such a small person, but the music was never beyond his reach and his performance of the second of Beethoven's concertos was amazing. Even in those early days his classical feeling was already to the fore—indeed, he is one of the few prodigies who have made good. Solomon was a genius and his playing of the great B flat minor concerto of Tchaikovsky took us by storm. What a *tour de force* for a boy of eleven! He has always had a marvellous physique and splendid health—essential factors in a public artist's work.

Strangely enough, only a few nights after Solomon's triumphant entry into the Promenade programmes Moiseiwitsch appeared. He was thirteen years Solomon's senior and had already established a reputation in England. He played *Suite fantastique*, a new work by Ernest Schelling. Moiseiwitsch has brought more new piano works before the public than any pianist I know, and I realize what a thankless task this is; for to memorize a concerto that may never be repeated is indeed an artistic sacrifice, and many composers owe Moiseiwitsch a very deep debt of gratitude.

That great English bass, Norman Allin, sang *O ruddier than the Cherry* at his first appearance which proved to be one of many during the wars years and since. I have always thought it a pity that Allin is of such a retiring disposition for, had he cared, he might have become one of the world's finest operatic basses. I believe his operatic rôles number fifty. I imagine he loved the English countryside and his home too well—and who can blame him?—but he always gives me the greatest satisfaction when he sings at any festival I direct. I can trust him with anything.

Nowadays we regard Béla Bartók as one of the leading forces in the development of modern music, but his works were unknown in England until 1914. On September 1 we played his suite for orchestra for the first time. This very original Hungarian composer's idiom was somewhat strange and brought forth a protest from one or two members of the orchestra who objected to 'playing such stuff' during the war—the only time, as far as I can remember, I ever received a complaint of the kind. I recall with amusement that A. E. Brain—brother of Aubrey

Brain, our present leader of the horns—stood up and 'went for' me.

"Surely you can find better novelties than this kind of stuff?" he said indignantly. I saw there was a call for a little tact.

"You must remember," I said, "that I must interpret all schools of music—much that I do not really care for—but I never want my feelings to reflect upon my orchestra. You never know, but I am of opinion this man will take a prominent position one day. It may take him years to establish it, but his originality and idiom mark his music as the type of novelty our public ought to hear."

This calmed Brain and, moreover, I have had the satisfaction of seeing my prediction fulfilled.

Herbert Heyner proved a success this season—an intellectual singer of the first rank, a good linguist, and a distinct personality. He eventually entered the army and rendered conspicuous service, but has suffered operation after operation owing to the amputation of a leg. He still suffers from it and I have always marvelled that, in spite of constant pain, he has achieved so much. I shall always be grateful to him for having introduced the first concert performance of *Amfortas's Prayer* which is now a regular and most useful item on Wagner nights. No one, to my mind, has ever sung it with such poignant feeling.

Frank Mullings was another artist who sang frequently during the war years. He was always assured of a good reception. I remember how beautifully he sang Bantock's *Ferishtah's Fancies* among many other works for voice and orchestra. As a Wagnerian singer Mullings, who is a dramatic tenor, won much fame; as Canio in *Pagliacci* his sense of drama was unequalled. During the last few years I believe he has devoted his time to teaching in Manchester and Birmingham, and I was delighted on hearing that his native Walsall has honoured him by conferring upon him the Freedom of the Borough.

During these trying days I introduced for the first time in England a suite by the French composer Florent Schmitt and, later on, performed selections from his ballet *La Tragédie de Salomé*. His works are, to my mind, a distinct blending of Latin and Teuton, but they always breathe romance. We produced a somewhat unusual novelty on September 17 in the form of an *Adagio* by Quantz, a prolific writer for the flute. Charles Souper stepped out of his seat in the orchestra and played this work on a bass flute, a beautiful instrument that had not been heard *solo* until then. In pitch the bass flute is a fourth lower than the ordinary flute, but I always feel it sounds much lower in quality than the mere difference of a fourth would seem to suggest. Rimsky-Korsakoff, Stravinsky, Ravel, and Holst have all made use of it, but this solo by Souper was a novelty at the time. This was indeed a year of first appearances of artists whose names are well-known nowadays. I remember with pleasure the appearance of Felix Salmond, who played the d'Albert 'cello concerto on September 22. Many people will remember the series of recitals he gave in London with his mother at the piano —an excellent and artistic combination. I was sorry when he decided to leave England for America where he now occupies a splendid position as professor in the Curtis Institute in addition to being, of course, a soloist.

Then there was Albert Sammons who appeared for the first time a week later to play Lalo's *Symphonie Espagnole*—a performance I shall never forget, for his tone was pure and his technique impeccable. I cannot understand why he has not made a world-wide reputation, for he is a born fiddler.

I remember finding myself seated next to Lionel Powell on a bus in Oxford Street about this time.

"I don't know how I can carry on if the War lasts," he said with a sigh. "I can't get the foreign artists; I can't even bring Kreisler over again until it is over."

"Then why don't you take up Albert Sammons and push him for all you're worth?" I said. "You could do it, and you would find he would never let you down."

His answer riled me.

"How can I push an *English* violinist?"

"Of course you can. He is rather retiring, but you can bring him out of his shell and, in a couple of years, you would be repaid. *Why* can't you push an English violinist? Nationality does not matter if the art is there. Anyhow, *who* made Paderewski? Daniel Mayer, of course!"

It never came off, but I am still of the same opinion.

I remember two outstanding novelties we produced during this very trying season. One was a most original symphonic poem by Eugène Goossens and the other a piece called *Conversations* (for piano and orchestra) by Walford Davies, the composer playing the piano part. This work is really a miniature symphony in four movements. Walford Davies wanted to point out the analogy between instrument and conversation, in which he but repeated what Bach told his pupils—namely, that he thought music was a conversation between separate voices representing characters. The titles of Walford Davies's four movements were *Genial Company, A Passing Moment, Intimate Friends,* and *Playmates.*

On October 17 Plunket Greene made his first appearance at the Promenades to sing Stanford's *Songs of the Fleet* which caused great excitement in the Promenade. The choir we had for the occasion was the Alexandra Palace Choral Society, trained by my old friend Allen Gill.

Altogether it had been an anxious time for us all but we worked together for the common cause of music in those dark days and, although the attendances were not up to usual Promenade strength, the public was evidently determined to help us carry on. I received letter after letter from the front telling me which day the writer hoped to be in London—and would I play this, or that? I should like to have done what was asked of me, but the programmes, of course, could not be changed. Many of our old artist-friends were unable to come to England—for the North Sea was no playground—but this fact had the desired effect of our making the utmost use of British artists. Concerts galore were being run up and down the country for various War funds, one of these being organized by Lady Randolph Churchill at which the great 'star' was to be no less a person than Adelina Patti.

My father always used to say that Patti's tone was like biting into a ripe peach. We never missed an opportunity in the old days of hearing her. Surely there was never such a 'golden' voice as hers! I was delighted when Lady Randolph engaged the Queen's Hall Orchestra and me for the concert at the Albert Hall on October 24, for I had always longed for the chance of accompanying Patti on the piano in a small room. The opportunity came when she asked me to meet her at the Carlton on the day before the concert. What an amazing career hers was! Fancy facing an audience as a child of seven (in 1850), retiring for three years to study at twelve, and coming out before she was turned sixteen to sing the part of Lucia in New York, creating such an impression as to be engaged for many other rôles for the next eighteen months!

Her wonderful little figure struck me at once when she entered her private sitting-room. Here was no low diaphragmatic breather, I said to myself, for Patti had a tiny waist and a very full bust. She had wonderful dark penetrating eyes that seemed to read your thoughts, and a delightful speaking voice. We rehearsed *Voi che sapete.* I felt the marvellous evenness of her warm quality. Her voice was not powerful but it excelled anything I had imagined in red-rose-like quality and voluptuous sweetness.

295

Patti was kind and charming to me during this long interview. As soon as I told her I had studied with Garcia, Randegger, Fiori, Duvivier, etcetera, she sang me some scales and arpeggios. Her flawless technique and even *timbre* throughout her compass were proof of the perfection of her training; no signs of headiness in the top notes nor 'mouthiness' in the medium, and certainly no over-brightness or vulgarity in her chest tones. Hers was my ideal of a great technique. Her vowel articulation was perfect and there was not the slightest trace of breathiness or jerking. It was truly wonderful and I was entranced. I believe she earned £35,000 a year by her singing. She deserved every penny of it.

I have never myself run a charity concert. On the other hand, I have given my services many times. And yet it comes to my mind that rarely have I heard *how much* has been given to an object or fund, and certainly I have never had a balance-sheet placed before me. I consider that when a charity concert is arranged all services should be given free of cost with the possible exception of expenses incurred for lighting, etc. Of one thing I am certain: *no artist taking part in a charity concert should be paid.*

I know how distressing it can be for the managements of charity concerts to find, near to the date of the concert, that the booking is small and that there will be rows of empty seats; but to put in an international 'star'—and pay a huge fee to him or her—is unfair to the supporting public who naturally think their presence is bringing in money to the charity and the charity only—even though their seats have only cost them half a crown. I wish the public would be a little more inquisitive regarding balance-sheets—some of which, I am quite sure, would be illuminating. So many charity concerts are run without due thought being given to legitimate expenses. It is the *extra* expenses with which I disagree.

So far as the sceptics were concerned I think we had an answer for them regarding music in the War years. Symphony concerts, Sunday concerts, and even a Provincial tour in November, 1914, proved that music was to keep its flag flying. I had only one cancellation—the Norwich Festival. I was completely in sympathy because it was obviously impossible with the ranks of both singers and instrumentalists depleted owing to the demands of war servies. On the other hand, the Manchester Hallé, the Liverpool Philharmonic, and the Sheffield Choral Union decided to carry on in the interests of the people at home and, incidentally, those away from home.

My work as a teacher of singing took many hours of the days on which I was free from other work, and were of great consolation to me; but I think I found the most perfect freedom from thoughts of the troubled world in the lectures I attended at the Royal Institution of which I have been a member for so many years. One of these, I remember, distressed me greatly; it was on the dreadful suffering of our men in France from 'trench feet'. This, however, was the only one of these lectures that did not bring to me the peace of mind I sought—for one short hour.

I am proud of the fact that Sir James Dewar invited me on more than one occasion to take office as one of the five annually-elected managers of the Royal Institution. Sir James evidently did not labour under the delusion that musicians are knowledgeable of nothing except just their job of music. These scientific lectures were the one outside interest I had—indeed I arranged my musical work in such a way that I could attend them as many as three times a week, and for many years never missed a Friday night invitation lecture. I especially enjoyed meeting scientific men in Sir James Dewar's drawing-room, a wonderful room situated on the first floor of the Royal Institution.

Sir William Bragg was Sir James Dewar's successor. Supported by Colonel Phillips, he conceived the idea of giving an orchestral concert in Queen's Hall as part of the Faraday celebrations which, it will be remembered, commemorated the discovery of electro-magnetic induction of August 29, 1831. In the programme appears the following note:

The President and Managers of the Royal Institution of Great Britain and the Council of the Institution of Electrical Engineers wish to acknowledge the courtesy of Sir John Reith and the British Broadcasting Corporation in allowing the season of Promenades to be interrupted to enable the Faraday Commemorative Meeting to be held in Queen's Hall. They are indebted to Sir Henry Wood for the arrangement of the programme.

Charles Woodhouse led the orchestra, and the organist was Berkeley Mason. The programme included the *Trumpet Voluntary* (Purcell), the Introduction to Act III of *Lohengrin*, Brahms's *Academic Festival Overture*, one of the *Enigma Variations* (Dorabella), the *Scherzo* from Mendelssohn's Octet, and Bach's Suite No. 6. The other part of the programme included tributes to Faraday paid by M. le duc de Broglie, Marconi, Professors Elihu Thompson, Zeeman, and Debye, and Lord Rutherford of Nelson.

The opening speech was made by Ramsay MacDonald, then Prime Minister, and the concluding address was given by the President, Lord Eustace Percy.

As an interesting memento of the occasion a miniature pocket knife (only an inch long) was presented to me after the concert. Its blade was made from the first bar of steel made (1819–24). There were only two of these little knives; the other was presented to Ramsay MacDonald.

I was most gratified at finding Marconi so interested in the musical part of the programme. I here met Rollo Appleyard who lunched with me here at my flat only a few months ago when I was actually writing this book. I told him that I had to rely on my memory for most of my facts for I have no detailed diaries (only engagements are recorded in them) and so my concert programmes are all I have to go upon. Mr. Appleyard then reminded me of the practical interest shown by King Edward VII in music in England and how he had spoken of me on a visit to Marienbad in 1907. I had to admit that I have never collected Press notices at any time and that I had completely forgotten the incident. Mr. Appleyard was good enough to search the files of *The Times* in the British Museum. He found the following (dated September 1, 1907) and had it reproduced by photostatic process:

In the afternoon His Majesty attended an open-air concert at the Cafe Bellevue. His Majesty appeared to be in excellent spirits and at the end of the concert sent Sir Stanley Clarke to Herr Schreyer, the conductor, to whom he expressed the pleasure the concert had given him. The King asked Herr Schreyer where he wintered. Herr Schreyer replied that he went to Vienna, Berlin, and Paris to hear the new productions. The King said: "Why do you not include London? Dr. Richter's productions are excellent; you should also hear Henry Wood's concerts."

Meetings between William Boosey and Robert Newman in order to discuss the coming season in view of the continuance of the War resulted in Newman's managing practically the same number of concerts as he had done in the past twenty-one years. Indeed, there were even extra Symphony and Sunday concerts. This showed truly national-spirited enterprise on the part of Chappell's who were in no doubt as to the falling-off of attendances during the season of 1914.

Early in 1915 Delius came to see me in the depths of depression. He told me he was very unhappy in France and intended coming to England—for a time at any rate. I was greatly troubled on his account and told him I should be only too pleased to offer him the loan of my London house, if he cared to accept it, for as long as he liked. He came with Mrs. Delius later and stayed at Elsworthy Road for a month while they made up their minds where they should reside permanently if they felt they could remain in England. Delius loved France.

Whether it was a case of the power of suggestion or not, I cannot say; but from the moment this interview ended I felt utterly depressed and worn out. Within a week I fell a victim to an epidemic of influenza which was raging at the time. I think I should never have risen above the depression that had taken complete hold of me, had it not been for the vital spark of music that still burned within me. I felt every minute of my forty-four years; in fact I felt older then than I do now, and (as I write these words) I am close on seventy. Early in 1917 I again felt fagged out, but the cause was certainly not overwork this time, for in no single year of my whole professional life had I conducted so few concerts. I imagine it was the outcome of the times; at all events, I was too ill to direct a Symphony concert on April 21, 1917. My friend Landon Ronald directed it in my absence.

To go back to 1915. On January 3 the Sunday Concert Society caught me on the hop and insisted I should compose a hymn tune for them (*O God our Strength*), words by Bishop Boyd-Carpenter. It was a *dreadful* tune, and my only consolation was that a footnote in the programme intimated that copies were purchasable at 1s. 9d. for twenty-five from the owners of the copyright, Skeffington's of Southampton Row. I never heard anything more of it.

On May 1, at a Symphony concert, we played my arrangement of Chopin's Funeral March for Scriabin who had died in Moscow on April 14. Two extra Symphony concerts were given at the end of the season to mark my twenty-one years' association with Newman. At the first of these (at Rosa Newmarch's suggestion) I made an orchestral transcription of Moussorgsky's *Pictures from an Exhibition* as so many musicians felt that the character and humour of the music could not be fully portrayed through the medium of the piano. It was produced on April 17, and never before had a Queen's Hall audience tittered so audibly—in fact, during the *Ballet of Chickens* real laughing was heard in all parts of the hall. I felt this to be a compliment to my orchestral version. Years before this Strauss told me that the audience ought to laugh in *Till Eulenspiegel*.

"If you can only make them laugh," he said, "that's what

I want, and you can rest assured you are giving a good performance."

Why not? If an orchestra can so touch an audience's feelings as to make them weep, why should they not occasionally present the other side of the picture and make them laugh? I agree with Strauss.

At the suggestion of Kussevitsky, Ravel scored *Pictures from an Exhibition*, produced in 1924, which was immediately published and therefore available to all conductors. I lent my orchestral transcription of it to several conductors in America but the expense and trouble involved made it impossible for me to continue to do so. After the publication of Ravel's own version I withdrew mine, but I shall always be grateful to Gordon Jacob for the many kind things he said about my orchestration of this humorous and delightful piece in his clever book on the orchestra.

During the twenty-first season of the Promenades, I introduced the name of Charles Martin Loeffler who was born at Mühlhausen, Alsace, in 1861, but who is French in sympathy. Notwithstanding, the country of his adoption is America. I met him in Boston when he presented me with three of his scores; they interested me and I produced them this season. The first was his symphonic poem *The Death of Tintagiles*, the important viola part in which was played by the now well-known composer Eric Coates. I always feel that Loeffler is, so to speak, the artist's artist. He was at this time in the Boston Symphony Orchestra but he resigned in 1903 to devote himself to composition. His forty orchestral compositions are really only known to his intimates as so few are published, but his work shows him to be visionary and a dreamer—a visionary whose thoughts are predominantly sombre and tragic. He is moved most by Verlaine, Poe, Maeterlinck, and Baudelaire—at least, this was the opinion of Lawrence Gilman, the great American critic, which he set down in his interesting book *Nature in Music* (1914).

The name of Joseph Jongen, the well-known Walloon composer (César Franck and Eugène Ysaÿe, by the way, were both Walloons), appears several times in the programmes this season. Jongen was a serious-minded composer who founded many of his orchestral pieces on Walloon folk melodies.

Here is a newcomer whose name is still well-known: William Murdoch. He came to us to play Liszt's *Danse Macabre* on August 23 (1915). Murdoch is, in my opinion, a very fine chamber-music player and his joint recitals with Albert Sammons and Lionel Tertis have proved him a fine, all-round artist. He played the *Emperor* concerto at very short notice, I remember, when Arthur Rubinstein was detained in Portugal. I also note that I produced a very original work by my friend Sergei Rachmaninoff—*The Island of the Dead* in which he portrays the feeling and emotion of Arnold Böcklin's great picture.

Owing to the air raids an announcement appeared in the programmes to the effect that on and after October 4 the Promenade concerts would be given on Mondays, Wednesdays, and Fridays at 3, and on Tuesdays, Thursdays, and Saturdays at 8.

The dignity and control displayed by the audience, night after night during the war years was amazing, and although I had my back to the people I was always conscious of what was happening. I could not actually hear the air raid warnings but I knew that the Promenaders were gradually receding towards the walls under the Grand Circle which was, of course, the natural inclination to 'take cover'. I never heard the anti-aircraft guns except in *pianissimo* passages. Every member of the orchestra behaved with exemplary calm. I remember with pride the marvellous *sang-froid* displayed by Wilfred James when shrapnel fell on the roof, dislodging part of the ceiling while he was playing the bassoon solo *Lucy Long*. The dislodged plaster fell at his feet, but he merely stepped aside without turning a hair, not even missing a quaver of these humorous variations.

In spite of these War conditions the Promenade concerts were so successful that, at the close of the season, Newman announced three special matinées on October 28, November 4, and November 11 (1915). This brought the season's concerts to sixty-six, so that our 'coming of age' at so serious a time in the country's history was surprising and worthy of the warmest congratulations.

On the back of the Symphony concert programme for February 12, 1916, a notice appeared to the effect that thirty-nine members had enlisted under the Derby Scheme and were now on active service.

It was now, if ever, that my policy of engaging women to play in the orchestra was justified; for the men, from time to time, had departed under the scheme of enlistment and women filled their places. Many were only engaged as a temporary measure, but the fortitude and loyal work were something I shall ever remember with gratitude and pride; though I shall never be able to understand why—considering I am the one English conductor who has successfully championed the cause of women in professional orchestras—I have never been invited to direct a single concert for the Women's Symphony Orchestra or any other women's organization. Goodness knows it is not the *work* I wanted, but the *compliment* would have been pleasant!

Incidentally, I made some excellent orchestral records for Columbia during the War years and whenever I put one on now it always recalls happy interludes in those trying times, and the jolly chats in the Studios with Arthur Brookes—then their manager.

The 1918 season opened a little guardedly in that we announced only a preliminary four weeks' season. I do not blame Chappell's for that because they were steadily losing money. However, the public response was so definite that, after the second week, the usual eight weeks' season was advertised, but it became more and more evident that we must shorten the concerts to allow the public to get home before the late-night (or early morning) aid raids began. We therefore began at 7.30 and finished at 9.30.

There is little of interest in the way of novelties or first appearances during the seasons of either 1916 or 1917, but we were grateful for such fine British artists resident among us as Irene Scharrer, Myra Hess, Daisy Kennedy, Gerwase Elwes, Carrie Tubb, Margaret Balfour, Rosina Buckman, Ruth Vincent, Robert Radford, Charles Tree, Louise Dale, Carmen Hill, Olga Haley and others.

Campina Granados' name turns up for the first time at the opening Symphony concert on October 28 with his important symphonic poem *Dante* in two movements, which made a deep impression. Granados was a Spanish composer of real distinction and the tragedy of his death—when the *Sussex* was sunk by a German submarine in the English Channel on March 24, 1916 —came just after the production of his opera *Goyescas* at the Metropolitan Opera House. His was indeed a Castilian temperament which is evident in all his works. I orchestrated five of his original piano dances and have played them for many years here, on the Continent, and in America.

A somewhat curious novelty was introduced by Moiseiwitsch at the first Symphony concert of 1917 in the shape of a new concerto in F sharp minor by Tchérepnin. This work suffered from too long *tuttis* in between the piano sections and lacked form and cohesion, but he played it magnificently. Albeniz's *Catalonia* made a much better impression at the same concert. I had played his works as far back as 1900 and knew him well in the old days when Mr. Money-Coutts brought him to London and he wrote *The Magic Opal* for the Lyric Theatre.

His serious Opera *Pepita Jiménez* was a fine work. Albeniz was himself a fascinating pianist and wrote over two hundred works for the instrument including a fine suite called *Iberia*. He led a roving and exciting life until 1883 when he settled down to composition.

The Promenade season of 1917 comprised sixty-two concerts. I remember that, after the first concert, Dora Garland led the Promenades for a week during Arthur Beck's absence on military duty. Miss Garland was a pupil of Maurice Sons and quite an old member of the orchestra. I remember how she surprised us all at the Bach concert in that week when she stepped out of her place among the first violins and put up a capital performance of Bach's *Chaconne* after which she led the orchestra in Mendelssohn's *Scotch Symphony*, an achievement of great moment and another feather to adorn the women's caps.

Malipiero's name first occurs this season. We produced his *Impressioni del Vero*. He is now regarded as one of the most advanced of modern composers but in those days he was a disciple of the modern Venetian school. These pieces displayed his faculty for suggesting the various aspects of nature.

My old friend Arthur de Greef appeared year after year, and perhaps we wearied a little of his reading of the Grieg concerto; but this may have been the management's fault and not his. At all events, we enjoyed producing his own concerto and gave several performances of his *Four Old Flemish Folksongs* which he often directed personally.

We do not hear much of Jaques-Dalcroze as a composer; rather do we hear of his Eurhythmics. Daisy Kennedy, however, played his concerto this season. It was a sad blow to Jaques-Dalcroze (and also to his associates) when, in 1914, he had to abandon the fine institute he had founded at Hellerau near Dresden. Another war measure. However, his system still flourishes in Switzerland, Paris, and London.

As musicians who could take no other part in the war, it was with humble gratitude that we gave a *Parsifal* concert on Good Friday of this year (1917) in the presence of H.M. Queen Alexandra. How wonderfully our Royal House singles out the right moment to express approbation of this or that undertaking! Queen Alexandra's presence in Queen's Hall was a kindly gesture to musicians at a time of much heartburning, just as King Edward's presence at a Sunday afternoon concert had silenced, once and for all, the criticism that had been levelled against them. This Good Friday concert coincided with the rallying of America on our side, and I was called upon to add yet another national anthem to my collection. I therefore scored 'The Star-spangled Banner' specially for this concert.

Boston had been wooing me for some time. After lengthy correspondence with the management of the Boston Symphony Orchestra I had an interview in London on May 1, 1918, with the Secretary, Mr. Higginson, and Mr. Grant, a wealthy lover of music who backed the Boston Symphony Orchestra much in the same way that Mr. Allan, the wealthy shipping magnate, backed the Scottish Orchestra for so many years.

The offer was tempting, and I carried in my mind the memory of that journey I had made so many years before at my father's instigation. I thought then that this body of musicians was the finest I had ever heard. So that musically it meant much to me, and the financial side was more than satisfactory, too. The question I had to answer was whether I could carry out the season's conducting at Boston each year and, at the same time, keep faith with the man who had helped me build up my career—Robert Newman—and Chappell's—to say nothing of my loyal public.

It was a very hard nut to crack, for I loved my English orchestra and the work which had now become a national institution. I knew that if I did not break away I should possibly remain tied more or less to routine-work year in, year out. Again, the musical satisfaction of a permanent orchestra run on lines permitting sufficient rehearsals to satisfy my yearning for perfection in performance was indeed a hard pull.

As such things do, this leaked out and the Press got hold of a story—one paper even announced the name of the boat on which I intended to sail. If ever I had had any doubt about my public it was dispelled now, for I was deluged with telegrams, telephone messages, letters and post cards, the most touching of all perhaps being those from the trenches. The Provinces showed the same concern as London. Deputations waited on me.

"*You must not leave us!*"—That was what they said.

Newman was inundated with letters from all quarters, the burden of which was: "London must not let Sir Henry Wood go to Boston to follow Dr. Muck at a time when the Queen's Hall was needed by thousands of troops returning for a few days' leave; and by war-weary citizens, kept hard at their several duties, to whom music is a solace and a help." One telegram from France summed up the situation in rather a cryptic fashion: "Surely Boston can find half a dozen conductors to take Muck's place—but hands off our Henry J."

The announcement in the Press resulted in rather a stormy interview with Newman and William Boosey, but I told them my mind was not yet made up and that the announcement was premature in any case. Their questions were somewhat searching.

"What do you intend to suggest about the Symphony and Sunday concerts which after twenty-three years have assumed as national a character as the Promenades? Who is to conduct these if you leave England for six months in the year? What about your provincial festivals and concerts? What about your pupils and all your other work?"

I realized that I could not relinquish my work in England for so long each year. Neither did it seem likely that I could retain the Promenade concerts if only for the reason that the programmes took time to agree upon, especially as the opening date and the duration of the season were subject to alteration.

My dreams pretty well vanished at this interview. It came to me that had it not been for Newman I should probably never have held the position or been accorded the esteem that was now mine. I also remembered that had it not been for Chappell's and Mr. Boosey the concerts might never have been continued during the anxious War years. It was obvious when Chappell's took over the concerts that they would lose money.

I had a further interview with Mr. Grant at St. James's Club on May 30. He suggested I should try a season and see how it worked. He was charming and persuasive, but I had to tell him that the difficulties would prove insurmountable and that if I went for one season I might as well go for three or more. On June 1, I was able to state definitely that I had decided against going to Boston. I had a Sunday afternoon concert the next day. As I walked on to the platform I received one of the most touching ovations of my life—indeed, the concert did not actually begin until ten minutes after the advertised time. It was the same at the Sunday evening concert, when the repetition of the afternoon's acclamations provided a touch of balm for my shattered hopes—my wistful musical hopes which I had sacrificed for what I knew was my duty.

The subject was destined to be re-opened in an unexpected manner. Mr. A. J. Balfour wrote to me and asked me to meet him at the Foreign Office. Wondering what he could possibly want with me I went to meet him on June 27. My surprise at his first words can be imagined.

"*Why* can you not take up the appointment at Boston?" he asked.

I told him that I had made no hurried decision and that, had the War been over, I might have been tempted to try a season at least, but I pointed out that my ties in England were holding me and the thought of what might happen to the musicians at Queen's Hall—my musical home.

Mr. Balfour then put forward diplomatic reasons.

"We want further friendship with America," he said. "I think, Sir Henry, you would be a great help to us in this."

I explained why, artistically, I had wished to go; how I had relinquished the idea when I remembered how many people were bound up in my musical associations here; and how, after twenty-three years, the representations of the public had decided me. "No, sir," I said. "I feel it is impossible for me to leave London at this time."

"I understand," he said. "But I wish it had been possible."

I parted from this charming, quietly-spoken diplomat feeling somewhat subdued and thoughtful, but also with a deep sense of honour and gratitude that he had even thought I should make an ambassador for British interests in America. He was kind enough to pay me a return visit when I was conducting the Handel Festival at the Crystal Palace, and reminded me of our interview at the Foreign Office. He often attended concerts of mine and was a lover of Handel in particular.

After this episode I felt much happier, for it had set the seal on my work in England. The season of 1918 was in no way different from its predecessors of the war years, but a less doubtful and anxious atmosphere could be sensed regarding the eventual outcome.

Delius wrote to me in the autumn and told me he had just completed a new orchestral work, suggesting I should produce it for him. The upshot of this was that I invited him to London and announced a date for the production of the work (Nov. 23). I arranged to meet him on September 30 when he crossed from France with his wife. I was deeply distressed with his tired and tragic appearance. He seemed to have aged terribly since our last meeting. We drove straight to Elsworthy Road which I was delighted to place at his disposal. Madame Delius was always anxious on his behalf and as soon as we were in the house she insisted on his resting.

"No, no!" said Delius. He then proceeded to unbutton his waistcoat, shirt, and top trouser buttons and to my astonishment pulled out sheet after sheet of manuscript which proved to be his new work which he had called *Once upon a time*.

"What a relief to get it safely to London!" he murmured, and subsided into a chair.

"I, too, am relieved," whispered Madame Delius. "I was so afraid they might search him and commandeer it."

This sounds almost melodramatic now, but at that time every possible means of avoiding being searched was resorted to. There was a rumour current that a certain German resident in America used to dispatch what he labelled *M.S. Composition* to Germany but which was found to contain information in code. Hence Delius's anxiety lest his manuscript should be confiscated.

A couple of days after they had settled in I called to make sure they were comfortable and happy, and was much disturbed to find every clock in the house stopped. I volunteered to wind and set them going again.

"Oh, no, no!" said Delius. "I can't bear the ticking of a clock!"

I remember casting a sly glance at my grandfather clock which stood in the hall and which had been a family treasure since 1806, and which I am certain had never before been wilfully silenced. I saw a good deal of the Delius's during the month they remained at Elsworthy Road, and they often came to Queen's Hall with our mutual friend Balfour Gardiner. I am glad to think that the few weeks of the quieter atmosphere of London restored Delius's shattered nerves and comforted his devoted wife. He now decided to call the work he had brought with him so dramatically from France *Eventyr* instead of *Once upon a time* (as it had been advertised in a Symphony concert programme). As a matter of fact, that was not the only change for we had to postpone the performance from November 23 to January 11. The reason was a good one. The copyist experienced difficulty in deciphering the notes of this modern and complicated orchestral score. Not surprising, for it was written in faint *lead pencil!* and had suffered from its unconventional mode of transport.

This is the only orchestral work I have ever come across in which male voices are used—not to sing, but to give a wild shout, behind the orchestra and out of sight. We had thirty men to do it, and they did it remarkably well; but in subsequent performances this novel and exciting effect has been omitted.

Although they do not refer to this year I quote two letters I received from Delius and his wife. Both are dated September 21, 1931.

From Delius:

DEAR WOOD,

I listened to the concert the other night and everything came through most beautifully. The rendering you gave of my new work, *The Song of Summer*, was really beautiful, and the nuances and tempi were just right. I enjoyed the whole evening most thoroughly.

Please accept my very best wishes,

Yours very sincerely,

FREDERICK DELIUS.

From Madame Delius:

DEAR SIR HENRY,

I must add a little word to tell you how greatly I enjoyed the concert. The new work sounded lovely and Delius looked so happy listening to it.

I think you did the *Dance Rhapsody* and *Brigg Fair* more beautifully than ever before.

We meant to write at once but my husband was very unwell the day after the concert. It turned out to be an attack of shingles and I am only glad it did not begin the day of the concert.

With kindest regards from us both,

Yours ever,

JELKA DELIUS.

XLII

THE POST-WAR YEARS
(1919–1926 inclusive)

WHAT A RELIEF it was to open the first post-War season of 1919 with a newly-decorated Queen's Hall! A somewhat disagreeable blue-green, I must admit, but the walls had at least been purged of the awful memories of the past four years. Balfour Gardiner was the first to express his joy and relief, musically, in a new work called *The Joyful Home-Coming* which we produced for him on the opening night of the twenty-fifth season. It was a work imbued with real spirit of jubilation.

On September 10 we produced a new symphonic poem called *Lamia* by a young English girl—Dorothy Howell. The work made such an impression that it was repeated during the season no less than five times. This was indeed exceptional for a British composer's work—for a woman a triumph.

Up to this time Miss Howell had been known as a pianist only. She was a native of Birmingham and a pupil of Sir John McEwen at the Royal Academy of Music. We afterwards produced her piano concerto and some ballet-music. She was a fastidious composer, slow in production; consequently she has produced few works; but they are all of distinction, for her themes and orchestration show real thought and musical feeling.

Early in the season Solomon paid me a visit. He said he wanted to talk to me about his career. Candidly, he told me, he was utterly sick of the piano and hated his work. I looked at this mere lad of sixteen and was not surprised. He had been playing in public ever since 1911 when he was only eight. He had had no child-life, no boy's interests, no games. As he said, it had been piano, piano, and nothing *but* piano.

"Go away for two years," was my advice. "Don't touch a piano and forget every note of music you ever heard, if this is possible."

Solomon took the advice. He returned in 1921 refreshed, matured, and in full command of his destiny. There is hardly any need for me to tell his public what it already knows: Solomon is a favourite throughout the country, always sure of the success his finished playing commands. His interpretations, ranging over a wide field, are deeply thoughtful and intensely musical.

I have been looking at these early post-War programmes. I purposely gave particulars of first performances and the initial appearances of artists in pre-War years because so many of them are unknown to the present younger generation. From 1927 onwards—when the B.B.C. took over the management of the Promenades—it is a different matter: few names that I could mention are unknown today. I will therefore content myself with a few observations on the more important events between 1919 (the season after the War) and 1927 (the year of the B.B.C. *régime*) leaving my younger readers to remember for themselves the advent of the more recent artists who are now well-known for their splendid work.

It may not be remembered, for instance, that Charles Woodhouse first became my leader in 1920. My association with him was of the happiest and I greatly deplored his resignation in 1935 owing to a breakdown in health. After a few years with me he knew the repertoire so well and evinced such a flair for conducting that I was able to institute a system that proved most useful.

I had always wished I could hear the orchestra as it sounds in the body of the hall, which is so different from the rostrum.

I armed myself with my little handbell and gave my baton to Woodhouse (during part of the rehearsals) and repaired to the Grand Circle where I was able to take notes of this or that balance, expression, or quality of tone. I found that many effects which reached me easily enough at the rostrum did not reach me in the Grand Circle even with the hall empty. The little bell, as I have said before, was treated as a joke by the orchestra, but I preferred to use it rather than shout.

The Promenades had now been running for a quarter of a century. We were all immensely proud of the fact, especially when their Majesties King George and Queen Mary were graciously pleased to honour us with a visit.

There is no royal box in Queen's Hall. The only one we ever had was done away with after the first season because it took up so much room in the Grand Circle. In its stead we reserved the whole of Block A (the block on the extreme left of the hall nearest the platform) and, on this particular occasion, there was a party of about thirty people including Elgar who was there in his capacity of *Master of the King's Musick*.

During the interval King George sent for me and congratulated me on my work of the past twenty-five years. The last item of the programme was the *Fantasy on British Sea-songs*. After the concert was over, instead of leaving the hall, the King and Queen sent for me again. King George then told me how much he had enjoyed the Sea-songs.

"*Rule, Britannia!* is a jolly fine tune," was his Majesty's opinion. Then, looking at me with those blue eyes of his, he dug me in the ribs:

"A better tune than the *Red Flag*, eh, Sir Henry?"

"I agree with you, Sire!"

The present *Master of the King's Musick* is Sir Walford Davies, whose work in furthering the knowledge of music among the younger generation would of itself place his name high on the roll of honour in the interest of music in Great Britain. He is an indefatigable worker too for music in Wales; while his list of compositions makes one wonder how he manages to get it all in. Grove's Dictionary alone gives works from his pen as seventy-four. His broadcast talks on Music must have been invaluable to millions of listeners.

On February 28, 1924, I was elected a Fellow of the Royal College of Music. On February 23, 1927, a dinner was given by the Council to the Fellows of the College. At this dinner, in his capacity as President, was H.R.H. Prince Edward, then Prince of Wales. His Royal Highness had opened the new home of the Donaldson Museum and also a new entrance to the Concert Hall given by the munificence of Sir Ernest Palmer. The dinner was eaten in the hall itself and there was an entertainment afterwards in the Parry Opera Theatre. Incidentally, I recently heard from the Bursar (who kindly looked up the above dates for me) and was amused to find him requesting me to sign the Roll of Fellows, which of course, I ought to have done long ago. I have now made good the omission.

The Prince sat opposite me with Sir Hugh Allen on his right. I sat next to Lord Gladstone. During dinner the Prince noticed a new portrait (by Orpen) of Stanford which hung on the opposite wall.

"Who is that?" he inquired.

"I don't expect Your Highness will know him: he is Sir Charles Villiers Stanford," replied Sir Hugh.

"Of course I do. He wrote the *Hallelujah Chorus*."

"Oh, no, sir. Handel wrote the *Hallelujah Chorus*."

"Good Lord! What a bloomer!"

The Prince roared with laughter in which we all joined.

The Royal College of Music has been fortunate indeed in Sir Hugh Allen who has been Principal for twenty years. He retired at the end of 1937. I know of no musician with a greater capacity for making friends—and keeping them—nor yet a man of such a happy, genial temperament. Whenever I meet him his kindness and friendliness bring home to me the regret that I have, perhaps, not given sufficient time in my busy life to the happy relaxation that comes of such meetings with my colleagues.

I note a first appearance of interest to the present-day Promenaders—that of the charming Astra Desmond who looked as well as she sang. She made an instant success with her singing of *Erda's Warning* from *Das Rheingold*. She was a pupil of Blanche Marchesi who first introduced her to me. She is a most accomplished musician and few are her equal as a linguist.

Many concert-goers of the present day imagine that Prokofieff is a new-comer and that his works have only been recently introduced. That is not a fact. Ellen M. Jensen played his piano concerto in D flat as far back as August 24, 1920. At that time Prokofieff was undoubtedly one of the most interesting figures among the young Russian group. I actually introduced his *Scherzo* for bassoons in 1916.

The Danish Legation first brought to my notice that now world-famous tenor Lauritz Melchior who appeared in 1920. He was announced as principal tenor of the Danish Opera in

Copenhagen. He sang *Lohengrin's Narration*, making a tremendous success with it. His dramatic voice was afterwards heard in several scenes from the Wagner operas and I think his fine, manly appearance appealed almost as much as his voice. I remember how annoyed Newman used to get with Melchior—almost to a point of refusing to re-engage him after the first season—because he would insist on singing in Danish. Even in 1923, his fourth season, he sang the Steersman's Song (*Flying Dutchman*) in his own language. Not a word of English—or even German.

A young composer of seventeen whom I introduced to London —I think in 1920—was Eric Fogg of Manchester who came to direct a suite from his ballet *The Golden Butterfly* which he could already describe as Opus 40. I had known his father for many years as organist to the Hallé Society and now fulfilled a promise to take interest in his talented son. I was pleased when the B.B.C. brought him to London some years later and gave him a permanent position as conductor of the Empire Orchestra, after his experience of some years in the Manchester Studio. I admire his bassoon concerto which Archie Camden played so well at a Promenade Concert (in 1935 or 1936).

Another first appearance of interest in 1920 was that of Harriet Cohen. She came to us to introduce a fine work by Bax—his symphonic variations for piano and orchestra. This work has always remained in my memory as a notable achievement; it is a pity it has never been published. Harriet Cohen is the possessor of a most charming and attractive personality. Everybody seems to know her and she seems to know everybody. I have never met an artist with a larger circle of friends. Her devotion to the music of Bax has been a noble gesture and her continued and persistent interest in his splendid piano works is deserving of all praise. The Royal Academy of Music is justly proud to include Harriet Cohen's name in the list of past students.

I first conducted the R.A.M. Students' Orchestra in 1923 since when I have (when engagements permitted) rehearsed them six hours a week. I cannot express my delight at the progress these young people have continued to make year by year. Quite recently they put up a performance of the *Prelude and Liebestod* and the *Venusberg Music* in Queen's Hall that could rank with some of our most experienced professional orchestral performances.

Strauss visited the Academy in 1936 and directed my Students' Orchestra in a performance of *Tod und Verklärung* without a rehearsal. He was delighted with them and praised their flexibility. The mention of his name reminds me that I have not related the fact that my performances of *Don Quixote* are founded on the memories of an evening with him at 46, Grosvenor Street. Knowing that I was soon to direct his epic in character-study, he volunteered after dinner to play the work through to me on the piano from my full score. Never shall I forget how he played and acted and sang every mood portrayed in the variations. When Sancho Panza talked (*via* the viola solo) Strauss put words to the phrases: "Give me more money, money, more money!" This fitted exactly the particular musical phrase.

Thinking of this orchestra again, only a few years ago it was quite rare to get students for wind instruments. This year (1938) we have seven horns, six flutes, four clarinets, four trumpets, two bassoons, two trombones, one timpanist, and several studying the harp. At the end of last term we had to engage two professional horn-players for our concert because three of our young students had been snapped up by one of the established London orchestras. I attribute this success to the fact that the Directorate of the Academy has taken my advice and has secured the best professors—men like Aubrey Brain, Alec Whittaker, Stainer, Newton, Kell, Langston in the wind department, and O'Neill for the timpani.

There are some budding (and not-so-budding) conductors among the students. I should like to whisper the name of one or two who will, if they stick to it, go far; but they must take a leaf out of my book and conduct everything that comes their way.

As I write I have just heard of the death of Philip Agnew, a great patron of the arts. This is a sad loss for the Royal Academy of Music. He was such an enthusiastic chairman of the management, and it was entirely owing to his persuasive powers that I undertook the training of the Students' Orchestra in the first place.

Sir John McEwen resigned his post as Principal in 1936. In a letter to me, dated June 28, 1936, he says:

The difference between the condition of things today and that which prevailed when you took charge fourteen years ago is simply staggering, and the debt which I personally and the whole Academy owe to you can hardly be over-estimated. It has always been a great gratification to me that the relations between yourself and myself have been consistently and continuously of the friendliest nature, and I hope that whatever rearrangements are come to as the result of my resignation, the Academy will long continue to enjoy the advantage of your experience and sympathetic help with the orchestra.

The President of the Academy is the Duke of Connaught who has taken the deepest interest in the welfare of this, the oldest musical institution in Great Britain. The Duke has been extremely kind to me, personally, and has often been present at my concerts in Nice and Monte Carlo, and has regularly attended the prize-giving at the Academy each year. Last year (1937), however, he was absent through indisposition, but we were privileged to greet our charming Duchess of Gloucester who came in the Duke's place to distribute the year's awards.

We are fortunate indeed in Professor Stanley Marchant as our Principal. Never in my long association with the Royal Academy of Music have I met anyone more enthusiastic for this grand old institution. It pleases me greatly to find him encouraging such a happy social atmosphere in the Academy. He has conceived the idea of starting a museum and picture gallery (housed in the Academy itself), and I feel greatly honoured at his accept-ance of one of my own oil landscapes with which to start the collection. He himself is deeply interested in the art and spends much of his leisure—if indeed he has any since he became Principal—sketching in water colour. This little picture gallery is confined to musicians, of whom so many paint.

The list of distinguished names before the public today as performers or composers, of whom I have already spoken as being R.A.M. students, would not be complete without remind-ing my readers that Sir Granville Bantock, Sir Arnold Bax, Dame Marie Tempest, Eva Turner, Lionel Tertis, Roy Hender-son, Myra Hess, and dear Ben Davies are also past students. Myra Hess was of course the pupil of that great piano teacher Tobias Matthay—at the R.A.M. It is with pleasure I record the fact that Myra Hess has played at no less than ninety-two Orchestral Concerts with me—and reminded me of this wonder-ful record when we chatted over the past, a few days ago.

Another present-day favourite to appear in 1920 was Jelly d'Aranyi who played Lalo's *Symphonie Espagnole*. What a person-ality and what a born violinist! The Promenade audience was completely carried away by her fire and dash. Yet, when a concerto demands it, she can be the classical of the classical. It always gives me pleasure to accompany her because of the intensity of her musicianship. The performance by the two sisters (Jelly d'Aranyi and Adila Fachiri) of the Bach double violin concerto in D minor is a piece of *ensemble*-playing the Promenade audiences have been fortunate in hearing almost annually for some years.

It seems I have produced every orchestral work of Eugène Goossens at the Promenade concerts before the B.B.C. took them over. I wish he had devoted his energies to writing orchestral works that might have been played the world over. His grand operas appear from time to time, but they seem to be performed only once or twice at Covent Garden. I doubt whether any composer can hold his public by a dramatic work produced, say, once in five years. Strauss himself is no exception to that rule, for he owes his popularity to his early symphonic poems which have been played all over the world. They may have paved the way for his operas but, even so, only *Der Rosenkavalier* has ever really caught on. *Salomé* and *Elektra* have never shared the same success.

I think it must have been in 1923 that Isobel Baillie first came to us; at all events, I remember a young and pretty girl with masses of golden hair and a voice equally golden. She has steadily mounted the ladder of fame until, nowadays, a festival without her is almost unthinkable. I am certain she owes her position to sheer hard work. Success has never turned her head nor caused her to become either lazy or self-satisfied. I will say for Isobel Baillie that, in all my work with her I have never found her anything but note-perfect—whether in *The Wife of Bath* or Brahms's *Requiem*.

I was the first to introduce the music of Joaquin Turina, the delightful composer of whom Debussy, Ravel, d'Indy and Florent Schmitt thought so much. His splendid *Procesión del Rocío* has always met with a warm reception in London. I also gave the first performance in England of his *Danzas Fantasticas*. These three dances were founded on *La Orgia*, a novel by José Mas.

The name of Darius Milhaud appears for the first time in 1922. He was one of the notorious French 'Six' who lean so much towards sombre and violent expression in music: hatred, despair, fury, terror. He has obviously drawn his inspirations largely from Grand Guignol, but his experiments in both polytonality and atonality are of the deepest interest. Unfortunately, when I produced his second *Suite Symphonique* neither public nor press took interest in this really novel composer.

A little later in the season of 1922 I produced Ernest Bloch's *Schelomo* for 'cello and orchestra which was played by May Mukle. Ysaÿe was the first to show me this deep original work and I have taken interest in Bloch's compositions ever since. His second symphony (*Israel*) created a profound impression when I produced it at Queen's Hall; I cannot understand why it has not been revived. Perhaps the newly-founded Bloch Society will do something towards bringing about more performances of his larger works—*Trois Poèmes Juifs*, especially, for it is a fine piece. All Bloch's work has a strong racial quality, and even where no actual Hebraic themes are introduced he always seems to voice the ideals and aspirations of his race and creed.

I extracted a certain amount of private delight and re-assurance from the fact that several ultra-modern works this season were hissed in no unmistakable manner. It gave me enormous satisfaction to realize that the audience was not composed of a number of passive listeners or (shall I say) passive frequenters, but of a public capable of expressing their judgment. No one can be more interested in the advancement of musical ideas than I; indeed, my feelings are to oppose anything static or stationary where music is concerned; but these outbursts from the audiences in Queen's Hall proved to me that we had gathered together musical people trained in all schools of thought, real music-lovers. The knowledge of it made me feel that my twenty-eight years of sticking to my guns had been worth while. The War had cooled my ardour for wider fields, and this evidence of musical discrimination was in no small way a reward and seemed to tighten the bonds that held me to England.

José Iturbi, now well-known in America as a conductor-pianist, made his first appearance in London this season to play *Hispania*, a work for piano and orchestra by his compatriot Joaquin Cassado. Iturbi's brilliance marked him as a pianist of the first rank—a fact confirmed by his subsequent appearances. This is all the more remarkable because, as I have said before, an artist rarely succeeds in a dual capacity in England. I have already mentioned several really great men who have failed in this way. I think Ysaÿe suffered as much as any of them; for his reputation as a violinist, great as it once was, suffered a depreciation of fifty per cent as soon as he appeared as a conductor. Strange, but it is so.

Dora Labette's name is popular with London concert-goers. She came to us many times this season. I shall always remember her charming singing of Spohr's *Rose, softly blooming*, so unaffected and beautiful was it. The words *Living and dying, sweet Rose, like thee* seemed to fascinate everyone. Her girlish charm captivated the Promenaders.

We had a Danish pianist with us this season—Victor Schiöler who introduced Max Reger's colossal piano concerto in F minor. Rather a big pill, this, for the Promenaders to swallow, but they took it bravely—probably because Schiöler's performance was so masterly. I see he has lately blossomed out as a conductor in Copenhagen where I am sure he will make his mark if only because he is so sincere in all he undertakes.

Another pianist who became a conductor is Malcolm Sargent. To my mind, he is now one of the finest living conductors. I think it must have been in 1923 that he came to me to ask my advice about taking up conducting. I had seen him direct his *Nocturne* and *Scherzo* the previous year and, more recently still, his orchestral poem *An Impression on a Windy Day*. I was left in no doubt that he could easily become a first-rate conductor. It pleases me to think I was right in advising him to give up the piano. He has certainly fulfilled my expectations, for as a choral conductor he certainly excels. The life and vitality he had infused into the performances of the Royal Choral Society deserve gratitude and unstinted praise.

I have always been interested in Lord Berners both as a composer and as a painter. His musical works show such delightful *humour*. (How refreshing in these days when most orchestral colour is so gloomy!) His *Three Little Funeral Marches* are full of spontaneous, whimsical, though (maybe) ironical humour, and the same may be said of his ballet-music and his *Fantaisie espagnole*. I was very pleased with a most representative sketch of his which I purchased some years ago at an exhibition of his pictures in London and which still adorns my study.

Here is a name well-known to followers of modern music—Paul Hindemith. His first appearance was at a Symphony concert in 1923 when I produced his *Nusch-Nuschi Dances* from the Burmese marionette play. Since then I have produced everything he has written for orchestra including his oratorio *Das Unaufhörliche* (which I think is his best work) as well as the much-discussed Philharmonic Concerto. I shall always remember his first appearance because he played the solo part in his viola concerto. His facility was remarkable but he possessed very little emotional tone. That, however, was not significant, for his works do not call for any great emotional expression though there is an exhilaration about them that sometimes attracts. I feel it is necessary to *see* him when he plays his works; mere listening by wireless means being conscious of undecorated distortion whereas his peculiar personality softens much of what he has to say. Which reminds me that Mark Hambourg was playing at the Hull Philharmonic concert last year. After the concert we had supper together at the Royal Station Hotel. On passing the hall porter's black board on which names and messages had been written in white chalk and crossed off 'in straight lines with meticulous care, Hambourg clutched my arm.

"Look, Henry!" he said. ". . . *Hindemith!* That looks as he sounds sometimes."

Throughout those eight post-war seasons, the number of concerts given by the Queen's Hall Orchestra had not diminished, and the programmes show the gradual upward trend towards the ideal Newman had set before him when he instituted them over thirty years previously. After the War there had been, quite naturally, a good deal of re-adjustment, both in the personnel of the orchestra and in the matter of reappearances of foreign artists at the Symphony concerts, whereas the Promenades had given British artists *every* chance during the War years to establish themselves. So that there were now many additional artists to grace our programmes.

One of my chief activities of 1926 was the conducting of the Handel Festival at the Crystal Palace. The memory of it takes me back as far as 1899 when August Manns wrote to me saying he felt he was getting too old to take on the entire responsibility of the Festival the following year (1900) and asked me whether I would care to conduct the *Messiah* and *Israel in Egypt* in his stead.

My father and I had heard a performance of the former work under Manns some years previously, and I remembered how I disliked the way in which the accompaniments were scored. My father was of the same opinion.

"Henry," he said, "never direct a performance like that! No middle harmony, no balance between chorus and orchestra —all top and bottom and no middle!"

Remembering this, I wrote to Manns and said I should be delighted to conduct for him, but might I see the score before finally deciding. Olga and I were sitting at lunch a few days later when a small covered van drew up outside the house. I could not think why because we had not been buying furniture. It turned out to be the score and parts of the *Messiah*. I asked the man in charge to wait while I looked through the score. One glance was enough. I had turned to the Hallelujah Chorus and found that Costa (whose scoring it was) had inserted a part for bass drum and cymbals—an unthinkable liberty. And so inartistic!

That was enough for me. I sent the whole consignment back to the Crystal Palace and wrote to Manns saying I could not agree to conducting that arrangement. I re-scored the work and have been altering and modifying my scoring ever since—over a period of thirty years. I hope some great musician will one day bring out a performing edition with Mozart's superb additional accompaniments scored in a fashion that will preserve a perfect balance in a hall seating two thousand people, and a large chorus.

Public rehearsals are an abomination. This 1926 Crystal Palace Festival brought showers of censure upon me because I treated the morning public rehearsal as a *rehearsal* should be treated. I upset the management by stopping half a dozen times in the opening chorus of *Israel in Egypt*. They were all over the place and the contraltos decidedly flat. The manager came to my rostrum and told me that the habit had been to sing straight through the works at public rehearsals. I refused merely to 'run through' as many choruses as time permitted because this was the only meeting between chorus and full orchestra. How inartistic and altogether inadequate—and this, a great Handel festival!

Personally, I dislike strangers being present at rehearsals. I do not like to correct a soloist or a certain department of the orchestra in public—especially as descriptions are likely to be retailed afterwards. Richter never allowed an audience during rehearsals. Hans von Bülow held the same opinion, but he had to give way on one occasion during a rehearsal of the Meiningen Orchestra as he had been notified that Royalty would attend. Directly the royal party arrived he stopped the orchestra and, by a prearranged plan, called upon the second bassoon to play his part in a Brahms symphony—*alone*. He stopped him several times. Anything more boring or dull it is impossible to imagine; but it had the desired effect for the royal party did *not* remain.

This year (1926) for the first time in our long association, Robert Newman fell ill—so suddenly that for the moment I feared everything would come to a standstill, for I had never so much as engaged an extra player without having discussed it with him first. I had seen W. W. Thompson, his young assistant, in the office many times, but had no idea that even his close association with Newman—although it had extended over a period of years—could have fitted him for the difficult task that now faced him. However, he stepped into the breach and took over the management of the Queen's Hall Orchestra with assurance, tact and ability.

I cannot express here all I felt at dear Newman's passing. For thirty-one years we had worked side by side; we had been such firm friends. Our friendship had been built and maintained on an artistic and business basis even though neither of our private lives seemed ever to enter it. We never argued and we never fell out; the only words we ever had were over those Sunday evening concerts. Otherwise we discussed every detail from all angles calmly and in the kindliest spirit.

Newman's knowledge of music and musicians was always unbiased. In his dealings with me he was as straight as a die, and always enthusiastic. I feel I shall never look upon his like again.

XLIII

THE B.B.C. RÉGIME

I BROADCAST FOR THE first time on January 20, 1927, from the People's Palace.

When Chappell's took over the Promenade and Symphony Concerts the programmes after the interval at the Promenades included their publications, and every pianist was expected to play on a Chappell piano, though, later, this obligation was waived. The whole scheme, to my mind, was an astute stroke. It flourished for some years. The second half of the programme then gradually assumed the same musical interest as the first.

By this time broadcasting was in its fourth year. Since 1923 William Boosey, then managing director of Chappell's, had been fighting this new invention which, he maintained, threatened the entire concert industry. The following extracts from a letter written by him and published in the *Daily Telegraph* of May 19, 1923, makes quite amusing reading—today.

No one in the entertainment world is so foolish as to imagine that broadcasting can be opposed or wiped out. It has obviously come to stay. The objection of the entertainment world is against broadcasting under its present conditions. The first thing that the public should appreciate, and which they do not yet appreciate, is that the Broadcasting Company is a big commercial concern exploited by very able business men. In other words, the Broadcasting Company is a competitor of the entertainment industry, paying no entertainment tax, but being absolutely subsidized by the Government. It is in the extraordinary position that it has obtained from the Post Office a monopoly for trading, and the curious thing is that the bulk of its trading is bound at the present moment to be at the expense of other people's property. The very form of its licence, as drafted by the late Postmaster-General, who is now a director of the Marconi Wireless, states in so many words that although broadcasting must pay a subsidy to various Press agencies for cables, etc., it may use theatrical entertainments and concert matter without payment. This amazing licence, of course, cannot override the Copyright Act of 1911, which protects authors' and composers' rights, but for what it is worth it is part of this licence handed to this big trading company.

All points of controversy were eventually thrashed out but, had he lived, I fully believe William Boosey would still have been fighting a gallant, if losing game. I had several meetings at the time with Roger Eckersley and Percy Pitt with regard to the B.B.C.'s taking over the Promenades and, again, happy solutions were found to our problems, the only one which proved a little difficult being the title of the orchestra.

As I have already pointed out, the title 'The Queen's Hall Orchestra' was Speyer's. He refused it to Chappell's; now Chappell's refused the title of 'The *New* Queen's Hall Orchestra' to the B.B.C. The solution was found in 'Sir Henry Wood and his Symphony Orchestra'. This was again revised in 1930 and merged into 'The B.B.C. Symphony Orchestra'.

The solution, from my point of view, was indeed a happy one, if only because I was now free from the everlasting programme-versus-box-office problem for the first time for thirty-two years. When I walked on to the platform on August 13, 1927, for my first Promenade Concert under the British Broadcasting Corporation, I felt really elated. I realized that the work of such a large part of my life had been saved from an untimely death. I do not think I ever conducted Elgar's joyous *Cockaigne Overture* with greater spirit than on this occasion. I felt I was opening a book that, only a few months previously, had seemed to be closed for ever. Nobody can ever understand the relief I felt when discussing programmes for, although I did not get all my own way, I found everyone helpful and ready to study improvements in every shape and form.

And the joy of a *daily rehearsal* and, a little later on, *preliminary* rehearsals on four days before the opening concert! To me this was a real artistic advance. The opening, by the way, was now permanently fixed for the Saturday night succeeding August Bank Holiday.

When the B.B.C. took over the Promenade Concerts W. W. Thompson retained the management on their behalf. This was a relief to me for I was glad not to have to deal with an entire stranger and, as I have said elsewhere, Thompson had proved himself a capable and an astute man of business. Incidentally,

I think it is not generally known that he is an accomplished organist. He studied under Professor Stanley Marchant. The B.B.C. might have hunted through all the orchestral organizations and concert agents' offices in Great Britain and have failed to find a young man trained in the Robert Newman school—one conversant by personal touch and experience with the idiosyncrasies and peculiarities of the orchestral musician and the solo artist of every nationality. Thompson knows the terms these artists ask—and finally accept.

The thought brings to my mind an incident in New York a few years ago. I was walking along Fifth Avenue with a well-known Scots baritone. We met an equally well-known Welsh baritone who had arrived in New York only a few days previously. After greetings—all rather effusive—the Welshman said: "I sang *Elijah* at Brooklyn last night and had one of the successes of my life. What do you think they paid me?"

"Exactly half what you are going to tell me," snapped the Scotsman. Thompson knows such artists—and how to deal with them!

The position of Musical Director to the B.B.C. is, I am sure, no sinecure. It says much for Sir Adrian Boult that he is liked by one and all. When one knows how daily contact with all the varying factions under studio conditions so often leads to frayed nerves and edginess (both of musicians and general staff) Sir Adrian's popularity speaks for itself.

Boult followed me in 1923 as conductor of the Birmingham Festival Choral Society. He tells me that, as a small boy at Westminster School, he attended many of my Sunday afternoon concerts with a mutual friend, Mrs. Gillard. I first saw him conduct during the war (1918) when, by the generosity of Balfour Gardiner, the Queen's Hall Orchestra was engaged for two semi-private performances of Gustav Holst's *Planets* on the eve of the composer's departure for Salonika. To direct such a score, which was very complicated, was a great achievement. I recently attended a performance of William Walton's *Belshazzar's Feast* which he directed in a most convincing and masterly manner at a Symphony Concert.

Under the B.B.C. the production of novelties is a pleasure, for the daily rehearsals have given me more time for new works. As well, too, for composers are like goldfish with ants' eggs—never satisfied. Rightly so, perhaps; but Time, even now, is ever my master during the Promenade season.

I had directed the first performance in England of Mahler's First, Fourth, and Seventh symphonies prior to the B.B.C. *régime*.

322

I little thought in 1911, when I bought a full score of the Eighth symphony, that I should ever have the artistic satisfaction of producing such a colossal work. It is called the *Symphony of a Thousand* because Mahler wrote it for a thousand performers including a chorus of 400 children and an orchestra of 130 players. The B.B.C. invited me to produce this work in 1930 at a Symphony concert, giving me *carte blanche* in the matter of rehearsals. We repeated it in February of this year 1938. The success of the production gave me intense satisfaction. The Philharmonic Choir sang superlatively well (with faultless intonation) while the eight solo singers[1] were perfectly cast. The orchestral playing throughout proved once again that the B.B.C. Symphony Orchestra is the finest permanent orchestra England has ever had—in fact, it equals any of the world's famous orchestras today.

While on the subject of this Orchestra, and although to speak of the *Dream of Gerontius* on Good Friday, 1938, at Queen's Hall meant opening up this chapter, I felt I must speak of the most beautiful choral singing and orchestral playing I have rarely —if ever—directed. I must pay special tribute to Mr. Leslie Woodgate, the B.B.C.'s Chorus Master. I have *never* obtained such superb *pianissimo's* from such a large chorus, nor directed one with such evidence of sound knowledge of collective singing—their tone was a quality that only comes of careful training. This is not the first time I have recognized Mr. Woodgate's fine work, for so many choral concerts which I have directed during the past few years have given me the more artistic satisfaction from the fact that his singers *understand* a gesture —which speaks of good directorship in the studio rehearsals— they breathe correctly, and above all their *ensemble* is wellnigh perfect.

For perfect intonation, for emotional feeling and beauty of tone, the *Prelude* (indeed the whole work) was the most beautiful and finished performance orchestrally, it has ever been my privilege to direct. An unforgettable experience! An Orchestra that can give such performances as they have done under my direction during the months of February, March and April, 1938, of the Mahler Eighth Symphony, the *Dream of Gerontius*, and Rachmaninoff's Third Symphony makes it difficult for me to speak dispassionately. They are artists every one of them. Of Paul Beard, the leader, I will speak later, but such a body of musicians reflects the fine leadership of the various departments.

[1] Stiles-Allen, Margaret Balfour, May Blyth, Muriel Brunskill, Laelia Finneberg, Walter Widdop Harold Williams, and William Parsons.

Where does one find a finer artist than Robert Murchie (Flute) or such tone and finesse of phrasing as we have from Frederick Thurston (Clarinet) which places him on a plane second to none—a plane shared by Aubrey Brain (Horn), with his sureness, and velvet tone. Archie Camden (1st Bassoon) is an artist of the very first rank; Eugène Cruft (Double-bass) is yet another. Terence MacDonagh (Oboe) has recently taken over from Alec Whittaker and is doing splendid work. Ambrose Gauntlett ('Cello), Barry Squire (Second Violin) and Bernard Shore, form a quintette of principal strings unsurpassable and although I have already mentioned him Ernest Hall (Trumpet) perpetuates the long line of Great British Trumpet Players.

I have my anxieties regarding orchestral musicians; unemployment in their ranks today troubles me greatly. The craze for Mozart programmes just now has, to my mind, a two-sided argument—for and against employment of orchestral musicians. Managements welcome the lesser cost of the small orchestra required for Mozart, and thus one witnesses almost a greed for this much-neglected composer in past years; but is it wise to allow the craze to develop when one knows that the constitution of a Mozart orchestra requires only a few woodwind instruments with a proportionately small number of strings? Orchestral musicians—keep an eye on Mozart!

To return to Mahler's Eighth symphony. At the revival last February we had to limit the size of the chorus to the accommodation of Queen's Hall; but I am sure the B.B.C. would have given me my thousand performers if only the platform could have held them. Incidentally, I wonder whether someone will have the vision and courage to push back the organ a hundred feet or so towards Great Portland Street (where already exists the back entrance to the hall) and make room for a fine platform? This would also allow for an extension of the galleries.

The well-known actor Lewis Casson (whom in the old days I knew as an organ-builder) spoke after dinner recently at the *Dilettante* Club on that controversial subject: 'Do we want, or do we need, a national theatre?' He rounded up his discussion by saying: "Sir Henry should know *because he is a servant of the B.B.C.*"

I could not stand up and speak out of my turn and, as I do not like speaking in public, I am thankful to say my turn did not arrive; had it done so I should have replied something in this vein: "I am not a servant of the B.B.C. in the broad sense of the term, but have that honour only on certain nights when, under their management, that institution of persistent longevity The Promenade Concerts flourishes, also certain other concerts, both symphony and studio. On all such occasions the B.B.C. has found, and will continue to find, me their interestedly willing servant. I say *interestedly* because they are able to tap all schools of music, from the classical to the latest brainwave in modernism and atonality, without the hindrance of the 'box-office brake'."

Private enterprise could not have staged the Good Friday *Parsifal* of 1936 as did the B.B.C. with numerous chorus rehearsals with the Philharmonic Choir undertaken by Ritson Smith, Kennedy Scott, and myself. *The Flower Maidens* I rehearsed privately at my home several times; and they met half a dozen times prior to full rehearsals, having been coached with splendid result by Arnold Perry of the B.B.C. I have never heard a finer *ensemble* in this beautiful scene than the performance of 1936. Every voice was carefully chosen to match in *timbre* and weight —something not always so happily achieved. Soloists and orchestra were faultless, but it was a pity the boys' chorus was so poor. However, this defect was remedied in 1938 when the Boys' choruses were taken by the B.B.C. Singers, trained by Leslie Woodgate. Their singing was very beautiful.

The cast of 1936 was thus made up:

Muriel Brunskill	Herbert Heyner
Norman Walker	Victor Harding

Flower-Maidens

Elena Danieli	Kate Winter
Janet Powell	Helena Bromley
Molly de Gunst	Myra Owen

The Promenade audiences on Wagner nights have to thank the B.B.C. for the fact that I have been able to give excerpts from this sublime work (and many others) without—as I have said before—the curb of expense. I shall always be grateful for the consideration and artistic understanding of my ambitious desires to give such 'plums' during the Promenade season by all connected with the music and the finance of the B.B.C.

I always enjoy my concerts for the B.B.C. in Belfast, where the splendid Orchestra for so many years under the able direction of Mr. Godfrey Brown—who has now retired—is now directed by Walton O'Donnell. I shall always remember Mr. O'Donnell's Military Band, which he directed for some years for the B.B.C. in London—it certainly was the most beautiful I have ever heard. My journeys to Belfast are the more delightful, for in the Duke and Duchess of Abercorn I have staunch musical friends. They never miss my concerts—and I am always so kindly entertained by them at Government House.

There was a change in the B.B.C. Symphony Orchestra for the Promenade season of 1935. Charles Woodhouse had been compelled to resign owing to ill-health and the question of a new leader had to be discussed. Mr. R. C. Pratt, the able B.B.C. Orchestral Manager, came over to Ostend where I was staying for the last few days of my holiday. He put before me names of violinists who had been suggested as leaders for the Promenade Concerts. For years Marie Wilson had sat at the first desk with Arthur Catterall, and I knew she could be trusted with this exacting work. There was still doubt in some minds as to whether a woman could stay the course of the Promenade season, but Miss Wilson proved her powers and finally banished any fears of women not being able to hold their own with men in symphony orchestras. Her tone and technique were beyond reproach and she led the Promenades for two seasons with the greatest distinction. A great little woman this.

The Queen's Hall Orchestra was revived in 1935 for two main purposes: one to make a film and the other to record for Decca. The film, I understand, was beautifully produced; but I am sorry to say I never actually saw it as I was abroad when it was produced in London. The title was *Calling the Tune* and the subject dealt with the gramophone from its inception. It was produced at the A.T.P. studios at Ealing and I must say I thoroughly enjoyed the experience. The scene they built up of an orchestral platform was a model for architects to study.

George Robey and Sir Cedric Hardwicke figured in the cast. I believe one of the most beautiful spots in the film is the record of Melba singing *Oh for the Wings of a Dove*. I have recently seen a large orchestra staged in an American film, but the scene was nothing in comparison with that constructed by Reginald Denham.

Mr. Dreyfus (managing director of Chappell's) ran a series of Sunday afternoon concerts in Queen's Hall with the reformed Queen's Hall Orchestra during 1936. As the title of the orchestra belongs to me, about fifty of the old members formed the backbone of the orchestra together with several younger players. The Press was unanimous in its praise of their playing at these concerts at which appeared such artists as Myra Hess, Irene

Scharrer, Egon Petri, Moiseiwitsch, Lamond, and Pouishnoff. George Stratton—a most accomplished musician—proved a most excellent leader. I call him the Leader with the Beautiful Tone. The woodwind, also, was remarkably fine with Gordon Walker (flute), Miss Rothwell and Miss Boughton (oboes) and Miss Cain (cor anglais). I only wish we could have continued this series every Sunday, for it is only by pegging away that a Sunday afternoon audience in Queen's Hall can be regained. Half a dozen concerts, unfortunately, are not likely to re-create the habit.

This series of Sunday afternoon concerts was taken over by Harold Holt the following season. He introduced Ida Haendel who made her first appearance in London at one of them, playing the Beethoven violin concerto. The entire musical world is now watching the career of this remarkable child with the keenest interest. Although, at the time of writing, she is only fourteen, her interpretative ability is almost uncanny. She played the Brahms concerto at a Promenade Concert later in the year when her tone and feeling in the concerto were so beautiful that I seemed to hear dear old Ysaye at my side once again.

On March 6, 1938, at the Albert Hall, I had the pleasure of accompanying Menuhin who played the Mendelssohn, the Brahms, and the so-called 'lost' Schumann concerto. I am grateful for this last concerto as conceived by Menuhin. The first two movements are really fine; the *rondo finale* is certainly the weakest of the three but it is not given to every composer to write three movements in a concerto of equal merit. If the third movement had been as good as the first I am convinced the 'lost' concerto would have been acclaimed as a welcome addition to the violinist's repertoire. Menuhin's is a masterly control, and his tone faultlessly beautiful. No effort or playing to the gallery; no cheap effects or 'Paganini-swishes' of the bow; everything sedate and stately, as befitting the great artist he is. I found him charming—and so knowledgeable; he knew every note of the scores just as did Ysaye. The orchestra was the London Philharmonic, and to them I must add my tribute: they followed my every gesture, giving aesthetically beautiful accompaniments throughout.

I think I must have met almost every composer of note since Tchaikovsky and, perhaps more in one year than any other conductor in the world. I like to dwell on the thought of the many friendships I hold among British composers. What a list their names make!

Richard Strauss several years ago told me that the younger school in Germany was not to be compared with that of England —high praise from such a source. If British publishers would wake up and imitate continental publishers and allow directors of foreign organizations to see the scores of British composers' works, I am sure hundreds of performances would ensue. I have made inquiries in France, Germany, Italy, and America, and have been invariably told that publishers abroad rarely receive scores of British music. And yet no week in my life passes without my receiving scores from abroad. If it pays continental publishers to distribute scores, surely it would pay ours to do the same?

One of my oldest and most valued friends among British composers is Sir Arnold Bax whom I have already mentioned more than once. We are *very* proud of him. His brilliance and even his complexity are alluring, and his output is staggering. I have recently directed his *sixth* symphony as well as *London Pageant* (his latest work), while the *Garden of Fand*, *November Woods*, *Tintagel*, etc., take their place in my programmes year by year. The *Symphonic Variations*, which Harriet Cohen first introduced to the Promenade public in 1917, is another repertoire work.

Despite the complexity of his scores, Bax is (to me) a great Romantic. His Third symphony (which he dedicated to me) is perhaps my favourite. I have already mentioned the hostility it met with in Rome, but if ever I pay a return visit there I shall give it them again. Though the Italian people like to express their opinion when a work does not appeal to them (as they did definitely on that occasion) I had at least the satisfaction of the opinions of Respighi, Casella, Sinigaglia, and Santoli-quido, all of whom were present and spoke of the deep impression it had created on them. Casella, incidently, wrote to me in deep admiration of my performance of his transcription of the Bach *Chaconne* on the last night of the Promenade season of 1936. He played César Franck's *Symphonic Variations* at a Sunday afternoon concert some years ago—so brilliantly that I wonder he has not visited us again. His latest work—a *Partita* for orchestra —I consider most interesting.

Another old friend, already mentioned, is Vaughan Williams. It has been my privilege to present almost every work from his pen to Promenade audiences. He himself has invariably been at the rehearsals and always ready with a helpful suggestion; but I despair of ever being able to persuade him to use my little bell! His Fourth symphony in F minor (of which I have given as many as four performances in one season) is, in my

328

view, a vivid answer to some of our young moderns. To my mind, he has beaten these striving-for-originality moderns at their own game, but with a far stronger *musical* result. If that work had been signed by Berg or Schönberg the world would have been clamouring for it by now.

The *London Symphony* is now generally popular, and was received with great acclamation when I played it in Paris (La Salle Pleyel) as long ago as 1929. I recently heard from my old friend Madame Aubertin who resides in Paris, reminding me that at the conclusion of this concert Stokowski came forward and embraced me, saying: "This is the man who has taught me everything."

Stokowski was born in London and was educated at the R.C.M. under Hoyte and Walford Davies. He has often reminded me that he attended my Promenade concerts nightly for years in his younger days. This brings to my mind that after the Salle Pleyel concert I had supper with Madame Aubertin and Giulio Volterra, another friend of my younger days—a keen musician with whom I played many four-handed arrangements of orchestral works.

Roussel came over to our table.

"I am delighted to welcome you in Paris," he said. "And to thank you, for you are the only man who ever plays my music in England."

Roussel died in 1937 and I directed a memorial concert to him from the B.B.C. studio on December 14. Among other works of his I played the last from his pen—*Rhapsodie Flamande*, Opus 56. Roussel I remember as a little, dark man with a neatly-trimmed beard, who spoke fluent English. He had been a sailor in earlier life and had travelled all over the world. No doubt he spoke other languages with equal facility.

Another old friend whose memorial concert I directed was Glazounoff who died in 1936. Madame Glazounoff wrote to me after the concert, to which she had listened by wireless in her Paris home, and marvelled at the reception accorded to her husband's works. At the same time she thanked me for my long friendship and the many presentations of Glazounoff's compositions. I feel that his three Symphonies the Fourth, Fifth and Sixth will now take their place in the repertoire and, perhaps, the F minor piano concerto, which I produced in August of 1913. I remember that the pianist on this occasion was Alfred Quaife, a young and brilliant executant.

Another of the moderns is my friend Béla Bartók. I introduced his work to the Promenade public in quite early days. He visited

London when we performed his piano concerto in 1930, playing the solo part himself. He also supervised my performance of *The Amazing Mandarin*. Bartók is certainly an original composer, but he is a trifle too fastidious for Promenade productions, for he demands more time than it is possible to give him at rehearsals. However, I have always made a rule of having piano rehearsals at my house a day or two before a concert containing works of these foreign composers. I look upon this as valuable, not alone in the musical sense but in the personal. By means of these rehearsals I have come to know these men *well*—in some cases intimately; and this so helps one's interpretation of a work. Bartók has undoubtedly been influenced by the traditional melodies of Hungary on which he is an authority, but his rhythms and harmonies are quite individual and often most original.

In these days, when so much space is devoted to film and sport, our music critics have to be content with less space than they deserve. Men like Capell, Colles, Newman, Evans, and Toye have certainly *not* been given the space their writings merit. Some of them, fortunately, have a sense of humour—always to be desired. I was highly amused with a criticism (I think in the *Daily Telegraph* or *Morning Post*) the day after Heddle Nash had sung *Gerontius* so splendidly at the Albert Hall in 1936. Nash had been singing *La Bohème* frequently, and the writer said that his delivery of certain phrases made him fear that at any moment Gerontius would tell the Angel that 'her tiny hand was frozen'.

Speaking of critics behoves me to say that although I have not, since early days, subscribed to a Press Cutting Agency, I have always read the music columns of *The Times*, *Telegraph* and *Morning Post*—but have not kept many references to myself save one by Sir Hugh Allen on the twenty-fifth season of Promenade Concerts and one from the pen of Dr. H. C. Colles which appeared in *The Times* in 1931, at the opening of the thirty-seventh season of Promenade Concerts on August 7th. Any notices quoted in this volume have been sent to me by friends, and by searching newspaper files.

Here is Dr. Colles's article:

PROMENADE CONCERTS

A Musical Curator

Tonight Sir Henry Wood begins his thirty-seventh season of Promenade Concerts at Queen's Hall. Who else, one wonders, among the performers can claim it as the beginning of a fourth dozen? We know of none, and those of us were among Mr. Henry J. Wood's eager audiences of 1895 have mostly to admit that our 'assistance' has been intermittent. Year after year ever since that date Henry Wood has shouldered the responsibility for the most popular, as it is by far the most exhausting, series of concerts in London. He has remained undismayed by changes around him, by the loss of colleagues, chief among whom was Mr. Robert Newman, by changes in the orchestra, in those responsible for finance, by the air-raids of the War, and the hot-air opinions of the peace. To all the changes and chances of this musical life he has made but one answer: he has stuck a fresh carnation in his buttonhole, mounted to the conductor's desk, brought his *baton* down on the stroke of 8 o'clock.

Others have had from time to time, and presumably have now, a voice in arranging the Promenade programmes. Possibly every one of the high authorities of the B.B.C. thinks that he alone has made this year's scheme what it is to be, or at least has added the touch of distinction, and he may be right. But we owe it entirely to Henry Wood that for thirty-seven years the nightly series continued for two months or more has been a survey of all that is admittedly great in the art of orchestral music. Henry Wood has been in fact the curator of our musical National Gallery. He has seen to it that the great classics of all schools and countries are permanently hung in a good light, and that appropriate places are found alike for specimens of the primitives and for samples of the various modern cults. It is this representative character of the Promenade programmes which distinguishes them from those of the several institutions which engage attention through the rest of the year. The winter symphony concerts may offer stronger attractions to special tastes, may bring forward neglected works or revive again what the taste of the English public has hitherto rejected, the symphonies of Bruckner and Mahler for example. Or they may, indeed they must, be able to offer more finished performances than are to be obtained from an orchestra giving six different programmes a week. It is for them to ensure the satisfaction of those fine sensibilities to quality in orchestral ensemble which are supposed to have been awakened in the London concert-going public by the brief visits of foreign orchestras. The Promenades, although the orchestra employed is the bulk of the B.B.C. Symphony Orchestra (ninety-three performers), may not compete point for point with performances by the same players prepared in more leisurely conditions.

Indeed, looking at the matter from the personal point of view, it may be suggested that Sir Henry Wood's willingness to be known primarily as conductor of the Promenades has been a self-abnegating service. Herr Musikdirektor X pays us a visit in the winter to acquaint us with the soul shattering properties of his 'Choral Symphony' or his Brahms No. 1. The London audiences are duly impressed by the marvellous virtuosity of the foreign visitor. Sir Henry Wood is content to give all the nine symphonies and the four of Brahms not as his, but as Beethoven's and Brahms's. If they go well, to Beethoven and to

Brahms be all the glory; if ill, he will be told that he is not so great a conductor as Herr Musikdirektor X. Still, as Sir Henry Wood never has looked at the matter from the personal point of view in all his thirty-seven years, no doubt such comparisons trouble him not at all. Because he has taken the view of public service his personal reputation as an interpreter of certain works may stand less high than that of other conductors, either English or foreign, but he has attained a unique position as the well-nigh indispensable 'curator' of orchestral music in London.

The Promenades remain what they have always been, the chief solace of the music-lover whose work keeps him in London during August and September while others are holiday-making. But they are no longer the exclusive property of the Londoner since the B.B.C. happily acquired them for its patrons all over the country. A considerable part of them may now be switched on by everybody who owns a wireless set, and that means an incalculable increase in their sphere of usefulness. With their appeal to all and sundry, we may be a little anxious lest their primary purpose should come to be regarded as a secondary one, not by the London-bound audience, who are probably well aware that a symphony in the hall is worth ten on the wireless, and not by Sir Henry Wood and the orchestra, who, like all good artists, do not really play to an audience, either actual or potential, but by those who arrange or pass the scheme for the season. Is the increased specialization, one would like to know, to the taste of the present audience, or is it a concession to the supposed convenience of the switcher on and off? Save for Saturday nights, there is now scarce one which is not devoted to some special class of music, and a great number of programmes are one-man shows. Wagner, Haydn and Mozart together, Brahms, Elgar, Beethoven, fill the first week. Perhaps this is educational, but the Promenades used to educate us without our knowing it, and we preferred it that way. The earnest possessor of a four valve set may be in search of education, but hardly the tired Londoner standing on the floor of Queen's Hall. May not Brahms's first symphony come more freshly after a Mozart violin concerto than after his own, and an aria from *The Creation* follow 'Falstaff' better than 'Where corals lie'? Nevertheless we shall take what we are given as we are given it, and with gratitude to all concerned. Our first gratitude, however, on the opening of the season tonight must be to Sir Henry Wood, whose constancy has preserved all the best of his previous repertory, and who now brings the wealth of his long experience to bear in presenting it for the thirty-seventh time.

Up to 1929 I had only to announce that a certain work had been orchestrated by myself to call forth abuse from the Press and purists as having spoiled the original with heavy Wagnerian scoring, etcetera, etcetera. So much so that they very nearly disheartened me. I had heard Leopold Stokowski's transcription of the Bach *Toccata and Fugue* in D minor and determined to make a transcription of this superb organ piece that had been long in my mind. With my knowledge of the organ I knew just what was wanted for the right colour when given over to the wider scope of a full orchestra.

After many months of study I eventually finished the transcription to my satisfaction, but I knew I had only to place my name to it to receive the usual storm of abuse. I thereupon decided to have a little joke. Some months previously Glazounoff had visited me and had told me of the death of a promising young pupil of his by the name of Klenovsky. This name took my fancy and I presented the Toccata and Fugue under that name at a Promenade concert of October 5, 1929.

Klenovsky's success was unquestioned. Every season it is asked for and still finds a place in the Promenade programmes. Such was its popularity that in 1934 Hubert Foss, of the Oxford University Press, approached me in an endeavour to ascertain Paul Klenovsky's address—or that of his relatives from whom he could obtain permission to publish the work. I had to admit my pseudonym and quote here the notice regarding the publication of the Toccata and Fugue which appeared in *Oxford Bulletin* on September 19, 1934, which embraces all criticisms in one.

The publication of this work, which is the reason for the disclosure of the name of the true author, is an event of some importance. Not every new musical issue is rewarded by being given on the same day *The Times*' FOURTH LEADER and STRUBE'S CARTOON in the *Daily Express*, as well as leaders and 'top of the column' articles on the news pages of daily papers throughout the world. The English musical incident is more accustomed to the shade of the back pages or even the darker obscurity of neglect. Klenovsky has now become an historical if shadowy figure like Ossian; but his fame is the more enviable since he never earned it. He has passed into current speech (vide *The Times* Concert Notice of Sept. 6) just as he has passed into the current repertoire, blissfully unconscious of his success and with the ease of an accepted master.

Of the many classes of joke, there is one that is partly serious. This, like that of Henry Lawes, was a kind of protest against the attraction for the English public of a foreign name. Henry Lawes made a fashionable concert piece by setting to music the index of an Italian volume of songs in the Italian manner. Sir Henry Wood's joke is better, for he scored in his own manner but put a Russian name on, as if to say— "Well, you say I can't score—I wonder if Klenovsky can!"

The serious side is that even with forty years' experience of Promenade concerts, he cannot find *virtuoso* pieces for orchestra that will suit his audience. Some other pieces he has constructed have not met with sympathy from those who do not understand his problem and their purpose. Here, in Klenovsky, he has succeeded in the opinion of the public and critics alike. The score is published in miniature form so that everyone may see how he has done it.

The orchestra he demands is large, but his resources are fully employed. The organ for which the original work was written is never reproduced or imitated. For both these reasons the orchestration is worthy of study; for a third, it is the work of the most experienced orchestral conductor of our day. Of Sir Henry Wood we do not need to say more, for the doubly-dead Klenovksy alone has proved, without being able to take trouble, the great love for him the English people have.

My leg-pull greatly annoyed some but equally amused others, while it gave me enormous satisfaction. Some of my friends of the Press have never quite forgotten it and are ever watching for further evidences of an attempt to join the living with the dead.

An amusing instance of this appeared in the *Daily Telegraph* on February 3, 1936, under the heading of *In Memory of King George*. The review was written by one of my kindest critics and was of a memorial concert to the King at which I was present in the audience. Malcolm Sargent conducted.

Among the items was an arrangement of the *Dead March* (Saul) which somewhat puzzled me. It was certainly not Elgar's transcription and I was at a loss to guess the name of the transcriber. However, the Press settled it to their satisfaction the following morning, as follows:

'Klenovsky, we decided, had a hand in the arrangement of Handel's *Saul* March. The dynamic contrasts were fantastic.'

I knew quite well that Klenovsky was not guilty *this* time, but it so happened that I met Malcolm Sargent a day or two later.

"Do tell me," I said, "who scored that march?"

"*I* did," said Sargent.

The Duke of Kent was notably an understanding Royal patron of music. I am proud to quote from his speech at a dinner of the Worshipful Company of Musicians at Stationers' Hall on October 9, 1935. The Duke said:

To a great many people music is still not considered good unless it has been written by a foreigner, but the impression is gradually dying and British composers are receiving the recognition that is their due. If Mr. Klenovsky is dead let us hope that Sir Henry Wood will think it now time to give us some gems under his own name.

In Gordon Jacob's treatise on orchestral technique there is a list headed *Masterly Transcriptions* in which my transcription of the Bach *Toccata* is mentioned. This gratified me for it is pleasant to have the opinion of a real judge. In 1936 I was most agreeably surprised on receiving the following telegram from New York, dated February 21.

HAD GREAT PLEASURE CONDUCTING LAST NIGHT PHILHARMONIC BACH KLENOVSKY TOCCATA ORCHESTRATED BY YOU. AM VERY HAPPY IT MET WITH ENORMOUS SUCCESS. REGARDS.

TOSCANINI.

To turn to quite a different subject.

It distresses me sometimes when I look round the audiences at Symphony concerts to note how comparatively few people take the trouble to wear evening dress. Yet everyone wears it at the opera or even a prize-fight. I maintain that if we adopted a rule in the matter—in the higher-priced seats, at all events, our concerts would be attended more frequently by those who can afford to pay for good seats and who are always to be found in evening dress at their own dinner-tables. It is useless to deny the fact that the social element rules attendance at the opera and elsewhere. If patrons can be as sure of meeting their friends at the concerts—as at the opera, I am certain our symphony concerts, etcetera, would regain a lost audience. The twenty minutes interval recently inaugurated should help matters.

One evening not so long ago when Her Majesty The Queen attended a Symphony concert at Queen's Hall with a party including the Duchess of Kent, I felt quite sad to think Her Majesty looked down into the stalls and along the Grand Circle and found most of the audience in—to be quite candid—very dowdy attire. I wish managements would act boldly. A good opportunity will occur next year when Mr. Owen Mase inaugurates the London Festival of 1939. Incidentally, we shall owe Mr. Owen Mase much for he has recently been released from his duties with the B.B.C. in order to devote his whole time to founding this proposed festival and managing Sadler's Wells. It is good to know he has the full blessing of the B.B.C. What a chance is his to give once again to London a *real* musical festival such as has not been held since the days of Robert Newman!

I have never been able to travel for my music as I should have liked. London has always claimed so much of my time. On the other hand, I have managed at various periods in my career to conduct orchestras abroad, though most of my travels have been holidays. I see by my diary that I was in Paris in July of 1920. I remember that visit because Madame Aubertin took me to see Widor, the distinguished French organist and composer. He played to me for nearly an hour on a delightful little two-manual organ and naturally included his own favourite *Allegretto* and *Finale* from his fifth organ symphony. Widor was a musician of outstanding talents, and I have always admired his edition of Bach's organ works.

In 1921 I was in Zürich to direct a concert at the musical festival held in the *Tonhalle*. I found a fine orchestra under the permanent direction of the distinguished Swiss composer Volkmar Andreae, Director of the Zürich University and Principal of the Academy. Nikisch directed the concert the day before mine. I remember we went for a delightful boating excursion on the lake, lunching with some friends of Dr. Andreae. I was the guest of Mr. and Mrs. Hurliman who were very excited over their new Rolls Royce which had just arrived from London. In these days, when every third car is a 'Rolling Rollicker' one does not think so much of them, but in 1921 it was something of an event.

We started from Lucerne in perfect weather and I found the wonderful scenery and mountain air most exhilarating. The *Tonhalle* I considered a fine hall, and the audience might have been American, so enthusiastically was the concert received. I recollect a fine performance of Berlioz's *Faust* under Dr. Andreae.

I was in Zürich again in 1932 and was both pleased and surprised to be greeted by Harriet Cohen. She had been playing in Germany and was on her way to Geneva to meet her friend Ramsay MacDonald who was there for the disarmament talks. I happened to be performing Arnold Bax's third symphony, and Miss Cohen could not resist the temptation to come and hear it.

I am glad she has been recognized for her work for British composers. Her many friends and well-wishers were sincerely pleased when she was recently awarded the C.B.E. I remember with gratitude her enthusiasm for me when the Promenade concerts had been running nearly forty years. She raised a subscription and presented me with a silver salver on which were engraved the signatures in facsimile of over a hundred artists who had been associated with me at the Promenades. As the subscription exceeded the cost of this handsome gift (which is in daily use for coffee) I was also given a pair of gold cufflinks which I always wear.

In July of 1925 I was in Los Angeles conducting concerts, and only arrived back in London two days before the Promenade season opened.

I remember an amusing incident of which I was a witness while I was in Los Angeles. Two rival (*very* much rival) conductors met in a corridor after a concert conducted by one of them. The other gripped his hand in what was evidently intended to suggest warmth of congratulation. "It sounded . . . *it sounded!*" was all he said. I thought that the queerest congratulatory speech I had ever heard.

One morning in January of 1926 I received a letter from Mrs. Arty Mason Carter, wife of a well-known Hollywood doctor and president of the Hollywood Bowl Concerts. After some correspondence I agreed to her suggestion that I should conduct some of these concerts and actually directed my first on July 14.

Hollywood Bowl is unique. It is a natural amphitheatre seating twenty thousand people, with a park for about ten thousand cars. A splendid shell has been built to accommodate a large orchestra and the acoustic properties are perfect because there are no air currents and the sound is directed towards the audience. I tested the former fact with a lighted match. It is really a thrill when the lights are lowered and the music begins: very literally does the title *Symphonies under the Stars* apply. Naturally everyone in the cinema world attends these concerts. Charlie Chaplin was in my audience one night and I was delighted to find him so full of enthusiasm for British works.

I, for my part, had the pleasure of seeing old faces in the orchestra. Brain my first horn (brother of Aubrey Brain); Ferir the viola-player; de Busscher the oboist; Kastner the harpist; Conrad the bassoonist. It was all very pleasurable.

I think every artist should attempt to visit America. You are made so welcome there. You get the impression that you are the very person for whom America has been waiting. It may not always be quite sincere but it is very helpful.

I was surprised at Mrs. Carter's powers of oratory. Before the performance of Vaughan Williams's *London Symphony* she stood on my left and delivered a speech, an analysis of the work written by Olin Downes. Since my first visit the presidency has been passed on to Mrs. Irish who fills the position with every distinction.

We began our activities early in Hollywood.

The committee gave wonderful breakfasts in the grounds of the Bowl at eight o'clock before the orchestral rehearsals began. At these breakfasts the Mayor and other civic authorities spoke and eulogized these remarkable concerts in a wonderfully-arranged tent and under climatic conditions we rarely experience in England. At one of these breakfasts I remarked to my neighbour on the gorgeous banks of flowers behind the head table at which about sixty guests were seated.

"Yes," he said casually. "They *are* rather nice. I arranged them for my wife. I was here at four o'clock this morning."

America is certainly the land of speeches. I was amazed at the way society women bobbed up and talked at the various lunches and dinners I attended. They were most fluent and hurled superlatives about in a way that was really quite embarrassing, but after a season or two I became used to it and took it as a matter of course. The rehearsals finished about noon after which I was driven twenty or thirty miles to some luncheon club where I became used to seeing a notice in large letters:

LECTURE BY SIR HENRY WOOD

After a heavy rehearsal I am often a little tired and generally very thirsty, but I found I was given five minutes at the most to recover my wind, and then a secretary would come behind my chair and whisper "You *will* say a few words now, will you not, Sir Henry? You see, our three hundred members are so keen on hearing what you think about America."

It was useless to think I should be let off even as lightly as that. At half-past one I was whirled away to Luncheon No. 2—ten or fifteen miles away. There I read another notice:

LECTURE BY SIR HENRY WOOD

The second luncheon I found more leisurely than the first, but food played a small part in either of them. The speeches were more important, I found.

At three o'clock a car would take me off to some country house with a wonderful garden—perhaps thirty miles in another direction. Here I would be expected to shake hands with at least five hundred guests in the proportion of ten males to every hundred females. The actual introduction left me in no doubt about the names and places whence the guests came. It would be: "Allow me to present Mrs. Jones of Boston, President of So-and-so . . . *Sir Henry Wood* . . . *Mrs. Jones.*"

I just had time to say *Delighted!* (or something like that) before the next guest was presented. If I dared say anything more I should never have got through the 300 or so before half-past

338

five. After that I was whisked off to the Beverley Hills Hotel where, if I had any luck, I might arrive at 6.15. I would go straight to bed and be called at 7.15 for the 8.30 concert. Even then I had another seven miles to drive to get to the Bowl.

I was impressed with the Beverley Hills Hotel, especially with its twelve self-contained bungalows, each beautifully furnished and each with its own private staff. I could have taken my meals in the hotel itself had I wished, but I was greatly attracted to these bungalows which were surrounded by fascinating Oriental gardens. I was there again in 1930 but I took the precaution of asking Annie Friedburg, my most attentive American agent—to make it known that I could not again romp round the country in this fashion.

By further reference to my diaries I find I was conducting in Monte Carlo in January of 1928; in Montreux for a holiday during June of that same year; in Biskra for the same purpose in 1929; and in Paris in November to conduct the *Orchestre Synphonique*.

I left England again for a holiday in South Africa on December 12, 1930, and was not in London again until the following February. No sooner had I arrived in Capetown than I met a young man named Pickerill whose father and brothers had been connected with the Nottingham Sacred Harmonic Society. Pickerill told me he had attended my rehearsals with his father when he was only seven and that he now conducted the City Orchestra of Capetown. He asked me whether I would conduct four concerts while I was there. This was not what I had come for, by any manner of means. I wanted a holiday. I had one or two batons with me—merely because I always take them wherever I go in order to keep in practice.

Mr. Pickerill refused to take no for an answer, and was constantly with me during my three weeks' stay. He told me all about the city hall and its organ, and persuaded me to go and see it before I did anything else. We went in, I remember, by a door leading into the auditorium. Seated in the ten front rows of the stalls was a group of native schoolteachers listening to a native speaker wearing doctor's robes.

As soon as I entered he said: "Ladies and Gentlemen! Here is Sir Henry Wood of Queen's Hall, London." He then proceeded to give his audience an account of all I stood for musically, and begged me to address them. I am not given to speaking in public but what could I do! I told them how delighted I was to come and see their beautiful hall, even though I had only been in Capetown ten minutes. Before I knew what was happening

I found that Mr. Pickerill had already *arranged* these concerts. However, I said I would do them—and then the trouble began.

The Capetown broadcasting authorities began to worry me to allow them to broadcast the concerts. I told them I did not want anything of the kind. I had come there on a holiday and, while I was quite willing to help Mr. Pickerill, it must end there. I then learned that the news of my arrival had already been broadcast and that all South Africa knew about it.

The City Orchestra proved a pleasant surprise. It had been excellently trained and, to my delight, I found another old member of the Queen's Hall Orchestra—Britton—as leader of the 'cellos. He had gone out to South Africa some years previously on account of his health. The four concerts were a great success and the audience (which was composed of both whites and natives) was most enthusiastic. I had the pleasure of meeting Sir Abe Bailey at his beautiful house where he employed a first-rate French chef. I also met Mr. and Mrs. van de Byle who lived in a real old Dutch farmhouse. General Smuts paid me a visit and I was impressed by his charm of manner and his grip on world affairs which he discussed with the ease of the diplomat we knew him to be, as well as the fine soldier he is.

After the last concert I was presented with a silver cigarette box as 'a mark of esteem from the Musical Director and Members of the Capetown Municipal Orchestra'. The Manchester Philharmonic Society presented me with a silver cigarette box on my forty-seventh birthday (1916) and among many such gifts I possess a silver photo frame designed in the shape of a laurel wreath. This was presented to me in 1911 after the Sheffield Musical Festival.

I must admit great disappointment at having had to refuse an invitation to go to South Africa to open their great Exhibition in 1936; neither was I able to visit Australia and New Zealand in spite of many tempting suggestions both musically and financially. America now wants me for the World's Fair in 1939, tempting indeed!—But no, my commitments still hold me here.

I was on holiday in Costa Rica and Trinidad at Christmas, 1931, and home again on February 10, 1932; in Hamburg for a concert in November of 1933; in Copenhagen for three concerts a week later; and sailed for a holiday in Bermuda on December 21, leaving for New York on January 9, and was in Boston on the 12th to conduct three concerts during Kussevitsky's absence on his annual vacation.

I was really intensely gratified at conducting such a perfect orchestra or (shall I say) such a perfectly-*disciplined* orchestra.

They responded to my least movement and did not *reserve* anything for their permanent conductor. The term *reserve* is not mine: it is that of a London critic. He used it in a recent criticism of Menges conducting the London Philharmonic Orchestra. He said that Menges obtained from the L.P.O. some proportion at any rate of that quality usually reserved for their permanent conductor. I am left wondering how the orchestra manages to *reserve* quality in that fashion. At all events, the Boston Symphony Orchestra showed me generosity; nothing (so far as I know) was 'reserved' for Kussevitsky. Quite on the contrary, I had everything I wanted. I was conducting the London Philharmonic Orchestra quite recently and asked Leon Goossens what it was an orchestra reserved for its permanent conductor. He fondled his oboe for a moment.

"That's no compliment to any orchestra," he said. "I know that when I am in good form I play well; if I'm not, no conductor can make me play any better. I always give my best; we *all* do." I like to remember that Goossens started his career in London as a member of my Queen's Hall Orchestra—and what a beautiful player he is!

While I was in Boston I visited my friend F. Converse who has a lovely house. He taught at the New English Conservatory in Boston for some years and is really a product of Harvard. His hobby is making violins. He turns out some remarkably fine instruments but occasionally becomes very over-enthusiastic about them.

I think if I had to leave England and settle down abroad I should choose Boston. It is so artistic. I was delighted with its wonderful art galleries. Mrs. Gardiner's famous house has now been turned into a museum. I remember being much taken with Sargent's picture *The Spanish Dancing Girl* which is so beautifully lighted and so well hung.

I spent a day with Mr. and Mrs. Reutler in Boston, and I have a faint recollection of giving a talk on conducting in a store, but details of it elude me now. What I remember more clearly is that I stayed with Mrs. Harriet Foster—my old pupil—in New York towards the end of January and gave my first broadcast concert for the N.B.C. on January 28 from a studio in their marvellous Radio City.

I left again for South Africa on June 16 (1934) coming back via Canada where I visited both Montreal and Quebec, only reaching London on August 6 in time to take the first rehearsal for the Promenades the following morning.

I have stayed in many beautiful houses in my life, both here and abroad, but I think the real 'dream-house' was in Tunis where I visited Rudolph d'Erlanger (brother to Baron Frédéric) and his wife. I had met him in London years previously and had admired his delicious sketches; but to visit him in his amazing Oriental home, so romantically situated on the corner of a promontory overlooking the Mediterranean towards Sardinia was an exceptional experience. I remember how struck I was with the fact that, though Oriental in design—he was his own architect, and there was nothing gaudy or bizarre about it; rather was there evidence of the refined English taste. I was particularly taken with the little marble channel through which water ran in the main rooms, electrically illuminated by hidden lamps of soft greenish-blue. My host seemed to own quite a large strip of this promontory, including the lighthouse.

I had planned a short holiday in Switzerland in July, 1936. Perhaps a little late for this lovely land, but I have no choice in these busy days. It was lucky I was on the other side of our beastly little channel and able to fit in a week's conducting at Ostend *Kursaal*, though I must say the whole thing surprised me. Ostend itself, the orchestra, the management—everything. And the mosquitoes in my bedroom at the hotel were worse than anything I have experienced in the tropics. I only mention this week because it introduced me to one of Belgium's most charming musicians—Désiré Defauw, Director of the Royal Conservatoire in Brussels. He was there rehearsing. I look forward to the pleasure of meeting him again, especially if he is conducting, for he evidently knew what he wanted—and how to get it.

Another pleasure at the end of the Ostend week was that of directing a Sunday concert at Knocke. Here was a splendidly-organized orchestra, disciplined and composed of excellent artists. Their permanent conductor, K. Candael, is a remarkably fine director of an orchestra, and some of his compositions display real talent. It is curious that, though Ostend and Knocke are only three or four miles apart on the coast, they should be so many miles apart *musically*.

Many years ago I very nearly settled in Liverpool as so many of my pupils resided there. I had to spend several days every month there as it was. Liverpool is a city I have always liked. I have directed concerts for its Philharmonic Society for more years than I can remember off-hand, but what I particularly carry in my mind of the earlier days is that the Philharmonic Hall platform was the stage of the prima donna. That orchestra must have accompanied all the greatest artists in the world.

Nowadays, perhaps, the position is reversed, for orchestral items are the favourites. The orchestra is now led by that much travelled leader of the Hallé Orchestra, Alfred Barker, and with him at the first desk sat an old Queen's Hall player—A. J. Matthews. Barker was a pupil of Brodsky and followed Catterall as leader of the Hallé. He is a fine musician, has a beautiful tone coupled with excellent technique—and a very charming wife.

When time permitted I never failed to go and hear Goss-Custard play the cathedral organ. Nothing pleased me more than an invitation from him to listen to Bach on the organ at a time when the cathedral is empty and there is only a light at the organ console. I used to listen to Sinclair at Hereford under similar conditions.

I hope the new Philharmonic Hall (now being built to replace the one burned down two years ago) will prove an object lesson in Concert hall building, especially where the seating of the orchestra and the position of the organ are concerned. As for the cathedral, I think it finally explodes the fallacy that we cannot build cathedrals in these days. Sir Giles Gilbert Scott is a genius. The organ, too, is the most wonderful instrument in the country —the gift of a single donor at a cost of over £30,000. Such munificence for music in these days is amazing.

January 1 of this year, 1938, marked my fifty years of professional conducting in London. I spent the morning rehearsing the B.B.C. Symphony Orchestra at the Maida Vale studios for a Sunday afternoon concert the follwing day. I shall never forget the welcome I received from the Orchestra that morning. I was applauded for some minutes while the leader, Paul Beard, stood waiting to speak. He spoke of my fifty years' work in London, saying what a pleasure it had been to all of them to work with a conductor who understood the mentality of orchestral musicians and who made their task easy and pleasurable. He further said that the occasion was unique and concluded by wishing me a happy New Year which brought forth three of the heartiest cheers it has ever been my joy to hear.

The thought of this serves as a reminder that a conductor demands much from his leader. Not many are like Paul Beard whose presence is enough to prevent any slacking in the orchestra. His tone, technique, and extraordinary vitality stamp him a great leader, and his intonation is perfect. He never misses a note, and he does what some leaders do *not* do—he listens to the rest of the orchestra. Since Maurice Sons I have never met a leader with more grip and vitality.

One of the items of this programme was Bax's 'cello concerto magnificently played by Beatrice Harrison. I know Bax himself was carried away by her rendering of his highly original and exceedingly difficult work. He came to the final rehearsal on the Sunday morning and to the evening performance. I was delighted to find him so enthusiastic because I did not make the customary repeats in the first and final movements of a Beethoven symphony. I told him I had long since given up doing this. In my opinion the day has passed when it is necessary to make first-movement repeats in standard classical symphonies; to hear the first and second subjects *six* times over before the coda is reached is sheer redundancy. In 1895 it might have been necessary, but this is 1938.

Speaking of studio concerts reminds me that I directed Mendelssohn's violin concerto twice in one day—surely an exceptional experience. It was on March 6, with Menuhin in the afternoon in the Albert Hall and with little Ida Haendel in the evening at the broadcasting studio.

Another experience of yet more recent date is that of having directed seven orchestral concerts in various parts of the country in eight days, each with a different programme. Liverpool Philharmonic Society, March 21; Bournemouth Festival on the 24th; Bath Festival (two concerts) on the 26th; the London Philharmonic Orchestra on the 27th; the Hallé Orchestra's Benefit Concert in Manchester on the 28th; and the Royal Academy Students' concert in Queen's Hall on the 29th.

The first Bath Musical Festival (26th) created another record for me. I directed Tchaikovsky's fifth symphony (and it plays fifty minutes) three times in one day. The morning rehearsal which 700 children attended, and the afternoon and evening concerts. The young director here is a pupil of the Royal Academy and came under my instruction there with the orchestra—Maurice Miles. It was indeed a pleasure to meet once again my friend of the earlier days of my association with broadcasting—Gerald Beadle, now Director of the West Regional.

Bournemouth brings to my mind my old friend Sir Dan Godfrey. Marvellous pioneer work, his; and I know that up to the time of his retirement he did more to help the British composer than any other conductor. He had a splendid opportunity, with daily concerts all the year round. To Sir Dan Godfrey, Bournemouth owes its musical reputation—now in the safe keeping of Richard Austin. When conducting this splendid orchestra this year (now permanently enlarged to sixty-one players) I had the satisfaction of knowing I had brought some influence to bear and had helped towards this happy result in a little speech I made at the municipal luncheon at their festival last year. How wise Bournemouth is to have decided that really fine music can only make its appeal when presented by an *orchestra possessing instruments only too often cut out* on the score of expense!

Of other seacoast orchestras I have directed during their festivals that of Hastings under Julius Harrison cheers me as much as any. That it is musically well trained goes without saying, being in the hands of so gifted a musician and director. My visits to Hastings are always the more pleasant because Mrs. Andrews, Robert Newman's daughter—never fails to come and see me with her husband.

Eastbourne's orchestra, under the efficient Kneale Kelley, is doing splendid work; but why on earth a place like Eastbourne (which is residential as well as being an all-the-year-round resort) cannot employ its Symphony Orchestra for at least eleven months of the year passes my comprehension.

Torquay, again (situated as it is), could turn itself into a real Riviera (as it terms itself) by retaining a fine orchestra all the year round. No orchestra will ever pay for itself *directly* but in such a place, a good one would pay the municipality *indirectly*, I am sure. Cultured people require good music. Ernest Goss, as it is, is doing fine work, but I am sure he is being crippled by a short-sighted policy on the part of the authorities.

A conductor-composer for whom I have great regard is Constant Lambert whose exciting *Rio Grande* is now so well known that I need hardly say anything about it; but I should like to mention his book *Music Ho!* which should find a place in all musicians' libraries. Another book which greatly interested me recently was *Winged Pharaoh*, by Joan Grant, whose husband is an archæologist with whom she has travelled. Her vision of Egypt makes entrancing reading and the chapter on music is a beautiful thought. I first had the pleasure of reading this work in manuscript in Scotland last year when Dr. Marr, of Grantown-on-Spey introduced me to the authoress. As a first book—and from one so young—it is a triumph.

In my long life it has always been a joy to me to note the progress of young artists and to note how, as an artist of the older generation begins to recede or retire, a younger automatically takes his or her place. I am not going to fit a jig-saw puzzle together for my reader but will content myself with observing that some of these young people have attracted my attention. For instance, Clifford Curzon (has the *Wanderer*

Fantasia ever been played more poetically than by him); Cyril Smith, whose interpretation of Rachmaninoff's too-seldom-heard third concerto is so brilliant. Nan Maryska for the delicate Mozart arias; Michal Hambourg, the charming daughter of a famous parent from whom she has learned her artistry at the piano.

There is no doubt that the younger generation is being given a fine chance in the studios of the B.B.C., and although public concert-giving is at present deplorably neglected, the revival I see in progress will give them their chance in public so long as they continue to improve in their art. Patti and Melba have not been replaced; neither has Santley, and although Ffrangçon-Davies was angry when he asked: "Did the Creator exhaust himself when he created Charles Santley?" and I replied in the *affirmative*, I am still of the same opinion that the particular art that was Santley's has never been approached since. Nor has Melba's.

My dear friends—Singers-of-the-Present-Day—I beg of you almost to the point of praying that when success is yours, or seems to be yours, do not, I beseech you, give up your intensive study. Retain the services of a good accompanist; have lessons from every teacher of repute (from each you will learn something you can apply); above all, hear everyone and everything. Remember that even if a beautiful voice may carry you so far, it is the artistry of its management that eventually places you on the Melba or de Reszke plane. A Stradivarius is the most beautiful of violins, but it does not play itself.

You will forgive me for this advice. I know what I am talking about. I did not write *The Gentle Art of Singing*, which was the result of thirty years' applied study and thought, without taking deep interest in every singer who sets out on the rough road to success. When Hubert Foss knew of my labour of love—for I never anticipated publication—he asked that the Oxford University Press might publish it. This they did. It must have cost them a large sum, for the work runs into four volumes; embracing a graduated course. An instrumentalist will study a graduated course for years but rarely will a singer give the necessary time to study the *art* of singing. Because the voice is there it seems an easy thing; and if the voice happens to be beautiful it seems that all that is required is to *sing*. It is the argument of the Strad. over again; it requires the brain, the hands, and the musicianship to produce the music that made Kreisler and Ysaye famous.

The happiness that surrounds me in my work these days is

in no small degree due to the kindness and consideration of my colleagues, and all at Broadcasting House. I have just sat at a round-table conference on the forthcoming Promenade programmes and have come away feeling that a good season is in store for us all. Reflecting this spirit of friendliness I cannot do better than reproduce the following, taken from a broadcast talk in the *Music of the Week* series (February 13, 1938) given by Sir Adrian Boult:

The present high reputation of the Vienna Symphony Orchestra is due to Professor Kabasta who, with Sir Henry Wood and Dr. Mengelberg, commands our admiration by virtue of sheer mastery in the business of conducting. Quite apart from their merits as musicians and artists, they are superb craftsmen.

In these days one has to be careful of the time allotted to rehearsal: there is not always a generous allowance. The Promenade concerts are a striking example of this, and it is a continuous cause of astonishment and admiration to see how Sir Henry Wood after a half-day's preliminary rehearsal starts out on those eight weeks with only three hours a day to rehearse more than two hours' music.

You will be surprised to hear that every minute of the Promenade rehearsal is planned beforehand, and everybody knows exactly when everything is to be rehearsed. In particular I find myself marvelling at the way Sir Henry manages to insinuate a new or difficult work into the rehearsal scheme some days before its performance, so that it gets the benefit of several rehearsals with the result that even the worst performance of the whole Promenade season can still be called a fine one, and the average is something far finer than that.

XLIV

MY JUBILEE, MY SIXTY-NINTH BIRTHDAY, AND THE FORTY-FOURTH SEASON OF PROMENADE CONCERTS

Now THAT I have been conducting for fifty years I find myself surrounded by friends and colleagues who would do me honour. I suggested that the greatest they could do me would be to rally round and help me to return thanks in some practical form to the orchestral musicians through whom I have attained my position in the world of music today.

At the time of writing, a representative committee has been formed under the chairmanship of Mr. Robert Mayer which contains the names of old friends: Sir Hugh Allen, Sir Adrian

Boult, Baron Frédéric d'Erlanger (treasurer), Dr. George Dyson, Lord Horder, Sir James Jeans, Professor Stanley Marchant, and Sir Landon Ronald. A concert has been arranged for October 5, 1938, in the Albert Hall, the proceeds of which (together with subscriptions, the appeal for which will take me to the microphone for the first time as a speaker at a date not yet fixed) will go to endow beds in London hospitals for orchestral musicians.

A sub-committee is as follows:

The Royal Choral Society	Miss Tomlin
The Philharmonic Choir	D. Ritson Smith
The B.B.C. Choral Society	Leslie Woodgate
The London Symphony Orchestra	W. G. Wood
The B.B.C. Symphony Orchestra	R. C. Pratt
The London Philharmonic Orchestra	Frederick Laurence
Messrs. Ibbs & Tillett	John Tillett

W. W. Thompson (Chairman) by courtesy of the B.B.C.

A ladies' committee is being formed by Lady George Cholmondeley under whose chairmanship I know splendid work will be done and will go far to help me to help my musicians. The B.B.C. is not only giving the services of the Symphony Orchestra and Chorus, but the committee meetings are to be held in Broadcasting House and Sir Adrian Boult has placed his secretary (Mrs. Becket) at the disposal of the committee. Kennedy Scott has given the services of the Philharmonic Choir, and the Royal Choral Society is also coming to help. The London Philharmonic, the London Symphony, and the Queen's Hall orchestras are also giving their services as are the sixteen singers who will all take part in a new *Ode* now being written by Dr. Vaughan Williams for the occasion. How much I anticipate the pleasure of hearing this work! The singers are:

Isobel Baillie	Margaret Balfour
Stiles-Allen	Muriel Brunskill
Elsie Suddaby	Astra Desmond
Eva Turner	Mary Jarred
Parry Jones	Norman Allin
Heddle Nash	Robert Easton
Frank Titterton	Roy Henderson
Walter Widdop	Harold Williams

They are all now old friends who have sung under my direction with such distinction at Festivals—and of course the

Promenade Concerts. Words fail me to express my gratitude to all who have so generously given their services for the cause so dear to me.

While I was wondering as to whom I could ask to be the solo pianist, Moiseiwitsch made the original suggestion that Rachmaninoff's second piano concerto should be played by twenty-four pianists on twenty-four grand pianos placed in the arena of the Albert Hall. I can direct twelve trombones at a pinch but I doubt whether I can tackle twice that number *in pianos!* It might have been a way out—but how to choose *one*, and one only!

The problem is solved.

Rachmaninoff has written me a charming letter. He will come to England specially to play at this concert. Every artist in England will be gratified that so great an international figure will give his services to musicians in this country that evening.

When this Jubilee concert was first suggested I wanted it to take place on St. Cecilia's Day, November 22; but Rachmaninoff can only come during the first week of October, prior to his long tour in America. And now that he has generously consented to come and be the one *international* artist for my Jubilee concert I find it indeed difficult to put my gratitude into words. I am determined (and am glad that the committee agrees with me) that the balance sheet of this Jubilee concert, and subscriptions from those who cannot attend the concert, shall be made public; and I look forward with deep interest to the result which I hope may give many beds for the use of my beloved musicians.

As an inventive and original composer, I place Rachmaninoff in the first rank. His piano concertos are valued at their true worth throughout the realm of music. I imagine there is no living pianist who does not include at least one of them in his repertoire. His lovely choral work *The Bells* (of which I have already spoken) is a gem—so beautifully orchestrated and written with such knowledge of the voice. I wish I could do it more frequently. His songs are not often heard in England; strange, too, when one knows how singers revel in something beautiful and singable. The second symphony, with the composer's cuts, is now a repertoire piece.

I have recently had the pleasure of studying with him his third symphony in A minor, and have since directed it at the Liverpool Philharmonic Society's concert (March 22, 1938) and at a studio broadcast with the B.B.C. Symphony Orchestra (April 3). Rachmaninoff attended the morning rehearsal of the latter and expressed his unbounded satisfaction both with the playing and reading of his work, making a charming little speech to the orchestra. He had a special word of praise for Paul Beard's beautiful playing in the solo violin part in the slow movement. We are grateful for this new symphony and I, for my part, shall often play it. The work impresses me as being of the true Russian romantic school; one cannot get away from the beauty and melodic line of the themes and their logical development. As did Tchaikovsky, Rachmaninoff uses the instruments of the orchestra to their fullest effect. Those lovely little phrases for solo violin, echoed on the four solo wood-wind instruments, have a magical effect in the slow movement. I am convinced that Rachmaninoff's children will see their father's third symphony take its rightful place in the affection of that section of the public which loves melody. In fact, I go so far as to predict that it will prove as popular as Tchaikovsky's fifth.

Rachmaninoff's friend, Nicholas Medtner, attended the Sunday morning rehearsal.

It was a splendid gesture when Mr. Louis Dreyfus offered Queen's Hall for two successive nights, free of all charge, should it be decided to hold the Jubilee concert there; but I felt I could not undertake the emotional strain of two such concerts. At the suggestion of my committee, however, Chappell's have consented to a bust of myself (by Donald Gilbert) being placed in Queen's Hall. It is a very unusual experience surely to discuss the exact niche to accommodate it with Mr. C. S. Taylor, the Queen's Hall manager; and wonderful that such a mark of recognition should come to me during my lifetime.

Even in the days of all my choral and amateur orchestral societies (with their attendant rehearsals and travelling) I never remember being so pressed for a day's relaxation as during the early months of this year. However, I determined that one page should be left blank in my diary—that of my sixty-ninth birthday on March 3. This was satisfactorily arranged—until television sought me out and the young enthusiasts of the B.B.C.'s new department decided that I *must* have a new experience on my birthday. I found it difficult to refuse them—and secretly wanted to see what televising was like!

"There will be a small fee, Sir Henry," they told me. The actual figure was not mentioned, but I mentally allocated it to my Jubilee Fund. I televised at 9.30 and gained thereby two experiences: I saw for myself how everything connected with television is housed at Alexandra Palace, and I earned a fee exactly 50 per cent in advance of the first fee I ever earned as a conductor—fifty years ago.

But I have gone ahead of the beginning of one of the happiest birthdays of my life. I shopped all morning. Nothing gives me more pleasure than a visit to our fine London shops. Ties, shoes, ordering a fresh supply of cigars and cigarettes, and my one vice—*glacé* stem ginger. What a morning! The sun was so warm in Bond Street that my overcoat became a burden, but Hyde Park and St. James's Park were fresh and beautiful. And the Mall, with the Victoria Memorial gleaming in the morning sun —a reminder of the calm peaceful years of that great Queen's reign; this was London—*my* London—the London that has tied me to her and continued to support my life's work. My yearnings and ambitions in past years for wider fields and greater opportunities to express myself flashed before me then— only to banish in a sense of gratitude for all I have been able to accomplish here in the London of my birth. I thought of my cottage home in Oxford Street and of the home of my music— Queen's Hall. It is not given to many to live sixty-nine years within walking distance of the scenes on which the eye of a watchful public is focused, and still retain their respect—I might even say their love. On to my friends, Mrs. Flora Lion the artist, and her husband, in Chelsea for luncheon. I always think the portrait of her mother which Mrs. Lion painted in 1909, and which now hangs in the Tate Gallery, is one of the most touching pieces of portrait painting I know.

Home through Kensington Gardens (lest there might be no other opportunity, knowing my diary), along the Serpentine, blue under a cloudless spring sky.

Dr. Calthrop, a dear young friend of mine, decided that I must have a snack with him before going on to a cocktail party which Solomon was giving. This little repast with Dr. Calthrop and his charming wife ended with an equally charming surprise. As we were about to leave the dining-room I caught the strains of the *Bach Toccata and Fuge*—excellently played, too. On going into the lounge I realized that it was a record of my own with the Queen's Hall Orchestra. The room was in darkness except for a flickering blaze in the centre of the room where there was a huge cake with sixty-nine tiny candles—at least, they told me there were that number—but I counted them to make sure as I blew them out one by one, much to the company's amusement. A pretty sight and a pretty thought.

On to Quaglino's for dinner (after television)—and how hungry I was! A toast—"Your sixty-ninth Birthday!" I said I could not believe it. I still do not feel a day over fifty and am good for . . . well, you never know!

After all, did not Verdi write *Falstaff* at eighty, and the *Te Deum* and *Stabat Mater* at eighty-five? Tintoretto painted *Paradiso*, a canvas measuring 74 by 30 feet at seventy-four; Goethe completed *Faust* at eighty; Cato began to learn Greek at the same age; Tennyson wrote *Crossing the Bar* at eighty-three; Oliver Wendell Holmes wrote *Over the Teacups* at seventy-eight; Gladstone became Prime Minister of England for the *third* time at seventy-seven; and Titian painted that wonderful historic canvas *The Battle of Lepanto* (which hangs in Venice) at the age of ninety-eight. So what is a mere sixty-nine?

In looking forward to my forty-fourth season of Promenade concerts, due to commence on August 6, 1938, the cavalcade of a long vista of years passes before me. Some of the friends of my younger days are still with me: Dr. Cathcart, Mrs. Newmarch, Roger Quilter, Freddy Jonson. Many have passed on: Edgar Speyer; my cherished friend Siegfried Schwabacher; and dear Robert Newman whom I can still visualize with his bristling moustache and his blue eyes afire with enthusiasm that day in 1895 when he suggested I should direct Promenade concerts in the newly-built Queen's Hall. The hosts of composers I have met; the artists I have accompanied; the composers and artists to whom I gave their first chance; the orchestral musicians —from father to son and so on; and my friends of the Promenade Concerts.

And then my Jubilee concert—yet to come in October. The Promenade Concerts' Jubilee? Of that there is no question. Unlike the ever-changing map of Europe—they remain unchanged and will continue to be the rendezvous of the music-loving public of whom I feel very much the father. But *my* Promenade Concert Jubilee? Who can tell what may happen— six years hence? But rest assured I shall be there if I am on this side, perhaps with my carnation and my baton—but perhaps only with my carnation—to participate in the rejoicings that will be heard in Queen's Hall on that August night in 1944 to commemorate Fifty Years of Promenade Concerts.

APPENDIX

The following is a list of the more important novelties produced by Sir Henry Wood from 1895 to the end of 1937.

1895

Bunning, Herbert	Shepherd's Call
Clutsam, G. H.	Carnival Scenes
d'Erlanger, Baron F.	Second Symphonic Suite
Frewin, T. H.	Overture, The Battle of the Flowers
Halvorsen	Boyard's March
Kistler, Cyrill	Chromatic Concert Waltzes; March, Festklänge
Mackenzie, A. C.	Recitation with Orchestra, Eugene Aram
Massenet	Méditation (from Thaïs); Overture, Phèdre
Moszkowski	Malagueña (Boabdil)
Pitt, Percy	Suite in Four Movements
Rimsky-Korsakoff	Overture, Nuit de Mai
Scharwenka	Prelude, Mataswinka
Stanford, C. V.	Suite of Dances
Strauss, R.	Prelude to Act I, Guntram
Svendsen	Andante Funèbre
Tchaikovsky	March Solennelle
Vicars, Harold	Prelude, Rosalind
Wagner	Overture, Rienzi

1896

Ames, J. C.	Petite Suite
Arensky	Silhouettes
Chabrier, E.	Marche Joyeuse; Slavonic March
Chaminade, C.	Suite, Callirhoë
Dubois, Th.	Three Pieces (Xavière)
Dvořák	Der Wasserman; Die Mittagshexe
Elvey, George	Gavotte à la mode ancienne
Frewin, T. H.	Mazeppa
Glazounoff	Scènes de Ballet
Grieg	Two Norwegian Melodies
Guilmant, A.	March Fantasia
Itasse, L.	Rhapsodie Espagnole
Joncieres	Ballet, Le Chevalier Jean
Lalo	Namouna, Suite, No. 1
Lucas, Clarence	Minuet (Anne Hathaway)
Macbeth Allan	Serenata for Strings
Massenet	Overture, Le Cid; Rhapsodie and March (Le Cid)

Moszkowski	Introduction, Dance of Fairies, March of Dwarfs
Nicodé	Symphonic Variations in E minor
Pitt, Percy	Coronation March; Suite, Fêtes Galantes
Rimsky-Korsakoff	Capriccioso Espagnole; Scheherazade
Tchaikovsky	Casse Noisette Suite
Thierot, F.	Sinfonietta in E
West, J. E.	Recitation with orchestra: King Robert of Sicily

1897

Arensky	Symphony in B minor (Op. 4)
Becker, R.	Huldigungsmarsch (Frauenlob)
Bourgault-Ducoudray	Prelude, Thamara
Borodin	Danse Polovtsienne
Bunning, Herbert	Suite Villageoise (Op. 45)
Burgmein	Fantasie Hongroise
Crowther, G. W. F.	Concertstück in F minor
Cui, C.	Suite miniature
Dargomijsky	Cossack Dance
Draeseke	Tragic Symphony
Ford, E.	Scènes des Bacchanales
Franck, César	La Chasseur Maudit
Frewin, T. H.	The Seven Ages of Man
German, Edward	Three Dances from Henry VIII
Gilson, Paul	Symphonic Sketches
Glazounoff	Symphony No. 5; Carnaval Overture
Hartmann, E.	Overture, Runenzauber
Haydn, Michael	Symphony in C.
Horrocks, A. E.	Undine
Humperdinck	Intro. Act II, Königskinder
Iljinsky, A.	Allegretto, Gratulations, Menuet
Napravnik	Romance and Fandango
Pierné, G.	Suite, Izéyl
Pitt, Percy	Concertino for Clarinet and Orchestra
Saint-Saëns	Piano concerto; la Fiancée du Timbalier
Serov	Danse Cosaque
Squire, W. H.	Summer Dreams
Tchaikovsky	Suite, Mozartiana;
	Overture, Voyevode
	Fourth Symphony
	Overture, L'Orage
Umlauft, Paul	Prelude, Evanthea
Wagner	Huldigungsmarsch

1898

Coleridge-Taylor	Four Characteristic Waltzes
Elgar, E.	Three Bavarian Dances

Esposito, M.	Deirdre
Franchetti	Symphony in E minor
Frewin, T. H.	Overture, Bellona
German, E.	Bourrée, Gigue, Minuet from Much Ado About Nothing
Halvorsen	Norwegian Folksong
Liszt	Hungarian Rhapsody No. 6 in G
Lucas, Clarence	Overture, Othello
Massenet	Scènes Hongroises
Moniuszko	Mazur (Halka)
Moussorgsky	March in A flat
Parry, C. H. H.	Magnificat
Pitt, Percy	Overture, the Taming of the Shrew
Reed, W. H.	Valse Brilliante
Squire, W. H.	Sweet Briar
Strauss, R.	Festmarsch (Op. 1)
Tchaikovsky	Entr'acte, Airs de Ballet (Voyevode); Manfred; Waltz (Dornroschen) Fantasia, Tempest; Polonaise (Eugène Onegin)
Valentin, C.	Festmarsch

1899

Balakirev	Overture on three Russian Themes; Symphony in C
Bleichmann	Suite de Ballet
Block, J.	Five Flemish Dances
Chevillard, C.	Fantaisie Symphonique
Couldery, C. H.	Fantasia for Organ and Orchestra
Coverley, R.	Four Sketches for Orchestra
Cui, C.	Premier Scherzo
d'Indy, V.	Chanson et Danses
Dittersdorf	Actean
Dukas, P.	L'Apprenti Sorcier
Dvořák	Die Waldtaube; Heldenlied
Elgar, E.	Lux Christi
Erkel	Hunyady László
Glazounov (with Liadov and Sokllov)	Polka for Strings, Les Vendredis; Suite, Raymonda; Fantasia
Glinka	Russlan and Ludmilla
Goldmark, C.	Itron. Act II, Die Kriegsgefangene
Ippolitov-Ivanov	Caucasian Sketches
Holbrooke, J.	The Romaunt of the Page
Leo, L.	Sinfonia, Saint Elena al Calvario
Liadov	Valse Badinage
Lucas, C.	Overture, As You Like It
Mackenzie, A. C.	Prelude, Acts II and III, Manfred
Mascheroni	Grande Valse Espagnole
Massenet	Ballet Music, Herodiade; Le Sommeil de Cendrillon

355

Miguez	Ave Libertas
Moszkowski	Polish Dances
Olsen, Ole	Asgardareien
Perosi	Transfiguration of Christ; Resurrection of Lazarus
Pitt, Percy	Hohenlinden; Air de Ballet; Cinderella
Rabaud, H.	Poeme Virgilien
Reed, W. H.	Overture, Touchstone
Saint-Saëns	Prelude et Cortège (De janire)
Simonetti	Madrigale
Squire, W. H.	Slumber Song
Strauss, R.	Serenade for Wind Instruments
Tchaikovsky	Suite caractéristique; Les Caprices d'Oxana; Symphony No. 3; Danse Cosaque
Sinding	Episodes Schevelresques
Wagner, Siegfried	Intro. to Act III of Der Bärenhäuter
Wallace, Sutcliffe	Two Dances
Waud, J. H.	Comedy Overture
Wolkov, N. de	Cossack Dance

1900

Bantock, G.	Thalaba, the Destroyer
Beethoven	Duet for Two Flutes
Chevillard, C.	Le Chêne et le Roseau
Coleridge-Taylor	Overture, Hiawatha
Fox, G.	The Boy and the Butterfly
German, Edward	Nell Gwynn Dances
Glazounoff	Ruses d'Amour
Holbrooke, J.	Variations, Three Blind Mice
Lalo	Suite No. 2, Namouna
Moreau, Ll	Sur la Mer lointaine
Pitt, Percy	Serenade; Le Sang des Crépuscules
Rachmaninoff	Piano Concerto No. 1
Reed, W. H.	Valse Elégante
Rimsky-Korsakoff	Symphony No. 2, Antar
Ronald, Landon	Suite de Ballet

1901

Ames, J. C.	March, Last of the Incas
Bell, W. H.	A Song of Morning
Bloch	Suite Poétique
Celega, N.	The Heart of Fingal
Cowen, F. H.	The Butterfly's Ball

Elgar, E.	Chanson de Nuit et du Matin; Elevation; Two Military Marches; Prelude and Angel's Farewell (Gerontius)
Floersheim	Miniature Suite
Glazounoff	Chant du Menestrel; Ouverture Solennelle; Ballet, The Seasons
Klughardt	Festival Overture
Lekeu	Adagio for Strings
Liapounoff	Ouverture Solennelle
Lucas, C.	Ouverture, Macbeth
McDowell, E.	Indian Suite
Mackenzie, A. C.	Coriolanus
O'Neill, N.	Overture, In Autumn
Pitt, Percy	Ballet Suite, Dance Rhythms
Roze, Raymond	Sweet Nell of Old Drury
Saint-Saëns	Africa
Saint-Saëns-Ysaÿe	Caprice sur L'Étude en forme de Valse
Schumann, George	Amor and Psyche
Sibelius	King Christian II
Steggell, R.	Oreithyia
Tchaikovsky	Ballet, Swan Lake; Schäferspiel
Volbach, F.	Es waren zwei Königskinder; Ostern
Wagner, Siegfried	Introl Act III, Valse at the Fair
Weingartner, F.	Das Gefilde der Seligen; Symphony No. 2
Woods, Cunningham	Suite in F

1902

Averkamp	Elaine and Lancelot
Blake, Ernest	Elastor
Bruneau, A.	Six Chansons; Four Preludes from l'Ouragon
Coleridge-Taylor	Meg Blane
Coward, H.	Gareth and Linet
d'Indy, V.	Wallenstein
Enna, Auguste	Overture, Cléopatre
Franck, César	Symphonic Variations
Frischen	Herbstnacht; Rhenish Scherzo
Goetz, H.	Francesca da Rimini
Holbrooke, J.	The Skeleton in Armour
Huber, H.	Symphony No. 2 in E minor
Järnefelt	Krosholm
Koessler, H.	Symphonic Variations
Reed, W. H.	Among the Mountains of Cambria
Saint-Saëns	Phregné
Schillings, Max	King Œdipus

Schumann, George	Symphonic Variations; Overture, Liebesfrühling
Schytte	Piano Concerto (Op. 28,
Sinding, C.	Violin Concerto, No 1 in A
Strauss, R.	Wanderer's Storm Song; Hymnus; Pilgers Morgenlied
Tchaikovsky	Piano Concerto in E flat; March, Entr'acte and Overture, Hamlet; Coronation March
Thuille, F.	Romantic Overture
Wood, A. H.	Suite

1903

Arensky	Piano Concerto
Bainton, E. L.	Pompilia
Bantock, G.	Russian Scenes
Becker, H.	'Cello Concerto in A
Bowen, York	Lament of Tasso
Cox, G. W.	Suite, Ewelme
d'Indy	Entr'acte, L'Etranger
Forsyth, C.	Viola Concerto in G minor
Holbrooke, J.	Concerto Dramatique
Lekeu	Fantasia on Two Popular Anjou Airs
Lenormand	Piano Concerto in F minor
Handel	Concert for Two Wind Orchestras
Mahler, G.	Symphony No. 1 in D
Nesvera	Overture, Waldesluft
Pitt, Percy	Three Old English Dances
Raff, J.	'Cello Concerto
Rimsky-Korsakoff	Night on Mount Triglav
Scott, Cyril	Symphony No. 1 in A minor
Sibelius	Symphony No. 1 in E minor
Straesser	'Cello Concerto in D
Strauss	Aus Italien
Suk, J.	Suite, A Fairy Tale
Wallace, W.	Pelléas et Mélisande

1904

Bossi, E.	Organ Concerto in A minor
Converse, F.	Romance
d'Albert, E.	Two Songs with Orchestra
Debussy	L'Après-midi d'un Faune; Rhapsody No. 1
d'Erlanger, Baron F.	Andante Symphonique
Gardiner, Balfour	English Dance
Goens, van	'Cello Concerto No. 2 in D minor
Goldmark, C.	Overture, In Italien
Gouvy, Th.	Serenade for Flute and Strings

Handel	Air, Dank sei Dir; Concerto Grosso
Juon	Symphony in A
Learmont-Drysdale	A Border Romance
Macpherson, A.	Hallowe'en
Macpherson, S.	Violin Concerto
Miles, Napier	From the West Country
O'Neill, N.	Ballad, Death in the Hills; Overture, Hamlet
Schütt	Piano Concerto in G minor
Scott, C.	Rhapsody No. 1 in Op. 32
Sinding	Piano Concerto in D flat
Tchaikovsky	Battle of Poltava; Air, Dame de Pique; Air, Iolanthe
Vassilenko	Poème Epique
Volbach, F.	Alt Heidelberg; Easter
Walthew, E. H.	Caprice Impromptu
Weber	Theme and Variations
Zilcher	Double Violin Concerto in D minor

1905

Ahn-Carse A. von	In a Balcony
Bach	Brandenburg Concerto No. 6
Bantock	Variations, Helena
Bruch, Max	Suite on Russian Folktunes
Cliffe, F.	Ode to the North-East Wind
Draeseke, F.	Jubilee Overture
Franchetti	In the Black Forest
Gatty, N.	Fly, Envious Time
Liszt	Hungarian Storm March
Purcell-Wehrle	Three Pieces for Strings
Sibelius	The Swan of Tuonela
Strauss, R.	Symphony in F minor
Tchaikovsky	Three Poems for Violin and Orchestra; Intro. and Dance, Oprichnik; Ballade Symphonique, Le Voyevode
Wallace, W.	Symphonic Poem, Sir William Wallace

1906

Arensky	Variations for Strings
Bantock, G.	Prelude to Sappho; Hymn to Aphrodite
Boethe, E.	Episode from Odysseus
Borodin	Finale (Mlada)
Bruneau, A.	Messidor
Busoni	Suite; Eine Lustspiel, Ouverture
Enna, A.	Symphonic Poem, Märchen
Fibich	A Night at Carlstein

359

Glière	Symphony in E flat
Halford, G.	Overture, In Memoriam
Henriquez, F.	Suite for Oboe and Strings
Holbrooke, J.	Symphony No. 1, Les Hommages
Liadov	Eight Russian Folksongs; Baba-Yaga
Lalo	Violin Concerto in G minor
Mackenzie, A. C.	Ancient Scottish Tunes (Strings)
Moussorgsky	Gopak
Mozart	Concerto for Three Pianos in F
O'Neill, N.	In Springtime
Petri, Egon	Concertstück in C
Ricci	Two Forest Scenes
Sibelius	Finlandia; En Saga; Karelia
Williams, Vaughan	A Norfolk Rhapsody

1907

Arends, H.	Concertino for Viola and Orchestra
Austin, F.	Spring
Bach	Cantata, Amore Traditore
Bantock, G.	Lalla-Rookh
	Old English Suite
Barker, F. C.	Violin Concerto
Barns, Ethel	Concertstück for Violin and Orchestra
Brian, Havergal	English Suite; Overture, For Valour
Bridge, Frank	Isabella
Bruch, Max	Suite for Organ and Orchestra
Davies, Walford	Holiday Tunes
Delius	Piano Concerto in C minor
d'Indy	Symphonic Montagnarde
Dohnányi	Concertstück for 'Cello and Orchestra
Hall, Marshall	Symphony in E flat
Harty, Hamilton	Comedy Overture; Ode to a Nightingale
Hinto, A.	Three Orchestral Pieces from Endymion
Isaacs, E.	Piano Concerto in C sharp minor
Liszt	Concert Pathètique
Pezel, J.	Two Suites, Two Trumpets and Three Trombones
Pitt, Percy	Sinfonietta in G minor
Quilter, R.	Serenade
Ravel	Introduction and Allegro for Harp and Orchestra
Reger, Max	Serenade
Scott, C.	Overture, Princess Madeleine
Sibelius	Dance Intermezzo, No. 2; Violin Concerto
Verkey, Th.	Flute Concerto in D minor
Vreuls, V.	Poème for 'Cello and Orchestra
White, F.	Overture, Shylock

Bach	Brandenburg Concerto No. 1 in F
Bell, E. H.	Prelude, Agamemnon
Bowen, York	Piano Concerto No. 3 in G minor
Debussy	Le Jet d'Eau
Duparc, H.	Aria, Phidylé
Elgar, E.	Suite No. 2, the Wand of Youth
Gardiner, Balfour	Symphony in E flat
Leroux, Xavier	Song, Le Nil
Phillips, M.	Song, Fidelity
Pugno, R.	Concertstück
Selby, B. L.	A Village Suite

Bach-Wood	Suite in G, No. 5
Bantock	The Pierrot of the Minute
Bath, Hubert	Two Sea Pictures; African Suite
Berlioz	Aria, The Danish Huntsman
Borsdorf, Oscar, Jnr.	Concert Overture in D
Caetani, R.	Prelude Symphonique
Chadwick, G. H.	Symphonic Sketches
Coates, E.	Four Songs with Orchestra
Davies, Walford	Solemn Melody; Songs of Nature
Debussy	Song, Ces Airs Joyeux; Danse Sacrée; Danse Profane; Three Nocturnes
Dorlay, G.	Das Lied von der Glocke
Dvořák-Wood	Humoreske
Gracner, P.	From the Valley and the Heights
Hadley, H.	Salome
Haydn	Violin Concertos, Nos. 1 and 2
Herbert, V.	'Cello Concerto in E minor
Jarnefelt, A.	Praeludium
Liapounov	Rhapsody for Piano and Orchestra
Mahler, G.	Adagietto for Harp and Strings
Matthay, T.	Concert Piece for Piano and Orchestra
Moszkowski	Polish Dances
Moussorgsky-Wood	Song of the Flea; The Peepshow; King Saul
Noren, H.	Kaleidoscopic Variations and Double Fugue
Paderewski	Piano Concerto in A minor
Ravel	Rhapsodie espagnole
Reger, Max	Variations and Fugue; Symphonic Prologue to a Tragedy
Reinecke, C.	Flute Concerto in D
Rubinstein	Fantasie for Piano and Orchestra
Scheinpflug, P.	King Œdipus
Schumann, R.	Concertstück for Four Horns

Sibelius	Swanwhite
Sinigaglia	Danze Piemontesi (Nos. 1 and 2)
Stanford, C. V.	Songs, I think that we were children;
	O Flames of Passion

1910

Austin, E.	Variations, Vicar of Bray
Bantock, G.	Three Dramatic Dances;
	Dante and Beatrice
Bax, A.	In the Faëry Hills
Bryson, E.	Study for Orchestra, Voices
Davies, Walford	Festal Overture; Suite, Parthenia
Elgar, E.	Symphony in E flat, No. 2
Foote, A.	Suite for Strings
Hathaway, J. W. G.	Sketch, Sunshine
Hurlstone, W. Y.	The Magic Mirror
Jervis-Read	Two Night Pieces
Mack, A.	Song of the Shulamite
Martin, Easthope	Eastern Dances
O'Neill, N.	Four Dances from the Blue Bird
Pauer, E.	In der Natur
Pitt, Percy	Serenade
Rogister, J.	Fantaisie Concertante for Viola and
	Orchestra
Sibelius	Romance for Strings
Strauss, R.	Also sprach Zarathustra
Williams, Vaughan	Fantasy on English Folksongs

1911

Akfvén, H.	Symphony No. 2 in D;
	Midsommervaka
Aubert, L.	Fantasie in B minor, Piano and Orchestra
Bach-Mahler	Suite
Coates, E.	Miniatures
Davies, Walford	Parthenia; New Symphony
Debussy	Children's Corner; Rondes de Printemps
Delius	Sea Drift
Enesco, G.	Rumanian Rhapsodie No. 1; Suite
Gardiner, Balfour	Shepherd Fennels Dance
Harty, Hamilton	Three Pieces, Oboe and Orchestra
Mendelssohn-Forsyth	Small Suite
Mouguet, J.	Flute du Pan
O'Neill, N.	Variations on an Irish Air
Pitt, Percy	English Rhapsody
Raff-Wood	Cavatina
Ravel	Pavane
Reger, M.	100th Psalm

Rootham, C.	A Passer-by
Roze, Raymond	Antony and Cleopatra
Schumann-Pfitzner	Eight Female Choruses
Schumann-Sanders	Theme and Variation, Corno di Bassetto
Sibelius	Valse Romantique
Vogrich, Max	Memento Mori

1912

Ashton, A.	Three English Dances
Bach	Piano Concerto No. 2 in E
Bainton, E. L.	Celtic Sketches
Bossi, G.	Intermezzi (Strings)
Bridge, Frank	The Sea
Coleridge-Taylor	Violin Concerto
Dale, Benjamin	Concert Piece
Dubois, Th.	Fantaisie Triomphale
Elgar, E.	Crown of India
Enesco, G.	Rumanian Rhapsodie, No. 2
Fiocco-O'Neill	Three XVIII-century Pieces
Foulds, J. H.	Music Pictures (Group 3)
Glazounoff	Introduction and Dance, Salome
Hale, A. N.	Elegy for Organ and Strings
Harrison, Julius	Variations on Down among the Dead Men
Korbay, R.	Hungarian Overture and Entr'acte
Korngold, E.	Prelude and Serenade from Der Schnee-mann; Schauspiel Ouverture
Poldowski	Nocturne
Quilter, R.	Suite, Where the Rainbow Ends
Schönberg	Five Orchestral Pieces
Sinigaglia	Suite Piemonte
Wolf-Ferrari	Intro. to Acts II and III, The Jewels of the Madonna

1913

Bach	Aria, Hört doch der sauften Flöten Chor
Bach-Wood	Toccata in F
Bax, A.	Two Orchestral Sketches
Brian, Havergal	Dr. Merryheart
Clutsam, G. H.	Intro. and Dance, King Harlequin
Coates, E.	Idyll
Debussy	Iberia
Dohnányi	Suite in F sharp minor
Dorlay, G.	Concerto Passioné
Dunhill, T. F.	Prelude, the King's Threshold
Fairchild, B.	Tamineh
Fauré, G.	Suite Pelléas et Mélisande
Glazounoff	Piano Concerto, Op. 92

363

Goossens, E. Jnr.	Variations on an old Chinese Air
Grainger, Percy	Irish Tune and Shepherd's Hey
Hahn, R.	Le Bal de Beatrice d'Este
Keyser, H. A.	Prelude, Acts IV and V, Otello
Mandl	Hymn to the Rising Sun
Mozart-Pitt	Andante for Wind Instruments
Pitt, Percy	Aria for Strings
Purcell	Scena, from Rosy Bowers
Rachmaninoff-Wood	Prelude in C sharp minor
Ravel	Valse Nobles et Sentimentales
Scott, C.	Two Poems
Stravinsky	L'Oiseau de Feu
Vassilenko	Au Soleil
Williams, Vaughan	The Wasps
Zoellner	Aria, O, Buzzy Golden Bee

1914

Ashton, A.	Three Scottish Dances
Bartók, Béla	Suite No. 1
Borsdorf, Oscar, Jnr.	Glaucas and Ione
Boughton, Rutland	Love and Night
Bridge, Frank	Dance Rhapsody
Bruckshaw, K.	Piano Concerto in C
Coleridge-Taylor	Rhapsody, From the Prairie
Cowen, F. H.	Suite, Language of Flowers
Davies, Walford	Conversation for Piano and Orchestra
Davis, J. D.	Two Pieces for 'Cello and Orchestra
Elgar, E.	Sospiri (Strings)
Franck, César	Les Eolides
Gardiner, Balfour	In Maytime
Geehs, H.	Suite, Fairyland
Gooslens, E. Jnr.	Perseus
Grainger, Percy	Molly on the Shore
Holbrooke, J.	Imperial March
Liadov	A Fragment from the Apocalypse
Pitt, Percy	Suite, Sakura
Sacrati, F. P.	E Dove d'Aggiri
Schmidt, F.	Suite
Scott, C.	Britain's War March
Stravinsky	Scherzo Fantastique
Vivaldi-Siloti	Concerto in D minor
Walthew, R. H.	Overture, Friend Fritz

1915

Bach	Concerto, Two Violins and Strings
Bagrinovsky	Fantastic Miniatures
Bridge, Frank	Lament

Carr, Howard	The Three Heroes
Corder, P.	Prelude to Acts I and II, Rapunzc
Debussy	Le Martyre de Saint Sébastien
Delius	Eventyr
Jongen, B.	Fantasy on Two Walloon Carols
Mascagni	Introduction, The Sun (Iris)
Méhul-Wood	Le Chant du Départ
Purcell-Colles	Hornpipe
Rachmaninoff	The Island of the Dead

1916

Bach-Gounod-Wood	Ave Maria
Bach-Wood	Suite No. 6
Bridge, Frank	Sally in Our Alley;
	Cherry Ripe (Strings)
Bruneau, A.	L'Attaque du Moulin
Coates, E.	Suite, From the Countryside
Dorlay, G.	La Lutte et l'Espoir
Dubois, Th.	Three Orchestral Pieces (Xavière)
Glazounoff	Paraphrase, National Hymns;
	Song of the Haulers
Grainger, P.	Handel in the Strand
Granados	Dante
Handel	Concerto No. 6 in G minor
MacDowell	Two Poems
Moussorgsky	Intermezzo and Dance Khovantschina
Moussorgsky-Toushmalov	Pictures from an Exhibition
O'Neill, N.	Hornpipe
Pierné, G.	Prelude, Les Cathedrales
Prokofiev	Humorous Scherzo for Four Bassoons
Prowinsky-Wood	A Passing Serenade
Rebikov	Suite, The Christmas Tree
Reed, W. H.	Will o' the Wisp
Rimsky-Korsakoff	Pan Voyevoda; Prelude in C sharp minor
Rimsky-Korsakoff-Wood	Cradle Song (The Maid of Pskov)
Scriabin	Scherzo
Turina	La Procesión du Rocío

1917

Albeniz	Nivian's Dance; Corboda; Catalonia
Aubert	Suite Breve
Bridge, Frank	Two Poems
Bright, Dora	Suite Bretonne
Buck, Percy	Croon
Butterworth, Lieut. G.	A Shropshire Lad
Carr, Howard	The Jolly Roger
Chausson	Chanson Perpetuelle

Dubois, Th.	In Memoriam Mortuorum
Gnessin	Symphonic Fragment
Ireland, John	The Forgotten Rite
Kalemnikov	Le Déluge
Liadov	Kikimora
Loeffler	Pagan Poem
O'Neill, N.	Before Dawn
Ostroglazov	Illustrations d'après l'Apocalypse
Palmgren	Finnish Lullaby
Phillips, M.	Fantasy for Violin and Strings
Rabaud, H.	La Procession Nocturne
Rachmaninoff	Symphony No. 2 in E minor
Rimsky-Korsakoff	The Legend of the Tsar Saltana
Roussel	Les Dieux dans l'Ombre des Cavernes
Speight, J.	Queen Mab Sleeps; Puck;
	Joy and Sorrow
Tcherepnin	Piano Concerto in C sharp minor
Warner, W.	Three Elfin Dances
Zolotariev	Fête Villageoise

1918

Arcadelt-Wood	Ave Maria
Austin, E.	Stella-Mary Dances
Bach-Sanders	Passacaglia in C
Bridge, Frank	Blow out, you Bugles
Carpenter, J. H.	Adventure in a Perambulator
Dalcroze, J.	Allegory
Duparc, H.	Aux Etoiles
Gilbert, H. J.	Comedy Overture, Negro Themes
Laurence, F.	Legend
Malipiero	Impressione dal Vero (No 1)
Rootham, C. B.	Overture, The Two Sisters
Skilton, C. S.	Two Indian Dances

1919

Albeniz-Wood	Cordoba
Bainton, E. L.	Two Pieces
Berners, Lord	Fantaisie espagnole
Boyce, William	Suite in G
Butterworth, Lieut. G.	The Banks of Green Willow
Carr, Howard	The Jovial Huntsmen
Casella, A.	Le Couvent sur l'Eau
Debussy-Wood	La Cathédrale Engloutie
d'Erlanger, Baron F.	Sursum Corda
Delius	Eventyr
Gardiner, Balfour	The Joyful Homecoming
Golestan, Stan	Rhapsodie Roumaine

Grainger, Percy	Over the Hills and Far Away
Heath, J. R.	Rhapsody
Howell, D.	Lamia
Liszt-Wood	Idyll
Loeffler, C. M.	La Villanelle du Diable
Malipiero	Impressione dal Vero (No. 2)
Moussorgsky-Wood	Chansons Enfantines
Paderewski-Wood	Minuet in G
Poldowski	Pat Malone's Wake
Quilter, R.	Children's Overture
Scharwenka-Wood	Three Polish National Dances
Schmidt, F.	Rêves
Smith, D. S.	Overture, Prince Hal
Tcherepnin	Quartet for Four Horns
Widor	Sinfonia Sacra;
	Symphony for Organ and Orchestra

1920

Bax, A.	Symphonic Variations
Bowen, York	Violin Concerto
Casella, A.	Masques et Bergamasques
Catoire	Piano Concerto
Dorlay, G.	Valse Intermezzo
Faure, G.	Fantasy
Fogg, E.	Suite, The Golden Butterfly
Gibbs, Armstrong	Suite, Crossings
Goossens, E.	The Eternal Rhythm
Howells, H.	Merry-Eye
Laurence, F.	The Dance of the Witch Girl
Phillips, M.	Piano Concerto
Prokofiev	Piano Concerto
Ronald, Landon	The Garden of Allah
Strong, T.	Poeme di Guerra; The Night

1921

Bach-Goossens	Suite in G
Bainton, E. L.	Paracelsus
Bantock, G.	Coronach
Bartók, Béla	Rhapsody
Bliss, Arthur	Melée Fantasque
Carpenter, J. A.	Concertino for Piano
Howell, Dorothy	Koong Shee (Ballet)
Hughes, H.	Parodies for Voice and Orchestra
MacEwan, D.	Kam-Var
O'Connor-Morris, G.	Violin Concerto in A minor
Offenbach	Serenade (The Goldsmith of Toledo)
O'Neill, N.	Prelude and Call (Mary Rose)

Santoliquido	Crepuscule sur Mare;
	Il Profumo delle Oasi Saharianne
Sargent, M.	An Impression on a Windy Day
van Dieren, B.	Introit

1922

Aubert, L.	Habañera
Bloch, E.	Hebrew Rhapsody, Schelomo
Bridge, F.	Sir Roger de Coverley
Coates, E.	Suite, Joyous Youth
Farrar, E.	English Pastoral Impression
Gibbs, Armstrong	Ballet Music
Greenbaum, H.	Parfum de la Nuit
Holbrooke, Josef	Prelude, Bronwen
McEwen, J. B.	A Winter Poem
Migot, G.	Le Paravent de Lague aux cinq Images
Milhaud, D.	Suite Symphonique, No. 2
Molinon, B.	Sonata for Organ and Orchestra
Phillips, M.	Four Dances (The Rebel Maid)
Pierné, G.	Trois Paysages Franciscains
Roussel, A.	Pour une Fête de Printemps
Sargent, M.	Nocturne and Scherzo
Scarborough, E.	Promise
Wall, A. W.	Overture, Thanet

1923

Bach, C. P. E.	'Cello Concert in A minor
Bliss, Arthur	Colour Symphony
Bloch, E.	Trois Poèmes Juifs
Breton, T.	Violin Concerto in A minor
Davies, Walford	Memorial Suite
Dohnányi	Variations on a Nursery Rhyme;
	Violin Concerto in D
Foulds, J. H.	Keltic Suite
Gibbs, Armstrong	A Vision of Night
Greenbaum, H.	A Sea Poem
Heath, J. R.	Scherzo
Hindemith	Nusch-Nuschi Dances
Holst, G.	Fugal Overture; Fugal Concerto
Howell, Dorothy	Piano Concerto in D minor
Mackenzie, A. C.	St. John's Eve
Milhaud, D.	Suite Symphonique
Miaskowski, M.	Alastor
Novàk	Overture, Lady Godiva
Pick-Mangiagalli	Sortilegi
Rozycki, L.	Piano Concerto
Sainton, Philip	Two Orchestral Pieces

Saint-Säens	Grande Fantaisie Zoologique
Satz, I.	Suite, The Blue Bird
Schrecker	Chamber Symphony
Smyth, Ethel	Four Choral Preludes
Spilman, T. M.	Barbaresques

1924

Janacek	Sumarovo Dite
Korngold, Erik	Sursum Corda
Miaskowski, M.	Symphony No. 5 in D
Reger, Max	Romantic Suite
Respighi	Sinfonia Drammatica

1925

Coates, Eric	Two Light Syncopated Pieces
d'Albert, Eugène	Aschenputtel
Foulds, J. H.	Suite, Saint Joan
Graener, Paul	Variations on a Russian Folksong
Hales, Hubert	Overture, Twelfth Night
Hay, E. Norman	Dunluce
Ibert, Jacques	The Ballad of Reading Gaol
Kufferath, Camille	Mirages
McEwen, J. B.	Prelude
Pfitzner, Han	Palestrina
Schreker	The Birthday of the Infanta
Tcherepnin	The Romance of a Mummy

1926

Akimenko, Féodor	Ange
Austin, F.	The Insect Play
Bliss, Arthur	Introduction and Allegro
Boughton, Rutland	The Queen of Cornwall
Coates, Eric	The Three Bears
d'Indy, V.	La Queste de Dieu
Dohnányi	Ruralia Hungarica
Hanson, Howard	Pan and the Priest
Hindemith	Concerto (Op. 38)
Jacob, Gordon	Viola Concerto in C minor
Malipiero	Il Molino della Morte
Marx, Joseph	Romantic Concerto in E
Sibelius	Symphony No. 6 in D minor
Spain-Dunk	The Kentish Downs

1927

Alwyn, William	Five Preludes
Bridge, Frank	Impression
Dupré, Marcel	Cortège et Litanie

369

Haydn	Sinfonia Concertante
Hely-Hutchinson, V.	Variations; Intermezzo, Scherzo and Finale
Miaskowski	Symphony No. 6 (Op. 23)
O'Donnell, B. Walton	Songs of the Gael
Smyth, Ethel	Concerto for Violin, Horn and Orchestra
Spain-Dunk, Susan	Elaine
Walton, William	Portsmouth Point
Wood, Thomas	A Seaman's Overture

1928

Bach-Schönberg	Two Choralvorspiele
Bainton, Edgar	Eclogue
Benjamin, Arthur	Concertino
Casella, A.	Partita
Fogg, Eric	June Twilight
Goldmark, R.	A Negro Rhapsody
Howell, Dorothy	Overture, The Rock
Jacob, Gordon	Overture, Clogher Head
Kodály, Z.	Suite, Háry János
Sampson, Godfrey	Symphony in D
Sibelius	Tapiola
Sowerby, Leo	Overture, Comes Autumn Time
Strauss	Parergon (Sinfonia Domestica)
Tansman, Alexandre	Piano Concerto

1929

Arne	Piano Concerto No. 5 in G minor
Bax, Arnold	Three Orchestral Pieces
Berkeley, Lennox	Suite
Converse, F. S.	Flivver Ten Million
Hely-Hutchinson	A Carol Symphony
Honegger	Rugby
Howells, Herbert	Concertino
Lambert, Constant	Music for Orchestra
Miaskowski	Silentium
Moeran, E. J.	Rhapsody No. 2
Sainton, Philip	The Dream of a Marionette
Sowerby, Leo	From the Northland
Tommasini, V.	Prelude, Fanfare and Fugue
Walton, William	Viola Concerto
Wilson, Stanley	Piano Concerto
van Anrooij, P. G.	Piet Hein

1930

| Dupré, Marcel | Symphony for Orchestra and Organ |
| Goossens, Eugène | Oboe Concerto |

Grainger, Percy	English Dance for Organ and Orchestra
Honegger	'Cello Concerto
Ireland, John	Piano Concerto
Janacek, L.	Wallachian Dances
Kodály, Z.	Summer Evening
Krenek, Ernst	Potpourri
Maconchy, Elizabeth	Suite, The Land
Smyth, Ethel	Anacreontic Ode
Villa-Lobos	Chôros (No. 8)

1931

Berners, Lord	Luna Park
Elgar	Nursery Suite
Delius	A Song of Summer
Fogg, Eric	Bassoon Concerto in D
Walsworth, Ivor	Rhapsodic Dance
Webern, Ivor	Passacaglia

1932

Bainton, Edgar L.	Epithalamion
Beethoven-Manen	Concertstück for Violin and Orchestra
Hindemith	Philharmonic Concerto
Ravel	Piano Concerto for the Left Hand
Smyth, Ethel	Fête Galante

1933

Delius	Idyll for Soprano, Baritone and Orchestra
Gerhard, Robert	Six Catalian Folksongs
Goossens	Kaleidoscope
Honegger	Symphonic Movement (No. 3)

1934

Bach-Pick-Mangiagalli	Two Preludes for Strings
Bach-Respighi	Prelude and Fugue in D
Converse, F.	California
Cooke, Arnold	Concert Overture No. 1
Dale, B. J.	An English Dance
Kodály	Dances of Galanta
Moeran, E. J.	Farrago
Sinigaglia	Rondo (Violin)
Smyth, Ethel	Entente Cordiale
Tapp, Frankó	Metropolis
Taylor, Deems	Circus Day
Toch	Symphony for Piano and Orchestra
Williams, Vaughan	The Running Set

Bartòk, Béla	Hungarian Peasant Songs
Berkeley, Lennox	Overture
Bliss, Arthur	Suite from Film Music, 1935
Bush, Alan	Dance Overture
Fogg, Eric	September Night
Howells, Herbert	Elegy for Strings
Jacob, Gordon	Passacaglia on a well-known Theme
Larsson	Saxophone Concerto
Sainton, Philip	Serenade Fantastique
Shostakovitch	Symphony No. 1; Concerto No. 1 (Piano, Trumpet and Strings)
Stephen, David	Coronach
Tailleferre, G.	Concerto for 2 Pianos, Chorus and Orchestra

Bach-Casella	Chaconne
Bantock, Granville	The Frogs
Dohnányi	Minutes Symphoniques
Greenwood, John	Salute to Gustav Holst
Ibert, Jacques	Concertinóo de Camera
Ireland, John	Overture
Maconchy, Elizabeth	Piano Concerto
Marsick, Armand	Tableaux Grecs
Sibelius	The Ferryman's Bride
Vogel, V.	Ritmica Ostinata
Whyte, Ian	Three Scottish Dances

Austin, F.	The Sea Venturers
Bax, Arnold	London Pageant
Gibbs, Armstrong	Essex Suite for Strings
Handel	Five Choruses from the Operas (2nd Set)
Ibert	Escales
Jacob, Gordon	Variations
Kodàly	Ballet Music
Malipiero	Violin Concerto
Purcell-Herbage	Suite for Strings
Rossini-Britten	Soirées Musicales
Rubbra, Edmund	Violin Fantasia
Tailleferre, G.	Harp Concerto

INDEX

374

N

Nash, Heddle, 330, 348
Neilson, Julia, 34
Neruda, Franz, 44
Nesfield, Ernest, 25
Newman, Cardinal, 249
Newman, Ernest, 51, 224, 330
Newman, Robert, 60, 68, 71, 74, 83, 87, 88, 95, 101, 105, 108, 115, 118, 120, 122, 126, 129, 132, 137, 142, 143, 147, 150, 155, 156, 159, 162, 167, 172, 176, 190, 196, 200, 205, 211, 228, 232, 235, 240, 242, 250, 252, 254, 260, 266, 268, 272, 177, 279, 286, 288, 298, 304, 312, 318, 352
Newmarch, Elsie, 232
Newmarch, Rosa, 50, 127, 231, 239, 244, 256, 259, 299, 352
Newton (Bassoon), 313
Nicholls, Agnes, 208, 213, 251, 261
Nielsen, Carl, 174
Nietzel, Professor, 166
Nikisch, Arthur, 44, 159, 173, 212, 238, 239, 245, 266, 271, 322, 336
Norcross, 135
Nordica, Madame, 88, 245
Norelli, Jenny, 153
Norfolk, Duke of, 243, 248
Norfolk, Duchess of, 243, 258
Norman, Kate, 37
Norwich, Bishop of, 259
Novacs, Guiomar, 276
Noyes, François, 41

O

O'Donnell, Walton, 325
O'Mara, Joseph, 80, 85
O'Neill, Norman, 154, 202
O'Neill (Timpani), 313
Orpen, 311
O'Sullivan, Dennis, 85
Oudin, Eugène, 43
Ould ('Cello), 112
Ouroussoff, Princess Olga, 42, 89, 117, 119, 130, 135, 146, 148, 149, 155, 156, 164, 166, 175, 189 194, 205, 207, 240, 318
Ouroussoff, Princess Sofie, 242
Owen, Myra, 325

P

Pachmann, 109, 126, 266

Paderewski, 36, 108, 126, 238, 294
Pagani's, 68, 86, 99, 176, 195
Palliser, Esther, 138
Palmer (Brothers), 37
Palmer, Sir Ernest, 311
Parker, Fry, 70, 84
Parker, Horatio, 148
Parrot, Gurney L., 269
Parry, Sir Herbert, 87, 116, 184
Parry, Paul, 44
Parsons, Sir Herbert, 114
Parsons, William, 323
Patti, 57, 245, 295
Pattison, Mrs., 64
Pauer, Emil, 173
Paul, Lady Dean. See Mme. Poldowski
Paul, R. W., 93
Payne, Arthur, 70, 83, 136, 149, 155, 161, 183
Pearce, Faithful, 147
Percy, Lord Eustace, 298
Perkins, C. W., 281
Pernorma, 15
Perosi, Lorenzo, 126
Perry, Arnold, 325
Peterkin, W. A., 69, 74, 138, 151
Petri, Egon, 187, 327
Phillipi, Rosina, 180
Phillips, J. W., 208
Phillips, Montague, 234
Pickerill, W. J., 339
Piening, Karl, 167
Pierson, Henry Hugo, 268
Pike, 12
Pitt, Percy, 89, 116, 117, 155, 156, 162, 170, 188, 245, 252, 321
Pitt, Tom, 58
Plançon, Paul, 82, 88, 185, 206
Poldowski, Madame (Lady Dean Paul), 269, 275
Popper, David, 116
Portland, Duke of, 137
Possart, Ernst von, 85, 165
Pouishnoff, 102, 327
Powell, Janet, 325
Powell, Lionel, 294
Pratt, R. C., 326, 348
Price, Daniel, 149
Prokofieff, 311
Prout, Ebenezer, 29, 32, 79, 153
Prout, Louis B., 29, 31
Pugno, Raoul, 44, 142, 189, 267

381